Historical Atlas
of the
North Pacific Ocean

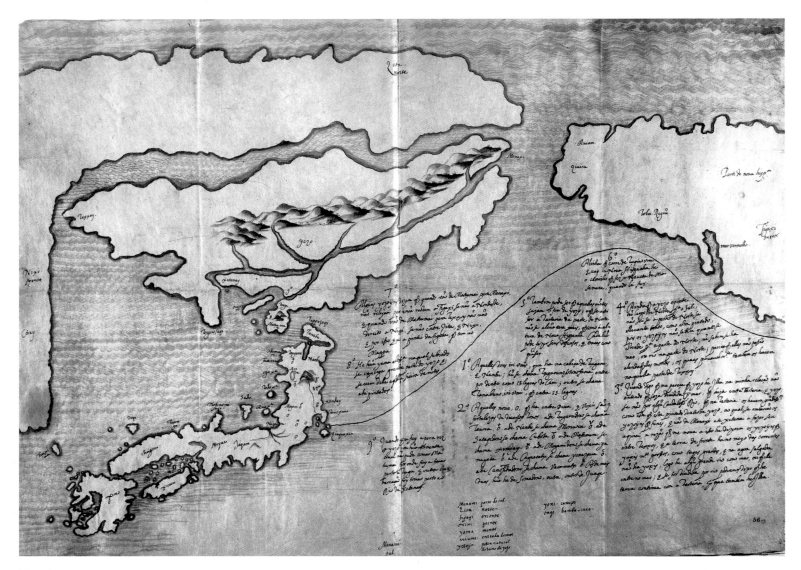

Map 1.
What today appears to us as a bizarre interpretation of the geography of the North Pacific Ocean was based on the latest information available at the time. Drawn in 1621 by a Jesuit missionary in Japan, Girolamo de Angelis, the map shows Japan, to the north of which is a grossly exaggerated Hokkaido, which was not at this time part of Japan. Asia is correctly shown separated from America even though the strait was as yet unexplored by Europeans. On the west coast of North America the peninsula of Baja California is shown; this was known from Spanish explorations from the previous century, but the rest of the west coast is essentially a blank. It would not be explored by Europeans until 1774.

Historical Atlas
of the
North Pacific Ocean

Maps of Discovery and Scientific Exploration
1500 – 2000

Derek Hayes

Published under the auspices of the
North Pacific Marine Science Organization

Douglas & McIntyre
Vancouver/Toronto

Douglas & McIntyre Ltd.
2323 Quebec Street, Suite 201
Vancouver, British Columbia V5T 4S7

National Library of Canada Cataloguing in Publication Data

Hayes, Derek, 1947–
    Historical atlas of the North Pacific Ocean

    Includes bibliographical references and index.
    ISBN 1-55054-865-4

    1. North Pacific Ocean—Discovery and exploration—Maps. 2. North Pacific
Ocean—Historical geography—Maps. I. Title.
G2862.N6S12H39 2001   911´.1644   C2001-910356-5

Originated in Canada by Douglas & McIntyre Ltd. and published
simultaneously in the United States of America by Sasquatch Books,
Seattle, and in the United Kingdom by the British Museum Press.

Copy editing by Naomi Pauls
Design and layout by Derek Hayes
Cover design by Karen Schober
Printed and bound in Hong Kong, P.R.C., by C&C Offset
Printed on acid-free paper

We gratefully acknowledge the financial support of the Canada Council for
the Arts, the British Columbia Ministry of Tourism, Small Business and
Culture, and the Government of Canada through the Book Publishing
Industry Development Program (BPIDP) for our publishing activities.

Derek Hayes
www.derekhayes.ca
derek@derekhayes.ca

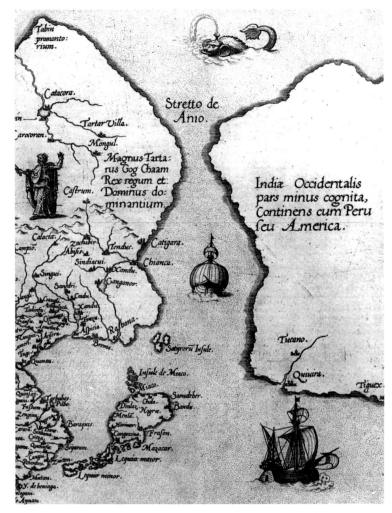

Map 2.
The Pacific Ocean as portrayed on a map from 1578 by Gerard de Jode.
The ocean was commonly shown as a relatively narrow sea in the
sixteenth and seventeenth centuries.

Published under the auspices of the
North Pacific Marine Science Organization (PICES)

With financial assistance from the
National Marine Fisheries Service,
National Oceanic and Atmospheric Administration,
U.S.A.

Acknowledgments

First of all I would like to thank PICES, the North Pacific Marine
Science Organization, for commissioning this book.
    Many people have assisted in its compilation and writing. In
particular I would like to thank the following: Alexander Bychkov,
Executive Secretary, PICES, and Robert Wilson and John Garrett of
2WE Associates, Victoria; Skip McKinnell, Assistant Executive Secretary, PICES; Edward Redmond and John Hebért, Geography and Map
Division, Library of Congress; Tony Campbell and his staff in the Map
Library at the British Library; Andrew Cook and Graham Hutt (Curator, Chinese Section), Oriental and India Office Collections, Brit-
ish Library; Jeffrey Murray at the National Archives of Canada; Adrian
Webb and Sharon Nichol at the United Kingdom Hydrographic Of-
fice; Brian Tynne at the National Maritime Museum, Greenwich; Alice
Hudson (Map Librarian), New York Public Library; Michel Brisebois,
Rare Book Curator at the National Library of Canada; Richard Smith,
Maps and Plans, National Archives and Records Administration, Wash-
ington; Sjoerd de Meer, Map Curator at the Maritiem Museum Prins
Hendrick, Rotterdam; Father Joseph de Cock, Archivum Romanum
Societatis Iesu, Rome; Catherine Hoffmann, Bibliothèque nationale,
Paris; Marina Smyth, Notre Dame University; Carol Urness, Map Cura-
tor at the James Ford Bell Library, University of Minnesota; Lincoln
Pratson, Earth and Ocean Sciences, Duke University, Durham, NC;
Shingo Kimura, Ocean Research Institute, Tokyo University; James
Gower and Howard Freeland, Institute of Ocean Sciences, Sidney,
BC; Warren Wooster, University of Washington; Walter Smith, NOAA,
and Davis Sandwell, Scripps Institution of Oceanography; Alfred
Mueller, Beinecke Library, Yale University; Fred Musto, Yale Univer-
sity Library; Susan Snyder, Bancroft Library, University of California;
Susan Danforth, John Carter Brown University, Providence, RI;
Herman Stapelkamp, Algemeen Rijksarchief, Den Haag; Diane
Shapiro, Wildlife Conservation Society, Bronx Zoo, New York; the
staff of the British Columbia Archives, Victoria, BC; and the staff at
the Vancouver Public Library Special Collections Division. In addition I would like to express my thanks to Naomi Pauls for her superla-
tive editing; and Scott McIntyre of Douglas and McIntyre, Vancouver,
and Joan Gregory of Sasquatch Books, Seattle, for their continuing
support.

Contents

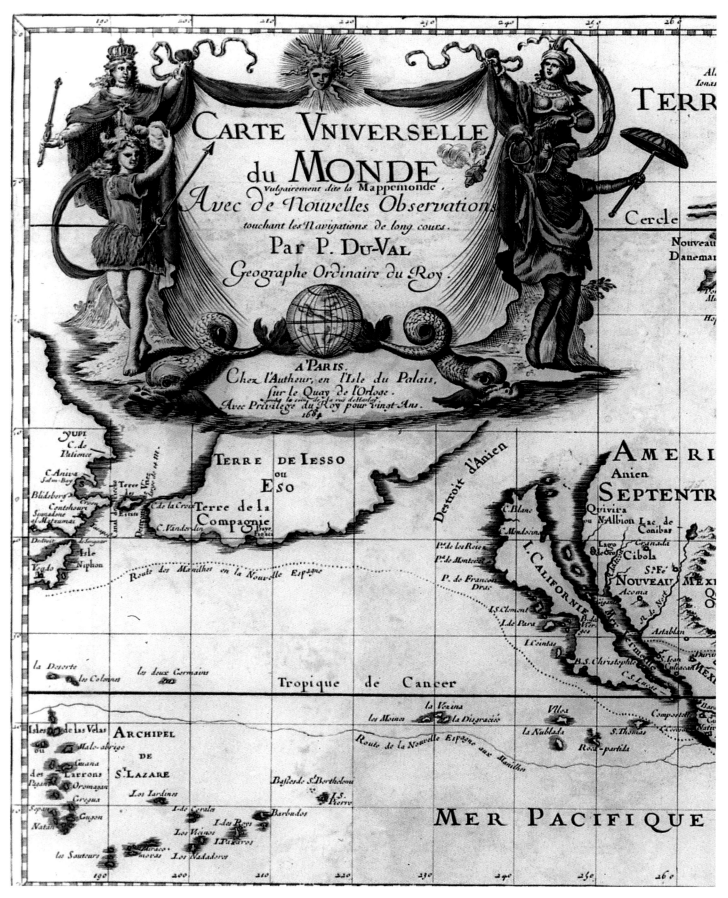

Map 3.

In many early views, the North Pacific Ocean was depicted as half land. In this 1684 map, part of a map of the world by French geographer Pierre du Val, a large continent, "Iesso" or "Eso," is a confusion with Hokkaido, the northernmost large island of Japan. "Company Land" ("Terre de la Compagnie") is one of the Kuril Islands seen by Dutch explorer Maerten Vries in 1643, but not defined on its eastern end. Some mapmakers interpreted this to mean it stretched to North America. The Strait of Anian ("Detroit d'Anien") separates Asia, or Jesso, from America, and California is shown as an island. In the west, Cape Patience, in reality on the island of Sakhalin, is shown as part of the Asian continent.

About the North Pacific Marine Science Organization (PICES)

This book was commissioned by PICES for its tenth anniversary in 2001.

PICES, the North Pacific Marine Science Organization, is an international and intergovernmental organization that was established and held its first meetings in 1992. Its present members are Canada, the People's Republic of China, Japan, the Republic of Korea, the Russian Federation, and the United States of America. The purposes of the organization are as follows:

- To promote and coordinate marine research in the northern North Pacific and adjacent seas especially northward of 30° N
- To advance scientific knowledge about the ocean environment, global weather and climate change, living resources and their ecosystems, and the impacts of human activities
- To promote the collection and rapid exchange of scientific information on these issues

The oldest intergovernmental marine science organization, founded in 1902, is the International Council for the Exploration of the Sea, ICES. This organization deals with scientific questions of its region, primarily the northeastern Atlantic and adjacent seas, and emphasizes science far more than political or administrative matters. The idea of a North Pacific analog to ICES was first proposed in 1973, but it was not discussed in any systematic way until the late 1970s. Several informal meetings, organized by the University of Washington's Institute for Marine Studies, were then held in Seattle, where scientists from Canada, Japan, the Soviet Union, and the United States exchanged views. Although many of the concepts that characterize the organization were developed in these discussions, the time was not propitious for bringing the idea to fruition. Impediments included the ongoing Law of the Sea negotiations and the difficult political relations between the U.S. and the U.S.S.R. in the early 1980s.

It was only in 1986, during an informal meeting in Anchorage that included Chinese participants for the first time, that agreement was reached to seek an intergovernmental discussion of a possible new regional marine science organization. Participants agreed to urge the Canadian government to convene such a conference, which was held in Ottawa in December 1987. A second conference, in Sidney, British Columbia, in December 1988, and a drafting meeting in Seattle in December 1989 were necessary before agreement was finally reached, in Ottawa on 12 December 1990, to establish the North Pacific Marine Science Organization (PICES). Representatives of Canada, China, Japan, the United States, and the Soviet Union initialed the draft convention.

The convention came into force on 24 March 1992 after ratification by three of the five signatory states, Canada, Japan, and the United States. The People's Republic of China ratified before August 1992 and participated as a member in the first annual meeting, in October of that year. Although the Soviet Union had participated in all of the intergovernmental discussions leading up to establishment of PICES, the new Russian Federation did not ratify until December 1994; the Republic of Korea became a member in midsummer 1995.

PICES held its first annual meeting in October 1992, in Victoria, British Columbia.

From the beginning, the approach of PICES has been multidisciplinary, with standing committees concerned with biological oceanography, fishery science, physical oceanography and climate, and marine environmental quality. There is growing interaction among these specialties, with joint scientific sessions and through the PICES Science Board, with interdisciplinary symposia and a broad study of Climate Change and Carrying Capacity (the CCCC program) in the region.

Most recently, PICES has taken the lead in joining forces with other international organizations to organize an intersessional conference entitled "Beyond El Niño," which was held in March 2000 and which looked at the evidence for and the consequences and implications of interannual, decadal, and interdecadal scales of physical and biological variability. While PICES is an infant compared with its prototype, ICES, which is about to celebrate its 100th anniversary, it has already become a major focus for international cooperation in marine science in the northern North Pacific.

Cartouche from a 1750 map of the Pacific Ocean by Dutch mapmakers Reinier and Joshua Ottens. The map is shown on page 85 (Map 122).

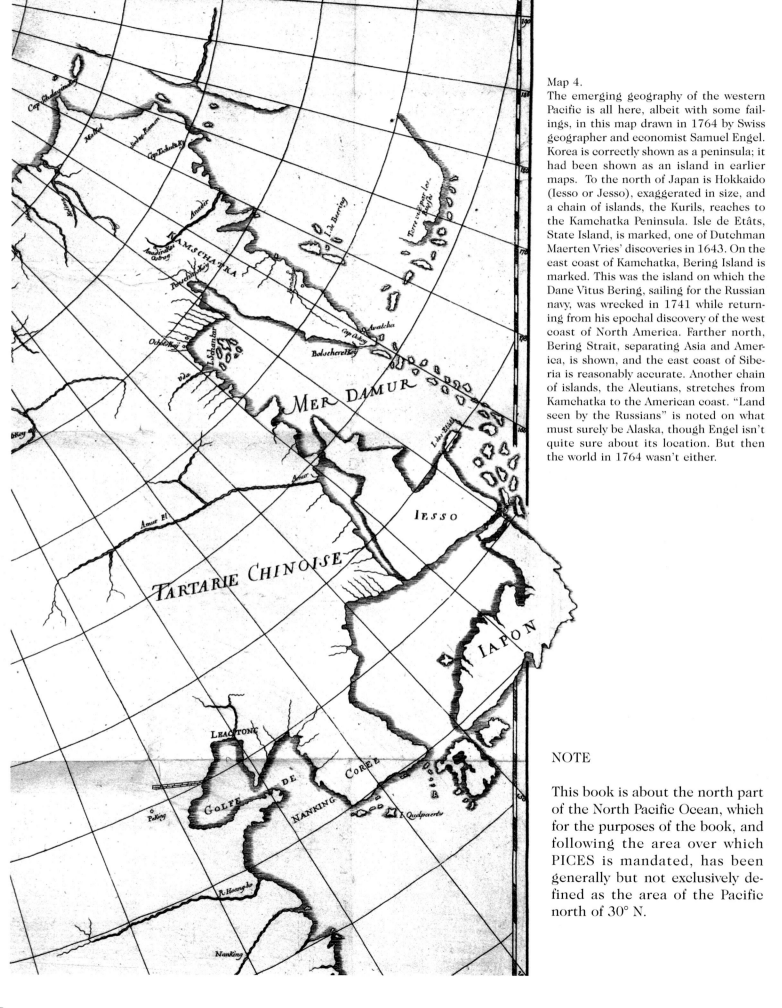

Map 4.
The emerging geography of the western Pacific is all here, albeit with some failings, in this map drawn in 1764 by Swiss geographer and economist Samuel Engel. Korea is correctly shown as a peninsula; it had been shown as an island in earlier maps. To the north of Japan is Hokkaido (Iesso or Jesso), exaggerated in size, and a chain of islands, the Kurils, reaches to the Kamchatka Peninsula. Isle de Etâts, State Island, is marked, one of Dutchman Maerten Vries' discoveries in 1643. On the east coast of Kamchatka, Bering Island is marked. This was the island on which the Dane Vitus Bering, sailing for the Russian navy, was wrecked in 1741 while returning from his epochal discovery of the west coast of North America. Farther north, Bering Strait, separating Asia and America, is shown, and the east coast of Siberia is reasonably accurate. Another chain of islands, the Aleutians, stretches from Kamchatka to the American coast. "Land seen by the Russians" is noted on what must surely be Alaska, though Engel isn't quite sure about its location. But then the world in 1764 wasn't either.

NOTE

This book is about the north part of the North Pacific Ocean, which for the purposes of the book, and following the area over which PICES is mandated, has been generally but not exclusively defined as the area of the Pacific north of 30° N.

A Pacific Ocean?

The Pacific Ocean as it is now defined did not exist in human mind before about 1500. Certainly the Chinese and Japanese knew that there was a vast ocean stretching far to the east, and similarly Europeans knew that there was an equally vast ocean to the west.

Those on the shores of Asia did not know how far the ocean extended, and those in Europe thought it extended to the east Asian shore. The idea that the sea all the way from Europe to Asia was "navigable in a few days if the wind is favorable" was the same idea that led Christopher Columbus in 1492 to sail westwards, as he thought, to the Indies. But even after having made a landfall he continued to think he was on the shores of Asia.

It required the European discovery of North America for there to be a Pacific Ocean. After Columbus, Cabot and many others thought they were sailing to the Indies, to Cathay, to Zipangu (or Chipangu, Marco Polo's name for Japan), and the Spice Islands by sailing westwards; but America "got in the way."

The Spaniard Balboa in 1513 crossed the isthmus at Panama and became the first European to confirm that another ocean lay to the west of America. There followed attempts to find a way through or round this inconvenient continent, a pathway finally being found by Magellan in 1520.

The Martin Behaim globe, famous as being the last European concept of the world before Columbus –

Behaim completed it while Columbus was still at sea in 1492 – shows well the Pacific and Atlantic as one sea extending westwards from Europe. The map shown here is a copy of the globe drawn on paper in 1730 by Johan Doppelmayer. If you look carefully, you can see that it is a map of a 360° globe; the Azores appear on the right-hand side of the "Pacific," as well as in their more correct position off the coast of Spain.

After Columbus and Cabot, many maps showed their discoveries as an extension of Asia. In particular, Newfoundland was considered to be at the far eastern tip of an Asian continent.

This view is well shown in the world map of Giovanni Contarini, drawn in 1506. On what to modern eyes is North America, he has clearly

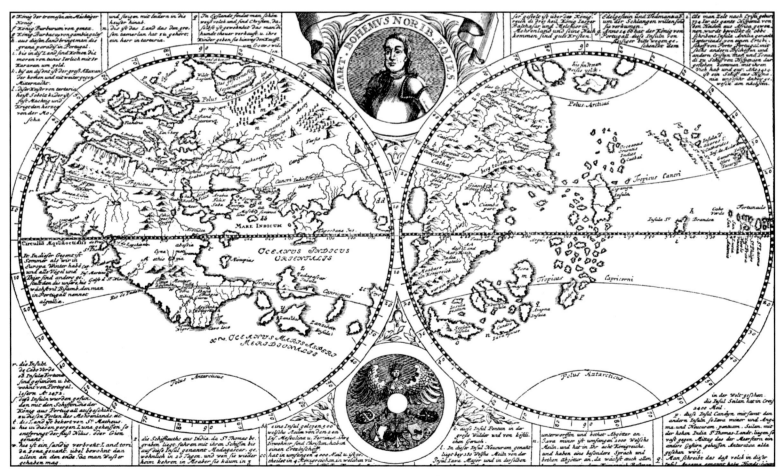

Map 5.
Map of the world according to the Martin Behaim globe, 1492, drawn by Johan Doppelmayer in 1730.

9

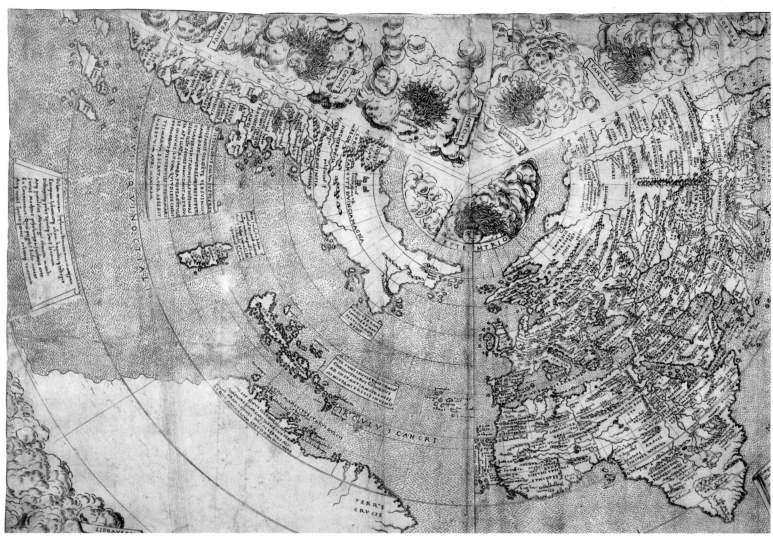

Map 6.
Giovanni Contarini's world map of 1506. The continents of North and South America are conspicuously missing, and the Pacific and Atlantic Oceans are one. Those parts of North America discovered by Europeans at this point are assumed to be an eastward extension of Asia. Ziapan – Japan – is in the middle of the pseudo-Pacific. This was the first printed map to show any part of North or South America. This map shows why Columbus thought he could sail westwards to the Indies. The map was engraved by Francesco Rosselli and is often referred to as the Contarini–Rosselli map.

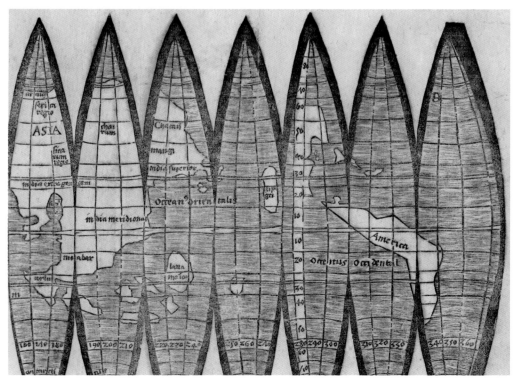

Map 7.
A world map by Martin Waldseemüller in 1506 was the first cartographic depiction of a Pacific Ocean. These are the gores for a globe drawn by Waldseemüller the following year, 1507. The depiction of an American continent necessarily broke the single ocean shown in maps like that of Contarini (above) into two: an Atlantic, and what would later come to be called the Pacific. Waldseemüller was the first to use the name "America" on a map, for South America.

marked Cathay; the island Zipangu is in midocean.

The first, and unusually early, portrayal of the Pacific Ocean along the lines of which we know it today was in a map drawn in 1506 by Martin Waldseemüller. It depicted the North and South American continents in perceptively reasonable form based on information available to him up to that time, and in particular the voyages of Amerigo Vespucci (after whom he coined the name "America"). In so doing, Waldseemüller's map, which has been called an inspired guess, showed a Pacific Ocean virtually by default. No matter that the west coast of his North America was almost a straight line, or that it must have been based on no more than an in-

tuitive guess; it stands as the first mapping of a Pacific Ocean. Apart from a huge Japan – Zipangu – again in the middle of the ocean, the map is a remarkably good delineation of an unknown sea.

Waldseemüller's map was a woodcut, a printed map, and as such was much more widely seen than previous manuscript maps. About 1,000 copies were produced. Thus it was relatively easy for other cartographers to copy Waldseemüller's ideas. The transcription of the Schöner globe, dating from 1520, shows a similar North American continent and Pacific Ocean

In 1529, a major cartographical step was taken in the map of the world drawn by Diogo Ribeiro. His

map is generally considered to be a copy of the secret official *Padrón general,* a large map that Spain constantly updated to make it the most complete map at any given time. Ribeiro was the chief cartographer of Spain and charged with its updating.

The breakthrough that Ribeiro showed on his map was the width of the Pacific Ocean. After two decades of Spanish exploration, Ribeiro finally reasonably correctly calculated the width of the ocean from the amount of longitude that must remain after all else was accounted for. This well-ornamented map has faded badly over the years, and a map redrawn for the Library of Congress in 1886 or 1887 is shown here.

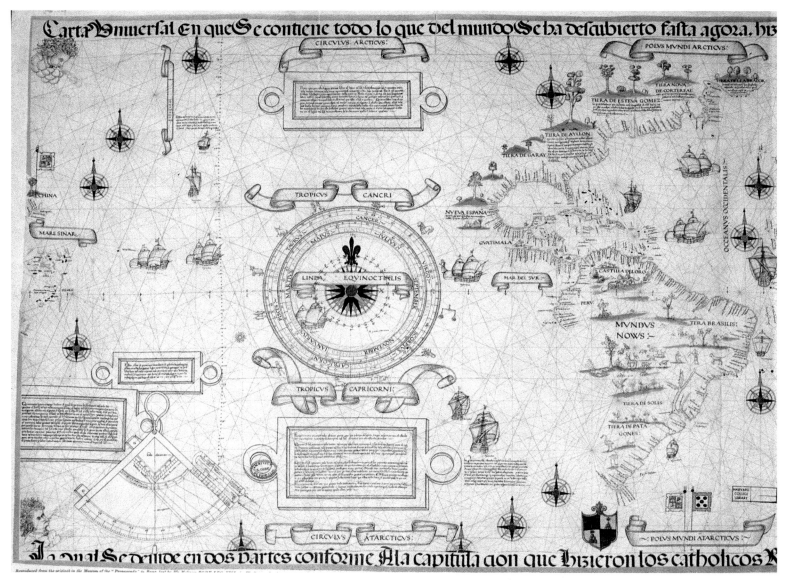

Map 8.   Western part of the world map by Diogo Ribeiro, 1529. This was the first map to show the width of the Pacific Ocean with reasonable accuracy. This is a copy made in 1886 or 1887. It is clearer than the original, which has faded.

Map 9.
Sebastian Münster's world map of 1546 showed a large island of Japan in the middle of a new Pacific Ocean and many other smaller, imaginary islands.

Map 10 (below).
The globe made by Nürnberg astronomer and mathematician Johannes Schöner in 1520 showed the imposition of a new continent – Cuba, not America – splitting the medieval world ocean into Oceanus Occidentalis and Orientalis Oceanus – the Pacific. Schöner was a bit liberal with his Pacific islands, the largest of which was Zipangi – Japan.

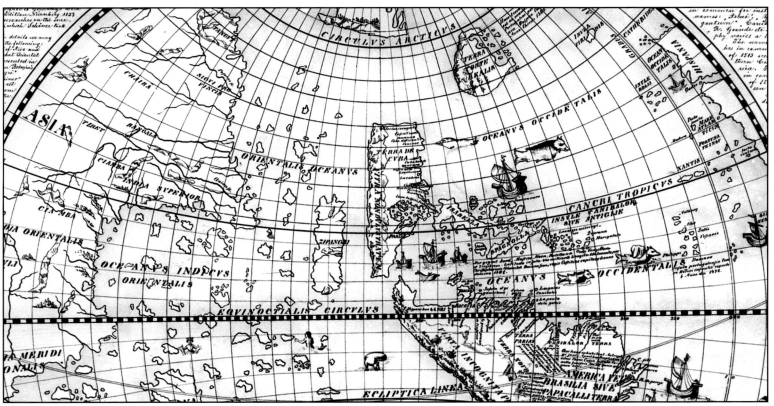

Triumphant Visions of the Boundless Ocean

The earliest recorded Chinese concepts of the world envisioned China at the center of the world surrounded by oceans. The oceans were the limits of the universe.

Early Chinese exploration of the Pacific was likely occasioned by religious motives. In 219 B.C. Hsu Fu was sent with several thousand men to search for a herb said to make one immortal, on "the great immortal island of the Eastern Sea," which has been interpreted to mean Japan. One Chinese theory – not generally accepted in Japan – is that Hsu Fu settled in Japan and set himself up as an emperor.

The most famous Chinese maritime explorer without a doubt was Cheng Ho, or Zheng He. In 1405 he was chosen as the leader of a large exploring expedition to the Indian Ocean. Cheng Ho was to lead six more expeditions after that, the seventh and last not returning to China until 1433. This final expedition was a massive affair, with 26,755 sailors, soldiers, and craftsmen. His expeditions reached Java, India, Arabia, Africa, and, some say, Australia. All were essentially westward expeditions, but all had to traverse the Pacific Ocean first.

As a result, Chinese knowledge of the Pacific and the other oceans he explored was immensely expanded, as were navigational techniques and experience.

Cheng Ho made maps, and one series in particular has survived, at least in a copy from 1621. Generally thought to have been drawn by some of Cheng Ho's men, this series of maps was reproduced in a book entitled *Wu Pei Chih* (literally "Notes on Military Preparation"), and are essentially navigational charts.

Twenty-four pages of maps cover an area from Nanking to the east coast of Africa, with 500 place names, including 200 in China itself. Perhaps not surprisingly, the maps of the coast of China are more detailed than other regions, presumably because Cheng Ho traversed the coastal seas twice for each of his seven expeditions. The tracks taken by his ships are shown as dotted lines, often accompanied by characters giving compass directions.

Cheng Ho's voyages gave rise to a number of early books in China, one of which, *Ying Yai Shêng Lan,* written in 1451, translates wonderfully as "Triumphant Visions of the Boundless Ocean."

Illustrations of ships contemporary with Cheng Ho from *Wu Pei Chih.*

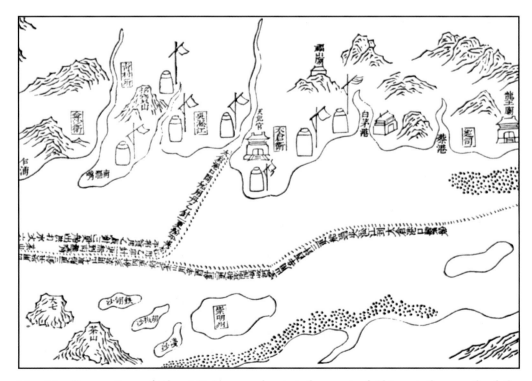

Map 11. Two sections of Cheng Ho's map, showing the coast of China at the mouth of the Yangtze River and part of the East China Sea. The dotted lines are Cheng Ho's tracks, and the Chinese characters give compass directions.

That Exceedingly Vast Sea – Balboa and Magellan

Late in 1512, the Spaniard Vasco Núñez de Balboa, an adventurer in the new Spanish colony of Darién, heard from the natives of a "land of gold, washed by a vast sea" a short distance to the west. In September 1513 Balboa crossed the Isthmus of Panama in search of gold and found a sea.

On 25 September 1513 Balboa and his men emerged from the jungle onto a mountaintop and beheld foaming breakers on a curving sandy shore, beyond which was an apparently boundless ocean. Thus he became the first European to see the Pacific Ocean.

An allegorical portrait of Magellan entering the Pacific Ocean, from Theodor de Bry's *Voyages*, 1592.

Balboa named it the Mar del Sur, the South Sea, because he had followed a southward route across the isthmus and it lay to his south from the point at which he arrived on the coast. Four days later, they were at the water's edge, where, tasting the water and finding it salt, he realized that he had found a new ocean and not just a large lake. He waded into the sea and ceremonially took possession of the ocean *and any coasts that it might wash* in the name of Spain, an action which would be cited later as evidence that the entire Pacific coast of North America belonged to Spain. This action of Balboa's was to mean that for centuries the Span-

ish would regard the Pacific as theirs: a Spanish lake.

When news of Balboa's discovery reached Spain it was received with great excitement. It was instantly recognized that this new sea would give Spain a chance at an even wider-flung empire. If Spanish ships now sailed westwards, the Spice Islands might be reached in a way that would circumvent the Portuguese claims to the East Indies, particularly if the islands lay farther east than thought. They might prove to be east of the Tordesillas line defining the boundary of Spanish and Portuguese spheres

of influence. Better yet, the new sea might lead to Terra Australis Incognita, the fabled Southern Continent that was considered at the time be required to balance the northern continents of the Earth.

After his discovery, Balboa made further plans for exploration, and in 1517 and 1518 two ships were built, *San Cristóbal* and *Santa Maria de la Buena Esperanza,* and began to coast the shores of the Gulf of Panamá in October 1518. Thus they became the first European ships to sail on the waters of the Pacific Ocean.

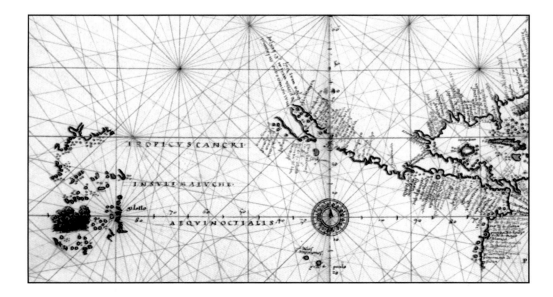

Map 12.
Part of a world map by Battista Agnese, 1542. This Venician map shows Balboa's isthmus and the Moluccas, the Spice Islands reached by Magellan. They had already been discovered by the Portuguese from the east. The Pacific Ocean is shown much narrower than it is in reality.

Fernão de Magalhães, better known by his anglicized name of Ferdinand Magellan, was a Portuguese navigator who was the first to act on the notion that although there was a continent blocking the way from Europe to the Spice Islands or Cathay, it might be possible to find a passage through the land and emerge into the ocean Balboa had seen.

The king of Portugal was uninterested in westward voyages because they would impinge on the territories given to Spain under the Treaty of Tordesillas in 1493 and 1494, when the two countries carved up the world as though it were theirs to carve. But the king of Spain, naturally enough, was interested when Magellan proposed a voyage to take possession of the Moluccas – the Spice Islands (now part of Indonesia) – for Spain by sailing west. He convinced the king that there was a good chance that the islands were on the Spanish side of the demarcation line. In fact it was difficult for either country to determine their position accurately as it involved calculation of longitude. Magellan was given command of five ships, which left Spain in 1519.

Magellan, of course, discovered a way around the southern tip of South America via the straits that today bear his name. Having emerged into the new ocean on an unusually peaceful morning in November 1520, after a long struggle to get through the Strait of Magellan, he named it Mar Pacifica – the Pacific Ocean.

We are fortunate to have the narrative of Antonio Pigafetta, an Italian nobleman who was, quite literally, just along for the ride. Pigafetta's narrative recorded:

Wednesday, November 28, 1520
We debouched from that strait [the Strait of Magellan] engulfing ourselves in the Pacific Sea. We were three months and twenty days without getting any kind of fresh food . . . We sailed about 4,000 leagues . . . through an open stretch of that Pacific Sea. In truth it was very pacific, for during that time we did not suffer any storm . . . Had not God and His blessed mother given us such good weather we would all

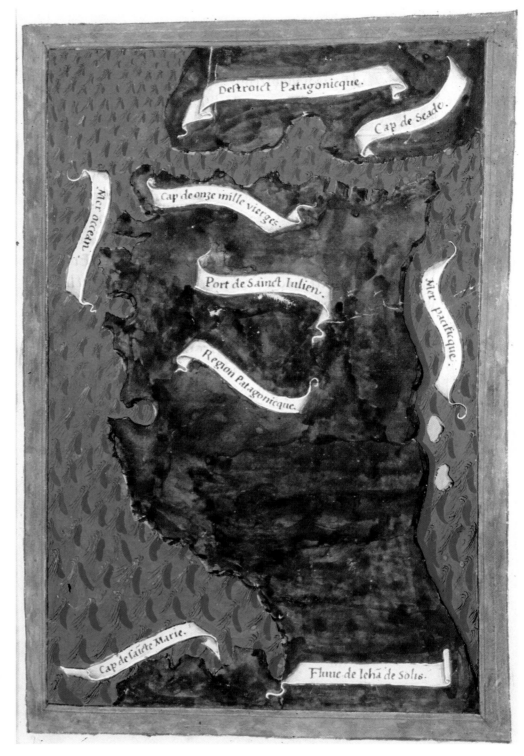

have died of hunger in that exceedingly vast sea. In truth I believe no such voyage will ever be made again.

In that prediction Pigafetta was wrong, but the vastness of the ocean would remain a critical factor in exploration and commerce until the age of steam, and sailors would soon learn that a knowledge of winds and currents was essential.

Magellan made it to the Moluccas, where he was killed by natives, but his

Map 13. The name Pacific Ocean first appears on a map. This "Chart of the Patagonian Region" is from the French edition of Antonio Pigafetta's book. South is at the top, with "Mer ocean," the Ocean Sea, the Atlantic, on the left, and "Mer pacifique," the Pacific Ocean, on the right. On the map in the Italian edition Latin is used; the Pacific is "Mare pacifico."

ship the *Vittoria* (*Victoria*), the sole survivor of the original five ships, continued westwards under Juan Sebastián del Cano and arrived in Seville on 8 September 1522, becoming the first to circumnavigate the world.

Voyage in Search of Gold

In the years after Balboa crossed the isthmus at Panama, the Spanish extended their explorations both north and south along the Pacific coast, their motivation, most of the time, being a search for wealth and riches. Peru was subjugated in 1533, and a Basque pilot, Fortún Jiménez, explored the coast of Baja California in 1533.

Spanish explorer Alvar Núñez Cabeza de Vaca arrived in Mexico City in 1536 with reports of pearls and emeralds to the north on the shores of the South Sea, and other tales of seven golden cities of Cibola

arrived with a Franciscan friar, Marcos de Niza.

In 1539 Hernando Cortés felt it worthwhile to investigate and sent Francisco de Ulloa in three ships north. Ulloa explored the head of the Gulf of California and rounded Cabo San Lucas and sailed north, discovering Isla Cedros, off the west coast of Baja, in January 1540. Ulloa only got as far as Cabo del Engaño, at 30° N, not finding gold or other wealth, but he did show that California was a peninsula, a fact that was to be overlooked by many mapmakers, who

would still insist on depicting it as an island (see page 45).

In 1542, Ulloa was followed by Juan Cabrillo, who got as far north as San Francisco. None of his maps have survived.

Map 14. Part of the fabulously illustrated wall map of Sebastian Cabot, drawn in 1544 and showing the discoveries of the Spanish in the Pacific up to and including that of Francisco de Ulloa in 1539–40. Spanish knowledge of the west coast of the Americas had proceeded faster southwards to Peru than northwards at this time, driven by the pursuit of gold. Nevertheless, a lot has been revealed since Balboa first saw the Pacific Ocean. Text and ornament fills the unknown Pacific.

Spanish Galleons Find Their Way across the Pacific

As early as 1522, when they had first arrived in the western Pacific, the Spanish had found it difficult to sail eastwards across the Pacific. One of Magellan's original fleet, *Trinidad*, under Gonzalo Gomez de Espinosa, left Tidore, one of the Moluccas, in April 1522 to attempt to sail east to Panama. He reached 42° N, seeing large whales and many flocks of birds, but could not make any headway eastwards and had to return to Tidore.

In 1527 Cortés, in Mexico, received directions from the king of Spain to assist ships he had sent to the Moluccas the year before to attempt to secure the islands for Spain. Cortés accordingly dispatched three ships, under Alvaro de Saavedra Ceron. He made it to the Spice Islands, but when he attempted to return by a route almost directly east, he was not able to do so. The following year he tried again, this time to the north, reaching 31° N, but the winds were always contrary and once again the ship had to return to Tidore.

In 1529 the king of Spain pawned any "rights" he may have had to the Spice Islands to the king of Portugal in return for a loan. In any case, by this time the Portuguese were in possession of the most important islands; but they could approach them and return by sailing east from Europe. Looking for other possible sources of wealth, the Spanish decided that the Philippines were within the Tordesillas-defined sphere of Spain and expeditions were mounted.

Sailing west across the Pacific at about 10° N was not a problem, but getting back again was a different matter.

Several unsuccessful expeditions were sent out, and then in November 1564 four ships commanded by Miguel López de Legazpi set sail from Navidad, on the west coast of Mexico, to take possession of the Philippines *and* solve the problem of getting back again. The pilot of the expedition was a friar, Brother Andrés de Urdaneta, a veteran of Pacific sailing, having

been with Juan Sebastián del Cano, the surviving circumnavigator of the Magellan expedition. In fact, Urdaneta had organized the whole expedition, even choosing the commander, a position a cleric was not allowed to hold.

Urdaneta had by this time formulated ideas about the circulation of the winds and currents of the Pacific Ocean, correctly realizing that there were both clockwise and counterclockwise rotations of air. He thus postulated that in order to pick up westerlies a ship would have to sail to higher latitudes, north or south. The question was: how far north or south?

Soon after sailing, one of the ships, *San Lucas*, separated from the rest of the fleet. Its captain, Alonso de Arellano, apparently wanted to reach the Philippines first and steal the glory and the choice spices; the real reason is not known. Whatever the reason, Arellano pulled ahead, reached the Philippines, and, fearing the arrival of the rest of the fleet, filled his ship's holds with cinnamon

Map 15.
A map of the Pacific and Atlantic Oceans made by Antonio de Herrera y Tordesillas. It was copied from a manuscript map of Juan López de Velasco, made about 1575 (see next page), and published in 1601. This map is from an edition of 1622. The Tordesillas demarcation line, the result of a treaty between the Spanish and the Portuguese to divide the world between them, runs through Brazil and also the Malay Peninsula. Spanish territory was supposedly west of the Brazil line and east of the Malay line. The Malay line was drawn as far west as possible by the Spanish (and this is a Spanish map) so as to include the Spice Islands in their domain, but at the time, no one really knew where it should be located.

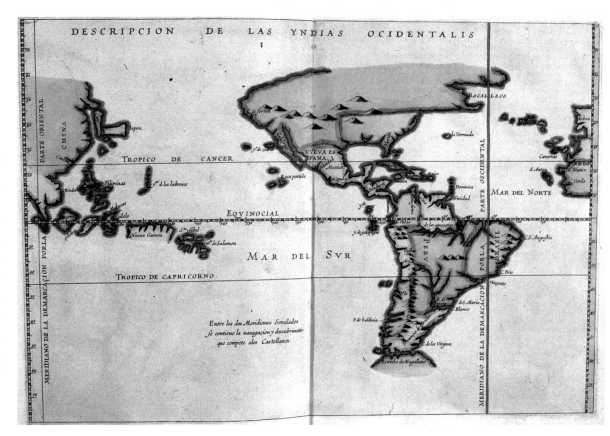

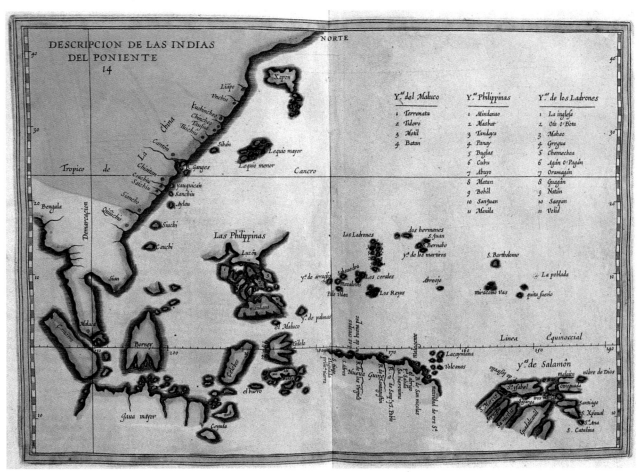

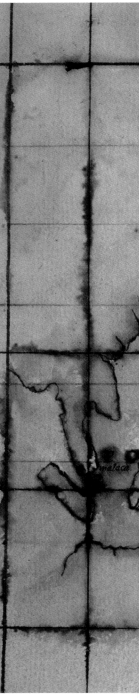

Map 16. A map of the western North Pacific made by Antonio de Herrera y Tordesillas in 1601 (1622 edition). It was copied from the manuscript map of Juan López de Velasco, made about 1575. The supposed location of the Tordesillas demarcation line runs through the Malay Peninsula.

Map 17 (right). Spaniard Juan López de Velasco's map showing the newly discovered sailing track eastward across the Pacific. The westward track is also shown. The map was drawn about 1575, ten years after the discovery of the wind pattern by Arellano and Urdaneta.

Map 18 (right, bottom). Track of the Manila galleon, from a captured Spanish chart. This map appeared in the English translation of the atlas of La Pérouse's voyage, published in 1798 (page 102).

and headed back. Arellano had been briefed by Urdaneta about his theory of wind circulation, so he headed north, hoping to pick up the westerlies.

At about 43° N, he found them. Triumphantly, he tacked east, and for twelve weeks ran before the westerly winds, reaching the North American coast at 27° 45´ N, in Baja California, on 16 July 1565. Turning southward, Arellano reached Navidad in August.

The rest of the fleet had in the meantime reached the Philippines, taking possession of the island of Cebu for Spain. The *San Pablo,* with Urdaneta on board, was sent back to Mexico to urge that reinforcements be sent to Cebu. Sailing north, the westerly winds were picked up at about 35° N, and again after sailing east for about twelve weeks, the coast of North America was sighted at 33° 45´ N, at Santa Barbara. Arellano had hoped, perhaps, to claim glory by being the first of the fleet to reach the Philippines; but he reaped a lasting place in history by becoming the first to sail across the Pacific Ocean from east to west.

Urdaneta, however, did not go unrewarded. A board of inquiry was established by the Spanish government to determine who was due the credit for solving the wind puzzle, and they decided in Urdaneta's favor. Arellano was disgraced and Urdaneta feted. But Arellano *did* the crossing first.

Soon after the establishment of the Spanish in the Philippines, a galleon made the round-trip every year, to supply the colony and bring back spices and gold to the coffers of Spain.

These galleons sailed every year from the Philippines between mid-June and mid-September, taking a route between 34° and 37° N; being able to quite accurately measure latitude, they could normally keep within these limits, where they knew the winds would be favorable. The passage across the Pacific then took about ninety to a hundred days.

The Manila galleons were not all the same by any means; they ranged from about 78 to 174 feet long. Though reasonably stable, they were not built for fast sailing nor for easy maneuvering. The square sails meant they could not sail into the wind at all, and even with fair winds they sailed at only about five knots. This is why the discovery of winds going in the right direction was so critical.

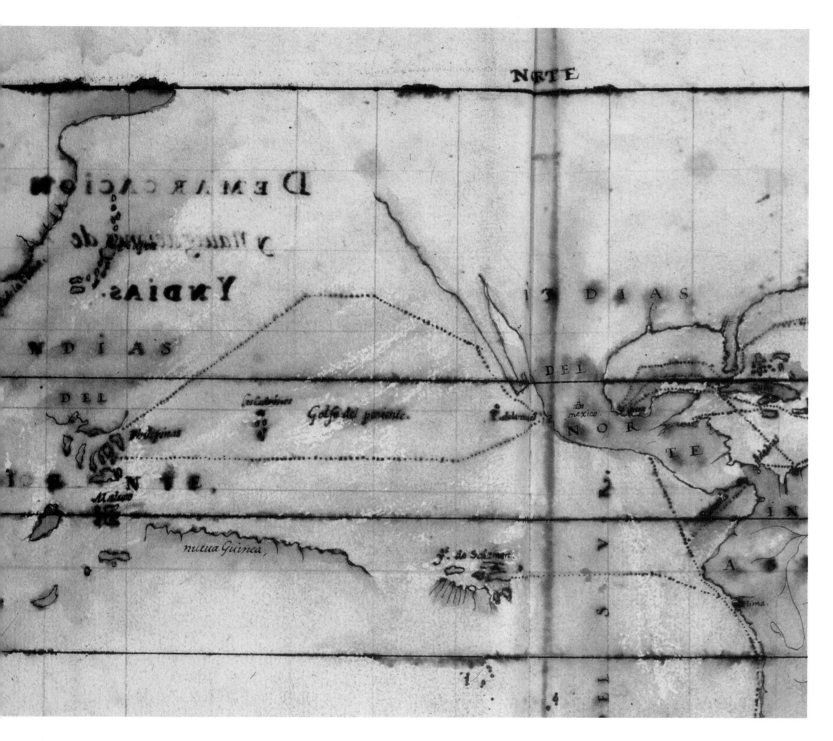

PART OF THE PACIFIC OCEAN BETWEEN CALIFORNIA AND THE PHILIPPINE ISLANDS.

from the Spanish Chart found on board the Galleon taken by Admiral Anson, in 1743, which exhibits the state of Geographical knowledge at that period,& the tracks usually followed by the Galleons, in their Voyage between Manilla and Acapulco.

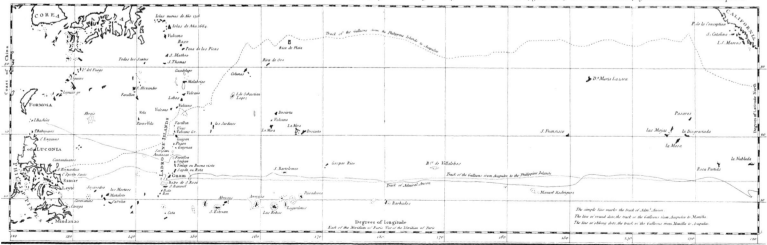

Japan and the Pacific

Map 19.
Based on information from Marco Polo, Japan sits in the middle of the ocean in this map, part of a world map drawn by Dutch mapmaker Abraham Ortelius in 1564.

The first European knowledge of Japan was from Marco Polo, who reported in his book, written at the end of the thirteenth century:

Zipangu [or Cipangu; Japan] *is an island far out at sea to the eastward* [of China], *some 1500 miles from the mainland. It is a very big island . . . they have gold in great abundance.*

This explains why the first depictions of Japan on western maps showed it as a large island right in the middle of the Pacific, as in the map by Abraham Ortelius, drawn in 1564, shown above. Sebastian Münster's

map, shown on page 12, likewise positions Japan in the middle of the ocean. Japan remained for many years one of the goals of gold-hungry European explorers.

The earliest surviving Japanese maps are the oldest of any country of the Pacific Rim; the oldest dates from 756, but is a map of landholdings. By the sixteenth century Japanese maps showed islands and terri-

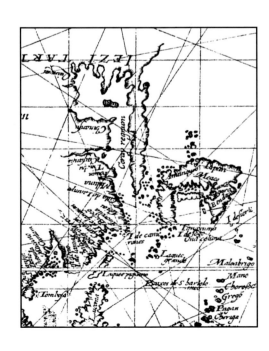

Map 20.
Japan, China, and Southeast Asia on an English map of 1599, drawn by Emery Molyneaux and published in Richard Hakluyt's *Principall Navigations.*

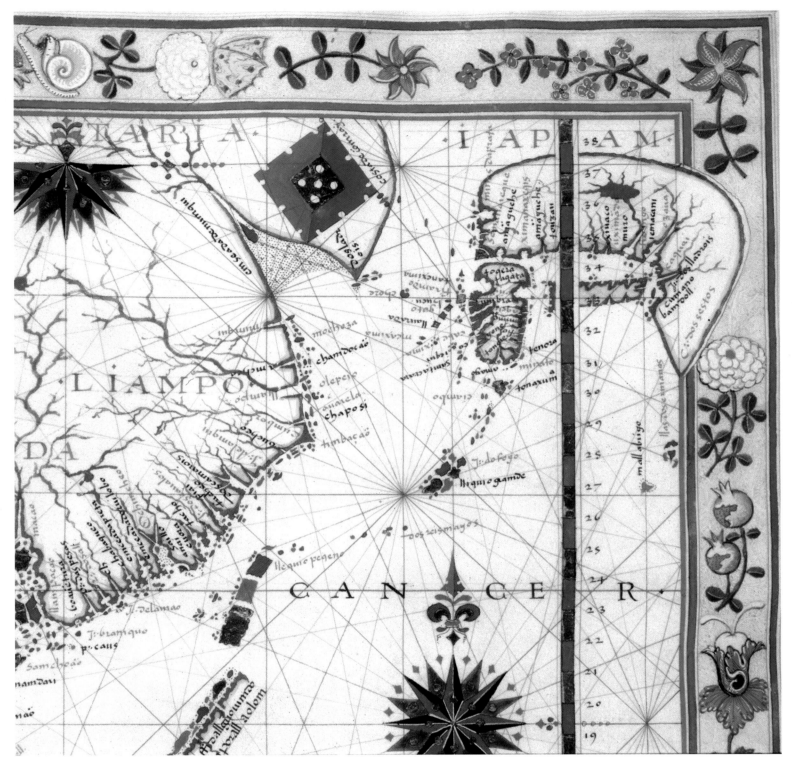

tories outside of Japan, but the maps were very impressionistic; they were works of art as well as maps.

Japanese knowledge of the Pacific was at this time very limited. It took the arrival of Europeans to make the Japanese more aware of the world beyond their shores.

The Portuguese were the first Europeans to arrive. The first documented ship was driven by storms to Tanegashima, just south of Kyushu,

in 1542. It didn't take Portuguese traders long to exploit what they saw as an opportunity, for from about 1544 on, Portuguese ships began to frequent Kyushu. Kagoshima, at the southern tip of Kyushu, became a trading port. The Portuguese would trade with the Japanese for almost a century, before being expelled in 1640. The map above is a Portuguese map of Japan, drawn by Fernão Vaz Dourado in 1570.

Map 21.
A stunning map of China and Japan drawn by Portuguese cartographer Fernão Vaz Dourado in 1570.

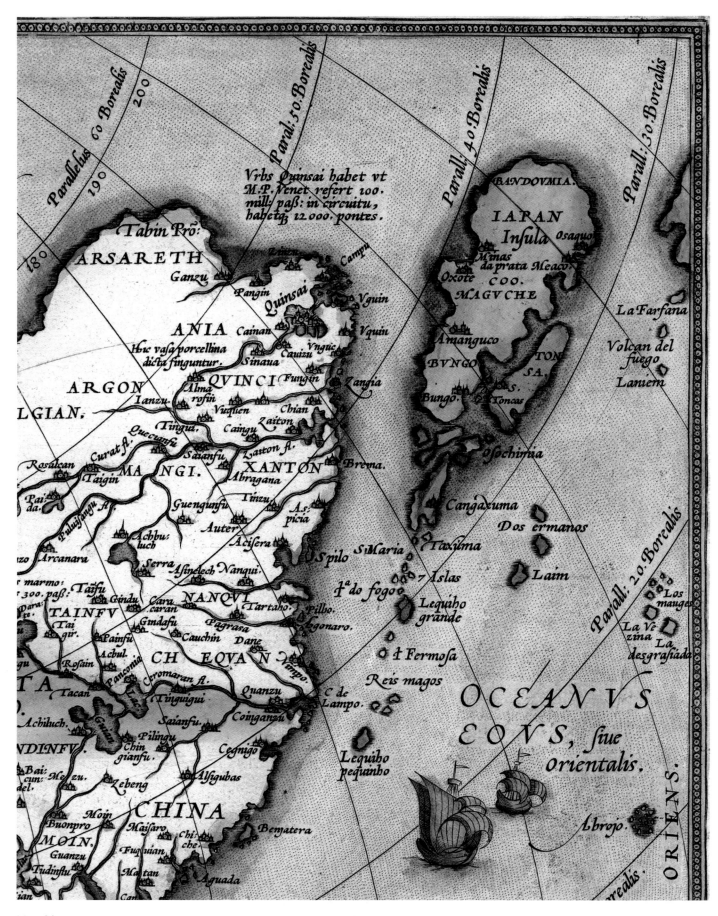

Map 22.
This rather beautiful depiction of Japan and the Chinese coast is from a map of Asia, *Asiae
Novo Descriptio*, drawn by Abraham Ortelius in 1570.

The Separation of Asia and America

When Columbus and Cabot first reached North America from Europe, they thought they had reached the Asian continent, and maps of the period reflect this view. The map by Giovanni Contarini, drawn in 1506 and shown on page 10, is typical.

After the discovery of the Pacific Ocean by Balboa and, in the years following, the realization of its immense width, many still assumed that the continents of America and Asia were joined. Maps such as that of Waldseemüller, who was first to show a Pacific Ocean (page 10), were not based on exploration but were merely good guesses.

The Pacific Ocean was assumed to be a kind of large gulf with North America and Asia as its shores. A map by Paolo Forlani, shown below, was published in 1562 and is typical of this school of thought. The ideas in this map were copied from a map by Giacomo Gastaldi published in 1546.

In the middle of the sixteenth century it was widely believed that there must be a northern strait, which would "balance" the Strait of Magellan at the southern tip of the Americas. But then it was realized that for there to be this strait – the Northwest Passage – there would have to be an outlet into the Pacific, which would necessitate that Asia and America *not* be joined. An interpretation of the works of Marco Polo is said to have given rise to the idea of (and the name of) a Strait of Anian,

Map 23.
Part of Paolo Forlani's 1562 map of the world, showing the Pacific Ocean as a gulf between America and Asia. A long "Colorado River" flows into the Gulf of California, not from the American West, but from China.

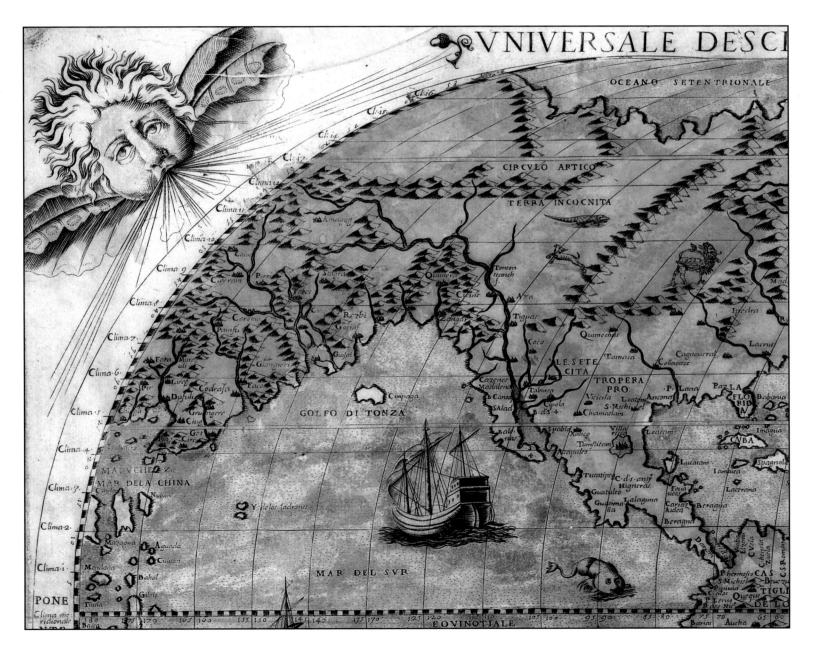

which was probably no better than a guess, but an intriguing one because of its clear resemblance to today's Bering Strait. Giacomo Gastaldi's world map of 1562, a revision of a 1546 map, seems to have been the very first to show this Strait of Anian, and once published, it was much copied, as was normal for the time.

Drawing a map showing a strait is one thing, proving it to exist quite another. It has never been proven that any of the mapmakers who drew a Strait of Anian on their maps derived their information from actual knowledge of what we know today as Bering Strait, yet theirs was a prescient guess.

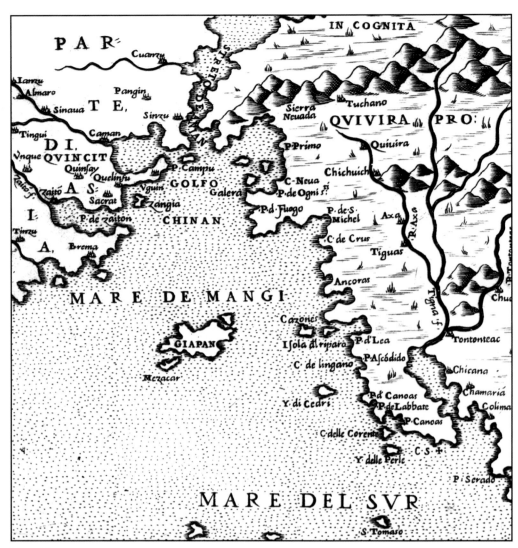

Map 25.
This map by Venetian mapmaker Bolognini Zalterii (but attributed by some to Verona mapmaker Paolo Forlani) was published in 1566 and is one of the first to show the separation of America and Asia. Was it a wild guess, or did he have some information we no longer know about?

Map 24.
Part of Giacomo Gastaldi's world map of 1562, showing a "Streto de Anian." This was probably the first depiction of a northern strait on a map.

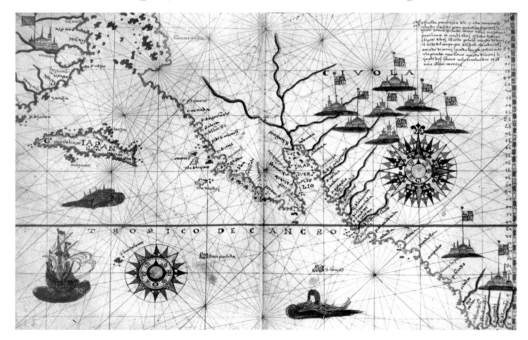

Map 26. A beautiful map of the Pacific Ocean drawn by Sicilian mapmaker Joan Martines in 1578. Japan sits splendidly in the center of the ocean, as Marco Polo's account suggests. Martines shows America and Asia separated, but hedged his bets by conveniently running the Pacific off the top of the map.

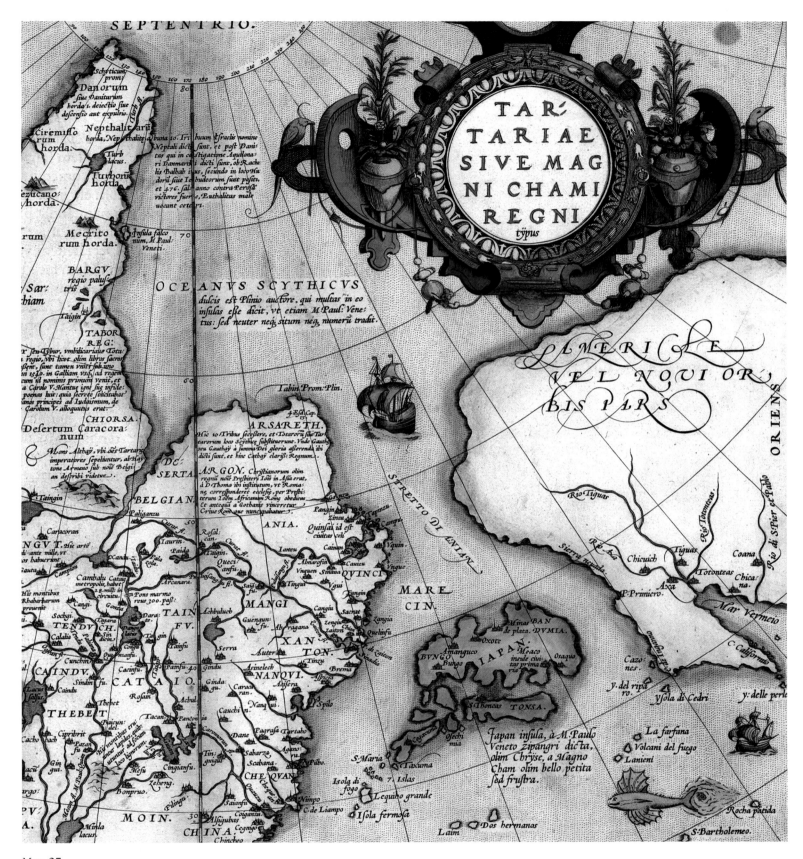

Map 27.
By 1570, when Abraham Ortelius published this beautiful map in his new atlas, *Theatrum Orbis Terrarum*, most mapmakers were incorporating the separation of the American continent from Asia into their maps. This map makes "Stretto di Anian" a major northern extension of the Pacific Ocean. Japan is massively out of scale.

Sir Francis Drake – How Far North?

Sir Francis Drake's so-called famous voyage, his circumnavigation of 1577–80, was the first circumnavigation by the English, the second after Magellan's, and the first in which the captain returned with his ship.

After sailing through the Strait of Magellan, Drake headed north, attacking Spanish towns and, in early 1579, attacking and plundering the annual Spanish galleon on its way to Acapulco from the Philippines. He then carried on northwards along the coast of California and, probably, farther north.

For a long time there has been debate about how far north Drake sailed. Some have claimed that Drake's voyage was deemed to have significant strategic value to England and the facts were altered or suppressed as a result, but unless clear archeological or documentary evidence can be found to show where he did get to, these claims will remain theories, albeit intriguing ones.

It does seem likely from the available evidence that Drake reached about 48° N. One recent claim was that he had reached as far north as 56° 40′, at the mouth of the Stikine River in the Alaska panhandle. Part of this hypothesis was based on a document called simply "The Anonymous Narrative," said to be the earliest written account of Drake's voyage; it is now in the British Library. An analysis of the written "48" revealed that it had been altered from 50, being changed to 53 on the way. Unstated, however, was the fact that the alteration had been made *before the ink dried*, making later deliberate change unlikely.

One factor used by some to indicate that Drake got much farther north than California is the evidence of cold temperatures. The account of Drake's voyage, *The World Encompassed*, has a section in it concerning the eastern Pacific Ocean, which may be viewed as the first climatological treatise on the region. It states:

Map 28.
Western hemisphere centered on the Pacific Ocean, from the title page to *Purchas His Pilgrimes*, published by Samuel Purchas in 1625. The map shows the explorations of Englishmen, including Drake and his ship in the eastern Pacific. John Saris, the first English East India Company trader to visit Japan, has his name marked on Japan.

Some of our mariners in this voyage had formerly been at Wardhouse, in 72. deg. of North latitude: who yet affirmed, that they felt no such nipping cold there in the end of Summer, when they departed thence, as they did here in the hottest moneths of June and July.

Drake's book offered a hypothesis to explain the cold:

The large spreading of the Asian and American continent, which (somewhat Northward of these parts) if they be not fully joyned, yet seeme they to come very neere one to the other. From whose high and snow-covered mountaines, the North and North-west winds (the constant visitants of those coasts) send abroad their frozen nimphes, to the infecting of the whole aire with this insufferable sharpnesse: not permitting the Sunne, no not in the pride of his heate, to dissolve that congealed matter and snow.

Many other navigators on the Northwest Coast have complained of cold, James Cook among them, but nevertheless the degree of cold does seem rather more than would be likely at 48° N; but then again, it also seems too cold for 52° N. And why would Drake, or his chaplain, who was responsible for the book, make a point of complaining about the cold if it showed they were farther north than they were allowed to say, unless they were trying to circumvent the edict in a roundabout way? There is also some evidence (from tree rings) that the climate of the region at this time was considerably colder than the period over which meteorological information has been gathered, and this could have been responsible for the cold. The year 1579 may have been exceptionally cold, but the lower temperatures presumably would have applied both to 48° and 52°.

Map 29.
Part of the "French Drake Map," drawn by Nicola van Sype about 1583. The virtues of ornament for hiding lack of information! Drake's track vanishes behind the cartouche.

There was more at Drake's elusive harbor:

In 38 deg. 30. min. we fell in with a convenient and fit harborough [harbor], and June 17. came to anchor therein: where we continued till the 23. day of July following. During all whiche time, notwithstanding it was the height of Summer, and so neere the Sunne; yet were wee continually visited with like nipping colds . . . we could very well have been contented to have kept about us still our Winter clothes.

And it was difficult to fix their position for, the book noted,

neither could we at any time in whole fourteene dayes together, find the air so clear as to be able to take the height of Sunne or starre.

Drake specifically states that he thinks no Northwest Passage exists:

And also from these reasons we conjecture; that either there is no passage at all through these Northerne coasts (which is most likely) or if there be, that yet it is unnavigable. [Due to ice; correct!] . . . Though we searched the coast diligently, even unto the 48 deg. yet found we not the land, to trend so much as one point in any place towards the east, but rather running on continually Northwest, as if it went directly to meet with Asia; and even in that height when we had a franke wind, to have carried us through, had there been a passage, yet we had a smooth and calme sea, with ordinary flowing and reflowing, which could not have beene, had there beene a srete: of which we rather infallibly concluded then conjectured, that there was none.

Long thought to have been located in California near San Francisco, Drake's harbor has more recently been considered by some to be at

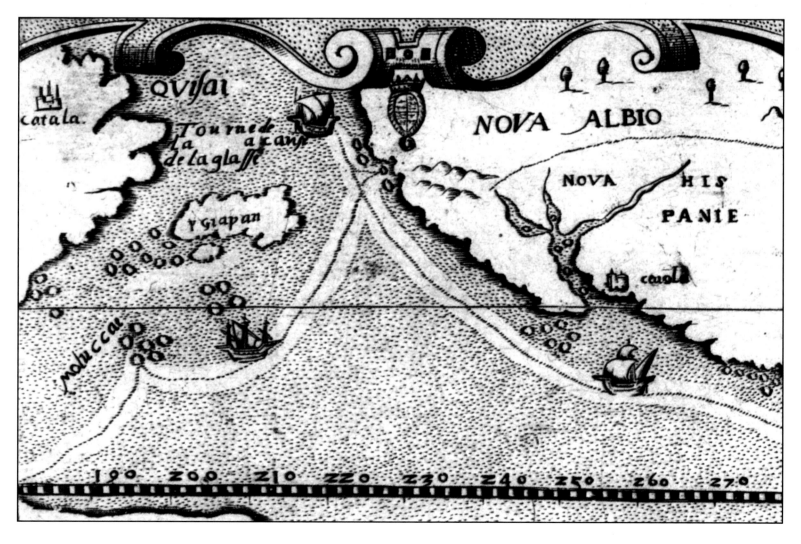

Whale Cove, in southern Oregon. Once again, this identification seems reasonable, even probable. But, like the theory that Drake sailed to 52° or 53° N, this idea is reliant on essentially circumstantial evidence. One favorite theory involves comparison of the coastline from Drake-derived maps with the modern coast; a perceived similarity is taken as evidence that Drake sailed past that location.

The "French Drake Map" (Map 29), drawn by Nicola van Sype about 1583, and supposedly seen and corrected by Drake himself, shows Drake's track disappearing behind a convenient cartouche. Four islands are shown on the western coast of America. The same four are shown on the "Dutch Drake Map," a similarly derived copy. These islands have been recently hypothesized to be crude depictions of (from the most northerly) Prince of Wales Island, the Queen Charlotte Islands, Vancouver Island, and the Olympic Peninsula. Of course, they could be, but without corroborating evidence, it is impossible to be definitive.

In 1647, Sir Robert Dudley, the son of one of Drake's financial backers, produced an atlas, *Dell' Arcano del Mare*, which was published in Florence. Some of the coastal features on the map of the northwestern coast of America (Map 30) have been compared to modern coastal features, specifically Cape Flattery, (at the extreme north of the coastline shown); Gray's Harbor (just south of the latter); and the entrance to the Columbia River (the large bay shown between 47° and 48° N).

Map 30.
Robert Dudley's map of western North America, 1647. It was one of the plates in his atlas, *Dell' Arcano del Mare*. Note the tip of Asia shown on the west side of the Pacific. The continuation of this map is shown on page 30 (Map 33), with more on Dudley's monumental atlas.

Drake's ship, *Golden Hind*, from the ornamentation on Hondius' 1589 map.

As one of Drake's financial backers, Dudley's father was in a position to have had direct information from Drake, which makes this map of particular interest. This is most intriguing, but is a similarity of coastal features sufficient to prove the map was drawn from a knowledge of the real coast?

A later printed map, presumed to have been derived from the "Queen's map," the original drawn for Queen Elizabeth I on Drake's return and now lost, is the 1589 world map by the famous mapmaker Joducus Hondius (Map 31). It has an inset map of Portus Nova Albionis in the top left-hand corner. This was derived from Drake's rendering of a harbor in which he careened his ship.

In showing the world as a double hemisphere Hondius created room for decorative devices and pictures. One is a picture of Drake's ship, *Golden Hind*. Hondius marked on the coast of Nova Albion – the name

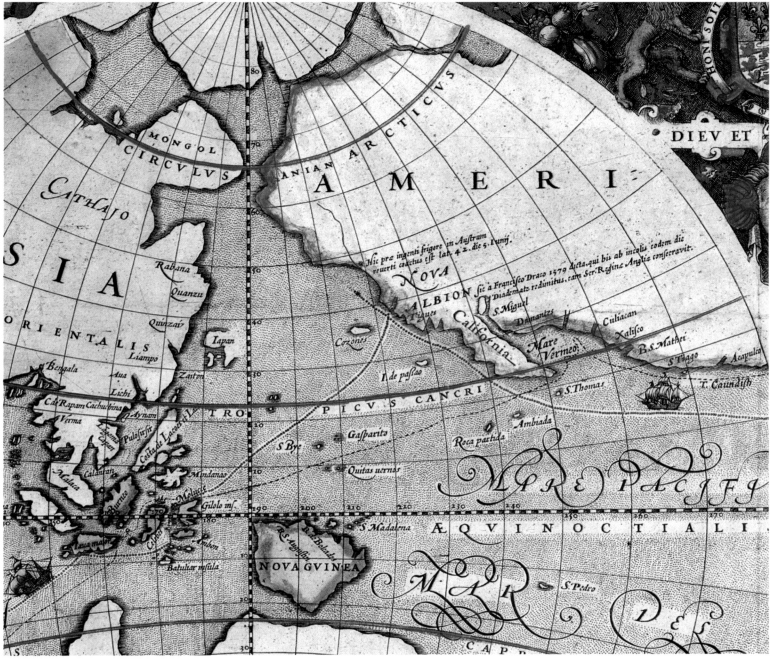

Map 31 (above).
The Pacific Ocean part of Jodocus Hondius' world map of 1589. Was the change that seems to have been made on Drake's track the result of deliberate secrecy? Hondius was Dutch, and unlikely to be concerned about English intrigues on his maps (although he was working in England at the time); the map or maps he copied might have been changed, but then why would he have *originally* drawn Drake's track reaching higher latitudes? Unless and until conclusive evidence surfaces, the controversy over Drake's route in the Pacific, and in particular how far north he reached, will likely continue to rage. The track of Thomas Cavendish, the second English circumnavigator, is also shown on this map.

Drake gave to the coast he claimed for England – that Drake turned back at 42° N because of the cold. There are indications on this map that the track was first marked continuing to about 48° N and was then partially deleted from the plate – an interesting correction indeed. Hondius may have corrected it after reading an account of the voyage by Richard Hakluyt, which itself may have been edited at the queen's direction.

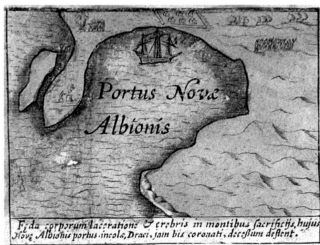

Map 32.
Drake's long-sought harbor on the west coast of North America, as depicted on the Hondius map of 1589. The location of this harbor has been the subject of endless debate among Drake aficionados.

Robert Dudley's Sea Atlas

Sir Robert Dudley produced his atlas, *Dell' Arcano del Mare* ("Concerning the Secrets of the Sea"), in Florence in 1647, and another edition in 1661. This huge and heavy tome was nevertheless specifically intended as a hydrographic atlas, to be used for navigation and carried on board ship.

Dudley's work was the first English sea atlas, the first sea atlas of the entire world, and one of the first to use Mercator's projection, on which straight lines are lines of constant bearing, an innovation which was an invaluable aid for mariners. A massive undertaking, the atlas comprised 146 charts, which took master engraver Antonio Lucini twelve years to engrave from Dudley's manuscript copies and utilized 2 270 kg or 5,000 lbs of copperplate!

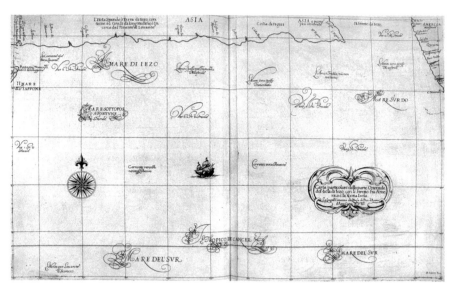

Map 33 (above) and Map 34 (below).
Two plates of the North Pacific Ocean from Robert Dudley's *Dell' Arcano del Mare*. The one below is the continuation westwards of the one above, which in turn is the continuation westwards of the map of the west coast of North America shown on page 28. A vast elongated Hokkaido ("Iezo") is shown extending westwards from the seas just off California. One wonders if Dudley had any knowledge of Maerten Vries' chart of 1643 (page 37), which showed Hokkaido as land with no definite eastward bound, and was to lead to other cartographers mapping a continent right across the North Pacific Ocean. These Dudley maps were first published in 1647 (the ones shown here are from the 1661 second edition of the atlas). On the map of Japan and the surrounding region, below, Korea is shown as an island, as it often was on maps of this period (see page 39).

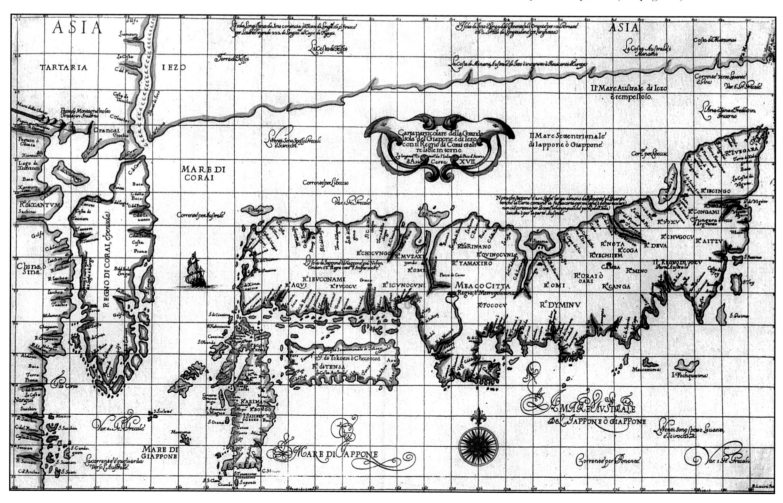

The Voyages of Sebastián Vizcaíno

Towards the end of the sixteenth century, new interest in the unexplored western coast of North America was stimulated by the establishment of the annual Manila galleon route southwards to Acapulco after crossing the Pacific in higher latitudes (see page 18). The appearance in the Pacific of English and Dutch "freelance adventurers" such as Francis Drake and Thomas Cavendish led to the suggestion that a port be established where the galleons could take refuge and where forces could be stationed to defend them.

In 1602 these considerations resulted in the Spanish navigator Sebastián Vizcaíno being given instructions to explore north from Acapulco. Vizcaíno was a merchant who had been involved in the Spanish trade with the Philippines and had sailed in a galleon in both directions across the Pacific; indeed, he had been aboard the galleon *Santa Ana* when it was captured by the English adventurer Thomas Cavendish in 1587.

He was to follow the course taken by Cabrillo some sixty years earlier (see page 16). However, following a common Spanish practice at the time Vizcaíno did not appear to have the previous expedition's charts with him, because he rediscovered San Diego, and the name is that which Vizcaíno gave to the bay. He also discovered the harbor at Monterey, and is again responsible for the name.

Vizcaíno, or at least his pilot or his cosmographer, made charts of the entire coast from Cabo San Lucas to Cape Mendocino, copies of which, made a year later by Enrico Martínez, "cosmographer to his Majesty in this New Spain," have survived.

One section, the northernmost chart of Cape Mendocino, is shown here. It took another two hundred years, however, for the long-lasting Spanish policy of secrecy to be revoked and it was not until 1802 that this summary chart of the entire voyage was published by the Spanish.

The reports of the details of this voyage are often contradictory, but it appears that one of the ships, commanded by ensign Martín de Aguilar, after being separated from the other ships in a storm, was forced northwards beyond Cape Blanco and, on returning southwards, came across a bay with a large river, which they named Rio Santa Ines. This river, because of its strong current and east-west direction, was thought to perhaps be the fabled Strait of Anian.

Many sailors had now succumbed to that scourge of long-distance voyages, scurvy, leaving the ship undermanned, and so no further exploration was carried out. But the reports of the Rio Santa Ines revived interest in a passage from the Pacific to the Atlantic, and this concept was to confuse the cartography of the Northwest Coast for almost two centuries. The "Entrada de Martín Aguilar," or "Opening discovered by Martin Aguilar" on English maps, was to show up on many maps for a long time after. Later, its supposed location somehow became about 43° N, and some thought it might be the Strait of Juan de Fuca.

In 1611 Vizcaíno took a pioneering Japanese delegation from New Spain (Mexico) back to Japan. Again with the idea of identifying potential refuges for the Manila galleon, in 1616 he surveyed several ports and carried out a hydrographic survey of the east coast of the island of Honshu, searching also for the fabled islands of gold and silver, Rico de Oro and Rico de Plata, which the Spanish thought existed in the ocean east of Japan. (These showed up on British Admiralty charts until 1875; see page 59.) Of course Vizcaíno did not find them, and none of the charts he made have survived, although perhaps one day they will be discovered in a Spanish or Japanese archive.

Maps of the coast of California at Santa Barbara and Santa Catalina (Map 35, left) and Monterey Harbor and the coast to Pillar Point (Map 36, right). From Vizcaíno's 1602 voyage, probably by Fray Antonio de la Ascension, copied by Enrico Martínez. These are part of a series of coastal maps drawn soon after the 1602 voyage.

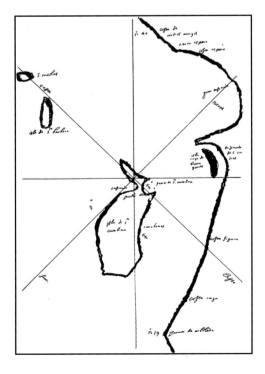
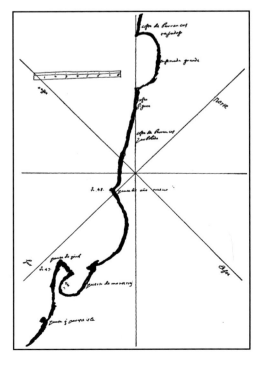

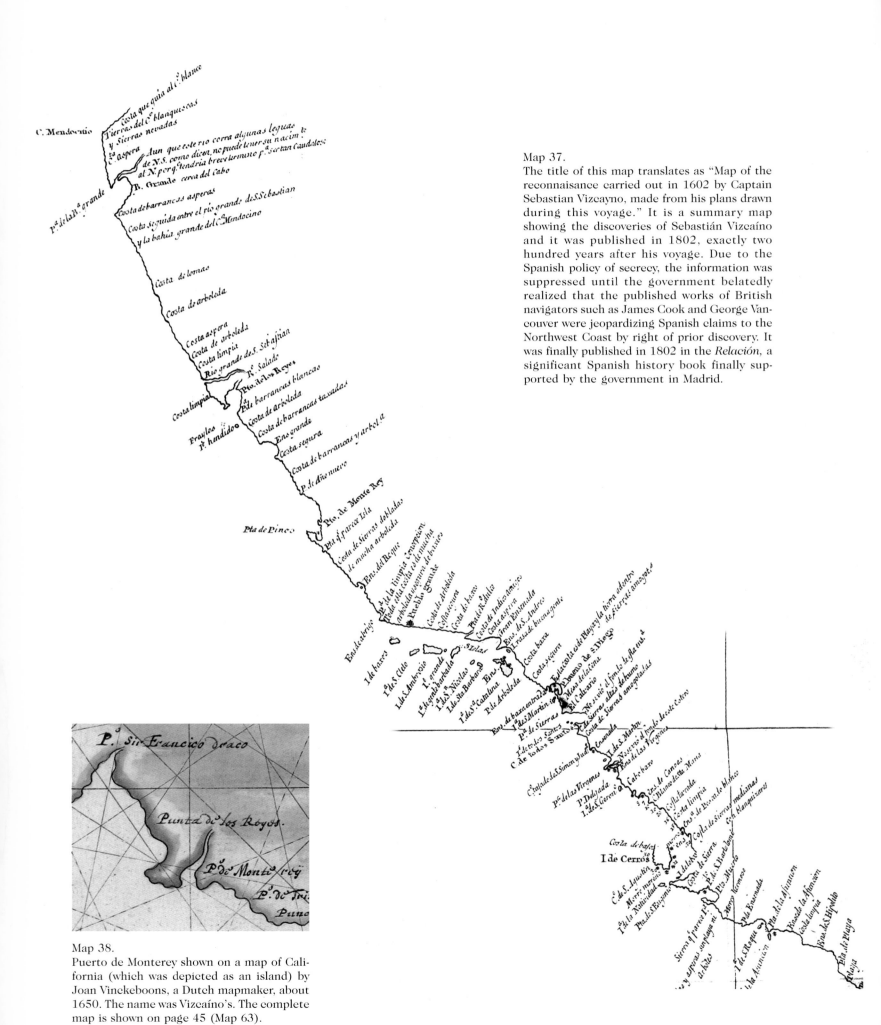

C. Mendocino

Costa que quia al C. blanco
Tierras del C.º blanquescas
y Sierras nevadas
P.ª aspera
P.ª de la B.ª grande
Aun que este rio corra algunas leguas
de N.S. como dicen, no puede tener su nacim.ᵗᵒ
al N. porq.º tendria breve termino p.ª ser tan Caudaloso
B. Grande cerca del Cabo
Costa de barrancas asperas
Costa de barrancas asperas de S.S. Sebastian
Costa seguida entre el rio grande de S.S. Sebastian
y la bahia grande del C. Mendocino

Costa de lomas

Costa de arboleda

Costa aspera
Costa de arboleda
Costa limpia
Rio grande de S. Sebastian
Rio grande de S. Salado
Costa limpia
P.ᵗᵒ de los Reyes
P.ᵗᵃ de barrancas blancas
Frayles
P.ᵗ hendido
Costa de arboleda
Costa de barrancas tasadas
Costa grande
Ens. grande
Costa segura
Costa de barrancas y arbol.ᵃ
P. de dio nuevo

P.ᵗᵒ de Monte Rey
Pta. á parece Isla
Costa de Sierras dobladas
Costa de mucha arboleda
Ens. del Reque

Pta de Pinos

A. de la limpia Concepcion
Toda esta costa es de mucha
arboleda y segura de brisas
Pueblo. grande
Costa de Arboleda
Costa segura
Costa de llano
Costa de Indios amigos
Costa aspera
Ens. de S. Andres
Gran Ensenada
Ens. de S. brose, gente
Ens. de brisa
Trasad.º biconagente
Costa baxa
Costa segura
Pta. la costa es de Playa y la tierra adentro
Bueno de S. Diego
Mesa de la cima
el Calvario
No sirvió el fondo de esta ens.ᵃ
Costa de Sierras altas de humo
Costa de Sierras anegotiadas
I. de barco
I. de S. Cielo
I. de S. Ambrosio
I. grande
I. Megrab barbada
I. S. Nicolas
I. de Sta Barbara
Islas
Ens.
I. de S. Catalina
Pta de Arboleda
Ens. de baxa central
I. de S. Martin
P.ᵗᵃ de Sierras
I. de tres Santos
C. de todos Santos
Costa de la Sierra
Enbiada de S. Simon y Judas
Ensenada
Costa de Sierras medianas
Ptas. de S. Martin
No cerro el fondo desde el Estero
Cortijada de S. Simon y Judas
Ensenada
No cerro el fondo desde el Estero
Ens. de las Virgenes
P.ᵗᵒ de las Virgenes
P.ᵗ Delgada
I. de S. Geron
Ens. de Cabo baxo
Pta. de Canas
Costa blanca de la Mesa
Costa limpia
Ens. de P.ᵗ de blanco
Costa de Sierras medianas
Costa de baxos
con blanquizares
Costa de Sierra
I de Cerros
C.º de S. Apustin
Morro marcado
I. de la Natividad
Pta. de S. Eugenio
Costa de Sierra
Pta. del Rio
Pta. de S. Pablo
Pta. Morro
Sierra á parece isla
y asperas son playa
de alto
I de S. Roque
Pta Bermada
Pta. de la Asuncion
I. de la Asuncion
Bias. de S. Hipolito
Costa limpia
Playa
Bias. de Playa

Map 38.
Puerto de Monterey shown on a map of California (which was depicted as an island) by Joan Vinckeboons, a Dutch mapmaker, about 1650. The name was Vizcaíno's. The complete map is shown on page 45 (Map 63).

P.ᵗᵒ S.ᵗᵃ Francisco draco

Punta de los Reyes.

P.ᵗᵒ de Monte rey

P.ᵗ de Tri
Puno

Map 37.
The title of this map translates as "Map of the reconnaisance carried out in 1602 by Captain Sebastian Vizcayno, made from his plans drawn during this voyage." It is a summary map showing the discoveries of Sebastián Vizcaíno and it was published in 1802, exactly two hundred years after his voyage. Due to the Spanish policy of secrecy, the information was suppressed until the government belatedly realized that the published works of British navigators such as James Cook and George Vancouver were jeopardizing Spanish claims to the Northwest Coast by right of prior discovery. It was finally published in 1802 in the *Relación*, a significant Spanish history book finally supported by the government in Madrid.

The Dutch Reach the Pacific

The Dutch first reached the Pacific Ocean in 1599, when a fleet of five ships from a Dutch trading company sailed through the Strait of Magellan.

One of these ships, *De Liefde* (*Charity*), arrived in Japan in April 1600. The pilot was an Englishman, William Adams, who established himself as an advisor to the shogun Iyeyasu and lived in Japan until his death in 1620.

Close behind this first fleet into the Pacific came Olivier van Noort, sailing on behalf of a rival Dutch company. He made it through the Strait of Magellan, intending to copy the English example and raid Spanish galleons and towns. Van Noort became the fourth to circumnavigate the world, after Del Cano, Drake, and another Englishman, Thomas Cavendish.

And then, in 1619, Jacob Le Maire and Willem Schouten rounded the southern tip of South America, determining that it was not contiguous with a southern continent and naming it Cape Hoorn in honor of their city in the Netherlands.

Dutch merchants had reached the East Indies by late in the sixteenth century and by 1602 had reached the Moluccas. Jan Huijghen van Linschoten published a book called the *Itinerario* in 1596 which summarized the Dutch knowledge of the region; it included the map shown here.

In 1600 the English East India Company was formed, and in 1602, the Dutch East India Company was created to compete with it.

The Dutch traders arrived in Japan first, in 1609, at Hirado, near Nagasaki, and received official trading privileges from the Japanese government, indeed, were encouraged to set up a factory. What a difference from what was to come in future centuries! The first English East India Company trader to arrive in Japan was John Saris, who arrived in Hirado in June 1613 only to find the Dutch already installed. However, with the help of William Adams, the English obtained similar trading rights to those of the Dutch. Saris' name is shown on the map of English explorations on page 26. The English, it seems, tried to sell the wrong goods to the Japanese, and were unsuccessful as a result; the Japanese did not want their woolens, and the English retreated in 1623, leaving the trade to the Dutch, who were destined to control it for more than two centuries.

Good Dutch relations with the Japanese did not continue long, however, and in 1641, the Dutch traders were required to relocate to the man-made island of Deshima, in Nagasaki Bay, where their activities could be monitored. They remained there until the nineteenth century.

Much of the subsequent Dutch exploration and expansion effort in the Pacific was directed to the south, towards Australia, the west coast of which was discovered in 1616.

Map 39

Part of a map of Southeast Asia published by Jan Huijghen van Linschoten in his *Itinerario* in 1596. Japan is shown hook-shaped, as it often was on early maps. Also of note is Korea, shown as a nearly circular island. East is at the top.

In 1638, the governor of the Dutch East India Company, Antonio van Dieman, authorized Abel Tasman to search the Pacific for "islands of gold and silver" rumored to lie east of Japan. Such non-existent islands were shown on maps in that location well into the nineteenth century, and were founded on the belief that silver and gold were most likely to be found in the latitudes of 31° to 42°. The rumor originated with the Spanish, but the Dutch knew of mines in northern Honshu that satisfied this criterion. Tasman, much better known for his later forays to the South Pacific (Tasmania is of course named after him), was captain of one ship, Mathijs Quast of another. They spent the second half of 1639 wandering over vast expanses of the Pacific east of Japan, reaching as far north as about 42° and as far east as about 177° W, finding no islands of silver or gold, and little land beyond the eastern coast of Honshu.

Not discouraged by this lack of results, van Dieman dispatched two ships in 1643, commanded by Maerten Gerritsz Vries. *Castricum* and *Breskens*

were to "investigate" the mainland coast of Tartary and carry out yet another search for the fabled islands of silver and gold.

Castricum, with Vries, lost contact with *Breskens* near the northern tip of Hokkaido and continued alone. Vries again of course found no islands of silver and gold, but he did discover some of the Kuril Islands and increased geographical knowledge of the western Pacific.

Vries sailed through a strait (now Vries Strait) between Ostrov Iturup, the Kuril Island immediately to the northeast of Hokkaido, and Ostrov Urup, farther to the northeast. The latter he believed to be not an island but part of a continent, which he named Companies Landt, after his East India Company. This was to add to geographic confusion for a century and a half, for a myriad of maps were later produced that showed Company Land or some variant of it stretching across the North Pacific to a Strait of Anian on a northwest coast of America (see Maps 43–47).

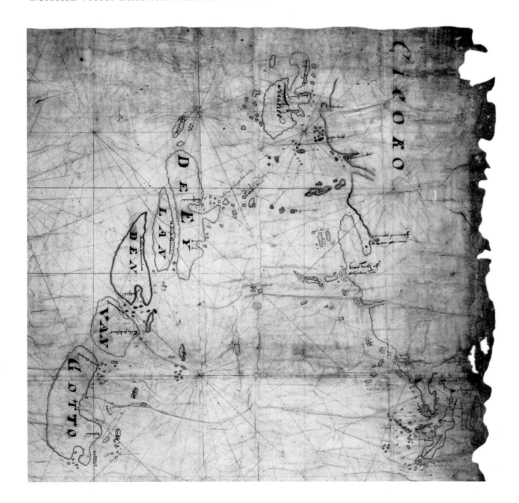

Map 40 (left).
A Dutch map of the westernmost part of Japan and the Gotoretto, the Goto Islands in Korea Strait, between Japan and Korea. Nagasaki is shown at bottom right; this was the location of the Dutch trading station in Japan. The map is undated but is believed to have been drawn about 1680.

Map 41.
Hessel Gerritz's monumental map of the Pacific Ocean, drawn in 1622 and now residing in the Bibliothèque nationale in Paris. It was drawn as the Dutch became more and more interested in the Pacific. The route of Jacob le Maire and Willem Schouten is shown around the southern tip of South America and into the Pacific past Cape Horn, which Schouten named Kaap Hoorn after his hometown in Holland. The fleet shown at the bottom of the map is that of Le Maire and Schouten. Hessel Gerritz was appointed cartographer to the Dutch East India Company in 1617. In this map drawn, or rather painted, in that capacity, the width of the Pacific is reasonably accurate, though longitude is not marked. One legend comments on the "great breadth between the most eastern and western places which are situated far south and north." The navigator portraits at top right are (from left to right) Balboa, Magellan, and Le Maire.

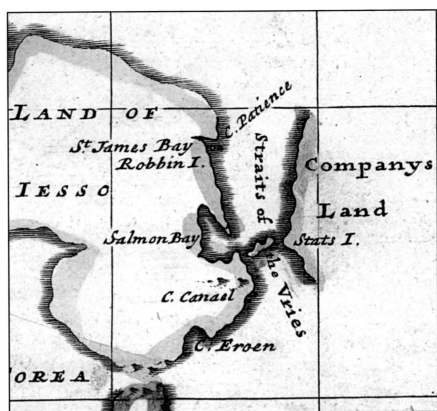

Map 42. A Japanese map of the harbor of Nagasaki, drawn about 1680. The artificial island of Deshima, where the Dutch traders were required to live, is clearly shown.

Map 43.
Maerten Vries' discoveries influenced mapmakers for a century and a half after his voyage. Hermann Moll showed a "Strait of the Vries" and "Companys Land" on his world map of 1719. (See also Map 79, page 55.)

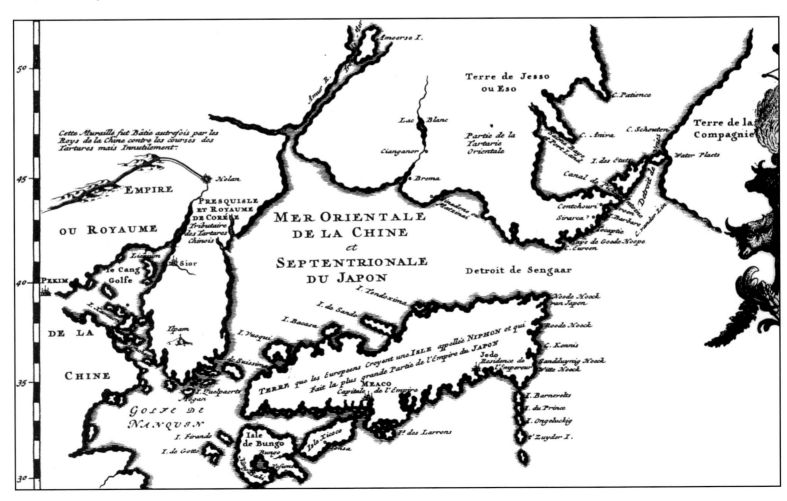

Map 45.
Maerten Vries' map, or at least a contemporary copy, showing his "discovery" of Company Land, actually one of the Kuril Islands. Compagnies Land was named for the Dutch East India Company, his employer. State Land was named for his country, or state, the Netherlands.

Map 44 (left).
This map, drawn by Henri Chatelain in 1719, illustrates the confused geography of the western Pacific at the time. It shows "Terre de la Compagnie" disappearing behind an ornate cartouche, a favorite device of cartographers when they had no idea what was really there. Hokkaido, shown here as "Terre de Jesso ou Eso," curves up to meet Company Land via what in reality are the Kuril Islands.

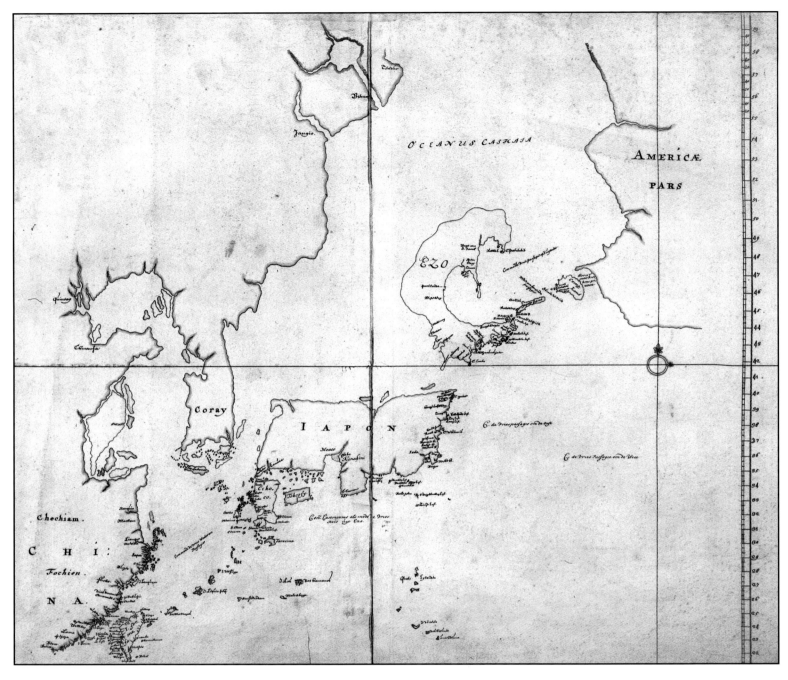

Map 46 (above).
A map contemporary with Vries' drawn about 1644 or 1645 by Isaak de Graaf. Suddenly Vries' Company Land has metamorphosed into "Americae Pars" – part of America. To make this work, mapmakers had to show a continent stretching right across the North Pacific, and many did just that.

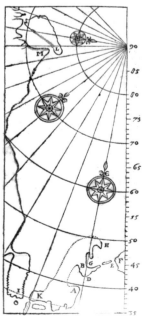

Map 47 (left).
A map drawn to illustrate a published account of Vries' voyage. I is Korea; K is Japan; A is also Japan; B is the capital of Jeso (Hokkaido); G is the bay reached by Vries; H is his northernmost point reached; E is "Vries Strait"; and F is "Kompagnies Lant in Amerika." It is easy to see how this idea confused Vries' Company Land with the North American continent. Being a printed book, this presumably had much wider influence than manuscript maps.

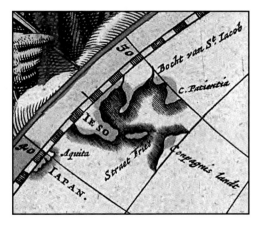

Map 48.
The first atlas depiction of Vries' discoveries was on a world map by Joan Blaeu in 1664. This small part of the edge of the western hemisphere is almost right off the map, literally!

Early Maps of Korea

Early mapmakers couldn't make up their minds as to whether Korea was an island or a peninsula. Because it was a tributary state of China, maps were not usually drawn only of Korea, but of larger areas. Abraham Ortelius' maps of 1570, shown on pages 22 and 25, didn't show Korea at all. Linschoten's map published in 1596 (page 33) showed an "Ilha de Corea" as an almost circular island .

By the middle of the seventeenth century, about half of the maps of the region showed Korea as an island, half as a peninsula, the latter winning out as time went on and geographical knowledge improved.

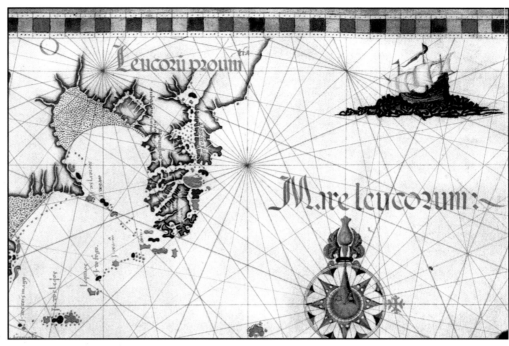

Map 49.
Diogo Homem's beautiful manuscript map of 1558 showed Korea as a peninsula and an archipelago; the large island at the southern end is Japan.

Map 50.
Luis Teixeira's map of Japan and Korea, showing Korea as an island, appeared in an addendum to Abraham Ortelius' *Theatrum Orbis Terrarum*, published in 1595. It was relatively widely circulated and much copied.

Map 51.
Korea as shown on Martino Martini's map of 1655. At this date some cartographers still showed Korea as an island, while others showed it as a peninsula.

Early Maps of China

Until relatively recently, maps in China have had a somewhat different role than those from western cultures. Maps were created as part of a larger intellectual and cultural undertaking that included more than geography and astronomy, encompassing philosophy, literature, art, and religion. Chinese maps often lack a fixed point of reference or change scales from one part of the map to the next, depending on the relative significance of the object being viewed, and often devote much space to text.

The ocean was seen as threatening and depicted with violent waves; more emphasis was given to (presumably less threatening) rivers.

After Cheng Ho's voyages in 1493, the Chinese emperor became increasingly concerned about foreign influences and in 1500 forbade anyone to put to sea on pain of death; foreigners were restricted to certain strictly controlled ports.

Even dynastic change in 1644 to the Manchu did not change the essentially land-emphasized view of the world. Early Chinese maps, then, tend to be depictions of the land, incidentally bordered by the Pacific Ocean. They were maps of the Chinese world, Sinocentric views of the land ruled by the emperor. This attitude, combined with that of the Japanese, meant that the Pacific was left to European powers to fight over.

One important early Chinese map is the *Huatyi tu*, a "Map of China and the Barbarians." It was carved in stone about 1136, though the map itself may date from even earlier: 1040 has been suggested. The 1 m (3 feet) square original is in a Chinese museum, and a paper transcript is shown here (Map 55). The Great Wall is prominent, and much text surrounds the map, describing the foreign countries.

A particularly beautiful example of the cartographic style developed during the Song dynasty (960–1279) is still evident on a world map drawn in 1743. In the section reproduced

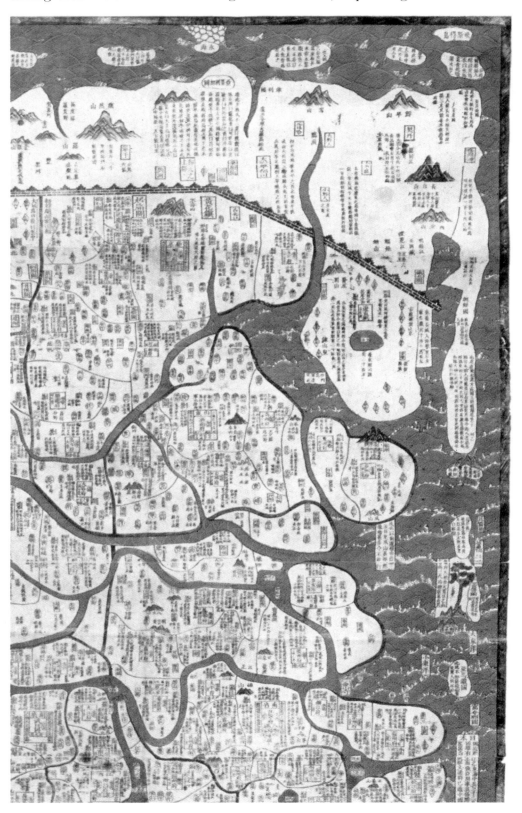

Map 52
Part of an anonymous, untitled Song dynasty Chinese world map, 1743. The map is about 1 200 x 1 370 mm (4 x 4½ feet). A gray-green multitude of "threatening" surf-topped waves uniformly depicts the seas. Rivers are almost as wide as coastal inlets, reflecting their importance.

Map 53. Pacific Ocean portion of a globe made in 1623 in Bejing by two Jesuits, Manuel Dias and Nicolo Longobardi; it is signed in their Chinese names, Yang Ma-no and Lung Hua-min. The globe is made of wood and is painted with lacquer. It is 592 mm (23 inches) in diameter.

here, from the northeastern part of the map, the coast of Asia is shown (Map 52). In the north, the Great Wall is again prominent. The map shows the Liaodong peninsula and then, farther west, a thin Korean peninsula. In reality, of course, the latter is much larger than the former, but it was not part of China, and this is a Chinese map.

The "threatening sea" of the Pacific Ocean is shown in the form of large stylized waves.

The arrival of Jesuit missionaries in China in the late sixteenth century is generally considered to have contributed a great deal to mapping in that country. The pre-eminent missionary was Father Matteo Ricci, who, in response to Chinese interest in Europe, produced a series of maps of the world that combined European techniques with Chinese. In order to please his hosts, Ricci placed China near the center of his maps. His first map has not survived but a close copy is illustrated in a book dated 1613.

The globe shown above was painted in 1623 by two Jesuits, Manuel Dias and Nicolo Longobardi.

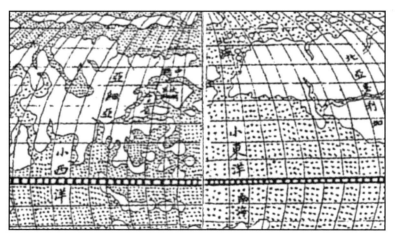

Map 54 (left). *Yudi shanhai quantu,* from Zhang Huang, *Tushu bian,* 1613.

(top left) Father Matteo Ricci, holding a map. From Du Halde's *Description Geographique . . . de l'Empire de la Chine,* 1735.

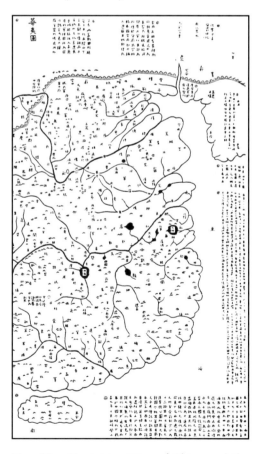

Map 55. *Huatyi tu,* "Map of China and the Barbarians." It was carved in stone about 1136, and probably reproduces a map drawn about 1040. This is a paper representation.

The Russians Reach the Pacific

An ever-expanding search for furs led Russian Cossacks eastwards across Siberia, and in 1639 Ivan Moskvitin reached the shores of the Sea of Okhotsk. In 1643–45 Cossack Vasilii Poyarkov reached the sea via the Amur River.

His exploration was followed in short order by a remarkable voyage by Semen Dezhnev.

The popular perception is that Vitus Bering was the first person to show that Asia was separated from America by a strait; after all, the strait in question is named after him.

However, this is a case of a relatively well documented exploration, that of Bering's first voyage, overwhelming relatively sparse information available about a predecessor. In fact the first (documented) person to sail through Bering's strait was an illiterate Siberian Cossack named Semen Ivanovitch Dezhnev, who in 1648 sailed from the mouth of the Kolyma River, which flows to the Arctic Ocean

at about 162° E, round the extreme northeastern tip of Siberia to a point near the Anadyr River, which flows into the Pacific at about 176° E. By so doing he proved, perhaps unwittingly, that Asia and America were separate.

The expedition consisted of seven small *kochas,* roundish-hulled ships that were well designed to deal with ice-filled seas, and ninety men. They left the Kolyma on 20 June 1648. We are not sure how long it took to get to the Anadyr, but we do know that only two ships completed the voyage, that commanded by Dezhnev and that by Fedot Alekseyev.

Because his voyage answered a significant scientific question – in this case whether Asia and America were joined – Dezhnev has been placed by some writers alongside Vasco da Gama, Christopher Columbus, and Ferdinand Magellan.

But Dezhnev did not draw any maps, or if he did, they did not survive; indeed it is far from clear whether any navigational log or other record was ever kept. This is generally a poor way to ensure your exploits are documented for posterity, but Dezhnev was only interested in the gathering of furs, and in survival, and probably did not view himself as an explorer.

Map 56.
The Godunov map of eastern Siberia, named after Petr Godunov, a Russian governor, who commissioned it in 1667. This is probably the earliest map to show the Russian Pacific coast based on actual exploration. The Kolyma and Lena Rivers are shown, incorrectly flowing to the Pacific. The map was drawn with south at the top but is shown here upside down, with north at the top.

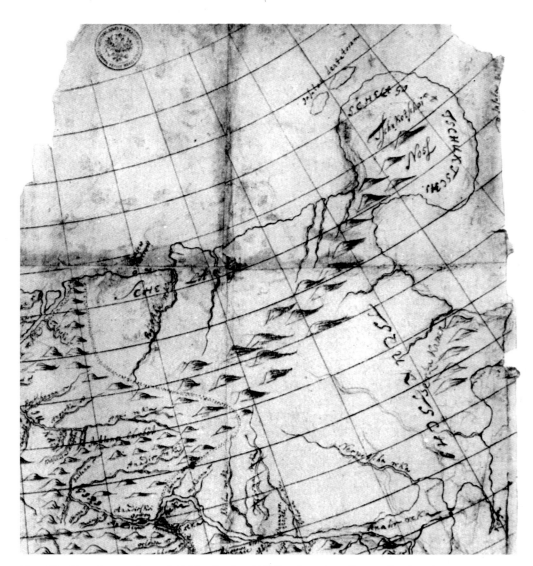

Map 57. Map drawn about 1736 by Gerhard Müller, based on Semen Dezhnev's reports.

It seems likely that Bering knew of his predecessor's achievement, for when the first public notice of Bering's voyage of 1728 (see page 63) was published in the *St. Petersburg Gazette* in March 1730, it contained the information that Bering had "learned from the local inhabitants that fifty or sixty years before a vessel arrived in Kamchatka from the Lena." Inaccurate and incomplete, this appears to have been a reference to Dezhnev's voyage.

In 1736, Gerhard Müller, one of the scientists attached to the Second Kamchatka Expedition, Bering's second voyage (see page 67), found a written account of Dezhnev's voyage in government offices in Yakutsk, in eastern Siberia. This account was sent back to St. Petersburg in 1737, and was published in Russian in 1742, but did not receive much attention until it was published in 1758 by the Russian Academy of Sciences.

By that time the name of Bering Strait had come into use, and Dezhnev Strait was not to be.

The first published information about Dezhnev's voyage appears to be that in a map by a Dutchman, Nicholaas Witsen, in 1687. In 1665 he visited Moscow and obtained geographical information sufficient to create a four-sheet map of Russia. The northeast section of this map appears to show both rivers, the start and end of Dezhnev's voyage, in more or less correct relative positions. Some of Witsen's correspondence also appears to contain knowledge of Dezhnev's voyage. All the information Witsen accumulated makes it hard to believe Dezhnev's voyage was entirely forgotten, at least until the end of the seventeenth century.

With his rediscovery of the voyage in 1736, Gerhard Müller drew a map based on his interpretation of Dezhnev's reports. The map he produced is shown on the previous page. Dezhnev's reports emphasized the Icy Cape, the Chukotskiy Peninsula, and this feature is shown grown large in the Müller-Dezhnev map. Both the Kolyma and Anadyr Rivers are shown.

Russians reached Kamchatka about 1690. Before the end of the

Map 58 (above).
Nicholaas Witsen's 1687 map, likely the first map to show Dezhnev's discovery of the fact that America was not joined to Asia but was separated by a strait, today called Bering Strait rather than Dezhnev Strait. Ironically, the map does not clearly show a strait, with the "Icy Cape" Dezhnev rounded being shown as a peninsula of indefinite length, but the map does show other features noted by the illiterate Dezhnev, notably the Kolyma and Anadyr Rivers, the beginning and end points of his voyage of 1648.

Map 59 (right).
Part of an anonymous map of eastern Siberia drawn in 1701 showing Kamchatka. Oriented unconventionally by modern standards, Kamchatka is the peninsula at the bottom of the map, and the island is Japan.

century, Kamchatka had been subdued by an expedition led by Vladimir Atlasov, in 1697–99. The first Russian discovery of Kamchatka has also been attributed fifty years before to Fedot Alekseyev, who was with Dezhnev but was killed by natives. He may have also been the first to find the northern Kuril Islands.

The map shown at the bottom of the previous page, certainly one of the first if not the first to depict Kamchatka, was drawn in 1701.

Shown at right is a map drawn in 1712 by Siberian mapmaker Semen Remezov based on information obtained from Vladimir Atlasov. Interesting, but unexplained, is the notation in Russian on the finger of land shown in the northwest part of this map: "recently reported land."

Russian explorers began to work their way south, "island hopping" the Kuril chain. About 1701 Ivan Golygin reached the first of the Kuril Islands, Ostrov Karaginskiy, and by 1712 A. I. Bykov and A. Krestianinov had reached Ostrov Shiashkotan, the third of the larger Kurils, going south from Kamchatka.

In 1682, Peter I ("the Great") had become tsar. He was interested in exploration, and in particular what the extent of his domains might be, or could be. As we shall see (page 62), it was he who sent out Vitus Bering to search for America. But the first

eastward expedition he sent out was that of Ivan Evreinov and Fedor Luzhin, to determine the extent of the Kamchatka Peninsula.

They crossed Kamchatka from west to east and back again, and in 1721 sailed to, by their calculations, the sixteenth of the Kurils. Evreinov's map was the first to show Kamchatka reasonably accurately, although his longitudes were incorrect.

Map 60.
Map of Kamchatka based on Vladimir Atlasov's expedition of 1697–99, drawn by Siberian mapmaker Semen Remezov between 1712 and 1714. Written on the long peninsula at top right are the words "recently reported land." It is tempting to assume that this must be Alaska, but it is more likely to be a misreported island in the Aleutian chain.

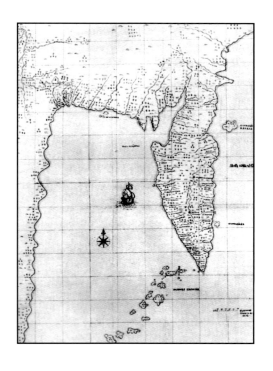

Map 61 (left).
Map of the Kamchatka Peninsula, the Sea of Okhotsk, and the northern Kuril Islands, drawn by Ivan Evreinov about 1722.

Early Mapping of the American West Coast

The shape of "the backside of America" – the west coast – was shrouded in mystery until the Spanish started to explore northwards from Mexico.

Hernando Cortés sent Francisco de Ulloa north in 1539–40, and he got as far as about 30° N (page 16), showing in the process that Baja California was a peninsula. No matter the facts! As early as 1542 one map (attributed to Alonso de Santa Cruz) showed the lower half of Baja as an island, and from there the myth grew, the depiction of California as an island becoming perhaps the most famous error in the history of the charting of the oceans.

Some mapmakers initially left a tentative opening at the head of the Gulf of California, and this seems to have propelled the concept that the land to the west of the gulf might be an island.

There was not much northward exploration by the Spanish in the latter half of the sixteenth century, and maps of that period still tend to show the California coast as part of mainland North America (for example, maps on pages 24, 25, 27, and 29). But by the seventeenth century the island myth had a resurgence of popularity and showed up in various forms on numerous maps, some of which are illustrated here.

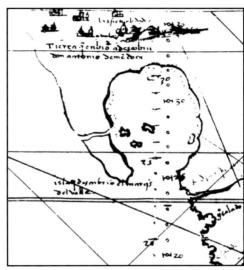

Map 62.
Alonso de Santa Cruz's map of 1542, showing the lower half of Baja California as an island. This seems to be the earliest depiction of any major part of California as an island.

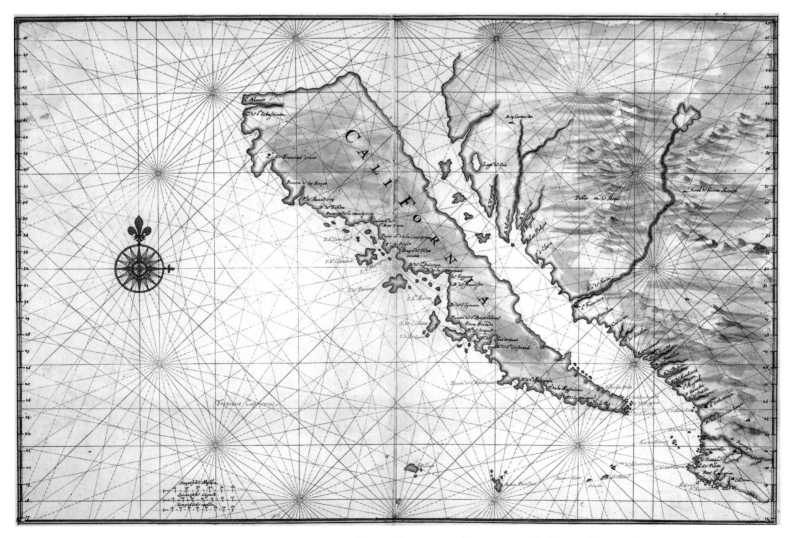

Map 63. A beautiful depiction of California as an island drawn by Dutch cartographer Joan Vinckeboons about 1650.

Now the island of California had become much larger, often encompassing the whole of the coast north to Cape Mendocino or beyond. No one had found a strait at the top of the "island," at about the latititude of Cape Mendocino, going southwards again, which would have been necessary if California really was an island, but this was simply because there was a 172-year hiatus in northward exploration after Sebastián Vizeaíno's 1602 voyage. How convenient for the wayward mapmaker. Just copy someone else's work, and perpetuate the island myth in the process!

In 1700 Jesuit Eusebio Kino explored the head of the Gulf of California and determined that it was a gulf rather than a strait; hence California could not be an island. But

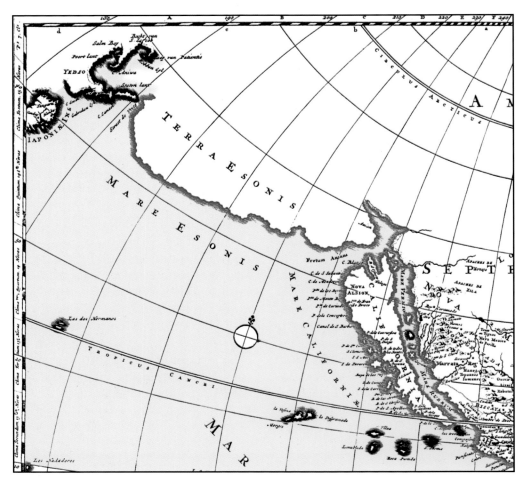

Map 64 (below).
Part of a map published by Henri Chatelain in 1719, from his *Atlas Historique*. The ship's track about a third of the way up the island of California is the eastbound Manila galleon route.

Map 65.
Recentissima Novi Orbis sive Americae Septentrionalis et Meridionalis Tabula, Carolus Allard, 1700. Wonderfully bizarre to modern eyes, this map shows not only an island of California but a continent in the Pacific Ocean, the extension of Maerten Vries' Compagnie Land (see pages 36–37), here named Terra Essonis, from "Yeso" or Hokkaido. Talk about confused geography!

Map 66 (below). Similar geographical ideas on a map by Johann Baptist Homann dated 1731, from a 1737 atlas.

Map 67 (above).
An early depiction of Island California drawn by French mapmaker Nicolas Sanson in 1696.

geographical myths, once established, die hard. Herman Moll, for example (map at right) clung to the island concept. But more scholarly mapmakers, such as Guillaume de L'Isle, did not slavishly copy others but mapped what was known through exploration and left it at that. At the same time as Kino's exploration de L'Isle concluded that California was not an island and showed it on his map of the same date as part of the mainland. During the eighteenth century some maps showed California as an island, others did not, but by the third quarter of the century the myth had finally died, except on the maps of a few regressive mapmakers.

Map 68 (above).
A superb depiction of California as a island by Herman Moll, published in 1719.

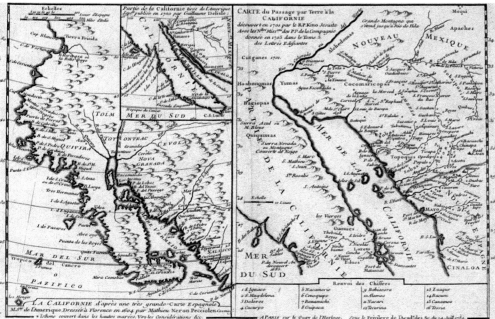

Map 69.
In 1752 French mapmaker Philippe Buache published his *Considerations Geographiques et Physiques*, which contained this "consideration" of whether California was an island or not. He seems to have correctly concluded that it was indeed a peninsula.

Van Keulen's Sea Atlases

Johannes van Keulen was a Dutch mapmaker who founded the van Keulen firm in the 1680s, a company that continued producing maps until the 1880s, a two hundred–year span. Van Keulen started his business by buying up all the plates of a friend, Henrik Doneker, who was retiring.

In the late seventeenth and early eighteenth centuries, as the operations of the Dutch East India Company expanded, the Dutch became pre-eminent in the production of maps, especially those used for navigation.

Van Keulen's grandson, also named Johannes, became the hydrographer for the Dutch East India Company and hence was privy to a considerable body of valuable information.

Van Keulen's "sea atlas" was called, aptly enough, *Zee-Fakkel,* or "Sea-Torch," and was a collection of maps intended to be used for navigation rather than just for perusal by armchair geographers.

The practical navigation maps van Keulen and others produced were nevertheless not the spartan affairs they are today. Ornamentation and

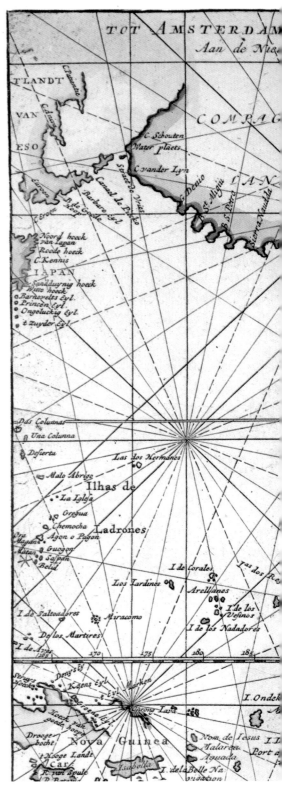

Map 70.
Part of Johannes van Keulen's *Nieuwe Pascaart Oost Indien,* 1680. Korea is shown connected to Hokkaido, as it was on many maps of this period.

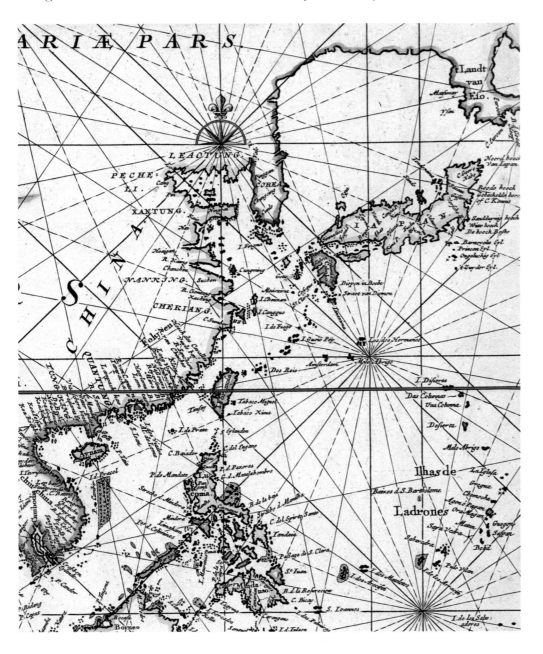

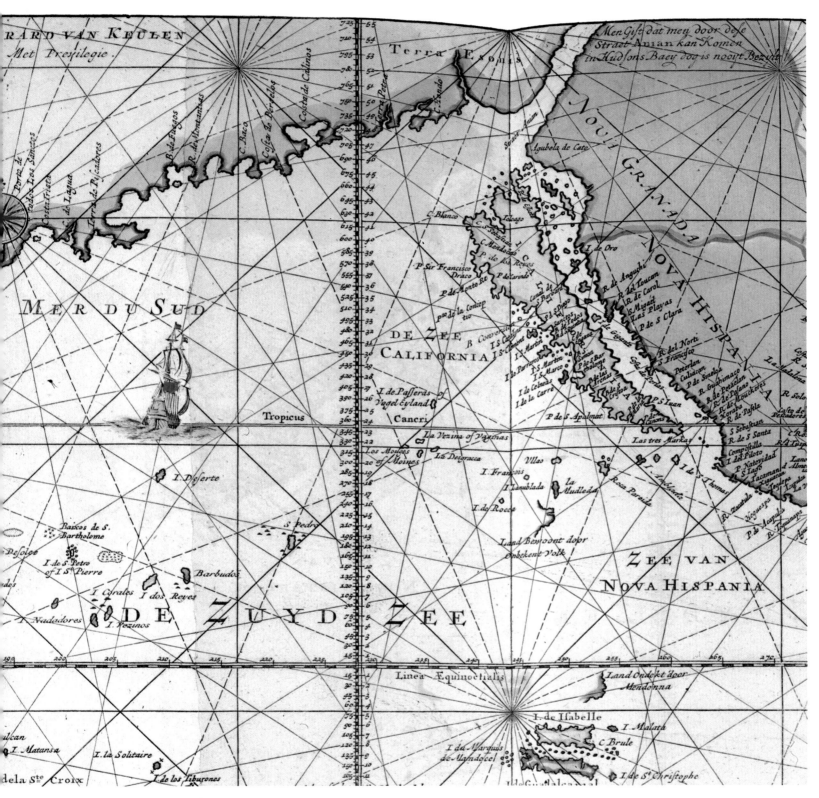

On the map, various labels are visible including:

RARD VAN KEULEN
Met Previlegie.

Men Gist dat mei door dese Straet Anian kan komen in Hudsons Baey dog is nooyt Bezeilt

Terra Esonis

NOVA GRANADA

NOVA HISPA

MER DU SUD

DE ZEE CALIFORNIA

ZEE VAN NOVA HISPANIA

DE ZUYD ZEE

Tropicus

Cancri

Linea Æquinoctialis

Land Bewoont door Onbekent Volk

Land Ondekt door Mendonna

Map 71.
The North Pacific Ocean as shown on a 1728 edition of van Keulen's atlas published by Gerard van Keulen. This map was published the same year Vitus Bering sailed into the strait separating Asia and America.

color were still seen as essential, so that many of the maps seem to us to be works of art. Shown here are two examples of the van Keulen firm's work.

The map of Japan, Korea, and China is part of a larger map of Southeast Asia published in 1682, a map that was remarkably accurate for its time. The North Pacific was still a mystery, and this is reflected in the other map, published by Gerard van Keulen, the older Johannes son, in 1728; it seems amazing to modern eyes that this map was actually intended for navigation. Maarten Vries' Compagnie Land stretches across the North Pacific, and California is shown as an island. Difficult navigation indeed!

Japanese Knowledge of the Pacific

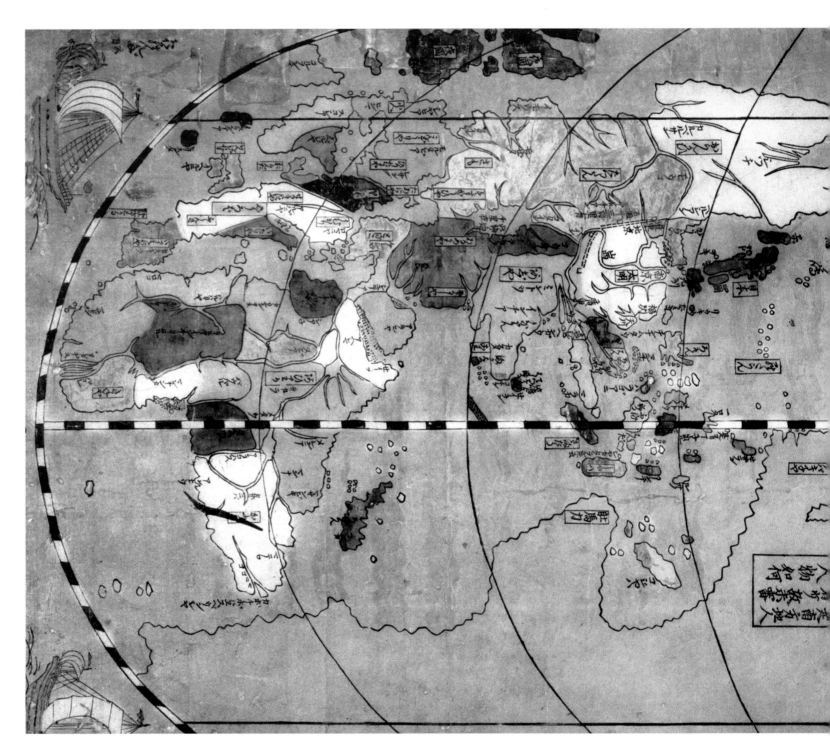

Japanese maps before the 1550s were generally conceptual rather than geographical. In the 1550s Jesuit missionaries arrived in Japan, even before they had reached China, and introduced a completely different view of the world. Japanese ideas of the Pacific Ocean actually came via China rather than directly from Europeans, and the result was a mixture of Western and Oriental concepts. The map shown here, *Bankoku-sozu*, was printed in 1645 from a woodblock in Nagasaki, the most westernized of Japanese cities due to the presence of Dutch traders on an island in the harbor (see Map 42, page 36). The map is centered on the Pacific, as were most Chinese maps. It is not known how widely this map and the geographic knowledge it represents were disseminated; however, those Japanese lucky enough to have seen this map would have had at least some idea that the Pacific was bounded by another continent to the east.

But ordinary Japanese mariners, at least until the 1850s, only got to know the extent of the ocean washing their shores through shipwreck or other mishap.

Map 72.
Bankoku-sozu, a Japanese world map printed from a woodblock at Nagasaki in 1645. The title means "Complete Map of the Peoples of the World," and the map was accompanied by a print of forty pictures of the peoples of the world.

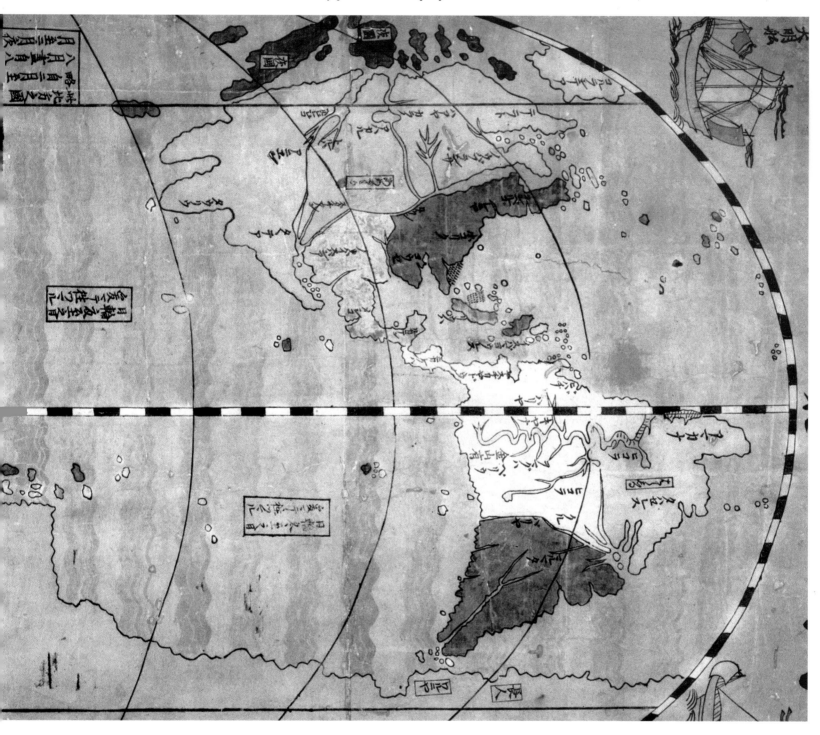

Early Japan was, to say the least, isolationist. An imperial decree in 1636 or 1637 disallowed the return of any Japanese citizen who had been abroad, prohibiting return on pain of death, and the same penalty awaited those who studied foreign languages or introduced foreign customs.

About 1689 the Japanese government ordered all junks to be built with open sterns and large square rudders, deliberately unfit for ocean navigation. They also commanded the destruction of all existing boats built on any foreign model. With these decrees, the government hoped to keep the Japanese people isolated within their own islands.

For, once these ships were forced away from the coast by the weather, their rudders soon washed away and they were soon dismasted. The result was that distressed mariners could only drift, at the mercy of winds and currents.

Thus the distribution of wrecked junks can be expected to tell of the ocean circulation in the Pacific Ocean, and indeed it does. It turns out that almost all of the known wrecks of Oriental boats on the coasts of North America have been Japanese junks.

This is explained by the Kuroshio and other currents that sweep in a northeast direction past Japan towards the Kuril Islands and the Aleutians, then continue east and south along the coasts of Alaska, British Columbia, and Oregon. These currents have swept junks towards North America at the rate of 16 km or 10 miles a day.

There are extensive records of Japanese junks washing up on North American shores, even before the

edicts. One came ashore at Acapulco in 1617; one arrived at Kamchatka in 1694 and a survivor was taken to Moscow; others drifted to Kamchatka in 1710 and 1729. Yet others washed up on the Aleutians in 1782; in Alaska in 1805; on Point Adams, at the mouth of the Columbia, in 1820; on the Queen Charlottes in 1831; and near Cape Flattery in 1833. In the latter instance, three sailors were rescued by the Hudson's Bay Company and sent to England to be returned to an uncertain fate in Japan.

The map below showing the distribution of Japanese junks wrecked and found drifting comes from a book by Charles Brooks published in 1876.

Map 73.
A map of the Pacific Ocean by Tsunenori Iguchi, from a Japanese book published in 1689. It is one of the first printed Japanese maps of the Pacific.

Map 74.
Distribution of Japanese junks found adrift or wrecked in the Pacific Ocean. The ocean currents are also shown, as corrected by George Davidson of the U.S. Coast and Geodetic Survey. From Charles Brooks, *Early Migrations: Japanese Wrecks Stranded and Picked Up Adrift in the North Pacific Ocean, 1876.*

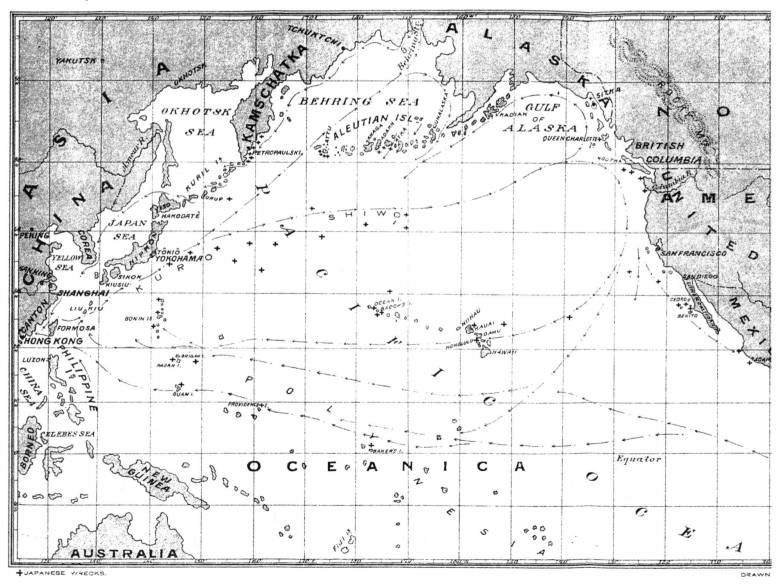

The East Asian Coast before Bering

The Dutch northward effort essentially stopped after Maerten Vries' voyage of 1643; they remained ensconced in Japan, seemingly content with the trade they found there. Then the Russians progressed eastwards in search first of furs and then, two decades into the eighteenth century and at the prompting of Peter the Great, in search of geographical knowledge, undoubtedly intended to later support imperial or commercial designs.

The information collected often was not published, but nevertheless, it often found its way into commercially produced maps and atlases. The pre-eminent commercial firm in this regard was the Homann firm of Nürnberg, whose founder and principal member was Johann Baptist Homann. After 1702 he was responsible for the creation of many fine maps that incorporated some of the latest information about the east coast of Asia. His maps, and those of others, record with increasing accuracy and detail the emergence of a real geography.

One of Homann's early maps was the one shown below, a map of Muscovy, which records a Pacific coast not much different from that drawn on the Godunov map of 1667 (see page 42). Other mapmakers soon added the peninsula first drawn by Nicholaas Witsen, reflecting knowledge of Semen Dezhnev's voyage in 1648 (see page 43).

Map 76 (above).
The east coast of Asia as shown on a map published in 1706 by French mapmaker Guillaume de L'Isle.

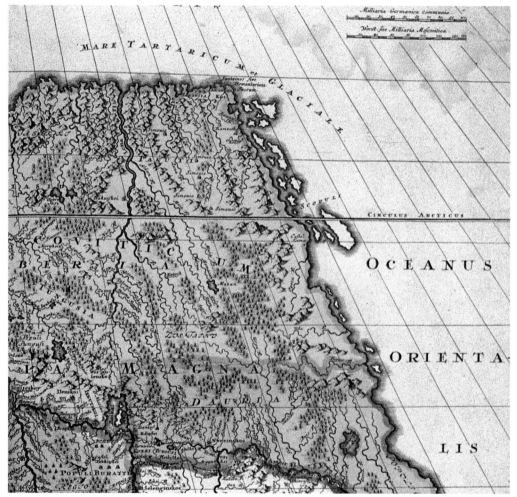

Map 75.
The northeastern corner of Siberia shown on a map of Muscovy by Johann Baptist Homann. The map is dated 1704, although this copy is from a 1731 atlas.

Map 77.
A map by Nicolas Sanson, published by Pierre Mortier in 1708, showing the addition of the Ice Cape peninsula, first drawn by Witsen in 1687 (see page 43).

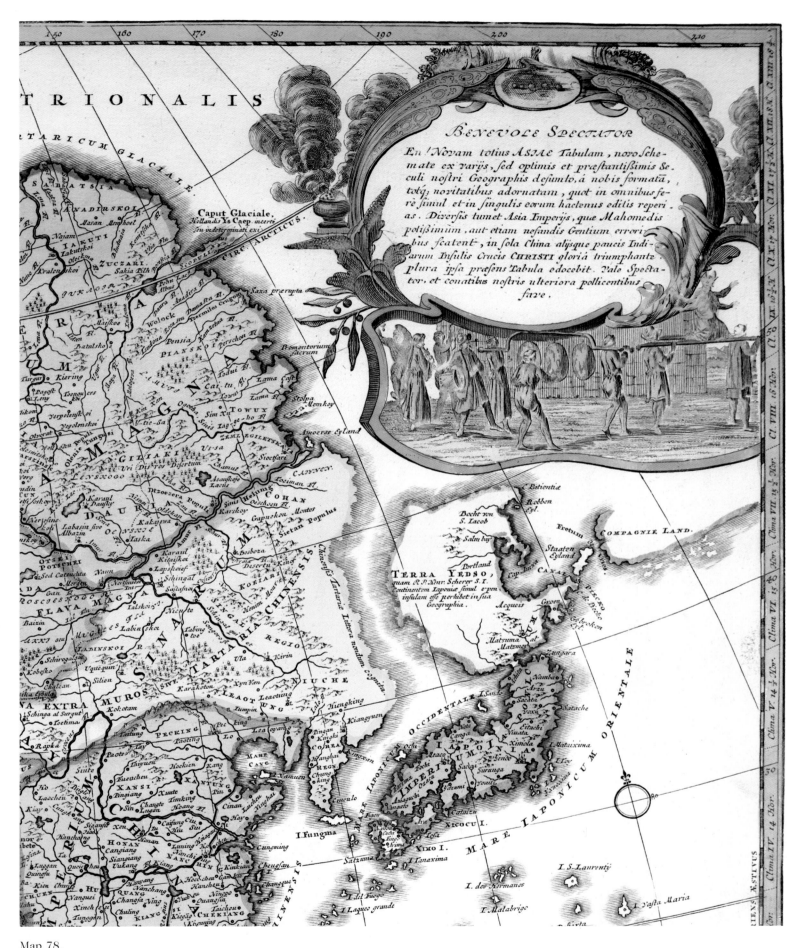

Map 78.
The northeastern part of Johann Baptist Homann's 1707 map of Asia, *Asiae Recentissima Delineatio*. The Nicholaas Witsen idea of an "Icy Cape" peninsula is well illustrated, corresponding to the Chukotskiy Peninsula of today, opposite Cape Prince of Wales in Bering Strait. Farther south the discoveries of Maarten Vries in 1643 are shown, in particular his "Company Land," stretching eastwards and conveniently off the edge of the map.

Map 79.

Herman Moll's map of 1719 was somewhat regressive, depicting geographical knowledge others knew by that time to be wrong. The coast of Siberia is similar to the Godunov map. The discoveries of Maarten Vries are well shown, complete with the de rigueur undefined "Company Land." Detail of the latter area is shown on page 36.

This peninsula was shown on a map published in 1705 by Guillaume de L'Isle, a respected French mapmaker (page 53). His notation records his uncertainty as to whether it was "joined to another continent." Yeso (Hokkaido) is shown as a landmass going off the edge of the map; all very indefinite.

Homann's beautiful 1707 map of Asia, part of which is shown here (left), also now shows the peninsula, called Ys Caep (Ice Cape), but much smaller. Vries' discoveries are shown, with a large "Terra Yedso" to the north of Japan leading to a huge and indefinite "Compagnie Land" to the east.

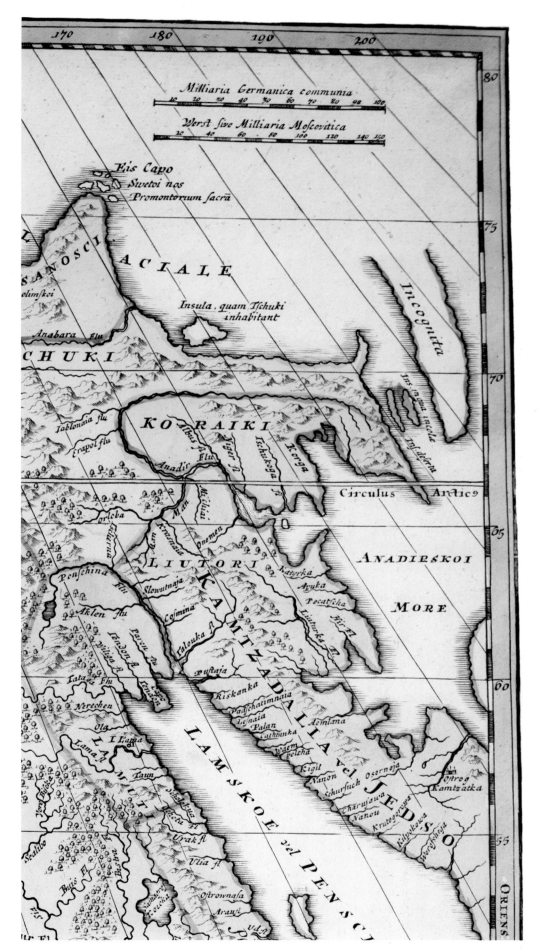

Map 80. Another map by Johann Baptist Homann, this one of Russia, drawn in 1723. The configuration shown, with islands in what might be Bering Strait, together with land marked "Incognita," which might be America, comes from a map by Ivan Lvov drawn in 1710.

The Homann map of 1723 (Map 80, page 55) shows a considerably changed conception of the coastal outline and may have been based on a map prepared by Ivan Lvov, a Russian geodesist, in 1710; the latter was obtained by Gerhard Müller from a retired Lvov in Yakutsk.

A similar configuration is shown in Homann's regional map of Kamchatka and the adjacent coasts (left), although this one defines Kamchatka as a peninsula instead of merely suggesting it. The significance of the 1723 map is that it is now thought to be the map Vitus Bering was carrying with him when he sailed in 1728 on his voyage to the strait that now bears his name (see page 63).

Map 82.
This map of Kamchatka appeared in Engelbert Kaempfer's *Historia Imperii Japonici*, published in 1727.

Map 81 (left).
This rather beautiful map drawn by Homann in 1725 contains similar information to his 1723 map overleaf, with one important exception: Kamchatka is shown clearly as a peninsula, together with a string of Kuril Islands southwards to Japan. Rather than a part of a larger map, this was specifically a map of Kamchatka and "Jedso" (Hokkaido).

Map 83.
This is a French copy of a map by Afanasii Shestakov, explorer of the Kuril Islands, about 1730. The line drawn across the Sea of Okhotsk shows the supply route from Okhotsk to Bolsheretsk.

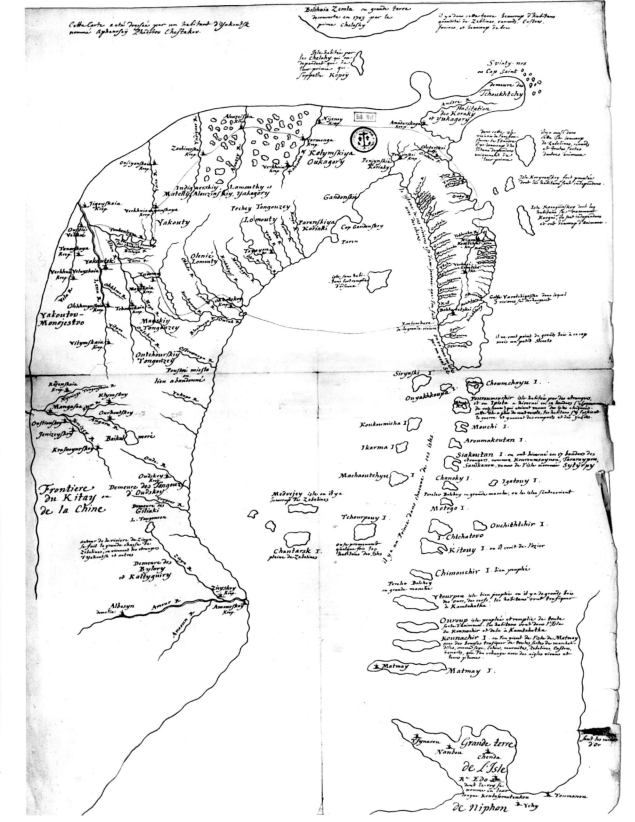

An eighteenth-century illustration of a Kamchatka volcano.

Another interesting map is that of Kamchatka, the Sea of Okhotsk, and the Kuril Islands drawn by Kuril Islands explorer Afanasii Shestakov in 1725, a copy of which is shown above.

Shestakov returned to St. Petersburg in 1725 to propose to the Russian government that they subdue the coastal natives of the region and also that he be allowed to search for land which was by this time believed to exist to the east – America. His proposals were welcomed, and he was named head of a special expedition. Two of the specialists assigned to his expedition were Ivan Fedorov and Mikhail Gvozdev, an assistant navigator and a geodesist, respectively.

Shestakov was killed in 1730 during a battle aimed at carrying out part of his first objective. But Fedorov and Gvozdev would achieve his second objective two years later, by finally becoming the first Russians to discover the Great Land – the North American continent (see page 65).

Lost Islands and False Continents

Over the centuries map and chart makers have, for a variety of reasons, often placed land where none exists. There were imaginative lands, exaggerated lands, and mistaken lands.

Until the end of the eighteenth century mapmakers who had poor information about what was in the North Pacific often resorted to filling up the "empty" voids, often with large decorative cartouches. Land was thought to have a "balanced" distribution so as not to disturb the rotation of the Earth, a common misconception leading in its most famous incarnation to the insistence on an unknown Southern Continent, Terra Australis Incognita. And in the North Pacific, the need to map an imagined Northwest Passage led to depiction of land in places it was not.

Land was often placed where mapmakers thought it might be,

based on their interpretation of the accounts of voyagers. The depiction of Japan as a large island in the middle of the Pacific was based on a reading of Marco Polo. The Spaniard João da Gama, on a voyage from Macao to Acapulco C1590, reported land in the northeastern Pacific, and "Gama Land" was shown on many maps for two centuries afterwards, leading even Vitus Bering to search for it.

But perhaps the most enduring exaggeration of all in the North Pacific was the depiction of Company Land, actually one of the Kuril Islands, by Maerten Vries in 1643, as shown on page 37. This map led other mapmakers for a long time thereafter to draw what was sometimes a vast continent stretching right across the ocean. Its eastern end formed a suitable west bank for a Northwest Passage, and it was named all manner of

names beyond various permutations of Company Land: Terra Essonis, the land of Yeso, came from a belief that the land was part of Yesso, or Hokkaido, one of the islands of Japan. The mythical continent was also sometimes labeled Gama Land.

And then there were mistakes. Under certain weather conditions it is quite possible to see the mirage of a considerable bulk of land at sea, from squall lines and other cloud for-

Map 84.
This wonderful representation of the North Pacific was drawn by an unknown mapmaker about 1702. Asia is a suitable distance from America, but a huge mythical land mass intervenes where ocean should lie. The "Land of Iesso" derives from Maerten Vries' depiction of an open-ended "Company Land" (see page 37); "Iesso" is one form of the ancient name for Hokkaido, the northernmost major island of Japan. Vries Strait balances the Strait of Anian on the other side of this dubious land.

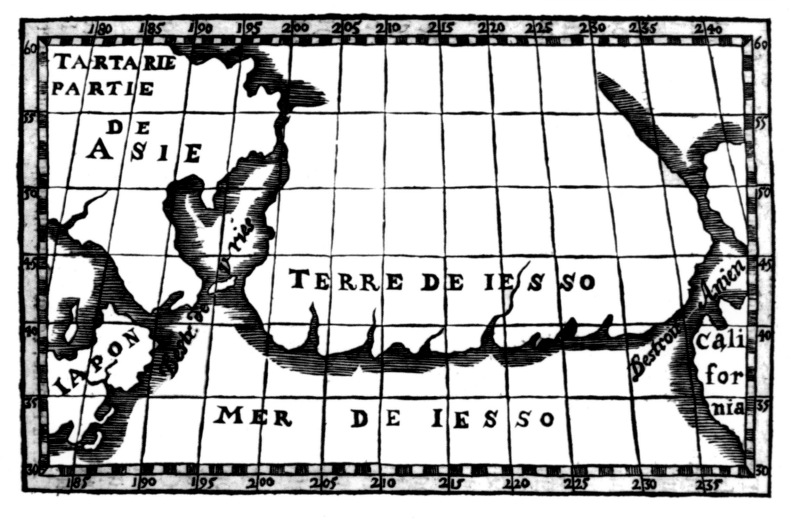

mations. Other sightings resulted from whales, floating seaweed, red tide, or even various debris floating on the surface. In an age of sail it was not usually practical to double back and check, assuming there were any doubts, and many sightings of reefs and islands were by commercial vessels more interested in getting where they were going than in investigating potential islands.

Interestingly, the more traveled the region, the more false islands reported in it; the Pacific north of about 40° suffered less than the zone from the equator to that latitude. For the false islands of the Pacific arose from someone reporting them to be there.

The North Pacific has had in its time hundreds of false islands, reefs or shoals – called *vigias* – mapped even on "serious" government hydrographic office charts, not just those of a commercial mapmaker with a good imagination and too loose with his pen. And many were there until quite recently.

In November 1875 the newly appointed Hydrographer of the Navy in Britain ordered what has been termed a "virtual massacre" of doubtful islands on Admiralty Chart 2683, a single chart that covers the whole Pacific Ocean. With a single stroke of the pen no less than 123 islands were removed, including, hilariously, three that were real and had to be restored again later!

Out went Todos Los Santos, Moor, Weeks, Morrell, Byers, Lots

Wife, Rico de Oro, Rico de Plata, and many more in the Anson Archipelago southwest of Japan; many of these had first found their way onto charts from one captured from a Spanish galleon by Captain George Anson and *Centurion* in 1743. In the eastern Pacific, out went Kentzell, Redfield Rocks, Philadelphia, and Maria Laxar. Exotic names for exotic islands that never existed.

Yet lost islands continued to be shown on charts. As late as 1982 the highly respected American oceanographer Henry Stommel, who wrote a whole book on the lost islands of the world's oceans, found Ganges Island in the Pacific, east of Japan at about 31° N, 134° E, on a globe in a Lufthansa office in Germany. He had originally found this island while leafing through a 1936 edition of the *Oxford Advanced Atlas* and thought it would be a good base for monitoring the Kuroshio Current. Further investigation revealed that the island was not marked on newer atlases, however, dispelling his hopes for a convenient location for his instruments.

Ganges Island had been the subject of numerous reports in the late

"I think I'll throw in a couple of extra islands on this map just for laughs!"

Map 85 (above).
An imaginary island at about 30° N, 140° W, from Thomas Jefferys' *American Atlas*, 1776.

Map 86.
Dutch mapmakers Reinier and Joshua Ottens drew this map in 1745. It shows lands discovered by "Dom Juam de Gama" southeast of Kamchatka. João da Gama was a Portuguese captain who sailed from Macao to Acapulco about 1590. Blown off course, he reported sighting land somewhere in the northwest Pacific. This land appeared on maps for two centuries thereafter!

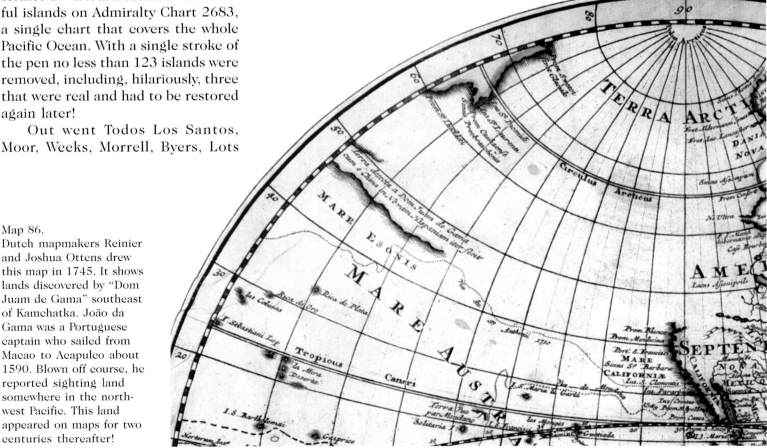

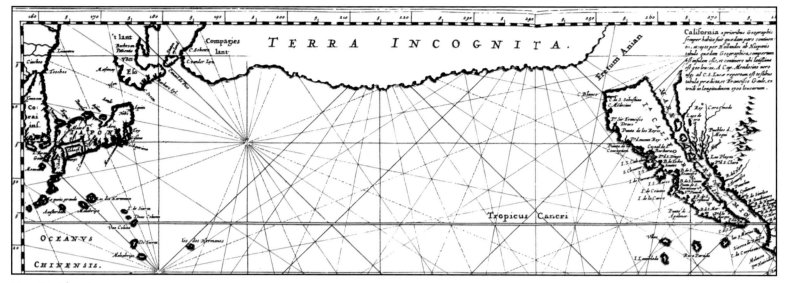

Map 87 (above).
Part of Joannes Jansson's map of the South Sea, 1650. Vries' "Compagies lant" (Company Land) has spawned a massive Terra Incognita continent clear across the North Pacific.

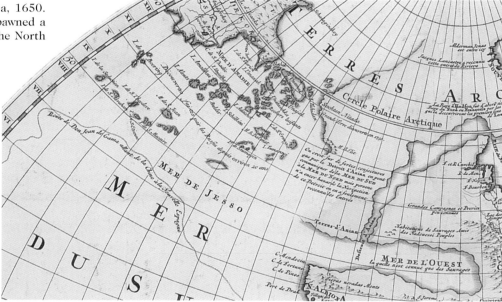

nineteenth century, the multiplicity of which convinced the U.S. Navy Hydrographic Office that they were "surely indicative of the existence of some danger in this region, the establishment of which was important." By 1880 the island was on a list of doubtful dangers to navigation, with the comment that Pacific Mail steamers had repeatedly passed over the position without seeing anything.

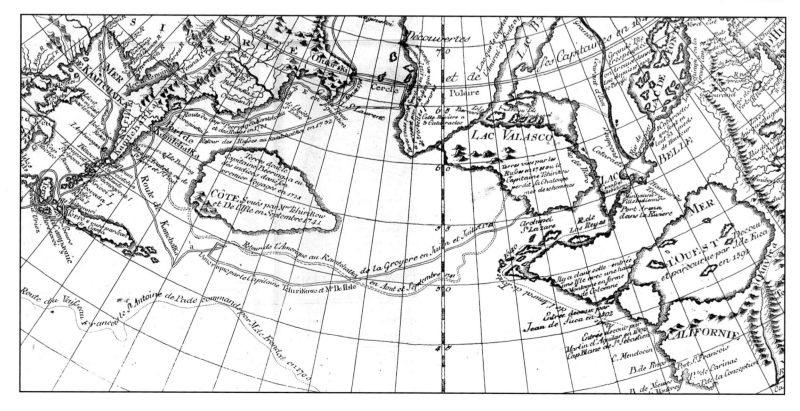

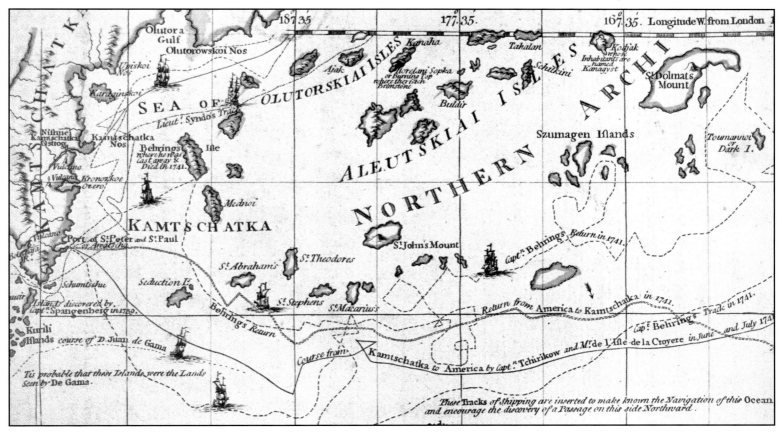

Map 90 (above).
A flurry of islands fills the northwest Pacific in this map by Thomas Jefferys, published in 1775. Some, such as Behring's Isle and Kodiak, are real; most are ficticious. The map is "authenticated" with multiple ship tracks.

Map 88 (left, center).
Jean Covens' and Corneille Mortier's superb map of 1780, showing a huge Sea of the West stretching east to Nebraska and a clear Northwest Passage to Hudson Bay. Alaska is an island.

Map 89 (left, bottom).
One of the most spectacular combinations of fact and fiction in a map of the Pacific Northwest. It was copied by Robert de Vaugondy from a map by Joseph-Nicolas de L'Isle, and published in 1755 in Diderot's *Encyclopedié,* a thirty-volume compilation of what was supposed to be the sum total of all the knowledge in the world. "Land seen by Jean de Gama" is just east of Company Land in the southern Kurils; a huge island attributed to Bering fills the western Pacific; and the coast of North America is a maze of islands, channels, peninsulas, and seas, including a large Sea of the West stretching to the Rocky Mountains. Interestingly, Sakhalin appears as an island off the Russian coast, which it is, but it was not known to be an island at this time. Make enough guesses, and one may turn out to be right!

Map 91 (right).
Part of a Spanish map of North America dated 1802. Large "Islas vistas antiguamente por los Españoles" inhabit the North Pacific Ocean. Also marked are "Dn [Donna] Maria la gorda" just north of Hawaii, and "I. de los Pajaros?" halfway between Hawaii and Baja California.

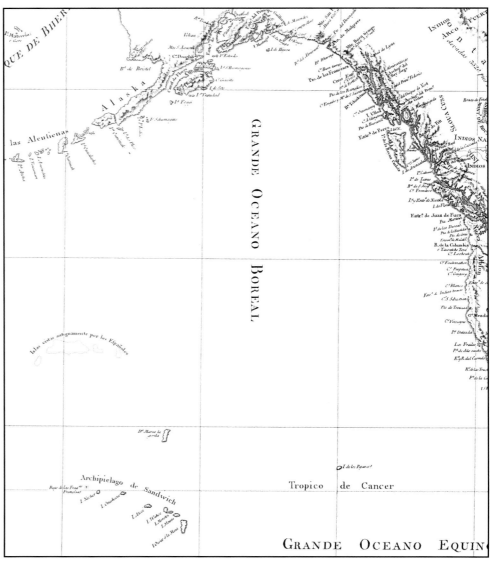

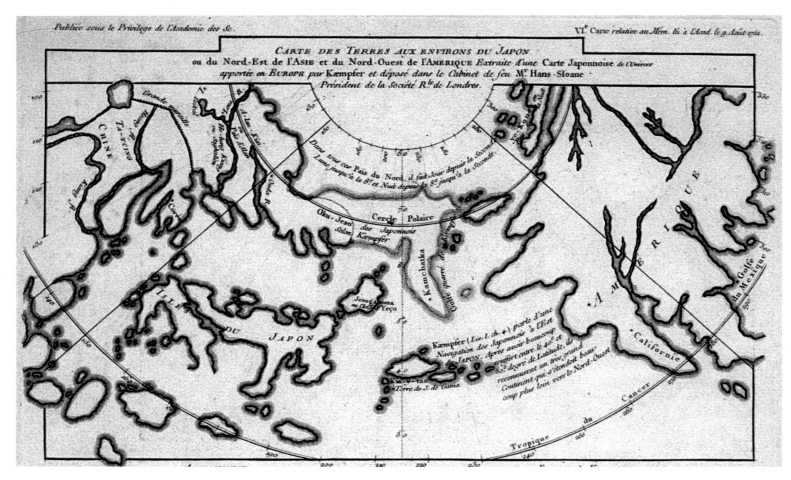

Map 92.
Perhaps the finest imaginary geography of the North Pacific, drawn by Philippe Buache in 1752 after a map belonging to Hans Sloane. All the essential geographical elements are present, however, and this is what makes it such an interesting yet bizarre map; they are almost all misplaced, missized, or misshapen.

Map 94 (right).
This map by Jean Nolin, drawn in 1783, has it all: continents where there are none, and non-existent islands in imaginary seas! In 1783 this nonsense was about to be torpedoed the very next year by the publication of the journals of James Cook's third voyage, spoiling the fun of armchair geographers forever.

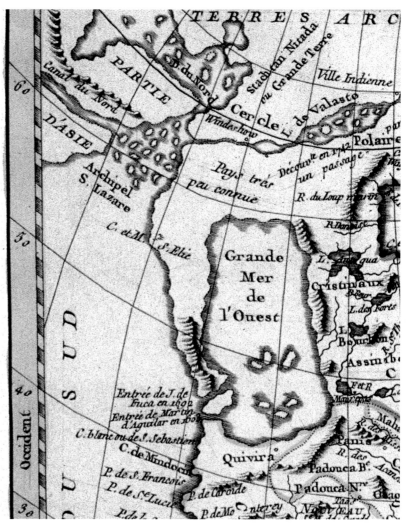

Map 93. Part of another map by Philippe Buache. Company Land, Gama Land, and "land discovered by the Russians" – the Aleutians as a continous coast – are all shown here.

Vitus Bering's First Voyage

The existence of a real Strait of Anian, shown on maps since the middle of the sixteenth century (see page 23), had never been proven when in 1697 the German philosopher-mathematician Gottfried Leibnitz suggested to a visiting Peter the Great that the Russians should be the ones to solve the mystery.

The exploration of the seas to the east of Siberia was a natural enough step for the Russians, who had advanced across Siberia in a relentless pursuit of furs.

As early as 1716 an expedition, called the Great Kamchatka Expedition, had been sent out to determine if there was any land opposite Chukotskiy, the eastern tip of Siberia. This undertaking had failed due to poor logistical planning.

Then, in 1719, the first scientific expedition was organized, that of Ivan Evreinov and Fedor Luzhin, who were sent by Peter the Great to (along with other instructions) "determine whether America is joined to Asia." They did not, but they did map Kamchatka and the Kuril Islands (see map at bottom of page 44).

But the first major scientific expedition to the Siberian Pacific was the First Kamchatka Expedition, initiated by Tsar Peter in 1725 and commanded by a Danish captain in the Russian navy, Vitus Bering.

Peter died a few days after the dispatch of the first detachment, but his wish to send the expedition was honored by Empress Catherine, who succeeded him.

The logistics of the expedition were intimidating. Alexei Chirikov, one of Bering's officers, was the first to leave St. Petersburg, on 24 January 1725, with twenty-five sleds of supplies; but Bering would not sail from Kamchatka until 14 July 1728, three and a half years later. The intervening time was spent in transporting men and supplies overland across an essentially roadless Siberia, dealing with unhelpful local governors, building ships, sailing across the Sea of Okhotsk, transporting everything across Kamchatka to the Kamchatka River, building another ship, more seaworthy than the others, and sailing down the river to – finally – the Pacific.

The new ship was named *Sviatoi Arkhangel Gavriil*. Bering's officers were Alexei Chirikov and Martin Spanberg, and Petr Chaplin was a midshipman, or officer-in-training. They only had eight sailors, but they had soldiers, who had to take over some of the sailors' duties.

They sailed at three in the morning on 14 July 1728, northwards. A careful record of wind directions and the course, speed, and drift of the ship was kept every hour in the watch journal, and at the end of every day the latitude and longitude were recorded, together with the compass variation and the distance computed to have been sailed. Also recorded were all shore reference points, when available, the current, and the weather. This care was to pay off later, enabling Bering to draw a quite accurate map of the Siberian shore.

Peter the Great's Instructions to Vitus Bering

1. You are to build one or two boats, with decks, either in Kamchatka or in some other place.
2. You are to proceed in those boats along the land that lies to the north, and according to the expectations (since the end is not known), it appears that land [is] part of America.
3. You are to search for the place where it is joined to America, and proceed to some settlement that belongs to a European power, or if you sight some European ship, find out from it what the coast is called, and write it down; go ashore yourself and obtain accurate information; locate it on a map and return here.

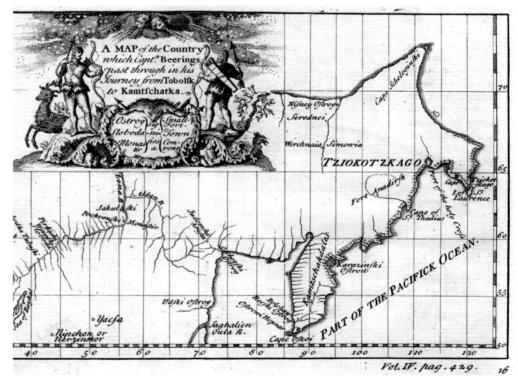

Map 95. This map, the first printed map of Bering's discoveries, was drawn by Joseph-Nicholas de L'Isle and was published in Jean Baptiste Du Halde's *General History of China*, in French in 1735 and in English in 1736. This is from the English edition.

By 27 July they reached Cape Navarin, at the southern extent of the Gulf of Anadyr. On 8 August, near Cape Chukotskiy, opposite St. Lawrence Island, at the very entrance to the strait that was to inherit Bering's name, they were approached by natives, Chukchi, in a hide boat, and through an interpreter were able to determine some features of the geography of the region.

By 13 August they were sailing past the easternmost tip of Siberia and Asia, Cape Dezhnev (East Cape), opposite Cape Prince of Wales on the American side. But they did not see the other shore or even the Diomede Islands, due to poor visibility; the strait is still 80 km or 50 miles wide at its narrowest point.

Now, with the Asian shore turning westwards, Bering requested from his officers Chirikov and Spanberg their thoughts on what course they should follow. Chirikov suggested they continue northwards in order to eliminate the possibility that a long peninsula (Shelagsk Cape) was connected to America. This peninsula was shown on many maps as continuing indefinitely to the northeast (see, for example, Witsen's map on page 43). Spanberg

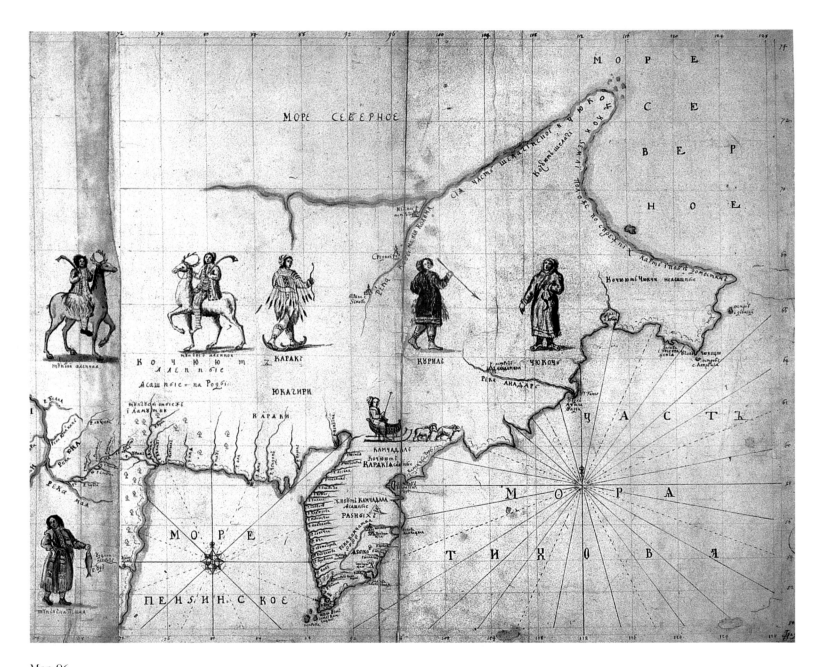

Map 96.
There are about fifteen copies of the map made by Bering of the western shore of the Pacific Ocean and the Bering Sea, which finally delineated Siberia more or less correctly. Because the members of the Kamchatka expeditions were drawn from a number of European countries, and because of the not inconsiderable interest from other nations, these maps found their way into archives and libraries in a number of countries. This one, a particularly handsome example, is from the Royal Library in Stockholm, Sweden. Note the notorious Shelagsk Peninsula, north of Bering's strait, which Bering failed to discredit, and indeed failed to prove it was not connected to North America.

was more conservative, suggesting they turn back in order to avoid the possibility of having to overwinter.

Bering did continue northwards, but only for a few days. On 16 August, pleading broken leeboards and keelboard, he finally decided that the strait had been discovered and gave the order to begin the return voyage. They had reached about 67° 25´ N, just above the Arctic Circle.

Sailing more quickly southwards, by 18 August they passed Cape Chukotskiy again and left Bering's strait.

On 20 August they again met Chukchi, and one of the questions they asked them was "Are there islands or is there land in the sea opposite your land?" But it was too late to be asking such questions; the Chukchi gave an indefinite answer, quite probably because they did not know, it being beyond their territory.

Continuing southwards, Bering reached Kamchatka Bay again on 1 September, entering the mouth of the river the next day. The expedition that had taken three and a half years of land travel (except for crossing the Sea of Okhotsk) was over after only fifty-one days at sea.

For all their care in plotting their route, Bering and his men apparently did not draw a map with their track shown, and as a result, there is still some controversy about specifics, and in particular the location of their most northerly point reached.

Whatever its precise location, the fact remains that Bering did not sail far enough north to conclusively prove the separation of Asia and America by the strait that bears his name today, but this would have been difficult in any case, as however far north he had gone, the connection could always have been at an even higher latitude. He did show that there was a body of water at the location of Bering Strait, but the proof that it was indeed a strait would come later.

It was left to Mikhail Gvozdev to actually sight the American coast, four years later. Even while Bering's expedition was under way, another under Afanasii Shestakov was being

organized. Shestakov was in Okhotsk when Bering returned, and it was to him that Bering handed over his ships and provisions. Mikhail Gvozdev and Ivan Fedorov were members of this new expedition, and it was they who sighted the Alaskan coast in 1732.

But it would be Bering again, with Alexei Chirikov, who would lead another expedition, to which is attributed the discovery of the main body of the North American continent from the west, in 1741 (page 67).

Map 97 (right).
Sketch by French geographer Joseph-Nicolas de L'Isle illustrating Bering's voyage in 1728. It was based on a conversation he had with Bering about 1732.

Joseph-Nicolas de L'Isle listed the signs that Bering had observed from which the conclusion could be drawn that he "had not been far from other lands":

1. At some distance from the shore he found the water rather shallow and the waves small just as in straits or arms of the sea.
2. He saw uprooted and other trees which were brought by the east wind, which trees are not seen in Kamchatka.
3. From the natives of the country he learned that an eastern wind brings ice in two or three days, while it takes a western wind four or five days to carry off the ice from northeast Asia.
4. That certain birds come regularly every year about the same month from the east and after having passed several months on the Asiatic shore they return with the same regularity the same season.

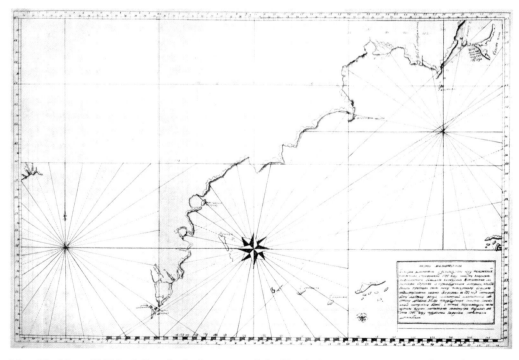

Map 98. Map of Mikhail Gvozdev's discovery of the North American continent, drawn by Martin Spanberg about 1734. The western tip of Alaska is shown in the top right-hand corner of this map, the first time it had been portrayed on a map as a result of exploration rather than conjecture. The Diomede Islands are shown, in Bering Strait.

Martin Spanberg's Voyage to Japan

When Bering presented the results of his first expedition to the Russian government, he also submitted a proposal for a second, more ambitious expedition, which came to be called the Second Kamchatka Expedition. It received preliminary approval in May 1731 but, like all these expeditions, took years to actually get off the ground.

Bering would not sail to America until 1741 (next page), but the Second Kamchatka Expedition also included proposals to explore southwards, to determine the true relationship of Japan to Kamchatka and the Kuril Islands. Martin Spanberg, who had been one of Bering's officers in 1728, was selected to command this effort.

It was June 1738 before they began their voyage to Japan from Okhotsk, in three ships, one of which was commanded by William Walton, an English captain also in the employ of the Russian navy. They had started late due to ice, and as a result got only as far south as about 46° N before the season ran out on them.

The next year they tried again, this time making it to Japan, though Walton became separated from Spanberg and they both made the voyage separately.

Another voyage was attempted in 1741, but a newly built boat leaked so much they didn't get very far. Nevertheless, Spanberg and Walton's voyages did allow them to determine reasonably accurately the position of Japan and most of the Kuril Islands; one of the maps that Spanberg drew is shown here. Russian knowledge of the west Pacific shore was to be more detailed for now than that of the eastern.

Map 99.
Martin Spanberg's map of Kamchatka, the Kuril Islands, and Japan, based on his 1739 voyage and that of William Walton.

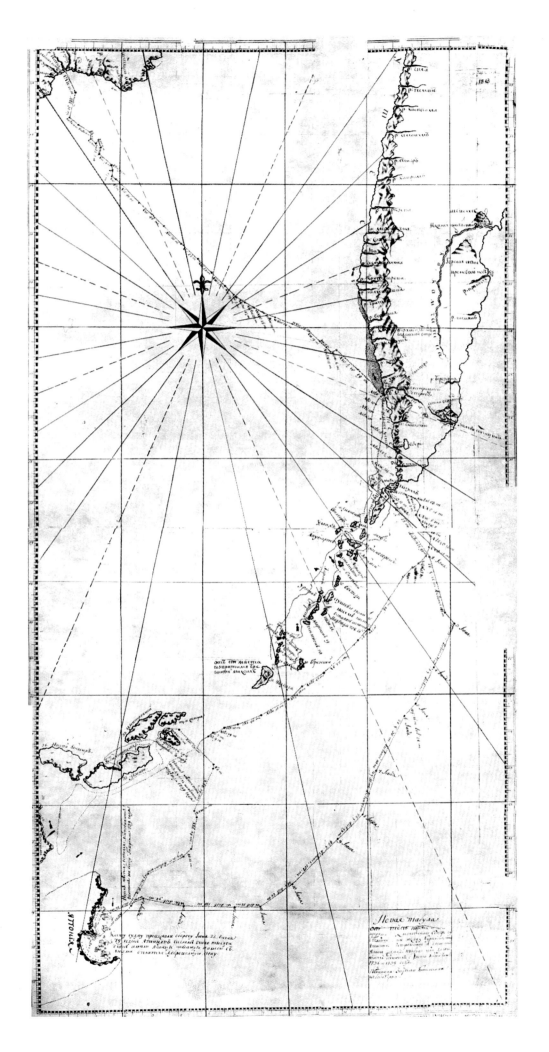

Vitus Bering's Second Voyage

As early as April 1730, when he submitted his report on his first expedition, Vitus Bering proposed to lead another, which would go much farther eastward and discover more exactly the position of North America. Bering clearly recognized that his first expedition had not been definitive in this regard. The proposed new expedition would be part of a larger scientific effort including the exploration of eastern Siberia, so that the whole scheme is often referred to as the Second Kamchatka Expedition; this name appears on some of the maps.

Bering's voyage would also discover whether the previously mapped speculative lands of Eso or Jesso, Gama Land, or Company Land existed. These were lands claimed to have been sighted by various nav-igators in the seventeenth century, in particular Maerten Vries in 1643 (see page 34), and they showed up on maps now and again either as islands or as part of North America, as cartographers strove to reconcile conflicting accounts.

After much preparation and years getting overland to Okhotsk and then to Kamchatka again, two ships, *St. Peter* and *St. Paul (Sviatoi Petr* and *Sviatoi Pavel),* under the command of Bering and Alexei Chirikov, sailed from Petropavlovsk in the spring of 1741.

When Bering and Chirikov sailed, they used as their guide a largely speculative map that had been prepared by Joseph-Nicolas de L'Isle, who was responsible for some of the worst – or most imaginative – of the speculative maps of the Northwest Coast. The map (below), drawn in 1731 and revised in 1733, was const-ructed, according to de L'Isle's own memoir, "for the purpose of helping in the discovery of the shortest route between Asia and America."

The map mercifully showed a lot of blank space in the regions that Bering's expedition was about to sail to, blank being better than totally hy-pothetical. The map did, however, show the speculative Gama Land – land supposedly seen by Jean de Gama – southeast of Kamchatka. De L'Isle's memoir had stated that these lands were "perhaps part of a large continent contiguous to America, joining it north of California."

In seeking these imaginary lands, Bering's officers – including Joseph-Nicolas de L'Isle's brother-in-law Louis de L'Isle de la Croyère –

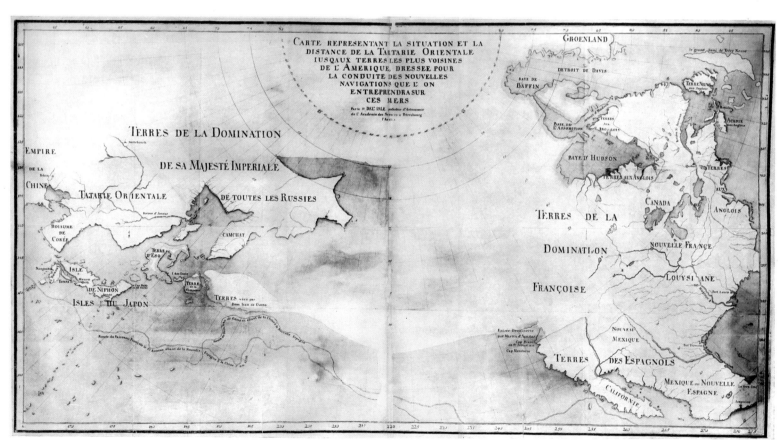

Map 100.
This map by Joseph-Nicolas de L'Isle was drawn in 1731 and was intended to summarize all knowledge of the Pacific Ocean to that date. It was carried by Bering on his second voyage in 1741 – to guide him! De L'Isle presented this map to the Russian senate with a memoir, which stated: "This map represents the true situation and distance of the eastern shores of Asia, known up to the present time, with that part of the continent of North America which is nearest to it. This map was made for the purpose of helping in the discovery of the shortest route between Asia and America."

decided, democratically, as was the custom at that time in such circumstances, to sail southeast towards this "land." The logic was that since the map had been provided to them by the Academy of Sciences, it must be correct.

What faith in government! The famous historian H. H. Bancroft put it succinctly:

The absurdity of sending out an expedition for discovery, requiring it to follow mapped imagination, seems never to have occurred to the Solons of St. Petersburg, and this when they knew well enough (from the first Bering expedition) that the continents were not far asunder toward the north.

Of course, the two ships found nothing, but as a result of this course, they ran into a storm and on 20 June became separated. After finding each other again, the ships once more lost sight of each other, this time for good. Bering's log, which was kept by assistant navigator Kharlam Yushin, recorded on 22 June:

Reef-topsail wind. We could have advanced on our course had we not been obliged to look for the St. Paul.

After wasting valuable time searching for each other, each ship continued by itself towards North America, and at this point we must consider Bering's and Chirikov's voyages separately.

Bering groped his way towards the American coast, beset by fogs, sounding all the time to determine if a coast was being approached. His log (Yushin's) is full of entries like the one for 28 June 1741: "Fog; sounded in 180 fathoms, no bottom" and, later the same day, "Topgallantsail wind, chilly, wet, foggy."

On 17 July 1741 Bering's log recorded sighting high, snow-covered mountains, and among them a high volcano. This was Mt. St. Elias; Bering had finally reached the North American mainland. On 20 July, some of Bering's crew, led by Fleet Master Sofron

Khitrov, were sent in the ship's longboat to land on an island, which Bering named St. Elias Island, as it was that saint's day. (Bering also named the island's most southerly point Cape St. Elias. Mt. St. Elias was given that name later. St. Elias Island is now called Kayak Island.)

Bering's scientist, Georg Steller, also managed a brief foray on shore (see overleaf).

Khitrov made a sketch map in his logbook to show "the position of the bay and the islands and their relation to the mainland." This was the first Russian map to show only part of the North American mainland (Map 101, below). The representation of the mountains, as seen from the side, laid down on the coast, is unusual. The set of cloud-capped mountains shown on the mainland are Mt. St. Elias and adjacent peaks.

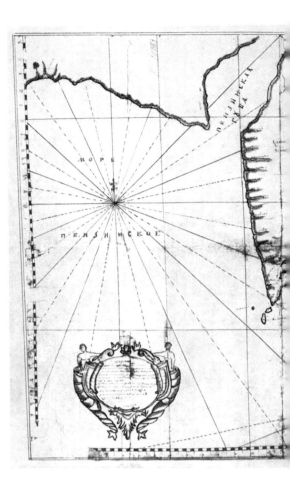

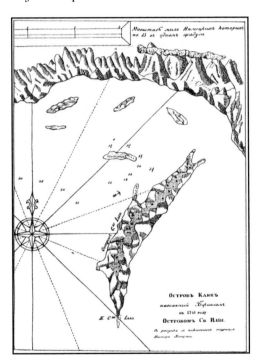

Map 101.
Sofron Khitrov's map of St. Elias Island, now Kayak Island, on the coast of Alaska near Mt. St. Elias.

On the way back towards Siberia, Bering halted at the Shumagin Islands, on the east side of the Alaska Peninsula; again Khitrov drew a map in his logbook.

But the season was drawing to a close and, partly because of the time wasted earlier, they had not arrived back at Kamchatka. The crew were

falling ill with scurvy, and the ship was becoming difficult to handle in poor weather.

Even Yushin, writing the log, noted, "I am altogether exhausted from scurvy, and I stand my watch only because of extreme necessity."

On 4 November, they sighted land: "We think this land is Kamchatka; it lies, however, between N and W, and it seems as if the end of it is not far." It was an island, now called Bering Island, only about 175 km or 110 miles from the Kamchatka coast, and less than three times that to Petropavlovsk, a

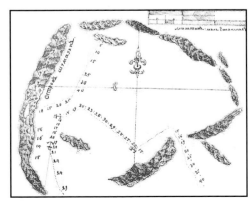

Map 102.
Khitrov's map of the Shumagin Islands.

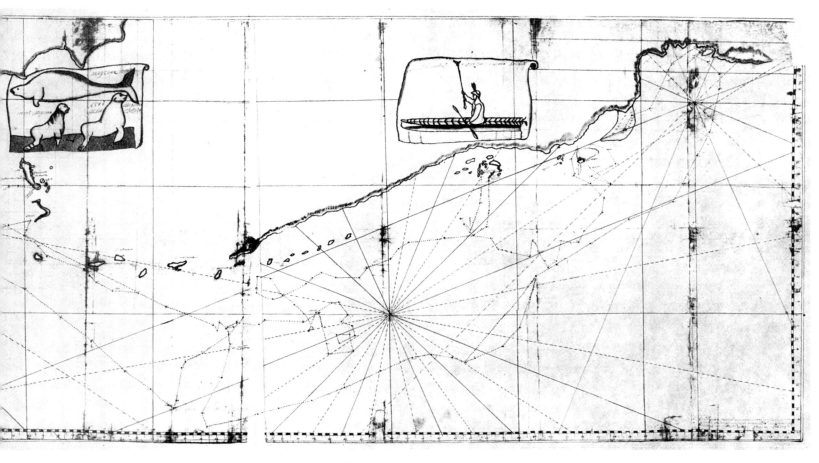

trivial distance compared to the vast space they had already covered.

A decision was made to land, with the intention of trying to save the men from scurvy. Yushin wrote that Bering, who was also ill, met with his officers and crew and decided on this course of action because of the lack of men to sail the ship. Twelve were already dead, and thirty-four completely disabled.

The ship was wrecked on the beach of Bering Island, unable to be properly anchored against the pounding surf. On 8 December 1741 Bering died, and many more of his crew perished over the ensuing winter.

By April, the survivors had determined that they were in fact on an island, and in May they began to build another ship from the wreckage of the first. Now commanded by Lieutenant Sven Waxell, Bering's second-in-command, they finally made it back to the harbor at Petropavlovsk on 5 September 1742.

Map 103 (above).
One of the maps made soon after Bering's voyage, probably by Sven Waxell in late 1742 or early 1743. The relationship of the Alaskan coast relative to Kamchatka is reasonably accurate, but the chain of Aleutian Islands has not been distinguished, so their coasts are plotted as a single shore. Bering Island is shown (close to the Kamchatka coast), and St. Elias Island (Kayak Island), where Bering finally reached North America, is also shown (at top right).

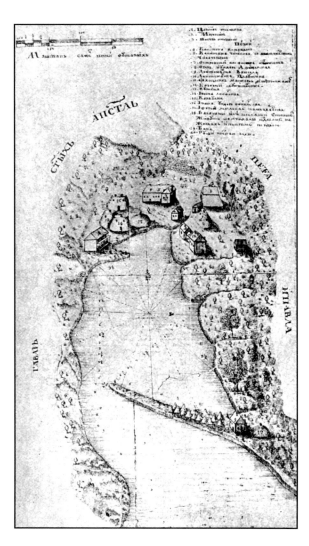

Map 104.
Survey of the harbor of Petropavlovsk, made in 1741, before Bering sailed.

Georg Steller – First Scientist of the North Pacific

Georg Wilhelm Steller was a German scientist who was part of the Second Kamchatka Expedition. This brilliant yet arrogant man was essentially the first scientist ever to be carried on a Pacific voyage, sailing with Bering himself on *Sviatoi Petr* (*St. Peter*).

He was one of Europe's foremost naturalists and was the first to record the unique wildlife of the coasts of Alaska and the islands of the Bering Sea. He was also a physician and a botanist, the multifaceted scientist of course being a common occurrence until well into the nineteenth century.

Steller was employed as personal physician to Archbishop Novgorov in St. Petersburg in 1734 when he heard of Russia's planned expedition to the Pacific. He wanted to be the first to report on the natural history of the region and so applied for a position as a botanist.

Steller wrote many botanical, zoological, and other reports during the expedition, only some of which have survived.

He was the first to describe the life cycle of the anadromous North Pacific salmon, realizing for the first time that this fish migrates from the ocean up rivers into fresh water to spawn and then die. In work with another scientist on the Kamchatka Peninsula, Stepan Krasheninnikov, Steller first identified its five species by the names still used today: *keta*, chum; *nerka*, sockeye; *kisutch*, coho; *tshawytscha*, chinook; and *gorbuscha*, pink.

Steller's name lives on in birds – Steller's jay being perhaps the most well known, but there are others, such as Steller's eider and Steller's eagle. Intriguingly, he also wrote of the Steller's sea monkey, which has never been seen by anyone else; either Steller for once was mistaken (which seems unlikely, as he studied it for two hours), or he saw one of the last of a now extinct species.

Steller is perhaps most remembered today for his descriptions of the also now extinct Steller's sea cow, the northern manatee, an ungainly sea mammal that was quickly hunted out of existence, mostly by Russian fur traders who took a liking to its taste.

Steller's journal, written while he was shipwrecked on Bering Island, describes the sea cow and its habits, notes which are extremely valuable given the extinction of the animal.

These animals, like cattle on land, live in herds at sea, males and females going together and driving the young before them about the shore. They are occupied with nothing else but their food. The back and half the body are always seen out of the water. They eat in the same manner as the land animals, with a slow forward movement. They tear the seaweed from the rocks with the feet and chew it without cessation. However, the structure of the stomach taught me that they do not ruminate, as I had first supposed. During the eating they move the head and neck like an ox, and after the lapse of a few minutes they lift the head out of the water and draw fresh air with a rasping and snorting sound after the manner of horses. When the tide falls they go away from the land to sea but with the rising tide go back again to shore.

Steller also noted the trait that was to doom the sea cow to extinction. "They are not afraid of man in the least," he wrote.

The sea cow must have appeared to the first fur traders to be an inexhaustible resource. Steller wrote:

These animals are found at all seasons of the year everywhere around the island [Bering Island] *in the greatest numbers, so that the whole population of the east coast of Kamchatka would always be able to keep itself more than abundantly supplied from them with fat and meat . . . The weight of this animal with skin, fat, meat, bones and entrails I estimate at 1200 poods.*

It seems that the sea cow provided a unique delicacy:

The meat of the old animals is not to be distinguished from beef; but it has this remarkable property that, even in the hottest summer months and in the open air, it will keep for two full weeks and even longer without becoming offensive, in spite of its being so defiled by the blowflies as to be covered with worms all over . . . All of us who had partaken of it soon found out what a salutary food it was, as we soon felt a marked improvement in strength and health . . . With this sea cow meat we also provisioned our vessel for the voyage [back to Kamchatka].

Steller only spent about ten hours on land once *Sviatoi Petr* reached Alaska, at Kayak Island, which he called St. Elias Island, below Mt. St. Elias. Bering, concerned only about the safety of his ship, sent Sofron Khitrov in the longboat to find a more secure anchorage but would not permit Steller to go with him, fearing that he would interfere with Khitrov's work. Thus there ensued a blistering argument between Steller and Bering in which Steller did finally prevail, as he was permitted to go ashore with a party sent to fill the water casks. There, working feverishly, he crammed days of work into his allotted ten hours. And it was Steller who first detected the presence of other humans, finding a recently used campsite, though no natives were seen. He found

utensils made of bark, filled with smoked fish of a species of Kamchatkan salmon called nerka [sockeye] . . . sweet grass from which liquor is distilled . . . different kinds of plants, whose outer skin had been removed like hemp . . . for making fish nets . . . dried inner bark from the larch or spruce tree done up in rolls and dried; the same is used as food in times of famine . . . [and] large bales of thongs made of seaweed which we found to be of uncommon strength and firmness.

After his return from Bering Island, Steller worked in Kamchatka and the Kuril Islands. In 1744, returning to St. Petersburg, he was charged with freeing some Kamchadal prisoners, and the stress associated with this led to his early death, in 1746; heavy drinking undoubtedly helped. He was only thirty-seven.

Steller measuring a sea cow on Bering Island. From Leonard Stejneger, in F. A. Golder, 1925.

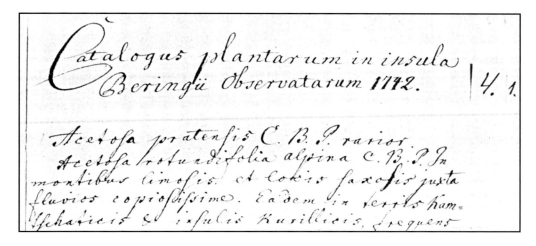

The beginning of the botanical catalog written by Georg Steller, including many plants new to science he found during his short stay in Alaska. Historian Frank Golder found the manuscript of Steller's journal, including the botanical catalog, in Russian archives in 1917. The copies he made are now in the Library of Congress, where this was found in Golder's files.

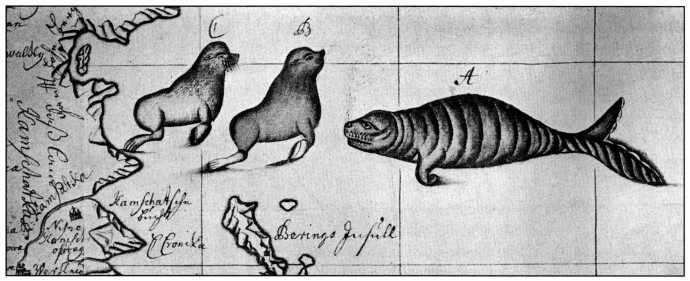

Map 105.
A tantalizing map whose current whereabouts are unknown. This is part of the map, reproduced in 1891. At that time it was in the Tsar's Library, which was broken up and sold in the late 1930s. The map was drawn by Sven Waxell, hence the Swedish language used. The animals shown are a fur seal, a sea lion, and a sea cow. Waxell had personally seen the sea cow, and thus his representation is important because it was drawn from life.

Alexei Chirikov's Voyage

Alexei Chirikov, in his ship *St. Paul*, fared better than Bering, reaching the North American coast ahead of Bering.

On 14 July 1741 Chirikov noted long broad white paths in the water, which he attributed to small fish in large quantities. This would, he thought, mean they were close to shore, and so he ordered systematic soundings to be made. The bottom was not reached at 100 fathoms.

That night, provision was made to be able to drop the anchor in a hurry should this be necessary. They saw ducks and gulls presumably flying from a shore, and they also saw whales and porpoises and three pieces of driftwood. Sure enough, they were at the North American coast; the next day land was seen.

Chirikov had made his landfall at 55° 20′ N, at Baker Island, on the west coast of Prince of Wales Island. The westernmost point of Baker Island is today named Cape Chirikof.

He was sure he had reached America. He had one of Johann Baptist Homann's maps with him. "Several known American places are not very far from this place," he wrote with confidence. He ordered it "placed on the map made of our voyage." Quite where he got his confidence from is a mystery.

They came within 3 km or 2 miles of the shore, and soundings were taken in order to find an anchorage, but none was found, because "everywhere the depth of water was close to 70 fathoms or more." A boat was sent to find a suitable bay and found none, but reports came back of great stands of fir, spruce, and pine on the mountains, and sea lions on the shore. From the *St. Paul* whales, sea lions, and walruses were seen.

Attempting to find an anchorage, Chirikov sailed northwards along the American shore, along the west coast of Baranof Island, past where sixty years later the Russians would establish the headquarters of their American operations, at today's Sitka.

Fleet Master Avraam Dement'ev was finally sent off in the ship's longboat with ten sailors to attempt to find an anchorage, and also to survey the land, as Chirikov had been instructed to do. Dement'ev was given all manner of gifts for any natives he might encounter. But the longboat did not return, and after a difficult week of attempting to stay in the same place, Chirikov and his officers decided that the reason Dement'ev was not returning was that his boat had been damaged. So Chirikov sent off another boat, the only one left, with the ship's carpenter and caulker and two others. But they did not return either.

Two boats did approach *St. Paul*, but they turned out to be natives in canoes, who could not be persuaded to come close.

Eventually, Chirikov could wait no longer; he had by this time concluded that his men had been attacked by natives, but the real reason for their disappearance will probably never be known. They might have been caught in dangerous surf, a whirlpool, or struck a hidden rock, much as a surveying boat from La Pérouse's expedition would do in Lituya Bay some forty-five years later (see page 102).

Now, unable to land and unable to replenish his water supplies, Chirikov reluctantly decided that he had to return immediately to Petropavlovsk, and on 27 July he sailed. Although land was seen at various places, they had no boats and could not land. Fog often constrained their view. Kenai Peninsula was seen, as was Kodiak Island. At Adak, the largest island in the Andreanov group in the Aleutians, natives approached and were given gifts.

Near Kodiak, a rapidly decreasing depth had caused alarm. They cast their lead frequently, and the water depth decreased to 55 fathoms, then 40 fathoms an hour later, then 30 fathoms an hour after that. "Every time the lead was cast," Chirikov recorded,

the soil changed. Sometimes it was fine gravel, sometimes coarse, which did not stick to the lead, and sometimes, fine gray sand, but the shore was not seen at night or in the fog, and even by day when the fog had cleared, it was not seen, and so it is realized that it is a bank far from the shore.

This was Albatross Bank, and Chirikov had discovered it just as surely as he had discovered the American shore.

With their water running critically low, they limped back to Kamchatka, arriving finally in Petropavlovsk on 12 October 1741.

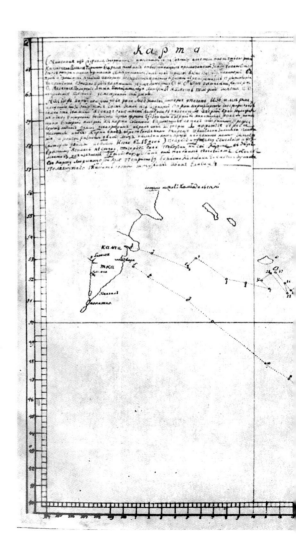

The information gathered by Bering and Chirikov was significant. It allowed a considerable amount of the map of the Northwest Coast to be filled in, and the position of the mainland in relation to Asia was now reasonably fixed, as much as it could be in a time of dead reckoning. Both Bering and Chirikov were out in their calculations of longitude.

It can be seen in Chirikov's map (below) that two American shores are shown. This is because dead-reckoning going eastwards produced a different location for the coast than that plotted going westwards, both positions being drawn from, or to, a known point, determined astronomically on land – that of Petropavlovsk. Currents adding to distance in one direction reduced it in the other. Hence they could not be *exactly* sure where they had been.

In any case, the fixing of points can still be, and was, misconstrued if the mapmaker wishes it. The map of the Northwest Coast copied by Robert de Vaugondy from Joseph-Nicolas de L'Isle and published in 1755 (Map 89, page 60, with caption page 61) marks the tracks of Bering and Chirikov reasonably accurately, but remains an utterly hopeless speculation as far as the west coast of North America is concerned.

Chirikov's maps, such as the one shown on this page, still show speculative geography south of his landfall.

Map 106.
Map of the voyage of Alexei Chirikov drawn by Ivan Elagin, Chirikov's pilot, in 1742. There are two coastlines plotted from Chirikov's track, with the coast on landfall being depicted west of that plotted from the return voyage. Dead reckoning, the method of plotting their position based on estimates of speed and elapsed time, produced different positions for the North American coast on the outbound voyage as compared with the return, both being measured from more accurate positions in Kamchatka. The track of Vitus Bering is also shown, with a North American landfall north of that of Chirikov.

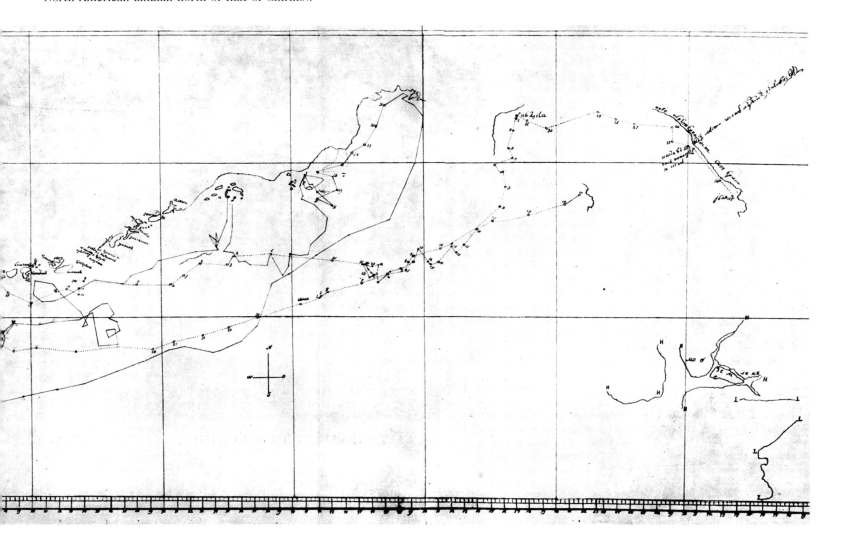

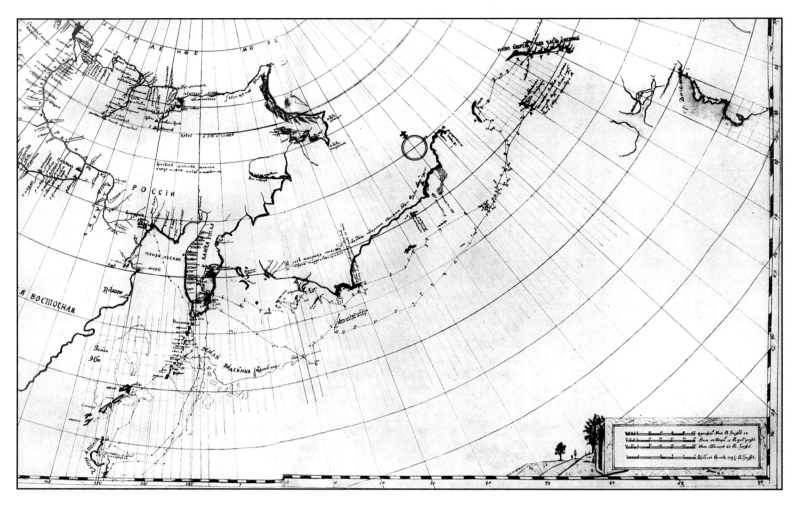

Map 107 (above) and Map 108 (right). Two Russian summary maps produced as a result of the Second Kamchatka Expedition, both drawn about 1742. It is not difficult to see how the sightings of land along the Aleutian chain manifested themselves on maps as a continuous peninsula. This idea would not be corrected cartographically until the arrival of James Cook in 1778, although by that time the Russians had realized that much of the peninsula was composed of islands.

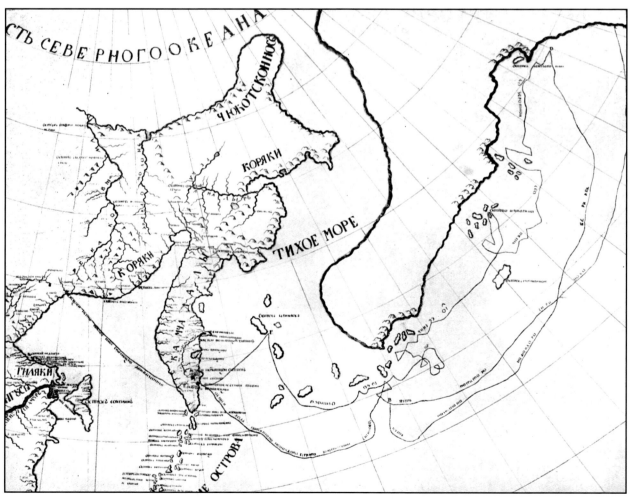

De L'Isle's Fantastic Map

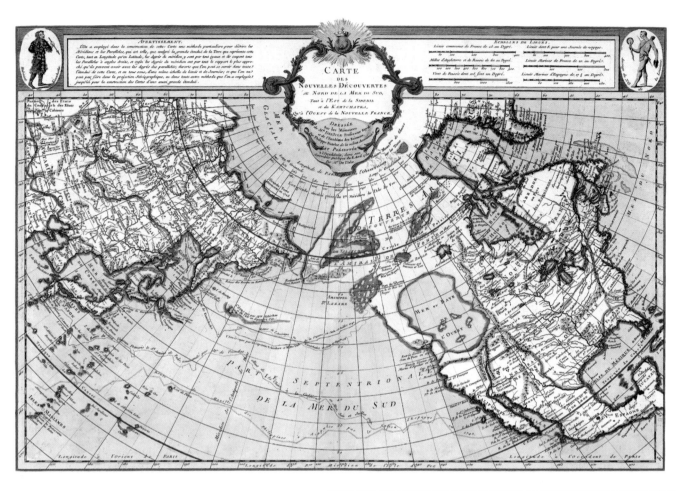

Map 109. Joseph-Nicolas de L'Isle's 1752 map. Despite its anomalies, the Siberian coast is shown quite accurately; the Russians were annoyed at de L'Isle for stealing their information. A missing continent, Gama Land, has only its south coast marked, in the middle of the North Pacific. A huge Sea of the West covers most of western North America.

Map 110 (below). A similarly bizarre map by Philippe Buache, brother-in-law of de L'Isle and partner in their map publishing business.

In 1708, a British magazine called *Memoirs for the Curious* published what purported to be a newly discovered account of a 1640 voyage to the northern Pacific Ocean by a Spanish admiral named Bartholemew de Fonte.

In sailing north along the coast, de Fonte was said to have entered a strait that led to a great inland sea and met a ship from Boston, which had supposedly arrived through a Northwest Passage. Inconsistencies in this story plus modern geography show that this voyage was fictitious. Nevertheless, this account was widely read and had an effect on later explorers and mapmakers.

The French geographer Joseph-Nicolas de L'Isle was a proponent of the de Fonte theory. He had spent twenty-one years at the Russian Academy of Sciences. When he returned to Paris to join his brother-in-law Philippe Buache to produce maps, he brought with him some maps he had acquired from the academy.

In 1752 he published a map which claimed to show the discoveries of the Russians. However, on the Northwest Coast of America he constructed an elaborate speculative map based on the de Fonte account and his own interpretation of Bering's discoveries. The academy was furious that de L'Isle had removed information to France, was further upset at his geographical speculations, and requested Gerhard Müller to refute them (see page 77).

John Green's Map of the North Pacific

A year after de L'Isle published his map of the Pacific, an Englishman, Bradock Mead, using the pen name John Green, produced a map of North and South America in six large sections in which he attempted to show the most recent discoveries of the Russians in the North Pacific in a much more responsible fashion, and which refuted the de Fonte idea of the geography of the North Pacific.

These important maps were published by Thomas Jefferys in London in 1753. They were an honest attempt to produce maps that only reflected exploration. The northern sheet (right) was the first map to call Bering Strait by that name. Mead had not heard of Semen Dezhnev; otherwise the name might well have been different.

The main North Pacific map (below) finally showed the trend of the North American coast correctly, but due to lack of information was still incorrect in many details, the most notable of which is the large island in the western Pacific "of which Capt. Behring found signs in 1728." Also shown is the strait Juan de Fuca "pretends he entered in 1594 [1592]."

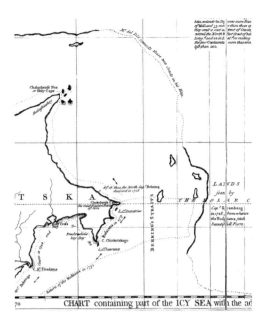

John Green's map of 1753: northern sheet (Map 111, above) and middle sheet (Map 112, below).

CHART, containing the Coasts of CALIFORNIA , NEW ALBION, and *RUSSIAN DISCOVERIES* to the North; with the Peninsula of KAMCHATKA , in ASIA, opposite thereto; And ISLANDS, dispersed over the PACIFIC OCEAN, to the North of the *LINE*.

Gerhard Müller's Famous Map

There were other dissenters to the de L'Isle view of the geography of the North Pacific Ocean.

Gerhard Müller, like de L'Isle, had been a member of the Second Kamchatka Expedition. Acting for the Russians, in 1753 he wrote an anonymous rebuttal, *Lettre d'un officier de la marine russienne,* based on Sven Waxell's journal, and in 1754, Müller constructed a map using information from Vitus Bering's voyages, adding to it other information that he had gathered, such as that about Semen Dezhnev's voyage of 1648. Müller wrote that he had had the map made "on the basis of my data and under my supervision."

He made the map to refute the geographical exaggerations made by de L'Isle on his map of 1752 (page 75). Because the Müller map was the first printed map to show Bering's 1728 and 1741 discoveries to the world in a reasonably accurate fashion, and also information from Dezhnev's voyage, the map assumed considerable significance.

The 1754 map, shown overleaf, had relatively limited circulation, but a 1758 revision was widely disseminated, and was included with a more extensive condemnation of de L'Isle contained in the third volume of a book written by Müller. This map was very influential and was widely copied.

Müller was at the time probably the one individual who knew the most about the geography of the North Pacific, and his map was a vast improvement on anything previously available. Despite this it contained many inaccuracies. The most notable was the enormous semi-tentative peninsula protruding from Alaska. This reflected the official Russian view that the land seen by Bering and Chirikov, which was actually the Aleutian chain, was part of a continent

Map 113.
French mapmaker Jacques Nicolas Bellin's rendering of Müller's ideas. The Aleutian Islands are shown as a peninsula. The tracks of Bering and Chirikov's expedition of 1741–42 are marked.

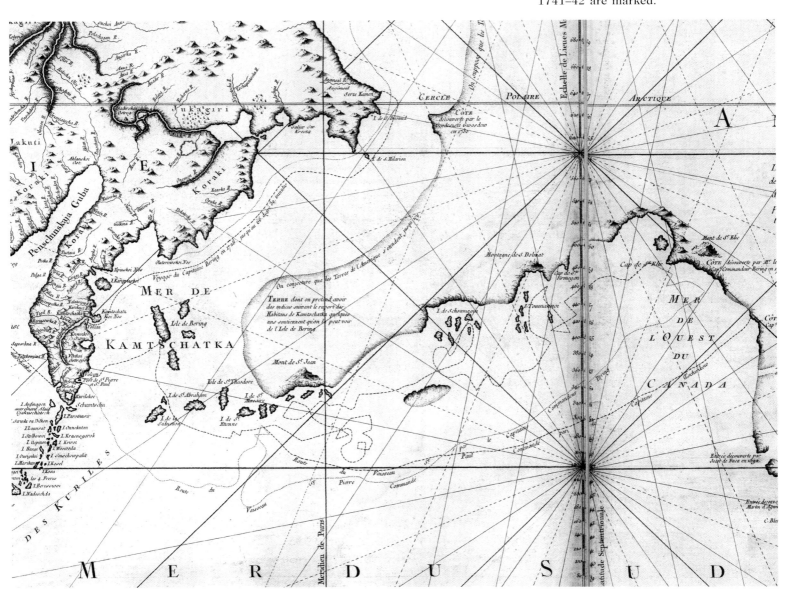

(see map on page 74, bottom). Given the information available, this was not a totally unreasonable assumption; even so, Müller only shows most of the peninsula with dotted lines rather than making bold with geography the way de L'Isle had done.

Another incorrect feature was the troublesome Cape Shelagsk, at the northeastern tip of Siberia, information for which came from Müller's interpretation of Dezhnev's account (see Map 57, page 42). The non-existent cape is shown as a huge mushroom-shaped peninsula extending more than 10 degrees east to west and almost to 75° N. If it had existed, the cape would have been the easternmost tip of Asia.

Müller's concept of the North Pacific remained the authority until James Cook's third voyage. It was modified to incorporate other discoveries, such as those of Ivan Synd (page 81).

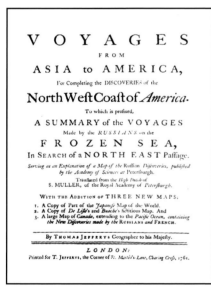

The title page of Müller's book, published in an English translation by Thomas Jefferys in 1761. Müller's map was first published in the 1758 German edition of the book. The 1754 map shown here is much rarer than the 1758 edition, as relatively few copies were printed. It took the publication of the book, and its translations, to widely disseminate Müller's map.

Map 114.
Gerhard Müller's influential map.
This is the original (and now rare)
1754 edition.

NOUVELLE CARTE
DES DECOUVERTES FAITES PAR DES
VAISSEAUX RUSSES AUX CÔTES INCONNUES
DE L'AMERIQUE SEPTENTRIONALE AVEC LES
PAIS ADIACENTS.
sur des memoires authentiques de ceux,
qui ont assisté a ces decouvertes, et sur d'autres
connoissances, dont on rend raison dans un memoire
separé
A St. Petersbourg a l'Academie Imperiale
des Sciences 1754.

BAFFINS BAY

DÉTROIT DE BAFFIN

LABRADOR

DÉTROIT DE HUDSON

HUDSONS BAY

ESQUIMAUX

NOUV SUD WALES

KRIS KRIK ou KILLISTINS

MER D'ANADIR

Tchuktschi

CÔTE
decouverte par le
Geodesiste Gwosdew
en 1730.

AMERIQUE

SEPTENTRIONALE

Mont de St Elie

CÔTE decouverte par Mr
le Capt Commandeur
Bering en 1741

CÔTE decouverte par Mr
le Capt Tschirikow
en 1741

Cap de St Elie

Cap de
St Ermogen

Montagne
de St Dolmat

Bering

Commandens

Pretendue R. de los Reyes
de l'Amiral de Fonte
en 1640 suivant Ms Delisle

I. de Schoumagin

la Capitaine

St Paul commandé par le Capt Tschirikow

Entrée decouv par
Jean de Fuca en 1592

Entrée decouv par
Martin d'Aguilar
en 1603

NOUV ALBION
decouverte en 1578 par
François Drane
Port de François Drane
Passement appelle de St François

PARTIE DE
CALIFORNIE

DU SUD

79

The Russians Discover the Aleutians

After Bering there were many enterprising individual fur traders and hunters who sought to exploit the new and rich resources to be found in the islands to the east.

As early as 1743–44, Emelian Basov sailed to Bering Island, site of Bering's demise, and Mednyy Island, close by, was also found by him in 1745. Before the end of the decade, the westernmost Aleutians, Attu, Agattu, and the Semichi group (all the Near Islands), were discovered by M. Nevotchikov. St. Matthew Island was discovered by S. Novikov and Ivan Bakhov in 1748.

Improvements in ship design (up till this point the hunters had been using *shitik*, boats made from wood planks sown together with lengths of twisted willow or fir) and rapid depletion of fur-bearing animals led in the next decade to voyages farther and farther to the east.

Evidence is generally inconclusive, because the fur traders and hunters often did not make maps or determine their positions accurately, but it seems the Andreanof Islands were reached by 1757; Umnak and Unalaska Islands, in the Fox group, by 1761; and the Alaskan mainland

also in 1761, by G. Pushkarev, although he thought it just another island. Kodiak Island was reached by Stepan Glotov in 1763.

These private explorations were supplemented by government-sponsored ones, and it is those that led to the drawing and retention of maps.

In 1762, Catherine II came to power in Russia. She wanted to renew the strength of the Russian navy and was responsible for a renewed interest in discoveries in the

Map 115.
Ivan Synd's map, showing the coast of Siberia from the Sea of Okhotsk to Bering Strait, including the Aleutian islands he discovered.

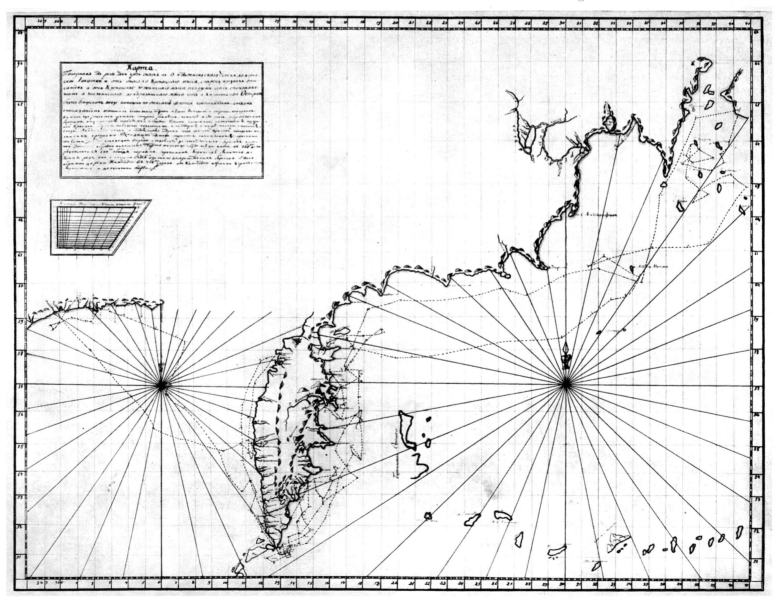

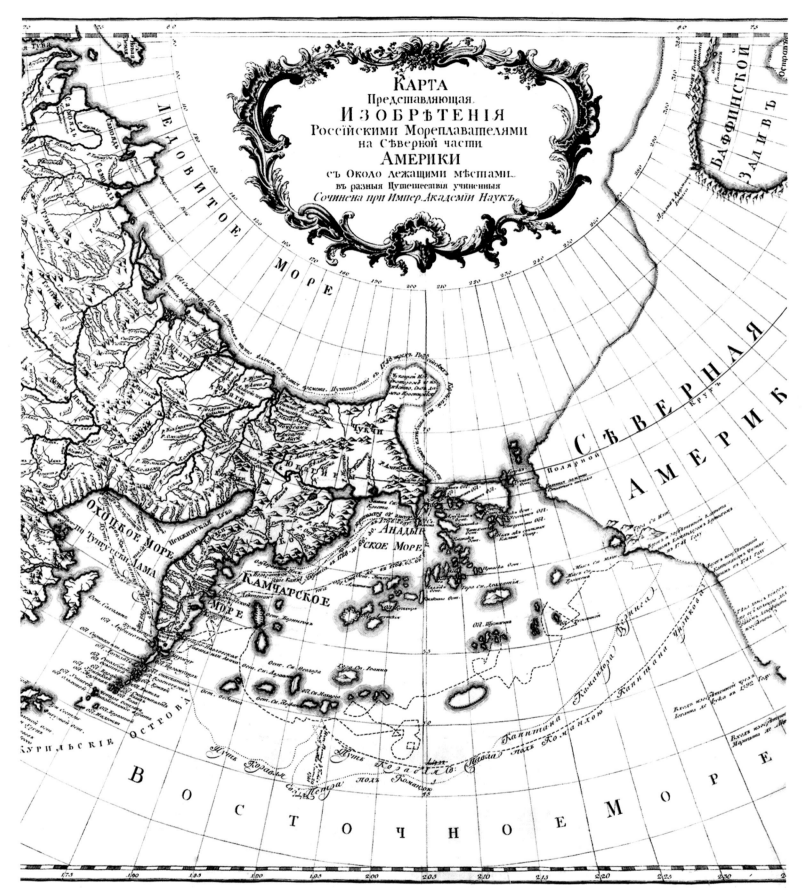

Map 116.
A Russian map from about 1773 showing Alaska as an island. This was Gerhard Müller's map of
1754 (pages 78–79) modified to include Ivan Synd's discoveries.

Map 117. Jacob von Stählin's map of the "New Northern Archipelago discovered by the Russians." Published in a book in 1774, the map was carried by James Cook, causing him to remark on its errors: "What could induce him to publish so erroneous a Map?"

North Pacific. In addition, she heard of the British plan to dispatch Commodore Byron to the North Pacific to seek a Northwest Passage; he sailed to the Pacific, but did not seek the passage.

As a result, in 1764 one of the survivors of the 1741 Bering expedition, Lieutenant Ivan Synd, was sent on a voyage into the Bering Sea.

Although he produced maps and a journal, all but one seem to have been lost. His map showed that there was a strait and showed that there was not a long peninsula from America almost to Kamchatka. The map he drew is shown on page 80.

On the basis of Synd's discoveries, Gerhard Müller's map was modified, and the overly long Alaska

Peninsula was shortened in favor of lots of islands, when reality lay somewhere between the two. The Russian version of this later map, dating from about 1773, is shown on the previous page (Map 116).

Also based on Synd, Jacob von Stählin produced a map in 1774, although it was hardly justified by Synd's own map. The latter showed

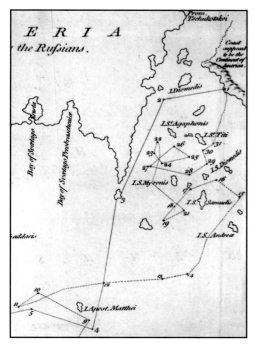

Map 118.
Synd's discoveries in the Bering Sea according to William Coxe, whose book was published in 1780. St. Matthew Island and the Diomedes are identifiable, but the other islands do not exist in the positions given. This map shows St. Matthew Island correctly at about 60° N.

fewer and much smaller islands in the northern Pacific. It was von Stählin's map that James Cook would carry with him on his third voyage, the map that would mislead him for some time (see page 98).

Catherine II was also concerned about possible Spanish designs on "her" northern territories. The voyages of Bering and Chirikov were in her eyes claims of sovereignty based on first discovery. There was also concern about potential British interest in the region following the end of the Seven Years War with France, which resulted in a strengthening of the British position in North America.

Petr Krenitsyn and Mikhail Levashev were ordered to visit the islands to the east in 1764 so that Catherine could find out if there was encroachment by other powers. For secrecy, they were instructed only to build ships if they had no other alternative; otherwise they were to "board a hunting ship or merchant vessel . . . in the general capacity of passengers" so they would attract as little attention as possible.

But there were no ships available, and Krenitsyn and Levashev had to build their own. Taking the maps of Vitus Bering, they explored the North Pacific until 1769, becoming separated a number of times and overwintering three times.

They charted a number of the Aleutian Islands and the western part of the Alaska Peninsula. They produced maps such as one of the Fox Islands, the easternmost of the Aleutians, shown here in a later English edition.

Between 1774 and 1779 Potap Zaikov explored most of the Aleutian Islands, and in 1779 drew the first reasonably accurate and complete map of the entire Aleutian chain (Map 120, overleaf).

Grigorii Shelikov, who would in 1799 be instrumental in the founding of the Russian-American Company; Gerasim Ismailov, who met James Cook at Unalaska in 1778 and exchanged geographical information; and Dimitrii Bocharov added to Russian knowledge of the Aleutians in the 1780s. A summary map by Shelikov, which includes a larger-scale map of Kodiak Island, site of the first permanent Russian settlement in North America, is shown overleaf.

Finally, mention should be made of Gavriil Pribilov, who in 1786–87 discovered the relatively isolated islands of St. George and St. Paul, today named, after him, the Pribilof Islands. These islands would later become economically significant, for they were (and are again) home to vast numbers of fur seals.

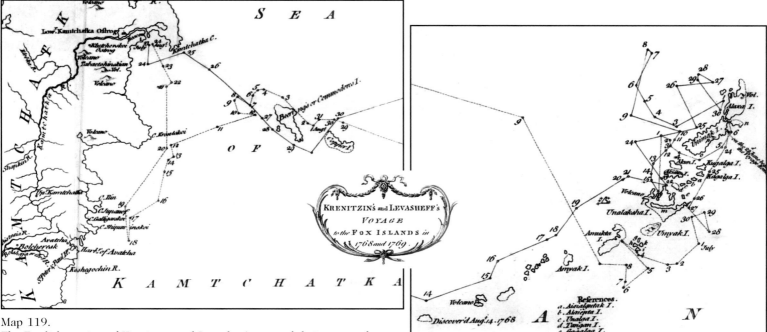

Map 119.
The English version of Krenitsyn and Levashev's map of their voyage from Kamchatka to the Fox Islands, the Aleutian Islands group nearest to the Alaskan mainland. It appeared in a book by Englishman William Coxe in 1780. It is more or less an exact copy of the Russian version, which shows that somehow Coxe, who visited Russia, gained access to the original. The map is long and narrow, with only the track of their ship connecting the detail from the Kamchatka side with that of the eastern Aleutians. The details either side of the map are shown here, and the map title cartouche inset.

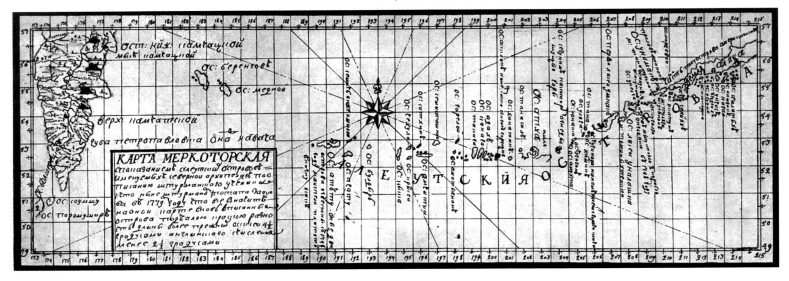

Map 120.
Potap Zaikov's map of the Aleutians, 1779.

Map 121.
A summary map by Grigorii Shelikov, one of the founders of the Russian-American Company. Drawn in 1787, the map was intended to promote trade possibilities in the North Pacific. It includes an inset map on a larger scale showing Kodiak Island, site of the first permanent Russian settlement in North America.

The Spanish Northward Voyages

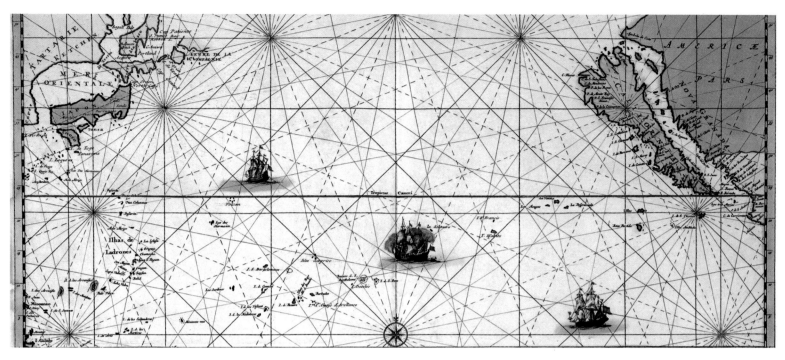

Map 122.
Knowledge of the Pacific Ocean, or South Sea, at the middle of the eighteenth century is shown in this map by Dutch mapmakers Reinier and Joshua Ottens, drawn in 1750. The magnificent cartouche from this map is reproduced on page 7.

Spanish knowledge of the Pacific Ocean north of the Tropics was much less detailed than what they knew of the tropical zone. Their main interest in the sixteenth, seventeenth, and much of the eighteenth centuries focused on the Philippines, and the routes there and back from New Spain. Only when their galleons were blown off course did they learn more, and this was not always interpreted correctly.

João de Gama, actually a Portuguese navigator sailing on a Spanish ship from Macao to Acapulco, is reputed to have seen land in relatively high latitudes in the western Pacific in 1590. Although more likely part of Japan or the Kurils, this gave rise to a "Gama Land" that was persistent on maps for two centuries, and was searched for by Bering and Chirikov in 1741.

Spanish explorations in the North Pacific were largely confined to the west coast of North America. By about 1768 they had decided to occupy Alta California, the California of today. In 1769 San Diego Bay, which had been found by Sebastián Vizcaíno in 1603, was settled by two overland expeditions meeting two ships which had been dispatched northwards by sea. One of the ships was commanded by Juan Pérez, who was to lead another northward thrust in 1774. The next year, 1775, Monterey was settled. That year San Francisco Bay was discovered by Gaspar de Portolá, who had led the overland expeditions to San Diego and Monterey.

Map 123.
Anonymous Spanish map, about 1779, of San Diego, "discovered by Sebastián Vizcaíno in 1603." North is to the left.

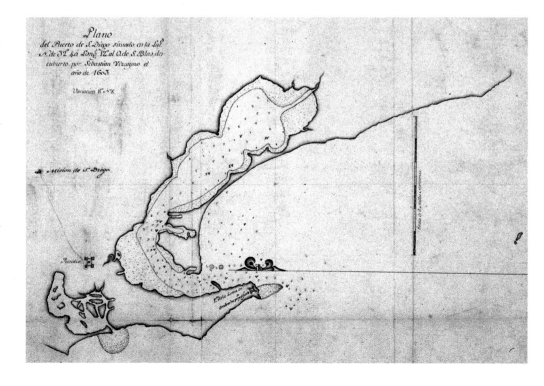

In 1773, the Northwest Coast of North America stood unmapped even in general trend, a major gap in the map of the world; only the polar regions were similarly unmapped. The reason for this state of affairs was a lack of motivation. No European power, up to that point, was really interested. There were no reports of gold to draw men northwards to these often unpleasantly chilly coasts, there were vast distances to cover in any case, and the currents and winds made sailing northwards along the coast next to impossible. Without motivation, no one bothered to try.

The Russian advance eastwards from Kamchatka to the Aleutians changed all that. The Spanish regarded the Pacific Ocean as theirs, and wanted to ensure that no other nation encroached on what they viewed as their own territory.

So in 1773 the Spanish viceroy in New Spain (Mexico) instructed one of his senior naval captains, Juan Pérez, to draw up plans for a voyage to the north to determine once and for all what the Russians were up to in Alaska.

Pérez had been involved with the Spanish advance into Alta California and had been the first Spanish captain since Sebastián Vizcaíno to enter the harbors of San Diego and Monterey, both in 1770.

Now those small settlements seemed reasonably secure, and the Spanish government considered the time ripe for a further northward thrust.

Pérez sailed from the Mexican port of San Blas in January 1774 in the *Santiago,* with a complement of about eighty-six men including, as second-in-command, Estéban José Martínez, and pilot Josef de Cañizarez. Both would feature in later voyages north.

The viceroy instructed Pérez to sail to 60° N. He was, on his southward return, to follow the coast, "never losing sight of it." Not only that, Pérez was to carry tropical spices such as cinnamon and nutmeg to show any natives he might encounter what the Spanish were looking for.

Clearly the Spanish at this time had little concept of the nature of the Northwest Coast!

Pérez reached Monterey on 8 May and finally sailed from this last outpost of Spanish power on 6 June, although adverse winds meant he did not actually leave the bay for another eight days.

Then, sailing offshore, he set a course to the northwest, changing to north at 50°. On 18 July they sighted land, off the northernmost point of the Queen Charlotte Islands, and the following day, near Langara Island (which was named Santa Margarita by Pérez) in Dixon Entrance, they met Haida in canoes, with whom they bartered. But, fearing treachery, they did not venture ashore. It was found that the natives already had some metal, and in particular half a bayonet and a piece of sword beaten into a spoon, which Martínez assumed derived from the abortive landing parties of Alexei Chirikov, just a little farther north, thirty-three years before. A feasible assumption, although the interlinked and far-ranging trading networks of native groups are often overlooked when this sort of "evidence" surfaces; the iron could have migrated a long distance, trading from native group to native group.

Remaining in the area for four days, Pérez was never able to anchor. His latitudes are confused. He maintained that he was at 55° 24´ when he saw and named a cape he called Santa Maria Magdalena; it is marked on the map (right) as Pᵗᵃ de Sᵗᵃ Maria Magdalena. But this has been identified as Cape Muzon, the southern tip of Dall Island, at almost exactly 54° 40´. Not coincidentally, this is also the southern tip of the Alaska panhandle. When the United States inherited the territorial claims of Spain in 1819 under the terms of the Transcontinental Treaty, they claimed the coast up to the magic 54° 40´, and in fact threatened to go to war with Britain in 1845–46 if they didn't get it. As it happened, of course, they settled for 49° instead. But 54° 40´ was accepted as the southern limit of Russian claims, so that when the United States purchased Alaska from

the Russians in 1867, this latitude became the boundary between British – now Canadian – territories to the south and American territories to the north.

Pérez gave up at this latitude; although he had been instructed to sail to 60°, he had seen no evidence of Russian encroachment. He tried to keep the coast in view as he returned southwards, without much success until he reached Vancouver Island. There he chanced on the entrance to Nootka Sound, which he named Surgidero de San Lorenzo. Unable to make it into the sound itself, he anchored outside on 7 August and again traded with natives. The latter encounter is significant in that it seems some silver spoons belonging to Martínez were pilfered, and four years later James Cook would trade for those same spoons; Cook mentions in his journal that he regarded them as proof that the Spanish had been at or near Nootka Sound.

The voyage farther south was uneventful and speedy; they arrived back at Monterey on 28 August. Martínez was later to claim that he had seen the entrance to the Strait of Juan de Fuca during this part of the voyage, but nothing in Pérez's account corroborates this claim.

Juan Pérez's voyage did not fulfill his instructions, but it was the first Spanish voyage north, and many others were to follow. The map opposite was drawn by Josef de Cañizarez and is the first map of what is now the coast of British Columbia, Washington, Oregon, and California north of Monterey drawn from actual exploration rather than from conjecture.

Map 124.
Map showing the west coast of North America from Monterey to the tip of the Queen Charlotte Islands drawn by Juan Pérez's pilot, Josef de Cañizarez. It is the first map of part of the coast of British Columbia and Washington State to be drawn from actual exploration. Pérez's anchorage off Nootka Sound is shown as "Surgidero de Sⁿ Lorenzo." "Pᵗᵃ de Sᵗᵃ Margarita" is the northern tip of Graham Island in the Queen Charlottes. "Cerro de Sᵗᵃ Rosalia" is Mt. Olympus, Washington.

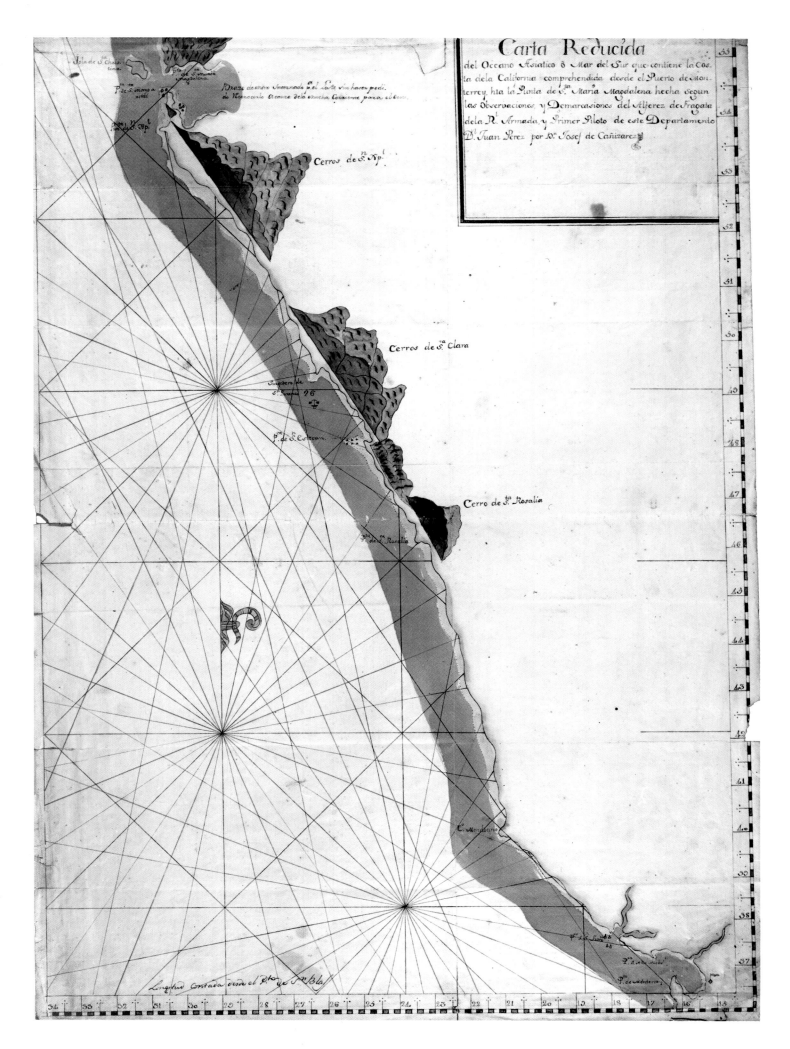

Carta Reducida

del Oceano Asiatico ô Mar del Sur que contiene la Cos.
ta dela California comprehendida desde el Puerto de Mon.
terrey, hta la Punta de Sta Maria Magdalena hecha segun
las Observaciones, y Demarcasiones del Alferez de Fragata
dela Rl Armada, y Primer Piloto de este Departamento
Dn Juan Perez por Dn Josef de Cañizares

Isla de S. Christina

Pta de S. Maria Magdalena

P. de S. maria a.bdell.

Pta N.
Pan del S. Bp.

Rmaze de mar Arremeada ô el Sular sin hacer pedi.
de Reonocerlo Ocaura dela mucha Coriaente para el bar.

Cerros de S. Npl

Cerros de Sta Clara

Surgidero de
St Simon 26

Pta de S. Estevan

Cerro de Sta Rosalia

Pta de Sta Rosalia

C. Mendocino

Pta de S. Luis

Pta de este insta
Pta de Relandorro

Longitud Contada desde el Pto ye Sn Blas

87

On 5 August 1775 the first Spanish ship anchored in San Francisco Bay. It was *San Carlos,* commanded by Juan Manuel de Ayala, and with him was pilot Josef de Cañizarez, who had been with Pérez the year before. Cañizarez's map of 1775 was the first of San Francisco Bay from actual survey. When he returned the next year, he drew another map, shown below.

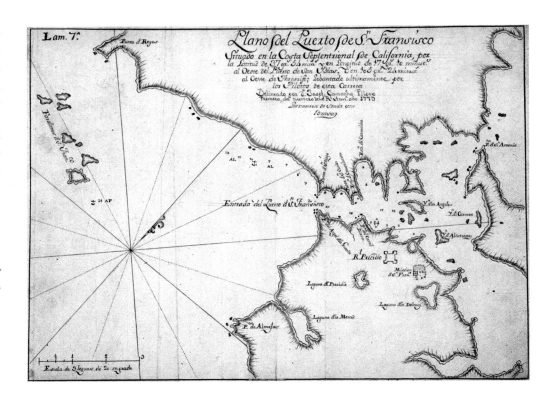

Map 125 (right).
A Spanish map of San Francisco Bay made by Josef Camacho, dated 1779 but probably a later copy.

Map 126 (below).
Part of *Plano del Puerto de Sn Francisco,* a map of San Francisco Bay drawn by Josef de Cañizarez in 1776.

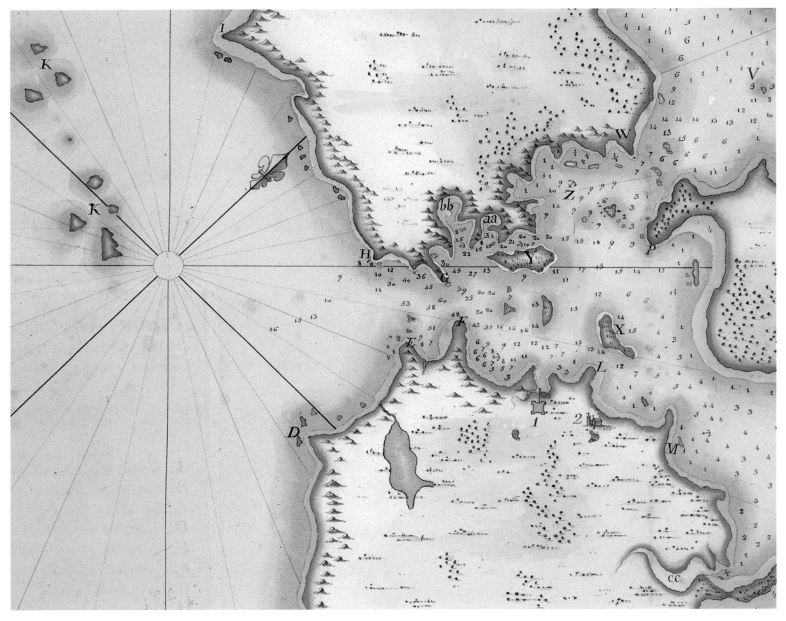

Bruno Hezeta Maps the Northwest Coast

Although it seemed unlikely that the Russians had settlements anywhere where they might threaten the Spanish, a second expedition was sent northwards in 1775, with instructions this time to reach 65° N. Two ships were dispatched: *Santiago,* with Bruno de Hezeta y Dudagoitia commanding the expedition and Juan Pérez now demoted to second officer because of his failure to follow instructions the year before; and *Sonora,* only 38 feet long, commanded by Juan Francisco de la Bodega y Quadra.

Heading offshore to sail northwards, the two ships made a landfall at Trinidad Harbor just south of Cape Blanco, and on 14 July 1775 landed on the Olympic Peninsula near Point Grenville, several miles south of the Quinault River.

Here Hezeta performed a formal act of possession for Spain. Bodega y Quadra sent some of his men ashore again later to fill their water casks, but they were all murdered by natives. Despite this and the short stay, Hezeta made a map of the area, which is shown here. This map is the first known map showing only the coast of Washington.

Leaving the coast and heading out to sea again, the ships were separated in heavy seas. Largely due to an outbreak of scurvy, Hezeta decided to sail the *Santiago* south again, but now he could follow the coast closely.

Map 128.
The first map of the Washington coast, drawn by Bruno de Hezeta y Dudagoitia, July 1775. The map shows today's Cape Elizabeth, the Quinault River, and Point Grenville.

A. Location of the cross (used in an act-of-possession ceremony)
B. Martyrs' Point (after the murdered sailors; now Cape Elizabeth)
C. Landing Island
D. Deceit Island

The river shown is the Quinault, and the dots extending south of Martyrs' Point show a reef on which the *Sonora* was temporarily stranded.

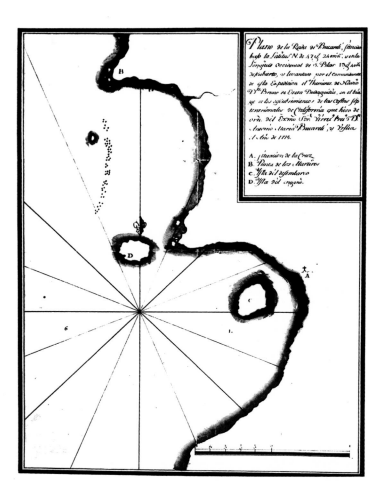

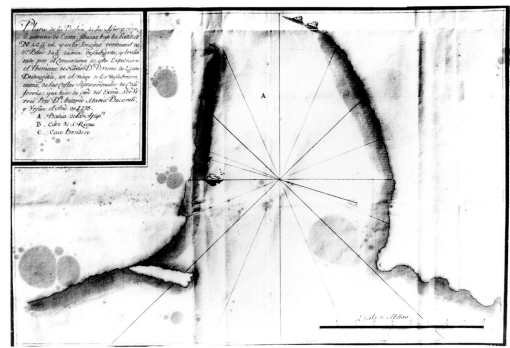

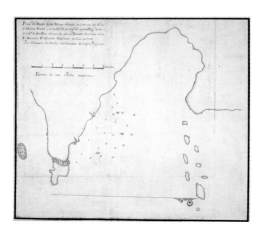

Map 127 (left).
A later Spanish map of part of the coast of Washington (as Map 128, above) either drawn in 1792 by Jacinto Caamaño or copied from him.

Map 129.
Map of Assumption Bay or [H]*ezeta's Entrance.*
Another of Hezeta's maps, drawn in August 1775. This is the first map of the mouth of the Columbia River.

On 17 August 1775, Hezeta came across what appeared to be a large bay, penetrating far inland. Hezeta tried to sail into the bay, but the current was so strong that he could not, even under a full press of sails. "These currents and seething of the waters," he wrote in his diary,

have led me to believe that it may be the mouth of some great river or some passage to another sea.

He decided it was the strait discovered by Juan de Fuca in 1592 and that the latitude had been misjudged. Hezeta named the bay Bahia de la Asunciōn after a holiday two days earlier.

This is the earliest recorded sighting of the mouth of the Columbia River by a European. It was a feature destined to be *missed* by many – including Cook in 1778, Meares in 1788, Malaspina in 1791, and Vancouver in 1792 – until finally being found and entered in 1792 by Robert Gray, in the *Columbia Rediviva,* from whence the river derives its name.

Hezeta was unable to anchor in the bay because he did not by this time have enough fit crew to handle the anchor, and he made directly for Monterey, reaching that port only twelve days later.

Hezeta prepared a map on the basis of what could be seen from outside the Columbia bar, and this is shown on the previous page. This was the first map of the mouth of the Columbia.

Map 130 (top).
Part of a Spanish map drawn in 1787 by Bernabe Muñoz that shows Hezeta's "entrada"; the Columbia now looks more like a river rather than just the bay Hezeta thought it was. It would not conclusively be determined to be a river until the American Robert Gray crossed the bar in 1792.

Map 131 (right).
A 1793 map by Esteban José Martínez shows "Entrada de Ezeta," the mouth of a recognizable Columbia River.

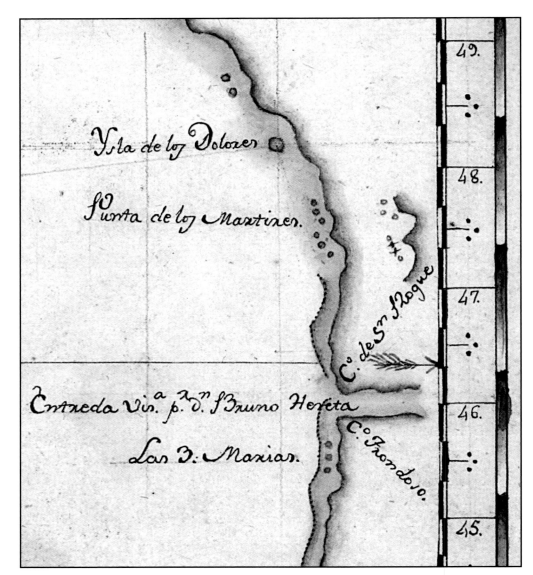

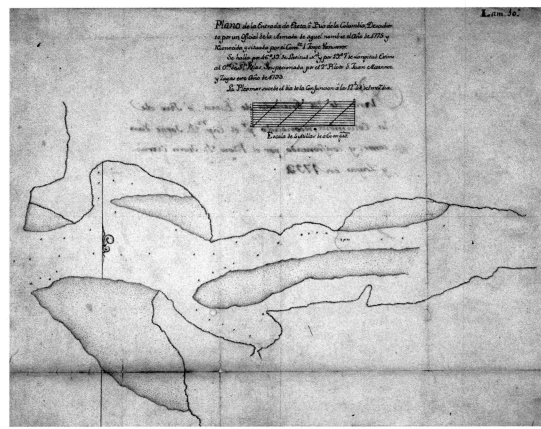

Bodega y Quadra's Epic Voyage

After separating from *Santiago*, Juan Francisco de la Bodega y Quadra in the little *Sonora* had decided to attempt to sail to 65° N, to follow his instructions. Indeed, it is possible that Bodega y Quadra, upset at Hezeta's lack of boldness, had deliberately separated from the other ship in order to be free to continue north. Francisco Antonio Mourelle, the second officer, wrote that they "formulated the temerarious project of separating and dying in their craft rather than return without enlightenment."

It was a brave act to sail from Washington to Alaska on the outer coast in such a small ship, particularly since navigation was little more than guesswork.

Sonora made a landfall on 15 August 1775 at 57° N, near a snow-capped peak they named San Jacinto – today's Mt. Edgecumbe, just west of Sitka. They eventually reached 58° N, just 2° south of the goal set for Pérez the year before.

Bodega y Quadra examined the coast in the area quite extensively, as he expected to find the mythical Strait of Bartholemew de Fonte. They did locate a good anchorage on the west coast of what is now Prince of Wales Island, at a bay they named (and which is still named today) Bucareli Bay, after the Spanish viceroy who had sent them. Francisco Antonio Mourelle performed possession ceremonies there, as Bodega y Quadra was ill that day. Scurvy was beginning to take its toll on the *Sonora,* as it had on the *Santiago.*

They limped back to San Blas via Monterey, arriving on 20 November 1775. A number of the crew died on the voyage, including Juan Pérez.

But enlightenment they found, for Bodega y Quadra was able to draw for the first time a reasonably accurate map of the west coast of North America.

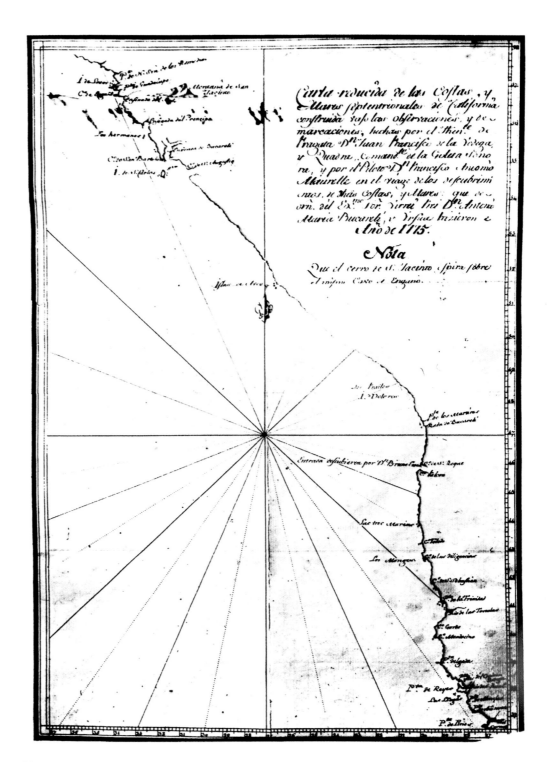

Map 132.
Bodega y Quadra's map of the west coast of North America, based on his discoveries and those of Hezeta. Detail is missing in the central part of the map due to the fact that Bodega y Quadra's ship was offshore at that time. This was a similar situation to that of James Cook in 1778, whose map of the Northwest Coast also shows little detail in the central part. Note the "Entrada descubierta por Dⁿ Bruno Ezeta," the "Entrance discovered by Don Bruno Hezeta," the mouth of the Columbia. Longitude is shown on this map, as it is on all Spanish maps of the period, as degrees west of San Blas, the Spanish naval port on the Mexican coast.

James Cook Defines the Northeast Pacific

The three voyages of James Cook were pivotal in the history of geographical knowledge of the Pacific Ocean. Before Cook there remained vast empty spaces on the map, where continents and straits may or may not have been.

After Cook, the essential outline of almost the entire Pacific Ocean had been mapped in sufficient detail to rule out most hypotheses of Southern Continents and Northwest Passages. Many details remained to be filled in, but the broad dimensions were now known for sure. And positions of islands and coasts had been fixed with remarkable accuracy; not only did Cook have an excellent ability to fix his position astronomically, but on the second and third voyages he carried some of the first examples of the new chronometers.

Cook's mapping of the west coast of North America demonstrated finally the width of the continent of North America, and by extension its corollary, the width of the Pacific Ocean.

Cook's uncanny surveying skills had been learned on the Atlantic coast of Canada and honed to perfection during his first and second voyages to the southern part of the Pacific. On his first voyage he mapped New Zealand and much of the east coast of Australia for the first time; on the second he disproved a popular theory regarding the existence of a Southern Continent by sailing where it was purported to be and in the process reaching beyond 70° S, farther than any had gone before.

In 1776, Cook set off on his third and final voyage, this time to the North Pacific. His instructions were to search for the Northwest Passage – to "find out a Northern passage by sea from the Pacific to the Atlantic Ocean." He was not to bother searching for such a passage below 65° N, as the British Admiralty knew from Samuel Hearne's expedition to the shores of the Arctic Ocean in 1771 that there could be no ocean passage below about that latitude. This is why Cook's maps of the west coast show only the trend of the coastline and not the details. From 65° northwards, Cook was instructed to

very carefully . . . search for, and . . . explore, such rivers or inlets as may appear to be of a considerable extent, and pointing towards Hudson's or Baffin's Bays.

Furthermore, if there should

appear to be a certainty, or even a probability, of a water passage into the aforementioned bays . . . [he was] to use [his] utmost endeavours to pass through with one or both of the sloops.

If he did not find such a passage, Cook was to winter in Kamchatka and then probe northwards to determine if there was a passage yet farther north.

All Cook's actions must be viewed with these instructions in mind.

Portrait of James Cook, painted by Nathaniel Dance between the second and third voyages. This famous painting hangs in the National Maritime Museum in Greenwich, England.

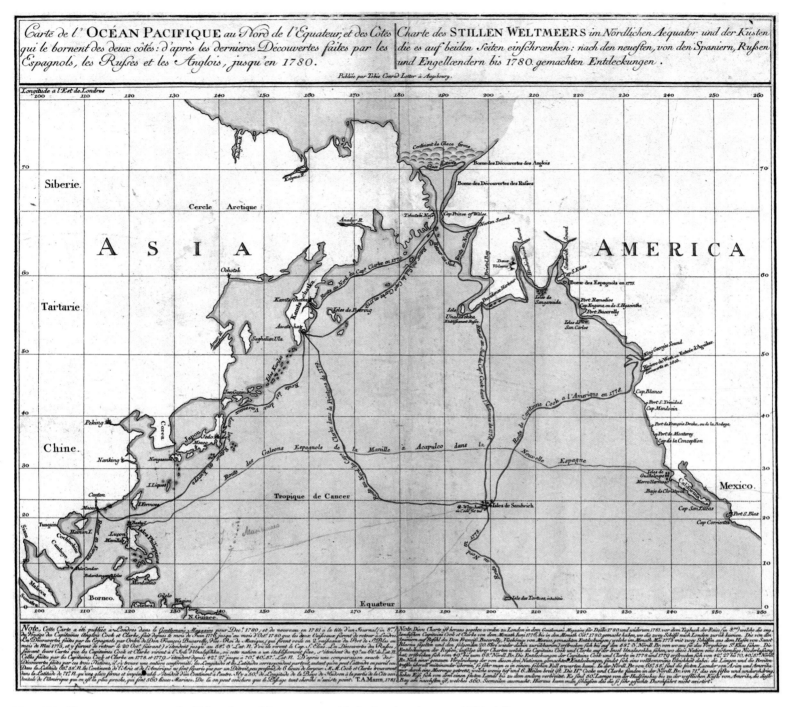

Carte de l'OCÉAN PACIFIQUE au Nord de l'Equateur, et des Côtes qui le bornent des deux côtés: d'après les dernieres Découvertes faites par les Espagnols, les Russes et les Anglois, jusqu'en 1780.

Charte des STILLEN WELTMEERS im Nördlichen Aequator und der Küsten die es auf beiden Seiten einschrænken: nach den neuesten, von den Spaniern, Rußen und Engellændern bis 1780. gemachten Entdeckungen.

Publiée par Tobie Conrad Lotter à Augsbourg.

Map 133. This interesting map by Tobie Conrad Lotter was published in Augsburg in 1781, fully three years before the appearance of the official edition of Cook's book *A Voyage to the Pacific Ocean*, which was published, posthumously of course, in 1784. There was enormous interest in Cook's third voyage, and the pressure was such that several maps and two books were published before Cook's, with the information coming, often anonymously, from members of Cook's crews.

After discovering and mapping Hawaii for the first time, he arrived on the west coast of North America on 6 March 1778, at a point near Cape Foulweather, in Oregon, at 44° 33´ N. Cook had been instructed to make a landfall at about 45° N, as this was north of any point felt likely to be considered subject to Spanish territorial claims. Britain had no wish to see the voyage cause an international incident. Bad weather did, however, force the ships southwards to about 43° N before they could begin to work their way northwards.

At about 48° N Cook located a headland south of Cape Flattery, which he so named because it "flattered us with the hopes of finding a harbour," but he failed to find the entrance to the Strait of Juan de Fuca. "It is in the very latitude we were now," Cook wrote in his journal, in where geographers have placed the pretended Strait of Juan de Fuca. But we saw nothing like it, nor is there the least probability that iver any such thing ever exhisted.

He did record "a small opening in the land" towards dusk. But darkness closed in, the weather deteriorated, and the ships were forced out to sea.

Much has been made of Cook's failure to find the strait, but in fact he was just following his instructions. He had been instructed not to look for a strait in this latitude; if he had,

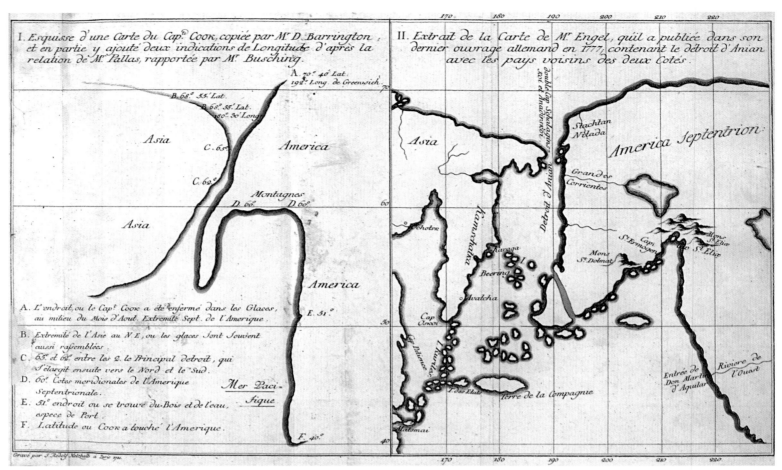

Map 134.
Not everybody got it right! These two maps were included in a book about Cook published in Geneva in 1781 by Swiss geographer and economist Samuel Engel. Clearly the information used was textual not cartographic, and descriptions, one must assume, can mislead. Both of these maps purport to be interpretations of Cook's third voyage. Their claim to fame is that they were apparently the first to be published.

his track record of meticulous exploration of coastlines suggests very strongly that he would have gone back to survey the coast once the weather allowed.

Cook's ships eventually found a harbor farther up the coast of Vancouver Island, at a place they called King George's Sound, later renamed Nootka by the British Admiralty.

Cook anchored his ships on the southeast side of Bligh Island (named after his sailing master, William Bligh, later famous by dint of the mutiny on his ship, *Bounty*) in a cove now named after Cook's ship, Resolution Cove. He stayed there most of the month of April 1778, repairing his ships, surveying, and observing the natives. During this time he surveyed the sound in the ships' boats, producing a map of it. Perhaps more important, he fixed the position of

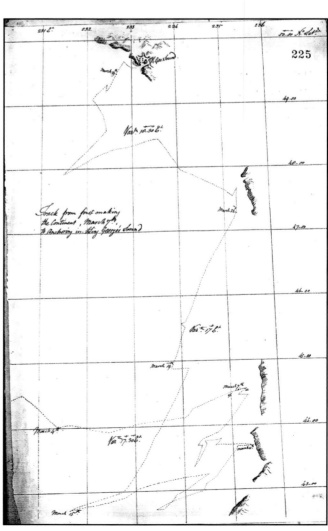

Map 135.
This page from James Burney's journal shows the track of Cook's ships from their landfall on the coast of Oregon northwards to Nootka Sound, Cook's King George's Sound. Clearly it was not all plain sailing! Burney was one of Cook's officers.

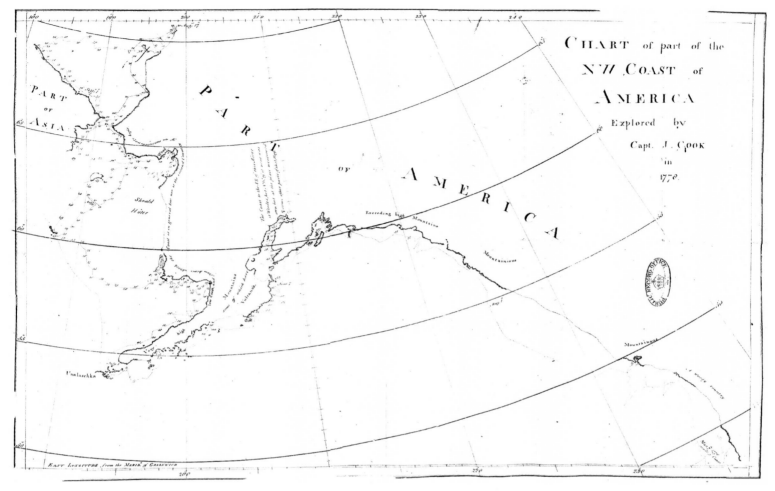

Map 136.
This map was drawn by James Cook and sent in a letter to Philip Stephens, Secretary of the Admiralty. The letter was given to the Russians at Unalaska. It was sent on 20 October 1778 (21 October in Cook's journal; he had sailed east from Britain and thus had gained a day but had not realized it) and arrived in London on 6 March 1780.

Nootka so that henceforth other ships would be able to find it.

At the end of the month, he sailed northwards towards Alaska, where he proceeded to map the coast in far greater detail than had ever been done before.

On his way, passing 50° N on 26 April, Cook noted in his journal that he regretted that again the weather was forcing him to stay away from the land,

especially as we were passing the place where Geographers have placed the pretended Strait of Admiral de Fonte.

Although Cook did not believe that such a strait existed, he wrote,

Nevertheless I was highly desirous of keeping the Coast aboard in order to clear up this point beyond dispute; but

it would have been highly imprudent in me to have ingaged with the land in such exceeding tempestuous weather.

North of about 55° N, Cook began looking for inlets that could be entrances to the Northwest Passage, and this was certainly the thought on his men's minds at this stage, because they would have shared in prize money – twenty thousand pounds – that had been offered by the British government for the discovery of such a passage.

Cook discovered and mapped a very large bay that he named Prince William Sound, and then, a little to the southwest, he found the large opening of Cook Inlet. Surely this was the long-sought Northwest Passage? Cook was not expectant, though many of his men were; naturally enough, they wanted their share of the huge reward.

Bucking the strong tidal rips for which the inlet is well known, they explored the opening: the northern part in two of the ships' boats, one under William Bligh east past the site of today's Anchorage, and the other under James King. They found that the water was turning fresh and the channels narrowing, so after sixteen days in this inlet, and the season running out on them, they gave up and left to resume their explorations westward.

Since Cook did not explore completely the northeastern end of Cook Inlet, and also because he named it Cook's River instead of Cook's Inlet, the possibility remained that a great river entered the sea here that penetrated the interior in such a way as to *still* provide a Northwest Passage, this time by river, and this was postulated by some, notably Canadian fur

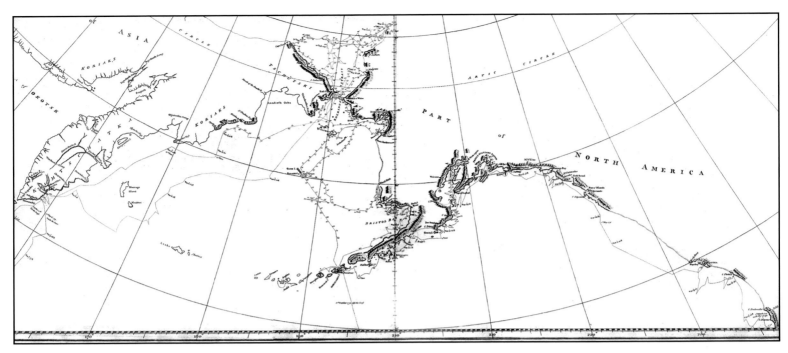

Map 137.
The summary map published in Cook's book in 1784. A coast revealed to the world in the true Cook tradition.

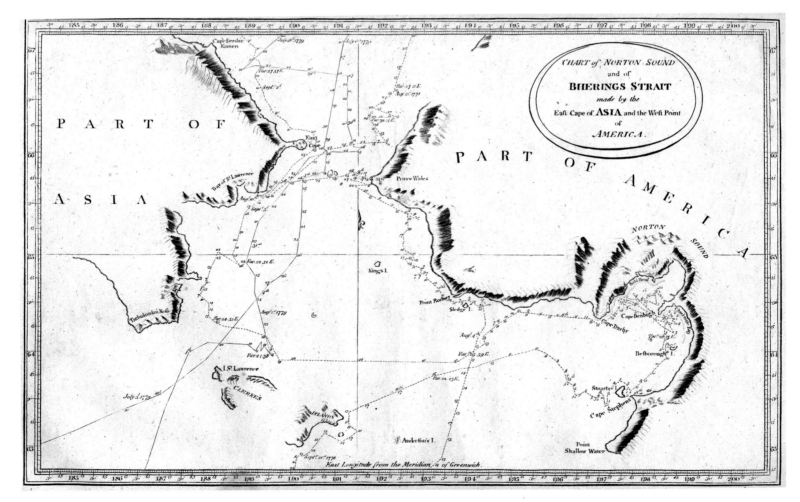

Map 138.
Considered by many to be the most significant map to come out of Cook's third voyage is this one of Bering Strait. Here the correct relationship of Asia and America is accurately laid out for the first time. This is the engraved and published map from the 1784 book.

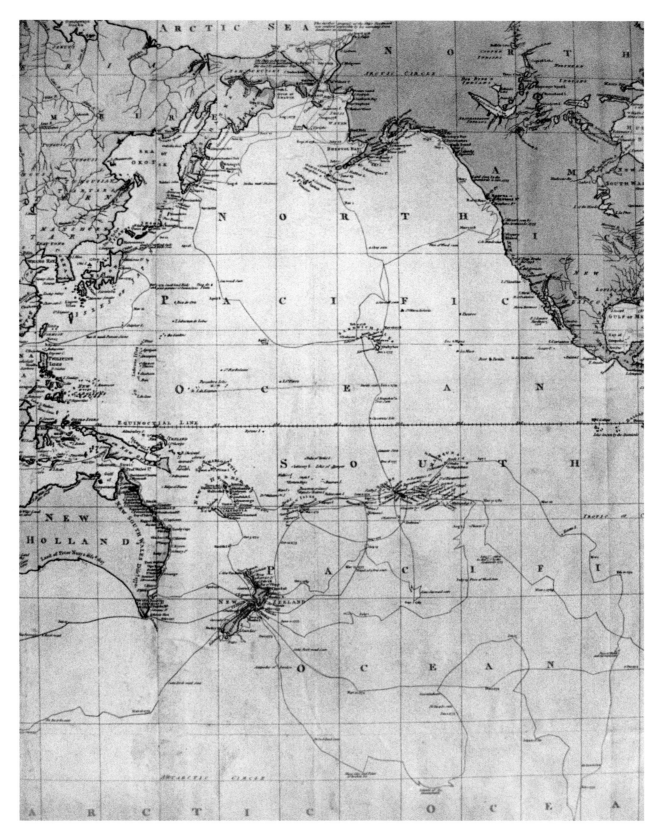

Map 139.

The Pacific Ocean arrives upon the consciousness of the world. This is part of a summary world map entitled *General Chart exhibiting the Discoveries made by Capt. James Cook*. It was published in 1784 by William Faden, but had been painstakingly assembled and drawn by Henry Roberts, who had been Cook's principal mapmaker during the voyage. Roberts had long been charged by Cook with making a world map with the tracks of all his voyages upon it; this was to be Cook's legacy to the world, and even after Cook's death, Roberts continued with this discharge of his instructions. The map attempted to show the relationship between Cook's coastal explorations and those of Samuel Hearne in 1771 and 1772 in the interior. Hearne's discoveries were, however, placed too far north and too far west. Nevertheless, here we have for the first time a reasonably accurate map of all of North America and the Pacific Ocean. Also shown here are the more extensive tracks of Cook in the South Pacific Ocean during his first and second voyages (1768–71 and 1772–75, including the southernmost point of 71° 10´ S reached during the second voyage at the end of January 1773.

trader Peter Pond. It was one of Cook's midshipmen, George Vancouver, who would finally put the myth to rest in 1794, changing the name from Cook's River to Cook's Inlet in the process.

Continuing to the southwest, they found a gap through the eastern end of the Aleutians and then sailed northwards.

South of Bering Strait, Cook reached a large, previously unmapped sound, which he named after the Speaker of the House of Commons, Sir Fletcher Norton. As the ships sailed up the sound, Cook noted a shoaling of the water that made him realize it was unlikely to be a passage. Nevertheless, it was explored and found not to divide Alaska from the rest of the coast.

On 9 August 1778, Cook reached the northwestern extremity of North America, which he named Cape Prince of Wales, after the heir to the British throne, despite the fact that it was already marked on Müller's maps of 1754 and 1758 (see pages 78–79), which he carried with him, as "coast surveyed by surveyor Gvozdev in 1730," actually 1732 (see page 65).

Cook then sailed through Bering Strait and reached 70° 44′ N before he was stopped by ice. This latitude was almost as far north as the equivalent southern latitude he had reached during his second voyage, 71° 10′ S, in January 1773.

On 29 August he decided to return to Hawaii to refit for a second season. While mapping some of the Aleutian Islands, Cook wrote in his journal:

In justice to Behrings Memory, I must say he has delineated this Coast very well and fixed the latitude and longitude of the points better than could be expected from the Methods he had to go by.

On his way he called at the island of Unalaska, where he met Russian fur traders. Unalaska was the site of the first permanent Russian settlement in North America. The senior Russian officer there, Gerasim Ismailov, allowed Cook to copy two Russian charts, showing, Cook wrote,

all the discoveries made by the Russians to the Eastward of Kamtschatka towards America, which if we exclude the Voyage of Behring and Tcherikoff [Chirikov], *will amount to little or nothing.*

Cook in turn presented Ismailov with a map of his explorations to date.

The following day, 20 October 1778, Cook gave Ismailov a letter that contained a map, addressed to the British Admiralty, with the request that they be forwarded by him to London. Cook obviously felt that they had a good chance of reaching London overland via the Russians before he could otherwise get a communication through to the Admiralty. The letter and the map did in fact get through, arriving at the Admiralty on 6 March 1780, and the map, probably drawn by Cook himself, is shown on page 95 (Map 136). This was the first map from Cook's third voyage, and the most complete map of Alaska and the Northwest Coast to date. It was to be much copied.

At this time, an interesting comment appears in Cook's journal relating to a map drawn by Jacob von Stählin (Map 117, page 82), which Cook had been using, or trying to use, up to this point. Von Stählin's map showed the Alaskan region broken up into many islands, including one itself labeled Alaschka. Cook wrote:

[The Russians] *assured me over and over again that they k*[n]*ew of no other islands but what were laid down on this chart* [the second of the two charts presented to Cook], *and that no Russian had ever seen any part of the Continent to the northward, excepting that part lying opposite the Country of the Tchuktschis* [across the Bering Strait]. *If M*ʳ *Staelin was not greatly imposed upon what could induce him to publish so erroneous a Map? in which many of these islands are jumbled in regular confusion, without the least regard to truth and yet he is pleased to call it a very accurate little Map? A Map that the most illiterate of his Sea-faring men would have been ashamed to put his name to.*

Second Lieutenant James King noted in his journal:

As far as we can judge, there never was a Map so unlike what it ought to be.

Cook also had Müller's map with him, but it proved to be not much better. King also wrote in his journal, on 23 July 1778:

As we have already Saild over a great space where Muller places a Continent, we can no longer frame any supposition in order to make our Charts agree with his.

Cook was killed by natives in Hawaii in February 1779, before he could return to complete the task he had been set. Captain Charles Clerke then assumed command, and the ships returned to Alaskan waters directly, principally to determine for sure that there was no practicable Northwest Passage through Bering Strait. Clerke was already ill by this time and he died in August 1779, command then being taken over by John Gore, who guided the expedition back to London. In this, both Clerke and Gore received a great deal of help from William Bligh, who was a brilliant navigator.

Map 140 (right).
During a stopover in Kamchatka in 1779, a midshipman, Edward Riou, surveyed the harbor and drew this superb map of what is now Avachinskaya Guba, Avatcha Bay, on which sits the modern Russian city of Petropavlovsk–Kamchatskiy.

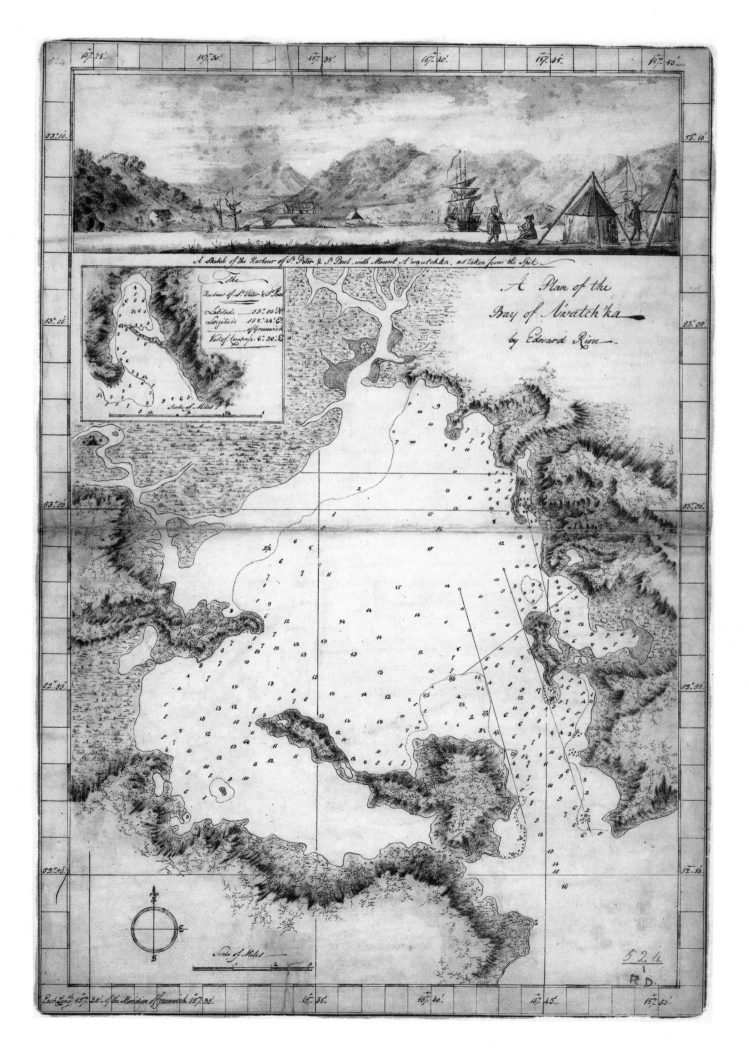

A Sketch of the Harbour of St. Peter & St. Paul, with Mount A'wautchka, as taken from the Spit

The
Harbour of St. Peter & St. Paul

Latitude ——— 53°. 00' N
Longitude ——— 158°. 44' E
of Greenwich
Var. of Compass. 6°. 20' E

Scale of Miles

A Plan of the
Bay of A'watch'ka

by Edward Riou

Scale of Miles

East Long.th 157°. 28' of the Meridian of Greenwich 157°. 30'.

The Lovtsov Atlas of the North Pacific Ocean

In the British Columbia Archives resides a beautiful and unique hand-drawn atlas of the North Pacific. It was drawn by Russian Fleet Navigator Vasillii Lovtsov in 1782.

Although it was based mainly on Russian sources, the atlas does incorporate information from charts and notes left at Petropavlovsk in 1779 by Charles Clerke, who had succeeded to the leadership of Cook's third voyage upon the death of Cook.

The Lovtsov atlas is an enigma. Many of the maps are far less detailed than the information available to Lovtsov would have allowed, and it

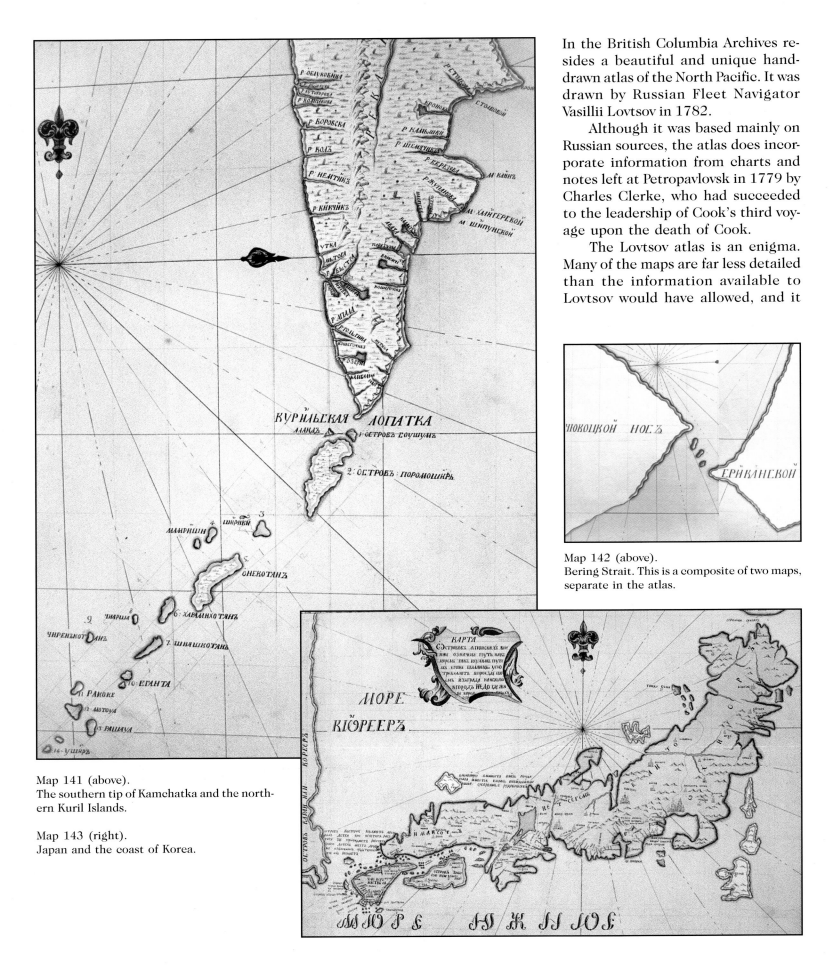

Map 142 (above).
Bering Strait. This is a composite of two maps, separate in the atlas.

Map 141 (above).
The southern tip of Kamchatka and the northern Kuril Islands.

Map 143 (right).
Japan and the coast of Korea.

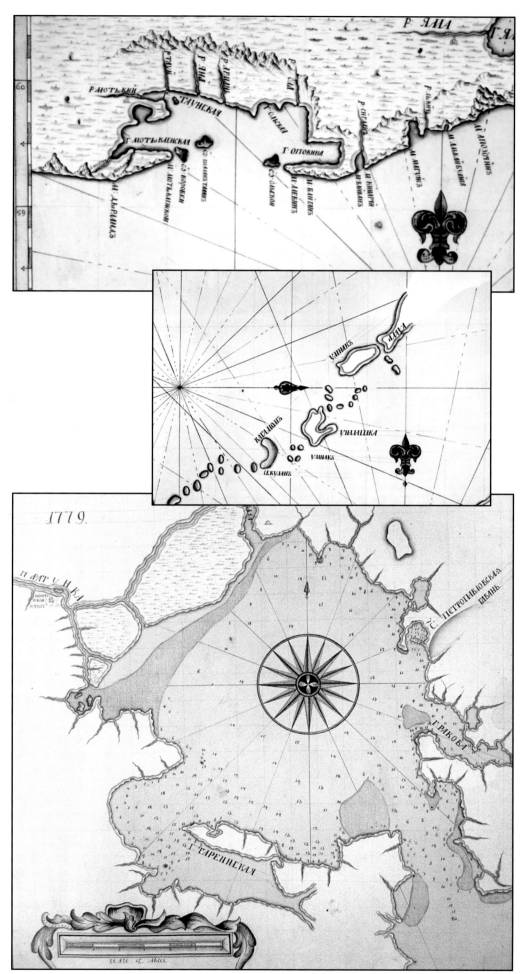

may be that some, particularly those of the west coast of North America, were simply drawn from memory, perhaps after being shown Cook's charts but not being allowed to retain them.

The atlas was drawn while overwintering "at the Bol'sheretsk ostrog" (fort), a Russian post on the west side of southern Kamchatka. Lovtsov is thought to have been in charge of supply vessels sailing from Okhotsk to Bol'sheretsk.

The eighteen charts in the atlas were drawn with pen and ink and finished with watercolors.

Maps from Vasilii Lovtsov's manuscript atlas (this page, top to bottom):

Map 145.
Northern part of the Sea of Okhotsk. This is Tauynskaya Guba, the bay on which the modern city of Magadan sits.

Map 146.
The easternmost Aleutians and the tip of the Alaska Peninsula.

Map 147.
Avatcha Bay on the Kamchatka Peninsula, site of modern Petropavlovsk. It is interesting to compare this map with Riou's (Map 140, page 99), with which it is contemporary.

Map 144 (below).
Part of the coast of the southern Alaska panhandle and northern British Columbia; the maps of the east Pacific are much less well defined than those of the west.

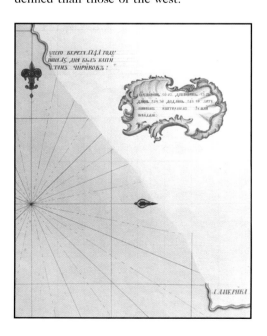

La Pérouse –
The French Answer to Cook

La Pérouse's ship, *Astrolabe*.

In the wake of Cook, the French organized a round-the-world scientific voyage designed to regain French prestige judged to have been lost to England.

Selected to command this expedition was Jean-François Galaup, Comte de la Pérouse, a highly regarded naval officer. Scientists from France and other countries, including Britain's Joseph Banks, assisted with the planning for the voyage. Banks even prevailed upon the British Board of Longitudes to lend the expedition two dipping needles (for measuring the direction of the Earth's magnetism) that had been used by James Cook.

Importantly, too, La Pérouse had some of the still scarce chronometers with him, including an English instrument.

La Pérouse sailed in August 1785 with two ships, *Boussole* and *Astrolabe*. In the North Pacific, La Pérouse was to determine the true position of the Aleutians and other islands to the west, whose positions were un-

known. He was also to survey the Kuril Islands, the coasts of Japan, and the Northwest Coast of America, altogether a massive undertaking which was to prove too much to achieve. His instructions stated:

We still lack a full knowledge of the earth and particularly of the Northwest coast of America, of the coast of Asia which faces it, and of islands that must lie scattered in the seas separating these two continents.

No less than eleven scientists and artists accompanied La Pérouse, and special quarters were added for them; this was a *scientific* voyage.

But there was more; La Pérouse was also instructed to determine just how far the Russians had pushed into North America. He was also to determine what kinds of furs received the best prices in China, and whether or not Japan might be tempted to open its doors to trade in furs. This was all a preliminary to a planned possible French commercial incursion into the North Pacific. Having lost their North American colonies in 1763, the French were on the lookout for new opportunities.

La Pérouse reached the North Pacific in July 1786, making a landfall near Mt. St. Elias on the Alaskan coast, then surveying southwards to Monterey. By keeping relatively close inshore, he was able to produce a superior chart to that of Cook, who, sailing northwards, had been forced to stay away from the coast more than he would have liked.

At Lituya Bay, which La Pérouse called Port des Français, his scientists went to work. A considerable record was made of native life and customs. But tragedy struck when twenty-one men drowned while carrying out a survey.

La Pérouse had been given three months to survey the entire Northwest Coast, a task that would consume three years of George Vancouver's life.

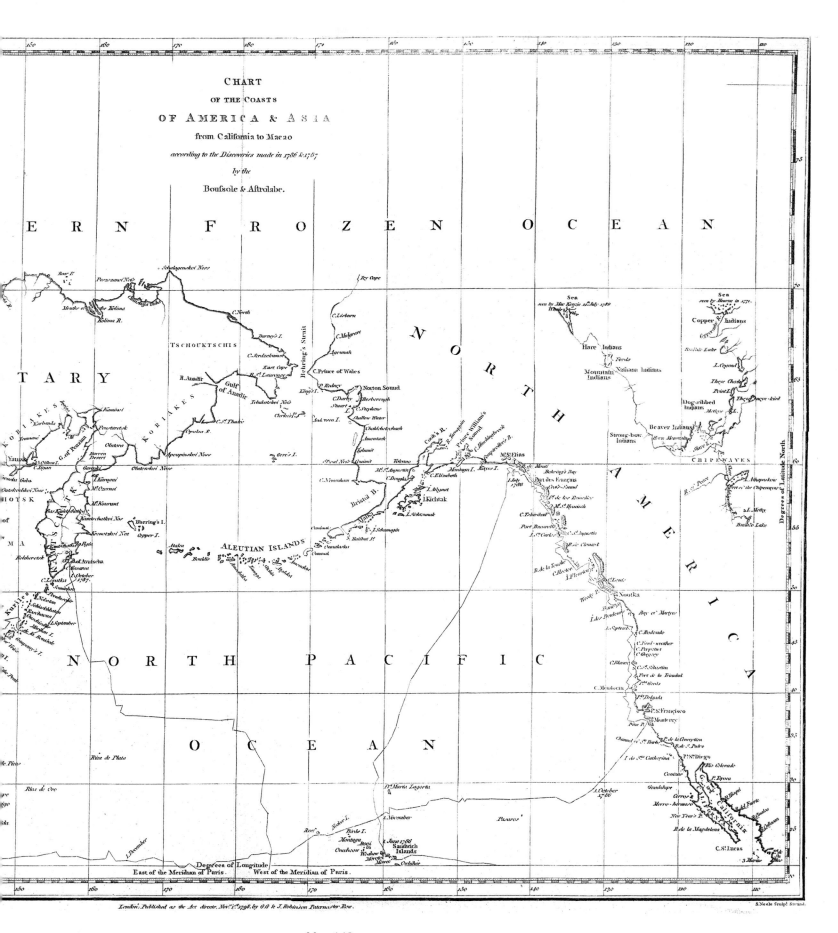

Map 148.
La Pérouse's summary map of the northern part of the Pacific Ocean, published in 1798, long after his disappearance. He had sent maps and data back to France from Australia, entrusting them to the British. Note that Sakhalin is shown as an island.

La Pérouse soon realized that his assignment was impossible. He gave up looking for a Northwest Passage, still thought perhaps to exist in these latitudes, and the quick survey he made of the coast led to the production of a remarkably accurate map.

Although he was well received in Monterey, the Spanish were alarmed that the French had arrived so soon after the British expedition of Cook.

After searching for lost islands in the central Pacific using a Spanish chart he had obtained (illustrated on page 19), La Pérouse visited Macao and then, in May 1787, sailed north into the East China Sea.

They surveyed the Korean coast, charting islands not already on the maps, and surveyed some of the coast of Japan, making no landings in either country due to their exclusion of foreigners.

Then the two ships sailed up the coast of Tartary, now part of Russia, into Tartar Strait, from approximately the position of modern Vladivostok.

La Pérouse sailed farther and farther north and the water became shallower and shallower. At Tomari natives informed him that Sakhalin was an island, not a peninsula. The illustration overleaf depicts this meeting. Another encounter confirmed the same thing. "I had gone too far not to want to explore this strait and ascertain whether it was passable," he wrote in his journal,

[but] *I was beginning to form an unfavorable opinion of it because the depth was lessening very quickly as one went north and the coast of Segalien Island was nothing more than drowned sand dunes almost level with the sea, like sand banks.*

Constant southerly winds presented a risk of being trapped at the north end of the strait, and so in the end La Pérouse decided not to risk his ships, turning south again without proving the insularity of Sakhalin, though he knew it to be an island and his charts show it as such.

Sailing south, hugging the west coast of Sakhalin, they found a strait – today called La Pérouse Strait – between Sakhalin and Hokkaido. Now

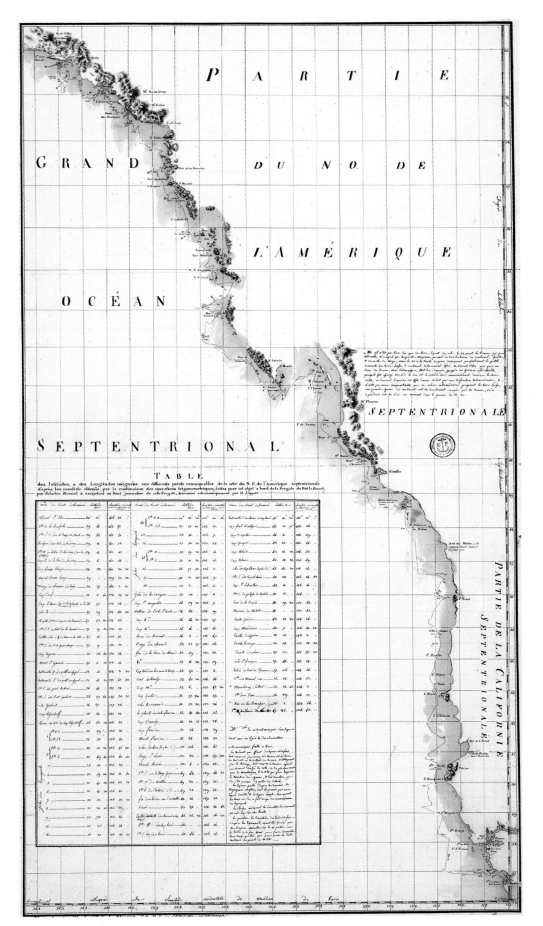

Map 149.

Map of the west coast of North America from Mt. St. Elias to Monterey, with the track of the La Pérouse expedition in 1786 and a table of positions prepared by two of the expedition's scientific staff, Gérault-Sébastien Bernizet, the surveyor, and Joseph Lapaute Dagelet, the senior astronomer. This survey was superior to Cook's or any other at the time; only Vancouver's exhaustive survey would prove more accurate. This is the original pen-and-ink map. It was not published until 1797.

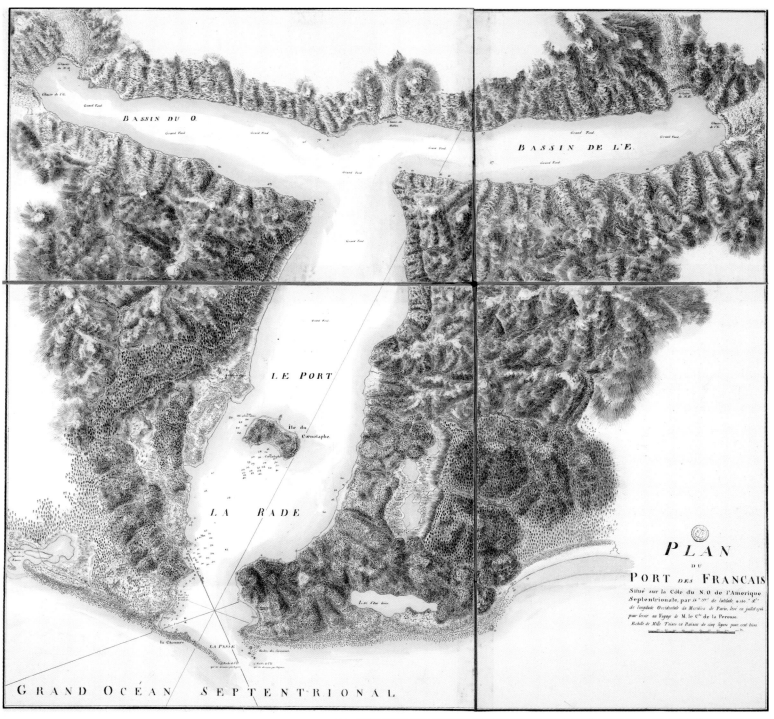

PLAN
DU
PORT DES FRANCAIS
Situé sur la Côte du N.O. de l'Amerique
Septentrionale, par 58°37' de latitude, et 140°5'
de longitude Occidentale du Meridien de Paris, levé en juillet 1786
pour servir au Voyage de M. le C.te de la Perouse.
Echelle de Mille Toises ou Raison de cinq lignes pour cent toises.

BASSIN DU O.

BASSIN DE L'E.

LE PORT

île du Coenotaphe.

LA RADE

GRAND OCÉAN SEPTENTRIONAL

LA PASSE

A spectacular view of Lituya Bay, Alaska (right), which La Pérouse called Port des Français, "drawn from nature by Duché de Vancy in July 1786." Gaspard Duché de Vancy had been appointed to *Boussole* as a "drawer of figures and landscapes." This inlet appeared on no chart and thus La Pérouse was interested in it as a potential base for any French fur trade establishment on the Northwest Coast. A map of the same inlet is shown above (Map 150). It was drawn by Gérault-Sébastien Bernizet and Paul Mérault de Monneron, *ingénieur en chef*. It was in attempting to determine soundings for this chart that disaster struck. A sounding party, which had been warned by La Pérouse not to go too close to the rocks at the entrance to the bay, did go too close and were caught by a strong tide. Twenty-one sailors lost their lives. In a sense this beautiful map lives on as their monument.

in seas mapped by Maarten Vries in 1643, they found a strait between two of the Kurils and sailed north to Avatcha Bay in Kamchatka, leaving there in September 1787 for the South Pacific.

By February 1788 they were in Botany Bay, Australia, and entrusted the British in Port Jackson, a few miles to the north, with their maps and journals, to be sent to France. It was just as well they did so, for after La Pérouse left Australia in March 1788, he was never heard from again.

The mystery of the disappearance of La Pérouse was solved in the 1960s, when the remains of both his ships were found on a reef on Vanikoro, in New Caledonia.

La Pérouse meets with natives of Sakhalin, who assured him of the island's insularity.

Map 151.
A map of La Pérouse's Castries Bay, now Zaliv Chikhacheva, on the coast of Siberia, drawn by Gérault-Sébastien Bernizet in July 1787. The name came from the French Minister of Marine, the Maréchal de Castries, and survives today in the town and port of De-Kastri, inside the bay. La Pérouse made many such detailed charts of bays and harbors. He had been specifically instructed "to draw careful plans of the coasts, bays, ports and anchorages he [was] in a position to inspect and explore; [and to] append to each plan instructions detailing everything relating to the approach and identification of the coast, the manner of anchoring and mooring and the best place to obtain water, the depths and the quality of the bottom; dangers, rocks and reefs; prevailing winds; breezes, monsoons, their duration and the dates of their changes; in short all the information that can be of use to navigators."

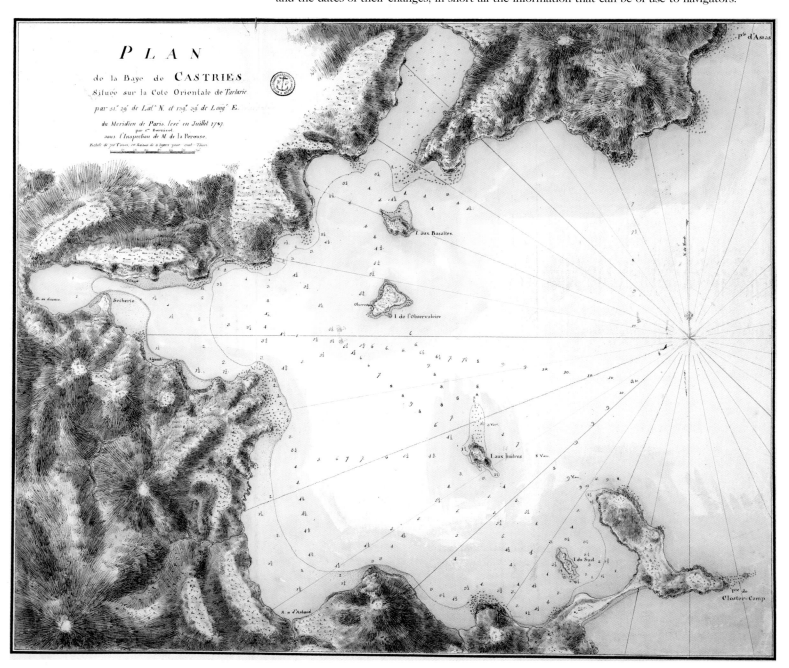

Billings and Sarychev

The publication in 1784 of James Cook's book on his third voyage was a matter of considerable interest to Russia's Catherine the Great. Here was documentary evidence of a major British incursion into what she regarded as her domain. There was also concern about Spanish northward voyages, and then, to cap it all, came news of the dispatch of the French expedition under La Pérouse.

In 1785, within a few weeks of La Pérouse's sailing, an expedition was organized to map "the numerous islands scattered in the eastern ocean, as far as the shores of America," and to obtain "a more accurate acquaintance with the seas separating the continent of Irkutsk from the coast of America."

To lead this expedition, who better than one of Cook's own? Joseph Billings had been a seaman, not an officer, with Cook, but he had offered his services to the Russians, who assumed that he would know what he was doing simply because he had sailed with Cook; such was the reverence in which Cook was held.

Fortunately for this expedition, a competent navigator and surveyor, Gavriil Sarychev, was appointed second-in-command. He would end his career an admiral and publish his own atlas.

Between 1787 and 1793, Billings and Sarychev sailed around the North Pacific, even marching overland at one point. Maps were drawn, and careful mapping allowed Sarychev to correct some of the mistakes made by Ivan Synd thirty years before, removing many islands from the charts.

Map 152.
Part of Gavriil Sarychev's map of the North Pacific, showing Bering Strait, Bering Island, and St. Lawrence Island, 1802.

One grand impediment to [previous expeditions'] success was the size of their vessels, which were very well adapted for crossing the main on voyages of discovery, but could ill serve the purpose of passing through shallows, and making minute observations of the shores. By the removal of this evil I flatter myself that not a single bay, island, or mountain, has escaped our notice, on the coasts of which we have taken a survey, and that we have, in addition to this, been enabled to rectify the mistakes of former navigators.

– Gavriil Sarychev, in the preface to his book, 1806

Fur Traders of the Northwest Coast

Fur traders, who invaded the Northwest Coast after James Cook looking for sea otter furs, tended not to draw very detailed maps, generally being content with a map that would allow them to find again a harbor or trading ground that had proved lucrative.

Nevertheless, because there were quite a few of them, and their maps were gathered by Alexander Dalrymple, soon to be Britain's first Hydrographer of the Navy, the information they contained expanded the geographical knowledge of the coast in the period between Cook and Vancouver.

One of these traders, James Colnett, who had been with James Cook on his second voyage but not his third, was given command of two ships to compete in the fur trade. Colnett commanded *Prince of Wales* and his associate Charles Duncan *Princess Royal*.

They were on the Northwest Coast in 1787 and 1788. Colnett concentrated on the coast north of the Queen Charlottes, Duncan on the coast to the south. Colnett's map and Duncan's map of the Strait of Juan de Fuca are shown here.

The intervention of Joseph Banks resulted in Colnett having aboard a scientist, Archibald Menzies, who was principally a botanist. Menzies would later return to the Northwest Coast with George Vancouver.

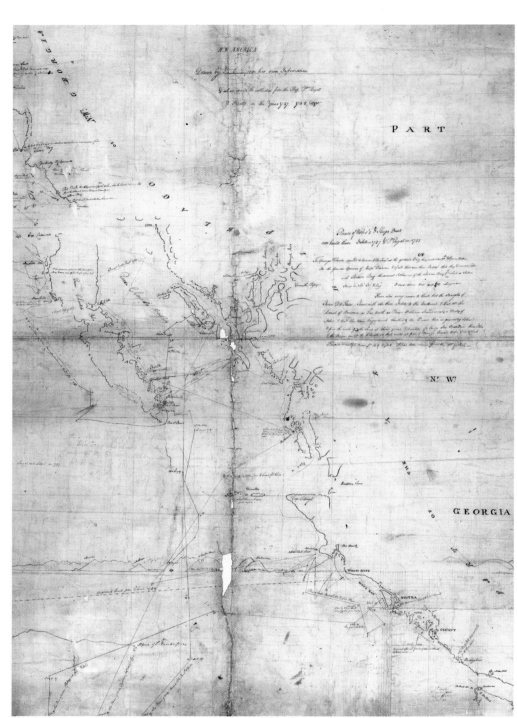

Map 154.
James Colnett's map of part of the coast of British Columbia and Alaska, 1788. Meticulously detailed, this map shows the considerable geographical knowledge of some British fur traders just prior to Vancouver's survey.
© Crown Copyright 2000. Published by permission of the Controller of Her Majesty's Stationery Office and the U.K. Hydrographic Office.

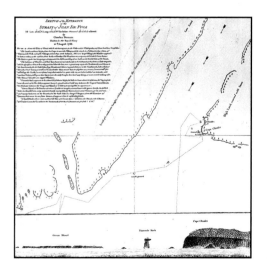

Map 153 (left).
The Strait of Juan de Fuca may have been discovered by the Greek pilot of a Spanish ship. He was born Apostolos Valerianos, but assumed the name Juan de Fuca when employed by the Spanish. However, no archival evidence of his discovery has ever been found. We do know that Charles Barkley, a British fur trader, rediscovered it in 1787. His chart of the strait is lost, and the earliest to survive is this one by Colnett's associate Charles Duncan. It is complete with a view, as a finding aid for this often missed strait. The Juan de Fuca account included a reference to pillars, at the entrance to the north side of the strait. There are pillars, but on the south side, as shown on Duncan's map.

The Sea That Never Was

John Meares was one of the fur-trading adventurers who followed in Cook's wake in search of the riches promised by the sea otter.

He also fancied himself a geographer-theorist, for when in 1790 he published a book about his voyages to the Northwest Coast, some of his maps contained a startling revelation. Meares drew an inland sea stretching from the Strait of Juan de Fuca northwards to a point approximating that of Dixon Entrance, north of the Queen Charlottes.

Not only did he show this sea on his maps, but also maintained that the American captain Robert Gray had sailed along this inland sea in his ship *Lady Washington* in 1789.

This was all a complete fabrication; not only did the sea not exist, but Gray did not sail there, and neither did he tell Meares that he had. George Vancouver was told this personally by Gray when he met him as he sailed towards the Strait of Juan de Fuca to begin his survey of the coast in 1792.

Nevertheless, at the time the story seemed quite feasible, and it misled many, even showing up on Russian maps soon after.

Map 155.
Part of Meares' map of the Alaska coast. Meares sailed here in 1788 and 1789.

Map 156.
One of John Meares' maps showing an inland sea stretching from the Strait of Juan de Fuca to Cross Sound. As the title suggests, Meares was also trying to promote the idea of a river route from the Pacific to Hudson Bay.

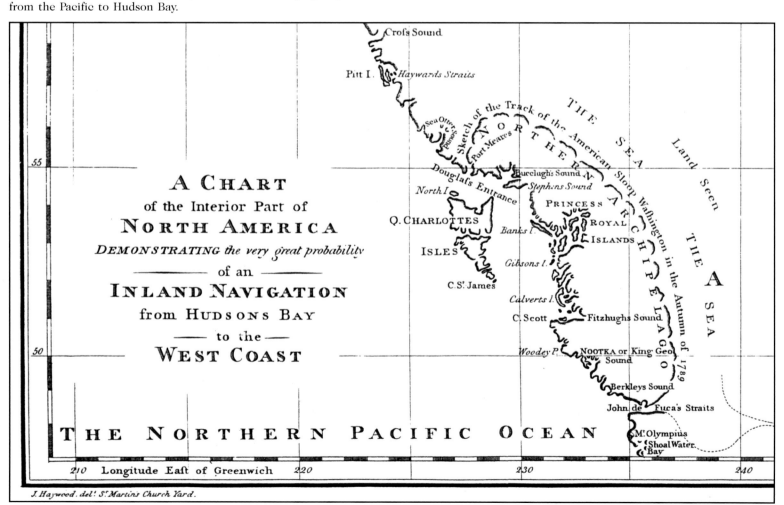

The Maps of Aaron Arrowsmith

Aaron Arrowsmith was the foremost mapmaker of his day, with a knack for collecting every bit of geographic information from whatever sources he could find. He managed to receive timely reports from many explorers, including most of the significant fur traders on the Northwest Coast of America, and from the Hudson's Bay Company, normally very secretive for competitive reasons. As a result, the maps he produced were by far the most accurate and comprehensive available.

Soon after Arrowsmith launched his own company producing and selling maps, he published a monumental map of the world. The 1790 first edition was followed in 1794 by an updated version, the Pacific part of which is shown below. Tracks are shown of voyages from Bering and Chirikov to Cook and the later fur traders. In the Pacific Northwest, the map shows the coastline as known to the British just before George Vancouver's arrival. The map shown here is an update published in 1794, a superb summary of all geographers knew about the Pacific up to that time.

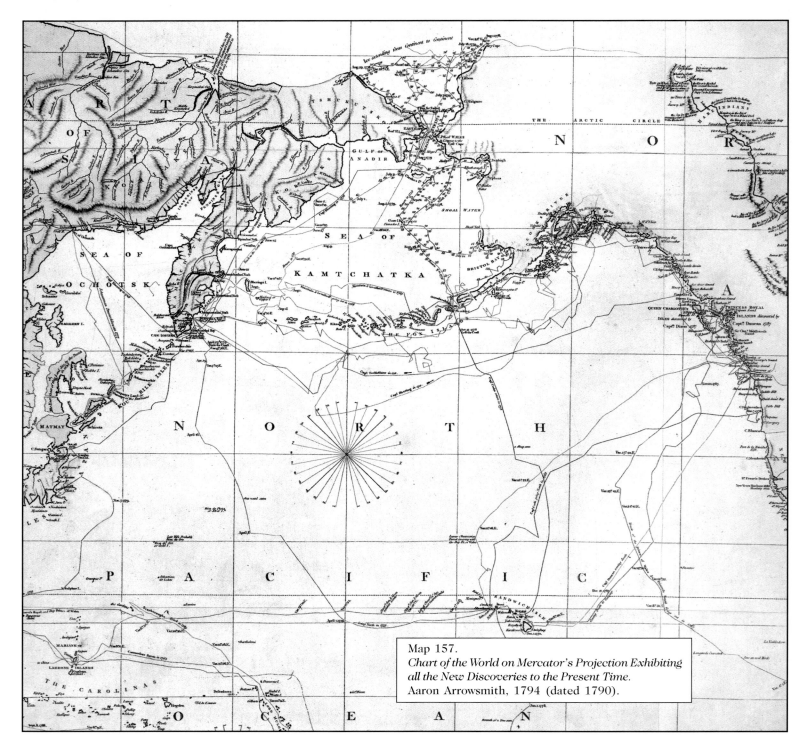

Map 157.
Chart of the World on Mercator's Projection Exhibiting all the New Discoveries to the Present Time.
Aaron Arrowsmith, 1794 (dated 1790).

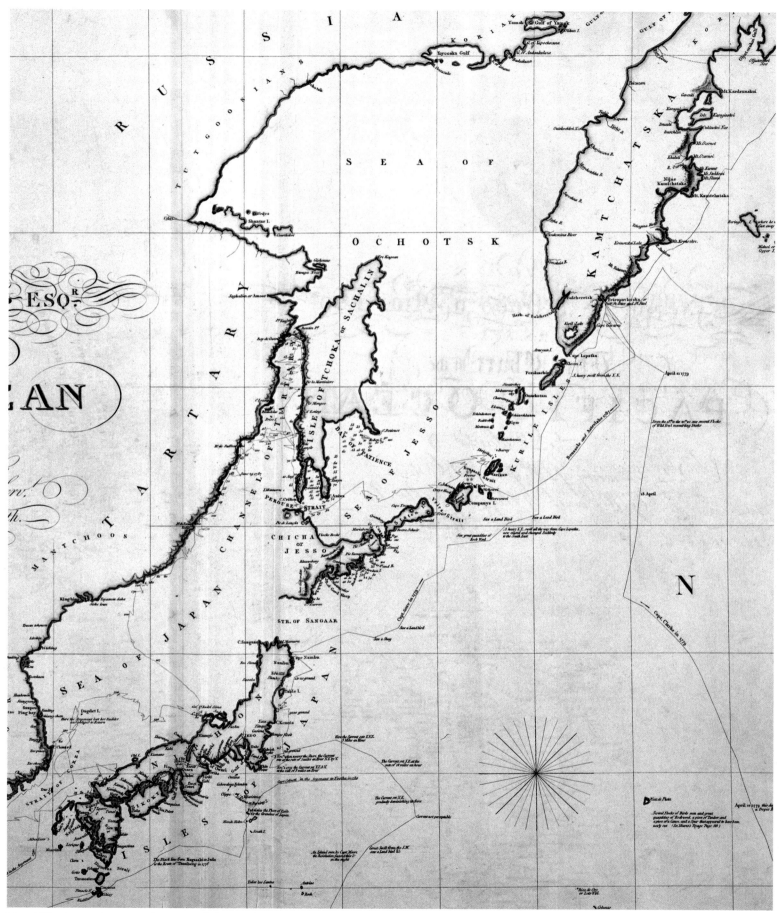

Map 158. Aaron Arrowsmith's map of the Pacific Ocean, published in 1798. Sakhalin is shown as an island, and the tracks of La Pérouse in 1787 are shown (see page 102). The latter's book had finally been published the year before Arrowsmith drew this map and thus the information was suddenly available. Hokkaido ("Chicha or Jesso") is undefined on its western side, and the southernmost two of the Kuril Islands are shown, after Maerten Vries' voyage of 1643, as "Staten Island" and "Companys Land," with Vries Strait between them. The southward track of John Gore in 1779 is also shown; Gore was in command of James Cook's third voyage after the demise of Cook and his second-in-command, Charles Clerke. Several imaginary islands are depicted, such as Rico de Oro (see page 59).

The Spanish Probe the Strait of Juan de Fuca

In 1790, the Spanish stepped up their pace of exploration in order to try to establish their claims to the Northwest Coast and at the same time make sure that no other nation discovered any possible Northwest Passage before them. Thus they began a series of voyages to determine the detail of the coast of the Pacific Northwest.

From a base at Friendly Cove in Nootka Sound, Spanish commander Francisco de Eliza dispatched an expedition to Alaska under Salvador Fidalgo. It was intended to counter any Russian presence.

Another expedition, under Manuel Quimper, was sent to probe the Strait of Juan de Fuca. In July 1790, just beyond the easternmost point that they reached, pilot Juan Carrasco sighted an opening that he thought was a bay, naming it Ensenada de Caamaño, after Jacinto Caamaño, a naval officer. It was in fact Admiralty Inlet, the entrance to Puget Sound, which was to be discovered and named by George Vancouver two years later.

The following year, 1791, Eliza himself wanted to discover the remaining unknown parts of the Northwest Coast. Unable to sail north due to adverse winds, he entered the Strait of Juan de Fuca. Clayoquot Sound, Barkley Sound and Esquimalt Harbour were examined, and a longboat commanded by José Verdía was used to explore north into Haro Strait. Verdía found this opened out into what the Spanish named the Canal de Nuestra Señora del Rosario, the Strait of Georgia. The Spanish name is still in use for the southern part of the strait, Rosario Strait.

Eliza then dispatched José María Nárvaez with pilot Juan Carrasco in *Santa Saturnina,* a small boat for exploring shallow waters, to accompany the longboat. Together they penetrated the Strait of Georgia as far north as Texada Island. They realized that this might lead to the open sea, and the presence of whales supported this idea. But their supplies were running low, and so they returned.

The superb map below is a summary map drawn by Nárvaez, the first map of the Strait of Georgia.

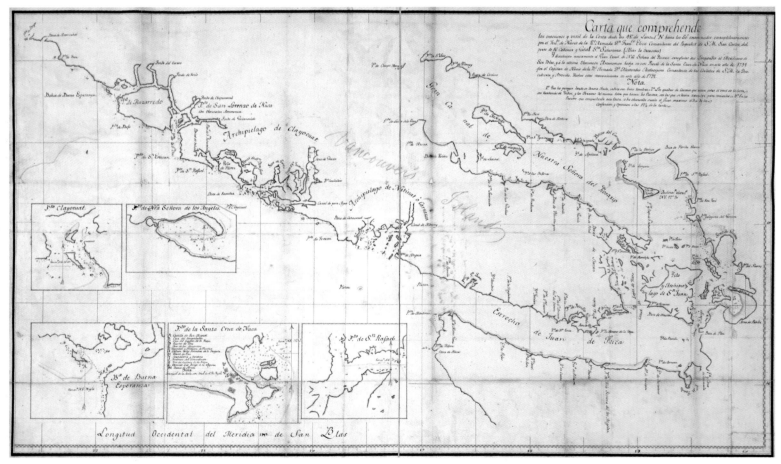

Map 159.
This *Carta que comprehende* – "Map of what is known" – of the Strait of Juan de Fuca and southern Strait of Georgia is the summary map drawn in 1791 after the probing expeditions of Manuel Quimper in 1790 and Francisco de Eliza in 1791. For the first time Vancouver Island is beginning to emerge as an island, but it is also becoming clear that it is unlikely these channels will lead to a Northwest Passage. This map graphically demonstrates the knowledge the Spanish possessed *before* George Vancouver began his survey the following year.

Malaspina's Voyage – The Spanish Answer to Cook

In the late 1780s Spain began to consider mounting a scientific round-the-world voyage to assert Spanish prestige after that of Cook for the British and in the immediate wake of the La Pérouse expedition for the French. This was encouraged by a seasoned naval captain, Alejandro Malaspina, who wanted to be the Spanish version of Cook and who managed to get himself selected for the task.

Not strictly just exploration, the voyage was to be principally one for more accurately charting the seas, using, for the first time comprehensively in a Spanish vessel, the new chronometers that had proven so successful for Cook.

Malaspina, like Cook, was sufficiently well regarded to be able to have a major say in his proposed route and objectives, though his actual instructions were brief and non-specific. "The project of circumnavigating the world has merited the acceptance of His Majesty, on the terms proposed by you," wrote the Minister of Marine.

That Malaspina considered his voyage a truly scientific one is witnessed by his behavior while in Alaska. Otter skins, the hot trading commodity of the day, and one with which they could have made money, were refused in favor of the deliberate collection of "artifacts for the Royal Museum," now part of the collection of the Museo de América.

Even the names of Malaspina's ships, *Descubierta* (*Discovery*) and *Atrevida* (*Audacious*) seem to be too close to Cook's *Discovery* and *Adventure,* on his second voyage, to be mere coincidence.

When Malaspina reached Acapulco, the Spanish government sent Malaspina orders to explore the Northwest Coast between 59° N and 60° N with particular care to ascertain whether an alleged Northwest Passage actually existed there, despite all the previous exploratory voyages that had not found such a passage. In 1770, a fictitious account of a voyage through the Strait of Anian had been published; it had been found in the archive of the family of one Lorenzo Ferrer Maldonado, who was later shown to have been an inventive charlatan. The strait was said to be between 59° N and 60° N.

Malaspina sailed directly from Acapulco to Yakutat Bay, at 60° N. This was Port Mulgrave, a name the Spanish accepted from fur traders. Here they stayed for more than a month, exploring channels and observing native customs. A map of Yakutat Bay was drawn. While the corvettes were anchored, two longboats were sent to determine whether some inlet contained a continental passage. Threading their way between the increasingly frequent pieces of ice in the water, they finally reached the front of a glacier (the Hubbard Glacier), from which large pieces of ice were breaking off. Malaspina named this Bahía del Desengaño, Disappointment Bay, because it was not a Northwest Passage.

The extensive research carried out by Malaspina's scientists meant that the report on the voyage would have been very large – seven volumes with seventy maps and seventy other illustrations – and correspondingly expensive. Nevertheless, the Spanish government approved the expenditure, because they wanted a work that would, in the eyes of the international community, surpass the British publication of Cook's voyages. It was never published, however, because on his return to Spain, Malaspina proposed that the king dismiss all his ministers, a plan that was judged seditious; he was thrown into jail, and his supporters and his work were scattered.

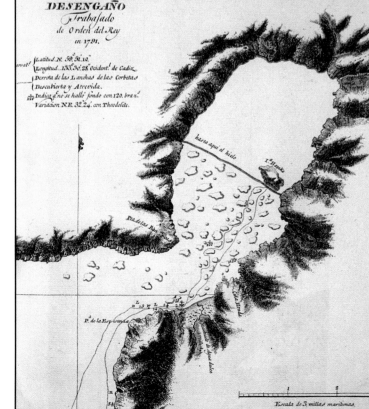

Map 160. Malaspina's map of Yakutat Bay, which he called Bahía del Desengaño, Disappointment Bay. "Up to here the ice" is marked at the boundary of the glacier.

Above is a sketch of a Tlingit warrior with wood slat armor, by Tomás de Suria, an artist with Malaspina.

The Last Spanish Explorations

The last Spanish expeditions to the Pacific Northwest took place in the eventful year 1792, the same year that George Vancouver started his major survey.

The Spanish knew of the maze of islands and channels that are the Alaska panhandle of today and thought it possible that they might still hide a Northwest Passage. Jacinto Caamaño was dispatched in 1792 to explore the region, although his ship, *Aranzazu*, was really too large for the job.

Caamaño entered Clarence Strait, thinking it might be a Northwest Passage; today it is known as part of the Inland Passage. He followed Clarence Strait north to 55° 30´ N before being prevented by bad weather from going farther. He returned to Nootka in September.

Caamaño's voyage showed that much of what had previously been considered mainland was in reality an archipelago, today called the Alexander Archipelago.

As it turned out, the voyage of two of Malaspina's officers, Dionisio Alcalá Galiano and Cayetano Valdes, was the last Spanish exploration on the Northwest Coast. They had two ships specially built for exploration, *Sutil* and *Mexicana.*

They were to determine whether or not there was a Northwest Passage from the Strait of Juan de Fuca to Hudson Bay. At least that is what the Spanish government thought they were doing; the instructions they received from Malaspina and from the viceroy were less specific.

Galiano and Valdes entered the Strait of Juan de Fuca in June 1792, and anchored briefly at the newly established Spanish post of Núñez Gaona – Neah Bay. There they learned that two large ships had already passed into the strait. These were George Vancouver's two ships.

Galiano decided not to investigate Puget Sound, probably because it appeared to go the "wrong way" to

that which they considered a Northwest Passage would have to run.

After entering the Strait of Georgia, they sighted William Broughton's ship *Chatham.* Broughton came aboard *Sutil,* and mutual assistance was offered.

On 14 June Galiano and Valdes found and entered the north arm of the Fraser River, anchoring there for the night. In so doing they became the first Europeans to find and enter the river.

A week later, Galiano finally met George Vancouver near today's city of Vancouver, B.C. Vancouver was shown Spanish maps, including the *Carta que comprehende* (page 112), revealing to him the fact that the Spanish had been here the year before.

Galiano and Valdes, like Vancouver, continued northwards, eventually circumnavigating Vancouver Island and establishing its insularity for the first time.

The summary map of Galiano and Valdes, as engraved and published in 1802, is shown here. It is detailed, accurate (they carried chronometers just as Vancouver did), and meticulously surveyed, a fitting end to Spanish efforts to define the Pacific Northwest Coast.

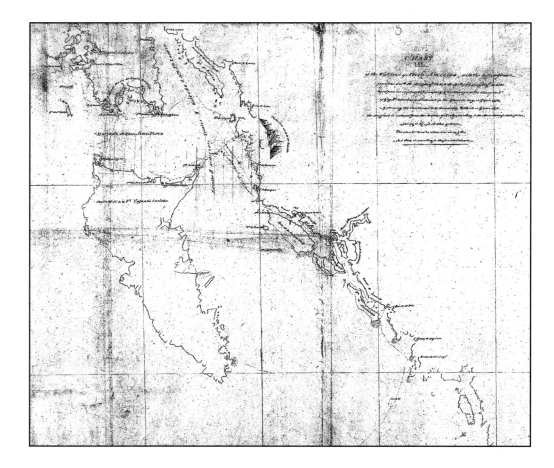

Map 161 (left).
An English copy of Caamaño's map of part of the Northwest Coast, showing the entrance to the strait he found. The Queen Charlottes are shown as a single island.

Map 162 (right).
This beautiful engraved map is a summary map of the voyage of Galiano and Valdes in 1792. It was not published until 1802, after Vancouver's book.

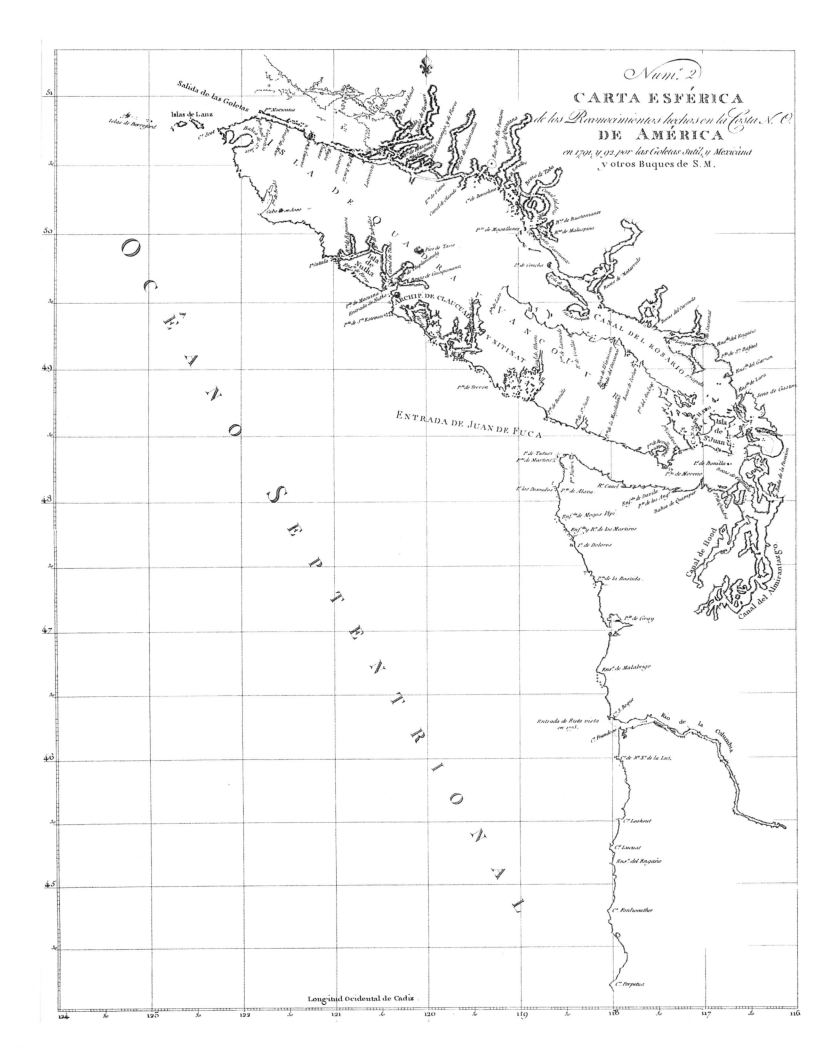

Num.º 2

CARTA ESFÉRICA
de los Reconocimientos hechos en la Costa N. O.
DE AMÉRICA
en 1791, y 92 por las Goletas Sutil y Mexicana
y otros Buques de S.M.

OCÉANO

SEPTENTRIONAL

ENTRADA DE JUAN DE FUCA

Long.itud Ocidental de Cadix

115

The Spanish Define the West Coast

In the period from 1769 to 1792 the Spanish essentially defined the shape of the west coast of North America north of the current Mexico–U.S. border. Some information, such as Sebastián Vizcaíno's discovery of the harbor at Monterey, was known before, but the major sweep of the coast was not.

Although the Spanish incorporated information from non-Spanish sources, their definition of most of the coast was carried out independently of the efforts of any other nation.

One man was there almost at the beginning and there at the end, a brilliant navigator in his own right and a daring one too, who rose to the position of overall command, below the viceroy. He also possessed the ability to put the information he had gathered together with that of others to create the most superbly comprehensive maps of the west coast, by far the best available until the completion of George Vancouver's survey in 1794.

That man was Juan Francisco Bodega y Quadra, who would be better known but for the overshadowing of his achievements by Cook and Vancouver.

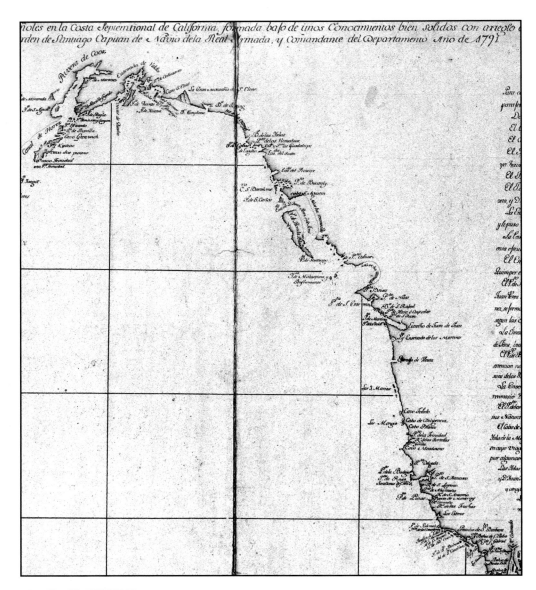

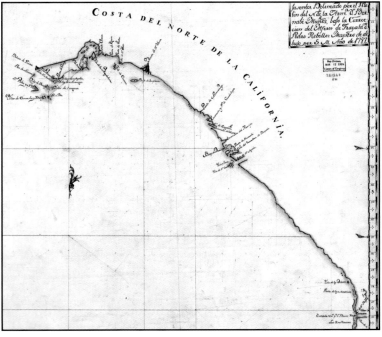

Map 163.
This map of the entire west coast of North America was drawn by Bodega y Quadra in 1791, before the Francisco Eliza expedition of that year revealed the Strait of Georgia; Vancouver Island is shown as part of the mainland. The mainland coast behind the Queen Charlotte Islands is tentative, perhaps holding the key to the elusive Northwest Passage. Jacinto Caamaño would be sent out the next year to investigate. The state of Spanish knowledge shown on this map can be compared with that later in the year, shown opposite. The vast improvement in knowledge in only sixteen years can be seen by a comparison with Bodega y Quadra's first map of the west coast of North America, shown on page 91.

Map 164 (left).
Spanish knowledge of the west coast before 1789 was limited to southern California and Alaska, the latter being the result of Bodega y Quadra's own explorations in 1775, on which others built. With one or two exceptions, much of the intervening coast was a blank. This map was drawn by Bernabe Muñoz in 1787.

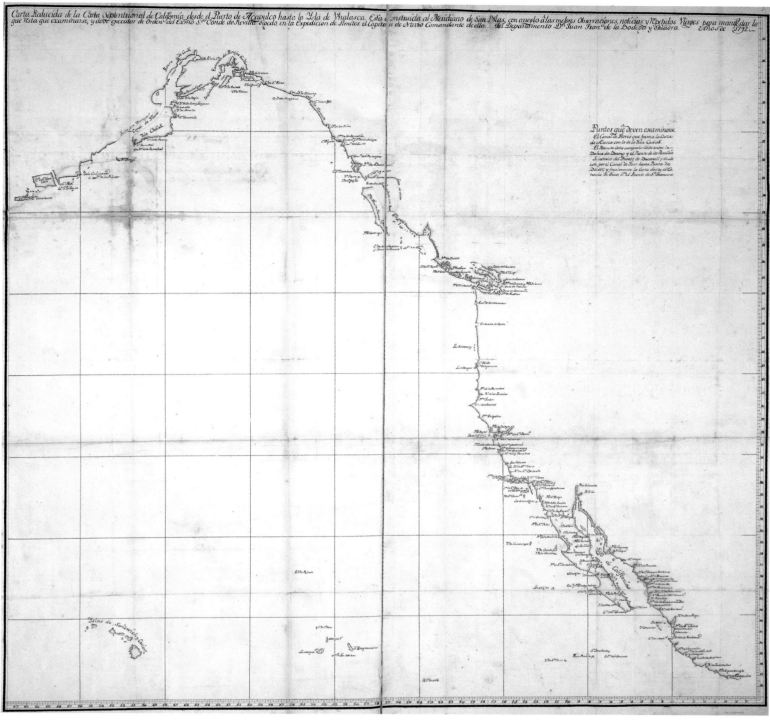

Map 165.
Bodega y Quadra's map of the west coast of North America drawn at the end of 1791 or beginning of
1792, before the explorations of Dionisio Galiano would demonstrate the insularity of Vancouver Island.

One of the reasons for this eclipse was the fact that the Spanish refused to present their findings to the world. The knowledge the world had of Spanish exploration was generally clandestine, except, notably, the cooperation with Vancouver. Spanish geographical knowledge otherwise seemed to surface in Britain in the hands of private individuals – Daines Barrington and Thomas Jefferys, for example.

Even Alejandro Malaspina's work, which was meant as a Spanish counterbalance to that of Britain's Cook, did not see the light of day because of internal political intrigues in Spain.

Only in 1802 would the Spanish government finally realize, somewhat belatedly, that their claims of sovereignty based on priority of discovery were in jeopardy because of the rest of the world's lack of knowledge of them. As a result they published in

that year the *Relación del Viage hecho por las goletas* Sutil *y* Mexicana *en al ano 1792 para Reconocer el Estrecho de Fuca,* ostensibly an account of only Galiano's voyage, but in fact a summary of all. The *Relación* contained an atlas with many of the significant Spanish maps in it, even Vizcaíno's map from as long ago as 1602.

Bodega y Quadra ended his days on the Northwest Coast at Nootka Sound, commandant at the Spanish

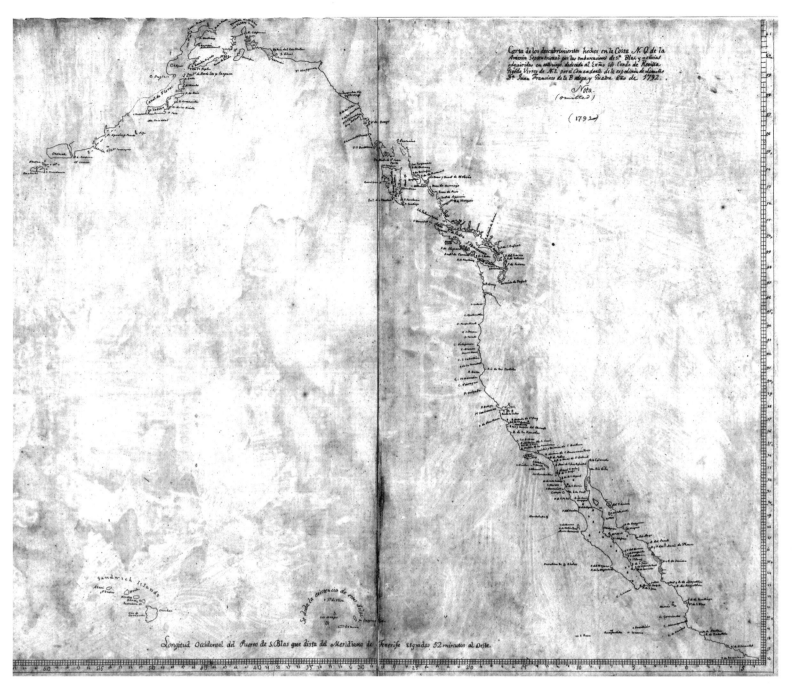

Map 166.
This map represents the cumulative peak of Spanish efforts to define the west coast of North America. It was drawn by Bodega y Quadra near the *end* of 1792, after the return of the expeditions of Caamaño and Galiano. Caamaño's strait (Clarence Strait) and Galiano's (and George Vancouver's) proof of the insularity of Vancouver Island are shown. The Spanish finally had a reasonably accurate map of the entire coast, though not without a lingering possibility that an entrance to a Northwest Passage could be found, a possibility that Vancouver would put to rest in the remaining two years of his survey. Spanish knowledge now extended from the tip of South America to halfway along the Aleutian chain.

headquarters there. It was in this capacity that he met with George Vancouver in 1792 in an attempt to finalize the wranglings over who owned the region contained in the Nootka Convention.

Bodega y Quadra was one of those all-too-rare individuals who seem to have been respected by all, whatever their nationality. When he finally left Nootka, one of Vancouver's men, the clerk of *Chatham*, Edward Bell, wrote:

Never was the departure of a man more regretted than that of Mr.

Quadra's. He was universally belov'd and admired and the only consolation we had was that we should see him again at Monterrey.

Bodega y Quadra died in 1794, sparing him from the war between Spain and Britain that began in 1796. Others, like Dionisio Galiano, did not avoid this fate. He died fighting the British fleet at Trafalgar.

George Vancouver's Epic Survey

The distinguishing feature of George Vancouver's work, as compared with all others', is its comprehensiveness. It is hard to see how without Vancouver's tenacity the Northwest Coast of North America would ever have been surveyed properly, for it is a tangled web of islands, inlets, bays, and promontories sufficient to tax the proverbial patience of Job.

Yet the man has received scant enough recognition in these politically correct days, recognition he is absolutely entitled to if for no other reason than his superb surveying achievement.

George Vancouver surveyed the eastern shore of the Pacific in three seasons, in 1792, 1793, and 1794. His survey was part of a final thrust by the British to determine once and for all whether the Northwest Passage existed.

His instructions were to acquire

accurate information with respect to the nature and extent of any water communication which may tend in any considerable degree to facilitate an intercourse for the purpose of commerce between the North West coast and the countries upon the opposite side of the Continent.

He was specifically directed

not to pursue any inlet or river further than it shall appear to be navigable by vessels of such burthen as might safely navigate the Pacific Ocean.

Vancouver was also instructed to share any survey information with any Spanish subjects he might meet, a tacit acknowledgment that Spanish maps might contain useful information, certainly a justifiable assumption based on the Spanish maps existing as of 1792.

Discovery, commanded by Vancouver, and *Chatham,* commanded by Lieutenant William Broughton, made their first landfall

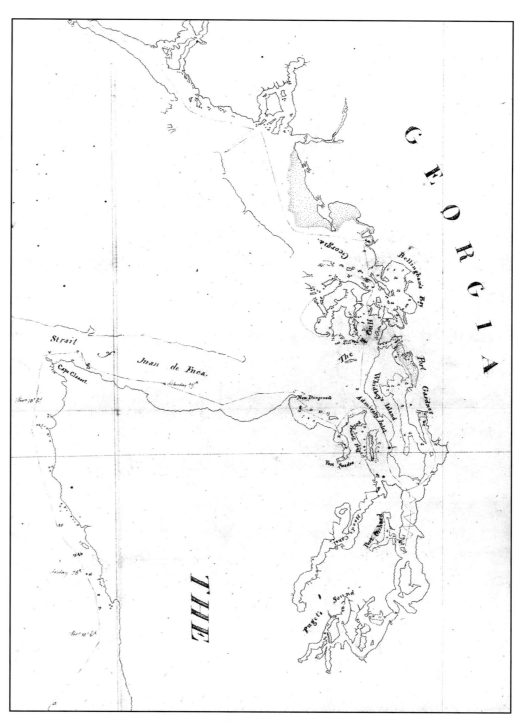

Map 167. Detail of George Vancouver's map of the west coast, showing Puget Sound and the southern part of the Strait of Georgia. Note the lack of detail for southern Vancouver Island.

about 175 km (110 miles) north of San Francisco, on 18 April 1792, on the coast of Drake's New Albion.

Sailing north, managing to stay inshore enough to survey, Vancouver somehow missed the mouth of the Columbia. Although he noted a change in the color of the water, he thought it the probable consequence

of some streams flowing into the bay. He did recognize Cape Disappointment, the headland on the north side of the river named by John Meares when he too could not find the river.

But he did find the Strait of Juan de Fuca, having Charles Duncan's map with him. In May and June 1792 Vancouver explored and mapped

Puget Sound, the southern part of which was named after Peter Puget, the officer in charge of the ship's boat that surveyed it. Over time, the name came to refer to the whole inlet.

It was Vancouver who named the waters to the north the "Gulph of Georgia," after the British king, despite finding that it was a strait rather than a gulf.

Near the site of the city that now bears his name, Vancouver did meet Spanish surveyors, Captains Dionisio Galiano and Cayetano Valdes, and they did exchange information. Galiano showed him José Nárvaez's map of Spanish explorations the year before (page 112), and Vancouver wrote in his journal of the "mortification" he felt at having realized that he was not the first to survey the southern Strait of Georgia.

Vancouver continued north, for some time in company with the Spanish ships, perhaps the first example of international cooperation in Pacific Ocean waters. It is therefore unfortunate to note that four years later, Spain and Britain were at war.

Vancouver concentrated on what he referred to as the "continental shore," because of his instructions to look for any possible opening which might be a Northwest Passage.

One of Vancouver's officers, James Johnstone, master of the *Chatham,* led many mapping parties to map inlets and ensure that they were not passages to the interior.

Finally, on one such expedition, Johnstone discovered a channel, which was named Johnstone's Passage and is now called Johnstone Strait, which led to the open sea, at last proving the insularity of Vancouver Island.

That season, the coastal survey was continued northwards to about 52° 20′ N, stopping just short of today's Bella Coola. Then they went to Nootka Sound, where Vancouver had some diplomatic business to attend to with the Spanish commander, Bodega y Quadra, and then they sailed south, first to San

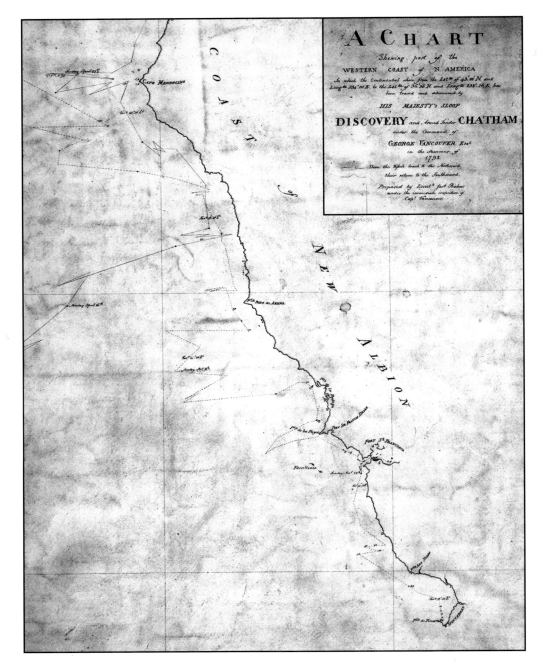

Map 168.
Part of George Vancouver's chart of the west coast of the United States, drawn in 1792 by Joseph Baker, one of his officers. The map shows the coast from Cape Mendocino south to Monterey.

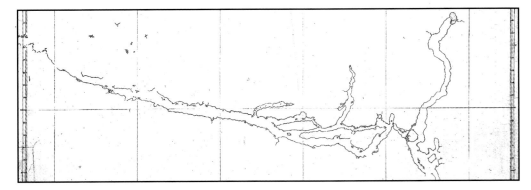

Map 169.
James Johnstone's original draft map of the passage he found and surveyed between Vancouver Island and the mainland, which established the insularity of Vancouver Island. The island is to the south, the "continental shore" to the north. The longest indentation shown in the coastline is Loughborough Inlet.

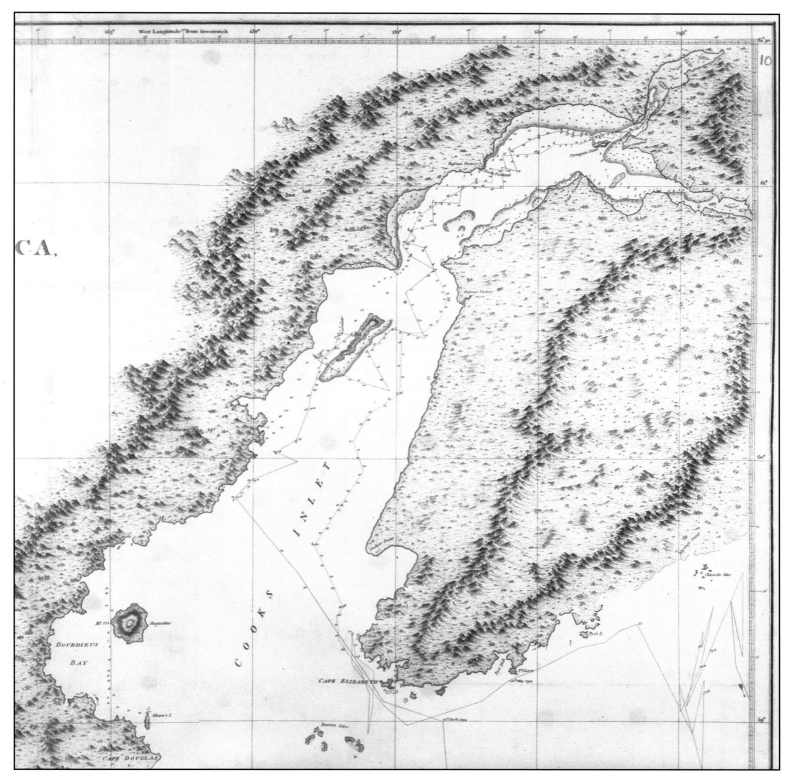

Map 170.
Vancouver's map of Cook Inlet, Alaska. He renamed it from Cook's River after determining that there was no outlet at the northeastern end. This map is from the atlas that accompanied his book, published in 1798. In the period between Cook and Vancouver, many speculative geographers, and notably North West Company fur trader Peter Pond, had considered that a large river which flowed from the western end of Lake Athabasca must reach the Pacific here. It was this river that Alexander Mackenzie explored in 1789 with the hope of reaching the Pacific Ocean. He didn't, of course, ending up in the Arctic Ocean instead; the river was the Mackenzie.

Francisco and then to Monterey. Vancouver was expecting further instructions from his government, which might have been sent to these places, but none were forthcoming.

After spending the winter in Hawaii, Vancouver was back again the next year, surveying northwards from the point he had left off the previous season. This time the coast to 56° N

was surveyed in four months – the intricately indented coastline of northern British Columbia and some of the Alaska panhandle, with too many islands to count.

They were back in Nootka by October. Then they surveyed the southern California coast until December, returning by January 1794 to Hawaii.

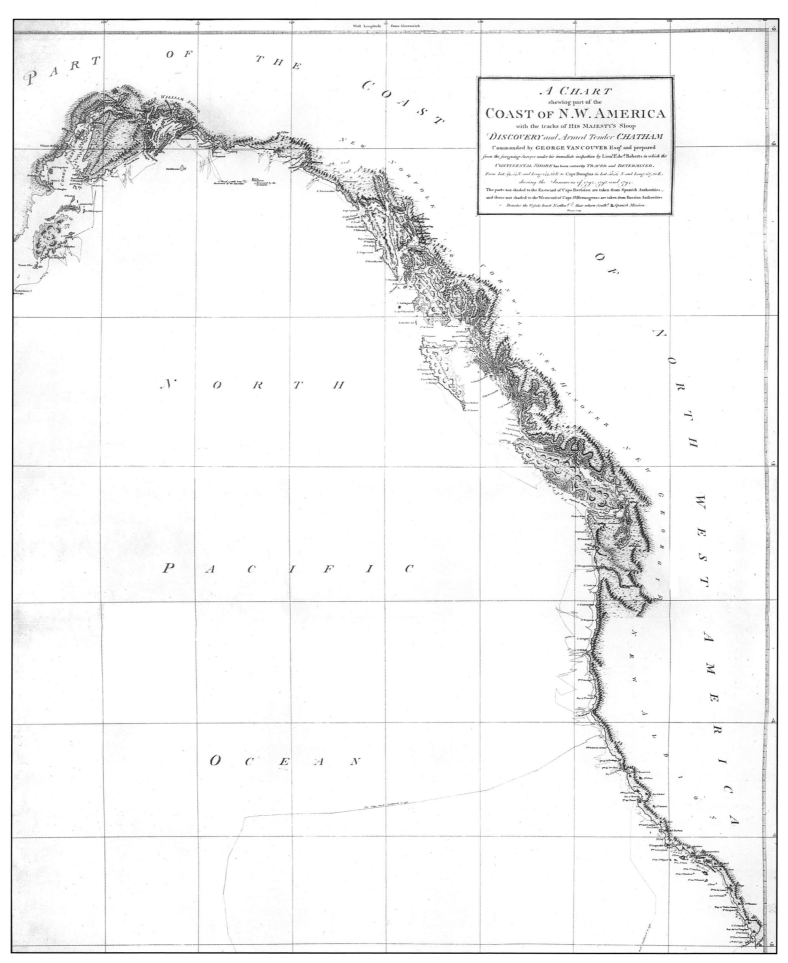

Map 171. The final result of George Vancouver's survey, the summary map of the west coast of North America. This was published in the atlas of his 1798 book. Most of the west coast is now shown accurately. Only relatively minor parts remain to be filled in.

Vancouver began his final season of survey, in 1794, from Cook Inlet in Alaska. They worked east and then south to join with the end of the 1793 survey.

One of the most significant results of this last survey was the determination that Cook Inlet, south of today's Anchorage, was indeed an inlet and not a river or other way to the interior. Cook had not explored the inlet to the very end and hence had left open the speculation that it was the mouth of a large river flowing from the interior. He similarly determined that Prince William Sound had no opening to the east.

Vancouver's superb three-season survey, much of it undertaken in small boats, for there was no other way to explore the detail of the deep inland indentations in the days of sail, was his magnum opus. He would not live even to see his work published; the job was finished by his brother John in 1798, achieving a worldwide recognition that has tended to overshadow the enormous contribution made by the Spanish in the years before Vancouver's arrival on the west coast.

Vancouver wrote:

I trust the precision with which the survey of the coast of North West America has been carried into effect will remove every doubt, and set aside every opinion of a north-west passage, or any water communication navigable for shipping, existing between the North Pacific, and the interior of the American continent, within the limits of our researches.

Pacific scholar J. C. Beaglehole noted that the Northwest Coast is

so remarkably complicated that Vancouver's systematic and painstaking survey ranks with the most distinguished work of the kind ever done.

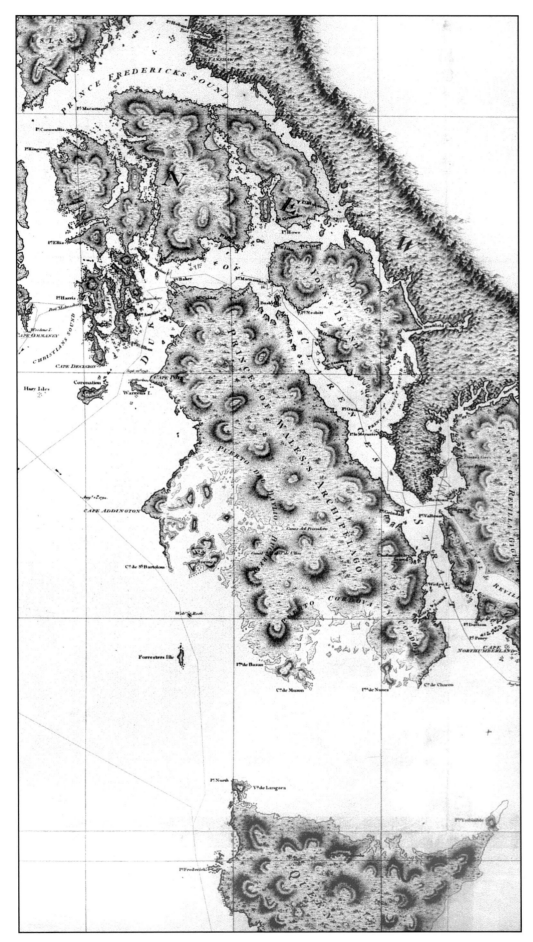

Map 172. Part of Vancouver's engraved and published map. This shows Dixon Entrance, the northern tip of the Queen Charlotte Islands, and the southern part of the Alaska panhandle. Juan Pérez's Langara Island is at the tip of the Queen Charlotttes; Vancouver did not change its name, though many names that survive are his, not Spanish ones.

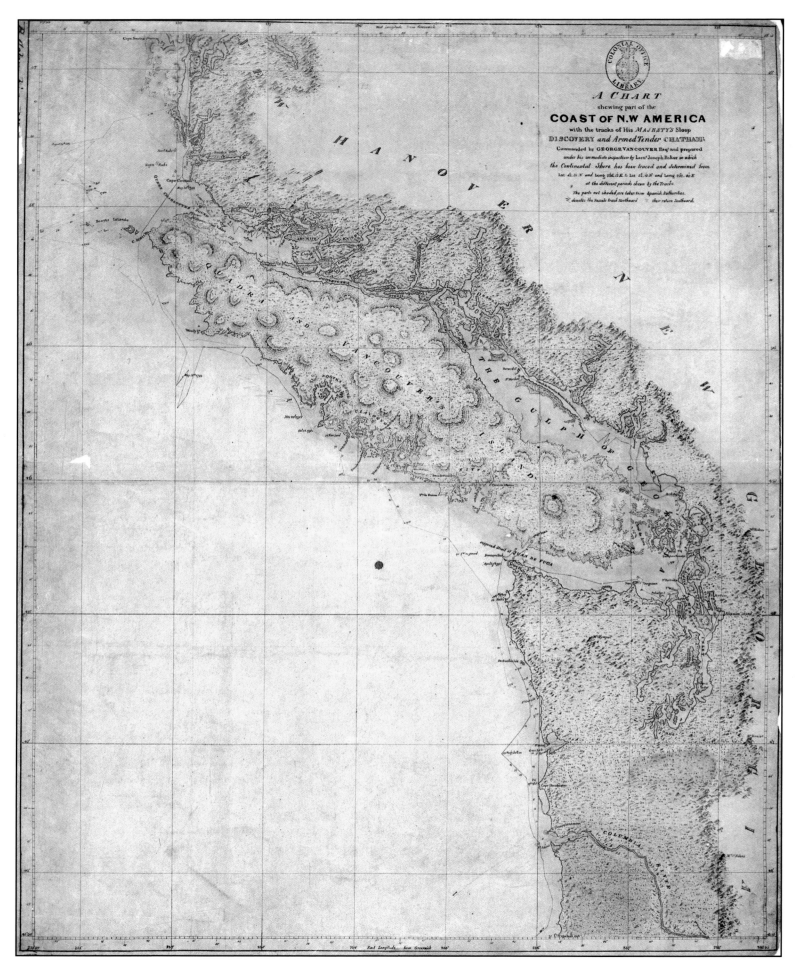

Map 173. This is one of the compilation charts for Vancouver's published atlas, showing Vancouver Island and adjacent coasts. It is a final manuscript map, which would have been sent to the engraver to make the plate for this sheet in the atlas.

Broughton Charts the West Pacific

Voyages of Discovery justly claim the public attention because they open new sources of knowledge and trade, and consequently are interesting to a scientific and commercial people.

– William Broughton, 1804

William Broughton was captain of *Chatham* for the first year of survey-ing on the Northwest Coast of America, 1792; he was sent back to England by Vancouver towards the end of that year to explain negotia-tions that had taken place with the Spanish. In 1793 Broughton was se-lected to conduct a survey of the southern part of the west coast of South America, which, it was as-sumed, Vancouver would not cover, despite it being in his orders. He was to proceed back to the Pacific by way of Nootka Sound, in case Vancouver was still on the Northwest Coast.

Broughton did not leave En-gland until February 1795, together with Zachary Mudge as second-in-command. Mudge had also been sent

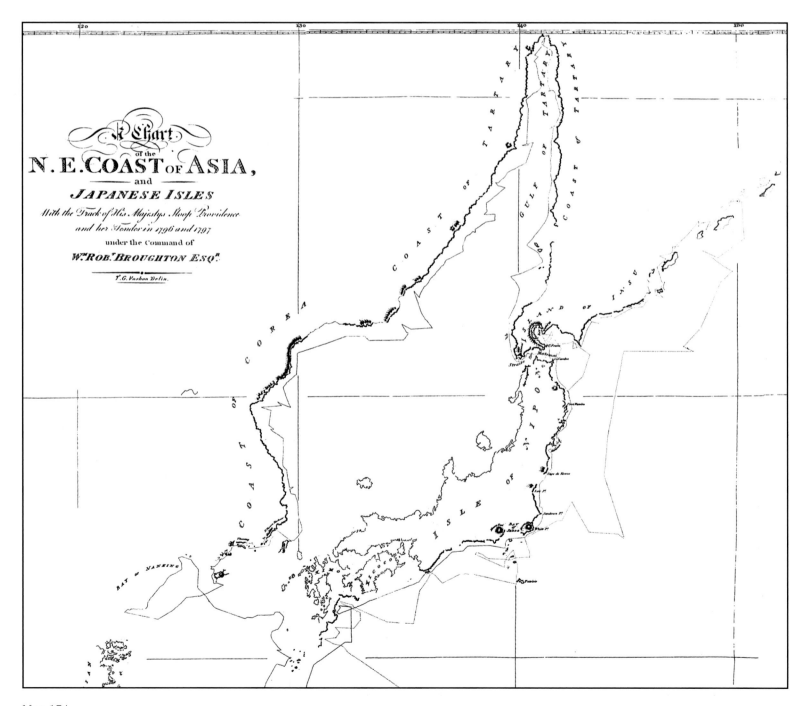

Map 174.
William Broughton's summary map of his voyage in 1796 and 1797. There is confusion between the northern islands of Japan and the Kuril Islands. Likewise, the insularity of Sakhalin is in doubt, with both the mainland and Sakhalin being labelled "Coast of Tartary."

home by Vancouver carrying information and maps.

The ship that Broughton commanded was *Providence,* the ship in which William Bligh, of mutiny on the *Bounty* fame, had returned to Tahiti to carry out the transportation of breadfruit to Jamaica, the task he had been trying to do in *Bounty.*

By spring 1796, Broughton was at Friendly Cove on the west coast of Vancouver Island. Because of the long time that had elapsed since Vancouver's original arrival on the Northwest Coast, Broughton assumed that Vancouver would have by this time carried out his instructions regarding the surveying of South America. Vancouver had not carried out this survey, but Broughton was unaware of this.

Broughton's instructions now left him to his own discretion; he could survey wherever he thought best "in such a manner as might be deemed most eligible for the improvement of geography and navigation."

Hence, in consultation with his officers, he decided to survey the only "blank" area left in the North Pacific at this time, the coast of Asia from Sakhalin, at 52° N, to the Nanking River at 30° N. He knew this area had been explored by La Pérouse, but his survey had not then been published.

Broughton arrived on the coast of Japan in September 1796 and charted the east coast of Hokkaido and Honshu. He determined that the rate of flow of the Kuroshio Current depended on the distance from the coast.

By the end of the year Broughton was at Macao. A smaller ship was purchased for surveying work in shallow waters, which was just as well, for the next year, *Providence* was wrecked south of Japan, the men being saved by the other ship.

After shipping some of his crew home from Canton, Broughton continued his survey, sailing up the east coast of Japan once more, through La Pérouse Strait separating Hokkaido from Sakhalin, and up the west coast of Sakhalin. Here he decided

there was no passage northwards between Sakhalin and the mainland, so he returned southwards along the mainland coast to Quelpart Island, off the southern end of Korea.

At the northern end of Tatar Strait, called the Gulf of Tartary on Broughton's map, he found extensive shallows that led him to believe there was no navigable channel any farther north. Broughton's map drawn at this time (Map 176, below) clearly shows Sakhalin as an island, yet his published map (Map 174, previous page) shows it as part of the "Coast of Tartary."

The schooner was taken to Trincomalee and its crew paid off. The lieutenant who drew Broughton's maps was Lieutenant J. G. Vashon. But he was also the officer of the watch the night the *Providence* was wrecked. As a result he was "discharged as per sentence of court martial."

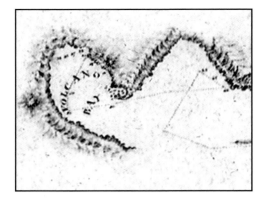

Map 175. Part of Broughton's 1796 survey of the east coast of Japan, showing Volcano Bay, on Hokkaido just north of Tsugaru Strait.

This illustration, entitled *Man and Woman of Volcano Bay,* appeared in Broughton's book. Note the smoking volcano in the background. The bay is on the southeast coast of Hokkaido.

Map 176.
Part of Broughton's map, showing the island of Sakhalin and the strait between it and the mainland, including the Amur River. The shape of Sakhalin is not correct, but the strait is relatively accurate.

The First Russian Circumnavigation

The first Russian circumnavigation had a dual purpose. It was planned as a voyage to rather belatedly recoup some prestige lost to other nations, coming as it did after the scientific voyages of Britain's James Cook, France's La Pérouse, and Spain's Malaspina. It was also a practical venture encouraged by the new Russian-American Company, which was now ensconced on the coast of Alaska complete with a monopoly on trade. Company officials had the idea that they could better supply their outposts with ships sailing from Russia's west coast outlet on the Baltic west around Cape Horn rather than overland through Siberia, which then still required a sea voyage.

The venture was approved by the new Tsar Alexander I as much because he was interested in expanding Russia's naval power in the North Pacific as for any scientific reason.

The voyage, which began in 1803 and lasted three years, did demonstrate the feasability of supply by sea, and numerous other Russian circumnavigations would follow, almost all calling at Sitka, the Russian settlement on Baranof Island in the Alaska panhandle, but food supply tended to be satisfied as much by traders of other nations as by Russian ships. A long series of Russian circumnavigations followed this first one, some of which were scientific. Accounts of two of the more interesting ones follow (pages 132–35).

Ivan Fedorovich Kruzenstern and Urei Lisianskii were appointed captains of two ships, *Nadezhda* and *Neva*, respectively.

The two ships were destined to investigate different areas of the North Pacific, although at first they sailed in concert. Lisianskii spent more time in the eastern Pacific. At one point he helped the Russian-American Company retake a fort lost to the Tlingit natives; he assisted with cannon bombardment from the ship.

Map 177.
The North Pacific part of Urei Lisianskii's map of the world, published in 1812.

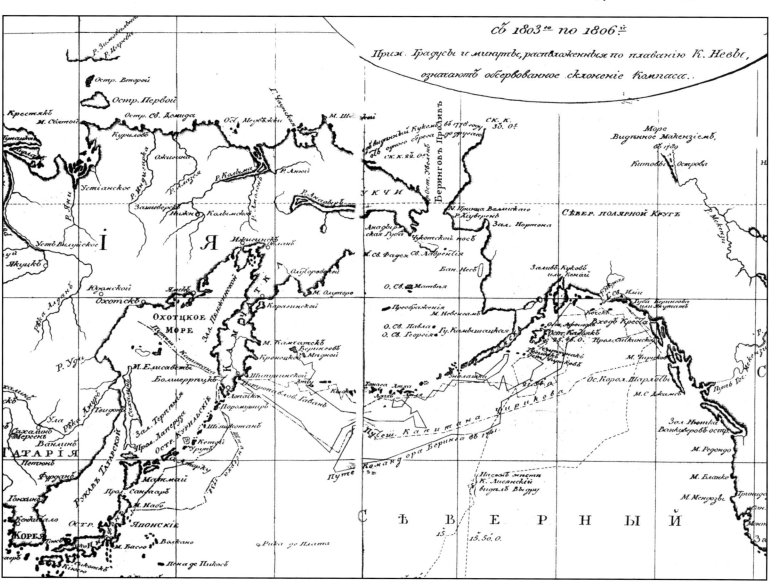

His account of the voyage, with maps, was published in 1812.

Ivan Kruzenstern spent more time in the western North Pacific and is best remembered for his explorations of the coast of Sakhalin.

Kruzenstern was the first to explore and map the north coast of Sakhalin. He wrote of the bay between Cape Elizabeth, the northeast point of the island, and Cape Maria, at the northwest point:

Should it ever be the intentions of Russia to plant a colony in the north of Sakhalin, this bay is the only spot calculated for such an undertaking.

Arriving at the north end of the strait between Sakhalin and the mainland, Kruzenstern sent out a boat to sound southwards, finding rapid shoaling to as shallow as three and a half fathoms (6 m). "I had every reason to believe we were near the mouth of the Amur," he wrote. He was right. In the middle of the channel, a bucket was used to sample the water. "It was perfectly sweet," Kruzenstern wrote. The ship's boat reported also that "the rapidity of the current from the southward had rendered the advance very laborious."

From these factors, Kruzenstern could not determine if there was a separation between Sakhalin and the mainland, although his map does show the island, but he could and did conclude that any passage wasn't safely navigable for *Nadezhda*.

Map 178.
Ivan Kruzenstern's explorations of Sakhalin, from his world map published with his book, 1813.

Map 179.
Part of a map by Vasili Berkh, who was one of Urei Lisianskii's officers.

View of Nangosaki from Kruzenstern's book. The Japanese port of Nagasaki was visited, but the Russians were not well received.

Mamiya and Sakhalin

La Pérouse, Broughton, and Kruzenstern were all undecided as to whether Sakhalin was a peninsula or an island, although all three had previously shown it as an island on their maps. The confusion is understandable, for the water shoals dramatically at the northern end of Tatar Strait due to the sediments from the mouth of the Amur River system. Here the Sakhalin coast approaches that of the mainland to within a few miles.

Japanese explorers were understandably interested in Sakhalin, which they called Karafuto, as an extension of the islands that form their own country. In 1785, ordered by the shogun to explore northwards, an expedition had sailed along the western coast of Sakhalin almost to 48° N; in two subsequent attempts they made it as far as 52° N, where the Gulf of Tartary narrows, and nearly 49° N on the eastern coast, at Cape Terpeniya. They also surveyed as far as Ostrov Urup in the Kuril Islands. Surveys by Mogami Tokunai were made into maps and submitted to the shogun.

Again by order of the shogun, who was interested in Sakhalin for reasons of defense, Matsuda Denjuro and Mamiya Rinzo sailed north in 1808. Matsuda sailed up the west coast, Mamiya up the east; near Cape Terpeniya Mamiya crossed the mountains to join Matsuda on the west coast. This convinced Mamiya that Sakhalin was indeed an island.

The next year Mamiya sailed into the mouth of the Amur River, reaching a Chinese trading post on the lower part of the river. In so doing he finally confirmed that there was a strait between Sakhalin and the mainland, and thus that Sakhalin was an island.

Western knowledge of Sakhalin's insularity did not come until considerably later. In 1852, Philipp Franz

Map 180.
Mogami Tokunai's maps of Sakhalin, published by Philipp Franz von Siebold in 1852.

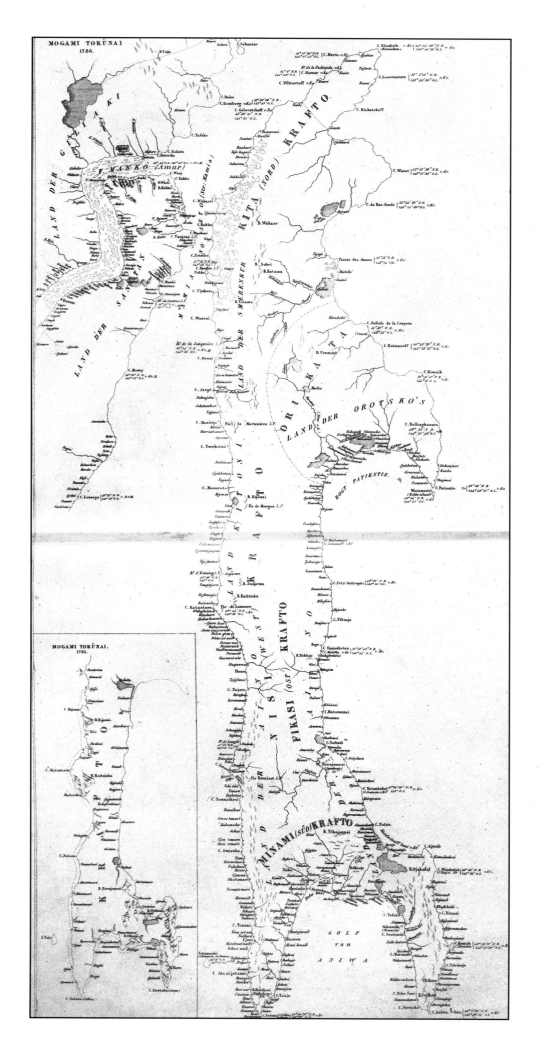

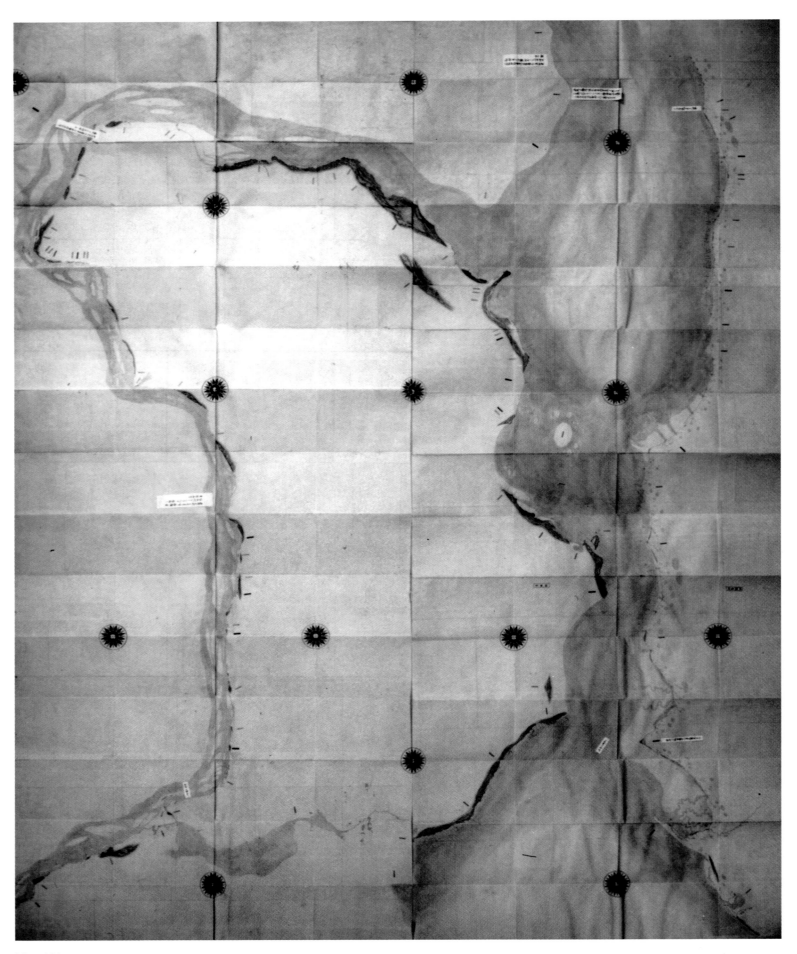

Map 181.
The strait between Sakhalin (Karafuto) and the mainland, as surveyed by Mamiya Rinzo in 1809. The Amur River enters the strait from the mainland side. Now part of Russia, the narrowest part of the strait is Proliv Nevel'skogo, and the wider part opposite the Amur is Amurskij Liman. The coast is highlighted by a band of blue, giving rise to the appearance on this map of an island opposite the mouth of the Amur, which was not intended.

von Siebold obtained copies of both Mogami's and Mamiya's maps and published a map incorporating their work. It was the first definitive proof of the insularity of Sakhalin based on actual penetration of the strait between the island and the mainland.

Map 182 (right).
Philipp Franz von Siebold's map of Sakhalin and adjacent coast, published in 1852, finally depicted Mamiya's survey of 1808 showing Sakhalin as an island. Although other maps had shown Sakhalin as an island, this was the first as the result of actual survey.

Map 183 (below, left).
A map by Jean Baptiste d'Anville published in 1737 shows that the idea of Sakhalin as an island had been around for some time.

Map 184 (below, right).
Aaron Arrowsmith's Pacific Ocean map of 1818 clearly shows Sakhalin as an island. The tracks are those of Ivan Kruzenstern.

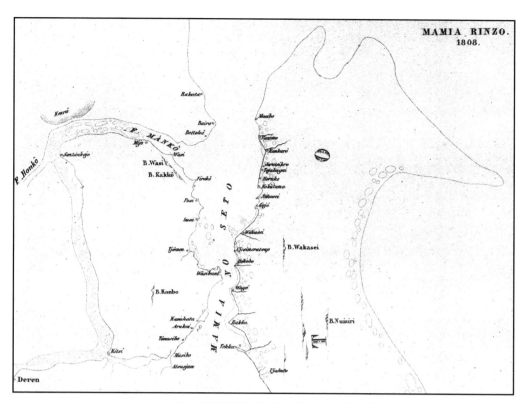

The Voyages of Otto Kotzebue

After the end of the wars against Napoleon, Russia was again able to turn its mind to round-the-world voyages of a scientific nature, although the first was initiated by a private individual, N. P. Rumiantsev. This voyage was to search for a Northeast Passage, which in this case meant that north of the North American continent usually referred to as the Northwest Passage. It was also to conduct scientific studies. Rumiantsev selected Otto Kotzebue, a naval lieutenant who had sailed with Kruzenstern on his round-the-world voyage in 1803–6.

Kotzebue took with him several scientists in his ship, *Riurik*. In the North Pacific in 1816, at a location given as 37° 30′ N and 199° 17′ (E; this is 160° 43′ W), Kotzebue made one of the first North Pacific measurements of temperature with depth, showing the following gradient:

6 June 1816	
	°F
Surface air temperature:	63.0
Surface water temperature:	61.0
At 10 fathoms:	59.5
At 25 fathoms:	56.8
At 100 fathoms:	52.7
At 300 fathoms:	43.0

Despite their value as pioneering efforts, these measurements were unfortunately not very accurate, due to poor instrumentation and research methods. Of the eight locations where Kotzebue measured temperature with depth, only the one noted above was in the North Pacific.

Proceeding northwards, Kotzebue thought he had discovered a fourth Diomede Island, which he named Ratmanoff Island "after the lieutenant of that name under whose command I was on the Voyage of Kruzenstern"; it is marked as such on his map (see facing page).

He thought it "singular that this island was neither seen by Cook or by Clark [Clerke], both having sailed close by it" and stated that he was "of the opinion that it has probably risen from the ocean." But Kotzebue in this instance was mistaken; there are only three islands in this location.

However, Kotzebue did make one major contribution to the knowledge of the geography of the coast of what is now Alaska. His own words tell the story best.

On 1st August, we observed that the coast took a direction to the east, the land continuing to be low. At eleven o'clock we were at the entrance of a large inlet . . . I cannot describe my feelings when I thought I might be opposite the long-sought-for N.E. Passage, and that fate had destined me to be its discoverer.

But the euphoria was not to last, for a week later Kotzebue recorded:

We had penetrated far enough to see that the land met everywhere . . . The depth had already decreased to five feet, and we gave up even the hope of finding a river.

Nevertheless, Kotzebue had discovered a hitherto unmapped bay which soon became known as Kotzebue Sound and is shown on his own map with this name.

The superb illustration of natives of Kotzebue Sound appears in Kotzebue's book, published in English in 1821. Kotzebue wrote that

they are above the middle size, of strong, vigorous, and healthy appearance; their motions are lively, and they seem much inclined to be jocose; their faces . . . are . . . distinguished by very small eyes and high cheekbones, and on both sides of their mouth they have holes, in which they wear morsebone, ornamented with blue beads, which give them a terrific appearance.

Kotzebue's voyage also visited more tropical areas of the Pacific Ocean, and he is known for his observations and theories regarding coral atolls, some of which were later accepted by Charles Darwin.

Kotzebue was called upon to command the ship *Predpriatie* on another Russian round-the-world voyage in 1823–26, which again had scientists on board, including E. Lenz, a physicist. This time he made no new geographical discoveries in the North Pacific, but did add considerably to scientific knowledge.

Kotzebue visited the Russian-American Company's capital at New Archangel'sk, now Sitka, and made observations on the habits of the sea otter. Perceptively, Kotzebue noted, "It

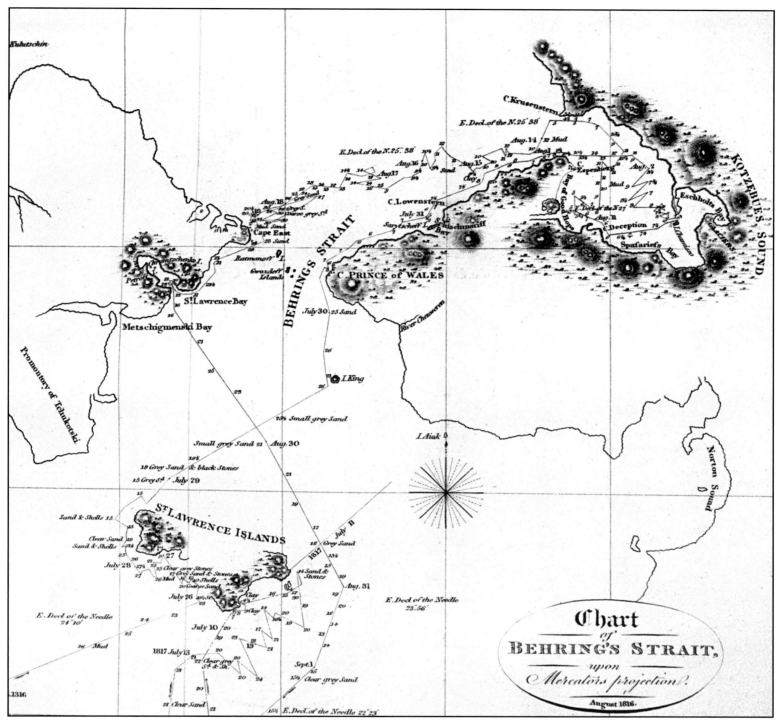

Within the map:

Kulutschin

C. Krusenstern

E. Decl. of the N. 25° 38'

E. Decl. of the N. 25° 38'

Aug. 14 12 Mud

Aug. 16

Aug. 15

KOTZEBUE'S SOUND

Aug. 17

Clay

C. Lowenstern

Espenberg

Aug. 18

Mud

Mud Sand

Cape East

28 Sand

July 31

Sarytscheff I.

Schischmareff Bay

E. Decl. of the N. 27'

Eschholtz Bay

BEHRING'S STRAIT

Deception

Spafarief's Bay

Ratmanoff I.

Gwozdeff Islands

Tschamisso

Ingenlook I.

Tschumtschenko I.

Peg.

C. PRINCE of WALES

St. Lawrence Bay

July 30 25 Sand

Metschigmenski Bay

River Choweren

Promontory of Tschukotski

26

25

I. King

28

26

28½ Small grey Sand

Small grey Sand 21 Aug. 30

Norton Sound

19½

18 Grey Sand & black Stones

15 Grey S⁴ July 29

21

15

L. Aiak

Sand & Shells 15

St. LAWRENCE ISLANDS

19

17

July 11

Clear Sand 19

16 Grey Sand

Sand & Shells

1817

13½

25

July 28 27½

Clear grey Stones

17 Grey Sand & Stones

15

Sand & Stones

39

26

25

Coarse Sand

20 Shells

Aug. 31

July 26

Clay

19

19

20

E. Decl. of the Needle 24° 10'

24

23

E. Decl. of the Needle 23° 56'

July 10 20

17

1817 July 13

Clear grey S⁴ & S⁴.

Sept. 1

15¾ Clear grey Sand

1816

21 Clear Sand

45¼ E. Decl. of the Needle 22° 23'

Chart
of
BEHRING'S STRAIT,
upon
Mercators projection.
August 1816.

Map 185.
Otto Kotzebue's map of Bering Strait.
Most detail is concentrated on his discovery, Kotzebue Sound.

(above, left)
Inhabitants of Kotzebue Sound,
an illustration from Kotzebue's book.

will soon entirely disappear, and exist only in description to decorate our zoological works." The sea otter did indeed almost disappear in Alaskan waters until its reintroduction in the twentieth century.

Kotzebue's physicist, Lenz, tried to overcome the poor instrumentation that had plagued Kotzebue on his first voyage, and designed a bathometer, which sampled water at various depths, and a winched depth gauge for lowering the instrument to a specific depth. These two inventions have been considered by some

to be the beginning of exact oceanographic technique.

From the data he collected with Kotzebue, Lenz formulated a theory of oceanic water circulation to explain the occurrence of lower temperatures at depth. Lenz was the first to establish the existence of lower salinity at the equator and higher salinity north and south of it, correctly explaining this as due to more intense evaporation in the area of the trade winds and less in the calmer regions around the equator.

Fedor Lütke's Scientific Voyage

Of the approximately fifty Russian voyages around the world that were undertaken during the tenure of the Russian-American Company in Alaska, the voyage of Fedor Petrovich Lütke was one of the most successful from a scientific point of view.

Two ships, *Seniavin,* under Lütke, and *Moller,* commanded by M. N. Staniukovich, left the Baltic naval port of Kronstadt in August 1826 with instructions to survey the Northeast Coast of Asia and the Northwest Coast of America. After treaties signed with both the United States and Britain in 1824 and 1825, Russia no longer had to provide warships to patrol the coast of northwest America, hence the instructions for a more scientific voyage.

Once in the North Pacific, the two ships separated and went about their own tasks. Staniukovich had little scientific inclination and only surveyed the north coast of the Alaska Peninsula, producing routine reports. Lütke, on the other hand, accumulated a vast amount of scientific data, and produced and later published several books with his findings, including a historical section with an atlas and a nautical atlas with more than fifty maps and plans.

Three naturalists were with Lütke. All were masters at several branches of natural history, as was common in their day. Friedrich Hienrich Baron von Kittlitz specialized in ornithology, Aleksandr Filippovich Postels was a mineralogist-naturalist, and Karl-Heinrich Mertens was the ship's doctor and, of course, another naturalist. Together they produced more than 1,250 drawings and sketches. They also took meteorological observations.

In 1827 Lütke visited the Russian-American Company's headquarters at New Archangel'sk (Sitka) and surveyed some of the coast. The winter of 1827–28 was passed farther south, in the Caroline Islands, and in 1828 the expedition surveyed the eastern coast of Kamchatka Peninsula and measured the heights of some volcanoes.

The scientists took daily observations of the temperature of the water on the surface and attempted to measure the temperature in deeper water; however, the first time they tried to do this, three thermometers were found to be broken when they were retrieved. Lütke was of the opinion that this was caused by water pressure.

Three hundred species of fish were preserved in alcohol, and Postels painted some 245 of them. Many of these were entirely unknown to science at the time.

The scientists certainly were collectors. The expedition also gathered 100 amphibians; 150 species of crustaceans, a hundred of which Mertens painted while they were alive; 700 species of insects; a "considerable collection" of shells; and 300 species of birds represented by 750 specimens. Mertens collected 2,500 plant specimens, and Postels collected 330 rock samples. Lastly, the expedition collected a "rich collection" of costumes, arms, utentils, and ornaments, and "some skulls of savages."

When the expedition returned to Russia, the specimens were all deposited with the Imperial Academy of Sciences in St. Petersburg.

View of the Russian Colony of Novo-Arkhangel'sk. The view, according to Kittlitz, who drew this picture, is of the interior of the town in its most populous and important place, from the door of the citadel. A Tlingit native looks on.

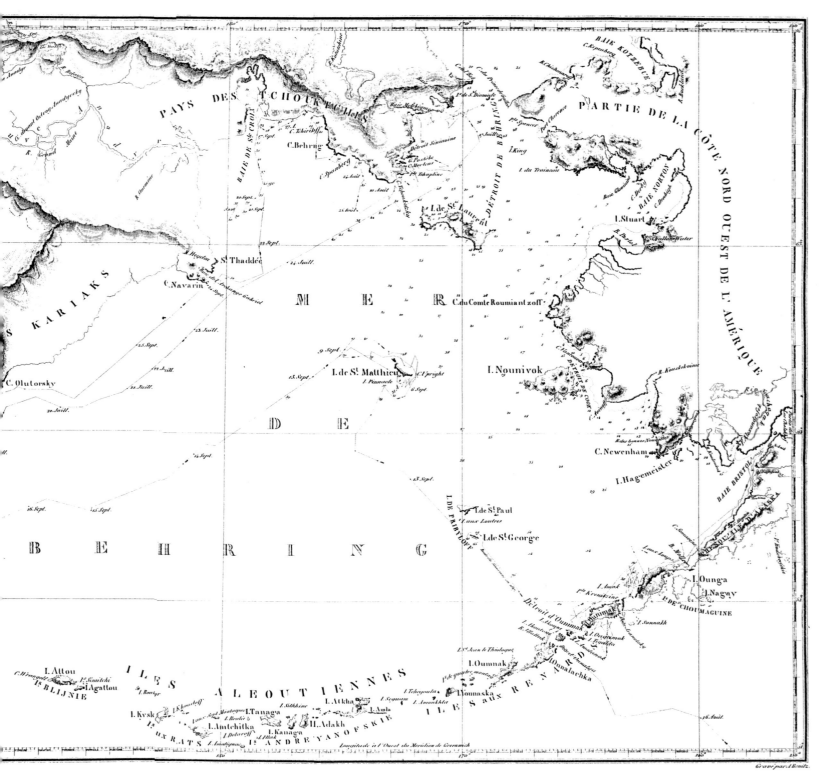

Map 186. Lütke's map of the Bering Sea, 1828, published in the French edition of his book.

(left)

Forest of Sitkha Island.
"In order to study as closely as possible the character of the vegetation we undertook an excursion to the summit of Mount Verstovaia, the highest of the island (3,000 English feet)," Postels wrote of this view from his own drawing. "The road through the forest . . . is represented in this picture."

(right)

Habitation at Unalaska, Aleutian Islands. Kittlitz drew this picture on Unalaska. He wrote:

The general appearance of the Aleutian Islands affords a striking contrast to that of Sitka. In place of the superb forest which covers the steep heights of this island from sea level, one does not see here the least small shrub; only the high grasses which extend to the arid region of a land composed likewise of high escarpments, presents an aspect more attractive than one might believe, like an immense carpet of velvet where the inequalities of the soil produce an infinity of nuances.

The United States Exploring Expedition

Porpoise.

In 1838 the United States Exploring Expedition, universally referred to as the U.S. Ex. Ex., was sent straggling round the world to collect scientific information both from lands and seas. It was a belated answer to the British and French expeditions of Cook and La Pérouse and, perhaps more immediately, that of Robert Fitzroy, with Charles Darwin in HMS *Beagle,* from 1831 to 1836.

Trade benefits were supposed to flow from this new expedition: new areas could be opened for trade, better routes found for New England whalers, and perhaps new islands would be discovered.

Charles Wilkes, though only a lieutenant, was appointed commander of the expedition. Wilkes had been appointed in 1833 the second superintendent of the U.S. Depot of Charts and Instruments, the predecessor of the U.S. Hydrographic Office. In twenty years of naval service Wilkes had proven himself scientifically. His affinity to the navy meant he preferred naval officers for scientific duties; "All the duties apertaining to Astronomy, Surveying, Hydrography, Geography, Geodesy, Magnetism, Meteorology, and Physics [are] generally to be confined to the Navy officers," he directed, which subjects "are deemed the great objects of this expedition." Only nine positions were given to civilians.

Six ships sailed from Norfolk, Virginia, in August 1838. By the time they had done their work in the Atlantic, rounded Cape Horn, and were finally in the Pacific, half of them were out of commission, and one, *Peacock,* was wrecked trying to cross the bar at the mouth of the Columbia River in 1842. All hands were saved, but the precious cargo of scientific specimens was lost. As a result, most of the work was done by two ships, *Vincennes* and *Porpoise.*

The expedition's most famous result was not achieved in the North Pacific but in the Antarctic, sailing within a mile of the coast of what Wilkes called "Termination Land," to this day named Wilkes Land. Wilkes claimed to have discovered Antarctica, a claim contested by Britain's James Clark Ross, whose own expedition sailed from 1839 to 1843.

Wilkes' expedition did not spend a large part of its time in the North Pacific. It visited Oregon and California in 1841, and Wilkes' reports were important in encouraging the United States to insist on holding the area that is now the states of Washington and Oregon against British demands.

Of importance were Wilkes' reports and survey of Puget Sound, which reemphasized the fact that it was the only significant harbor north of San Francisco.

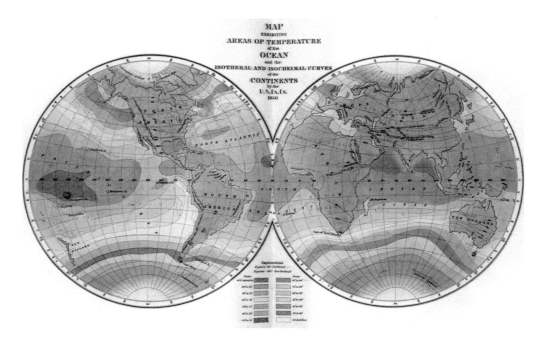

Map 187. *Map Exhibiting Areas of Temperature of the Ocean and the Isothermal and Isocheimal* [equal mean temperatures] *Curves of the Continents,* from a volume written by Wilkes himself, *Meteorology,* 1850.

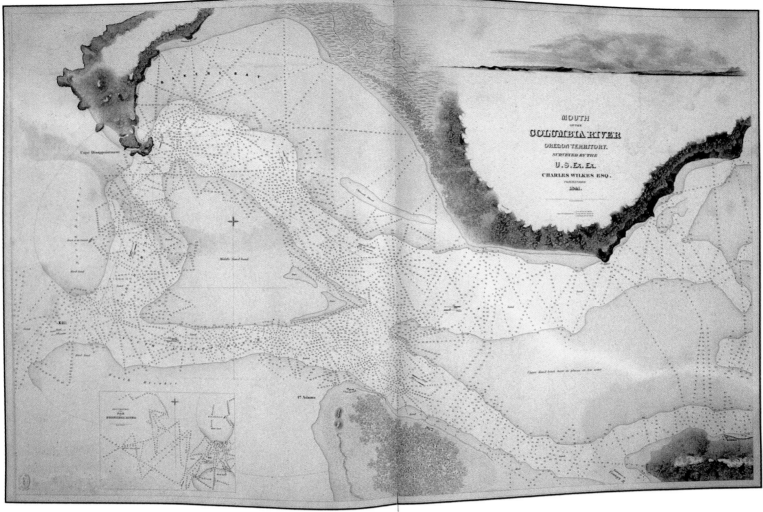

Map 188.
The survey of the treacherous mouth of the Columbia River, where one of the expedition's ships, *Peacock,* was destroyed trying to cross its notorious bar.

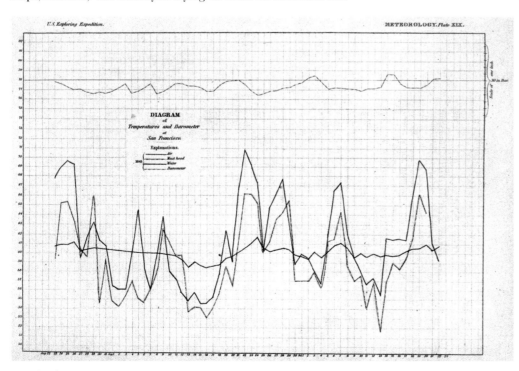

Graph of temperatures and air pressure recorded by the expedition while in San Francisco. The period covered is 22 August to 23 October 1841. Air temperatures at the surface and at the masthead were recorded, as was the surface water temperature.

Augustus Gould wrote the volume on *Mollusca and Shells,* from which these stunning engraved and hand-colored illustrations are taken. This plate, of *Pecten,* shows (at the top) two species from Puget Sound.

Many of the artifacts and specimens collected by the Wilkes expedition were sent to the National Institute, the forerunner of the Smithsonian, and promptly ruined. The curator also gave many away to his friends! Such was the respect for science. Plants from Oregon and California, neither at that time part of the United States, were shipped back to Washington on a ship which, after a voyage to China, was sold! The precious plants were dropped off in Havana, and did make it to Washington eventually.

Since his expedition was essentially a naval one, Wilkes needed government funds to process and publish the results of the voyage. Congress at first refused to pay, but due to Wilkes' persistence was at last persuaded to fund the preparation of some twenty-four volumes, twenty of which were ultimately published.

There was one catch: all had to be prepared by American scholars, which made it difficult for Wilkes to find appropriate scientists to do the job. He ended up writing several of the volumes himself, a task for which he was not unqualified. But it took a long time; Wilkes' volume of hydrography was not published until 1873, by which time new methods and better equipment had appeared.

In 1874, thirty-eight years after the start of the expedition, Congress cut funds for the remaining incomplete reports, and the United States Exploring Expedition was officially over.

Wilkes himself became a rear admiral and a significant backer of the new scientific oceanography. Towards the end of his days he toured the eastern United States with his sometimes unfinished reports urging scientists to consider "the vast space of

our globe occupied by the great ocean . . . It cannot but strike every one," he maintained, "what a wide field is open for investigation and experiment."

In some respects Wilkes was ahead of his time, advocating an invention to

obtain an echo from the bed of the ocean by the explosion of a shell just beneath the surface, the depth to be measured through the propagation of reflected sound.

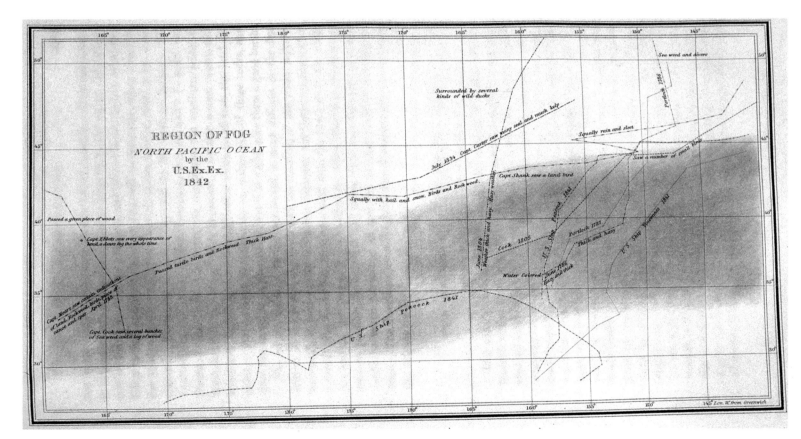

Map 189.
Wilkes wrote and published a book called *The Theory of the Winds*. This map of fog regions is taken from that book. Wilkes wrote: "All vessels may expect to meet with fogs and hazy atmosphere between latitudes 33° and 40°. This space might be very truly called the region of fog, the temperature of the water decreasing some 15°; and what is more remarkable, on a near approach to the coast, it again rises."

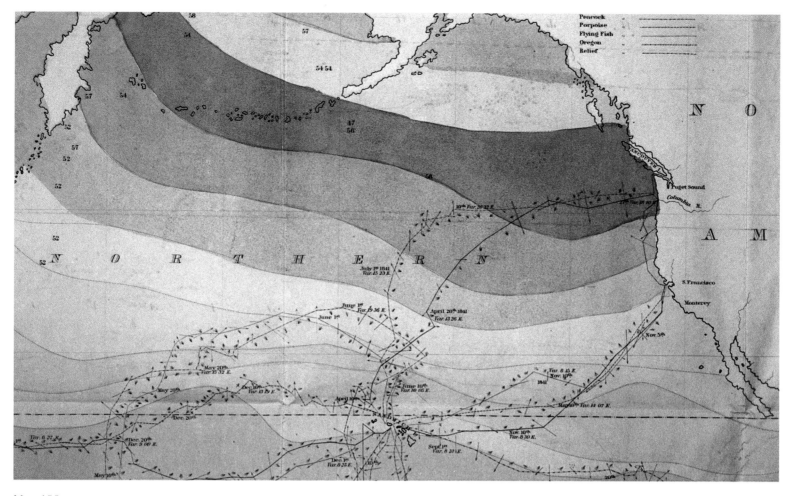

Map 190.
Track of the U.S. Exploring Expedition in the North Pacific, The map is from the *Narrative* of the voyage, published in 1845. The color bands are surface seawater temperatures. A lot of apparent information from so little actual data! Actually, the temperature distribution is not accurate, a consequence of too much extrapolation.

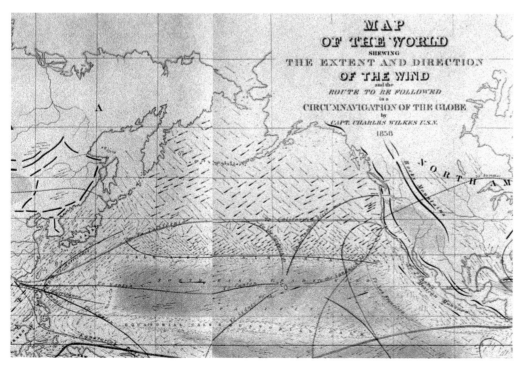

Map 191.
Part of a wind map of the world, from the volume *Hydrography*, written by Wilkes. The map was presented as a typical world map, running from 180° W to 180° E, but has here been cut and pasted to show the Pacific as a continuous sea.

Shells found in Puget Sound, from Augustus Gould's book *Mollusca and Shells*.

Mikhail Tebenkov's Atlas

Mikhail Dimitrievich Tebenkov's *Atlas of the Northwest Coasts of America from Bering Strait to Cape Corrientes and the Aleutian Islands* was published in St. Petersburg in 1852.

Tebenkov was a Russian naval officer who was manager of the Russian-American Company from 1845 to 1850. In 1831, he was responsible for building the Mikhailovskii re-

doubt, St. Michaels, near the mouth of the Yukon River.

In the 1840s, before and during his tenure as manager, Tebenkov organized several expeditions to survey the coasts of Russian America.

Over a period of twenty-five years, he had collected hydrographic maps that he had drawn, and added them to maps from other sources, in particular those of George Vancouver.

He also used ships' logs for information and verification.

In 1852, Tebenkov consolidated maps from these sources and published an atlas, which represents a superb collection of maps of the Northwest Coast from Russian sources. Three selections from his atlas are shown here.

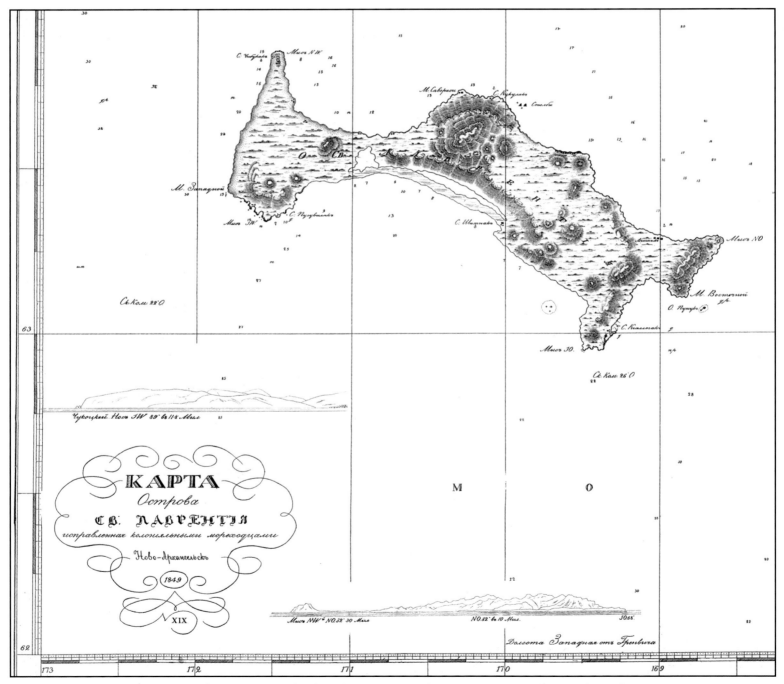

Map 192. Mikhail Tebenkov's map of St. Lawrence Island, in the Bering Sea, drawn in 1849. Note the soundings shown.

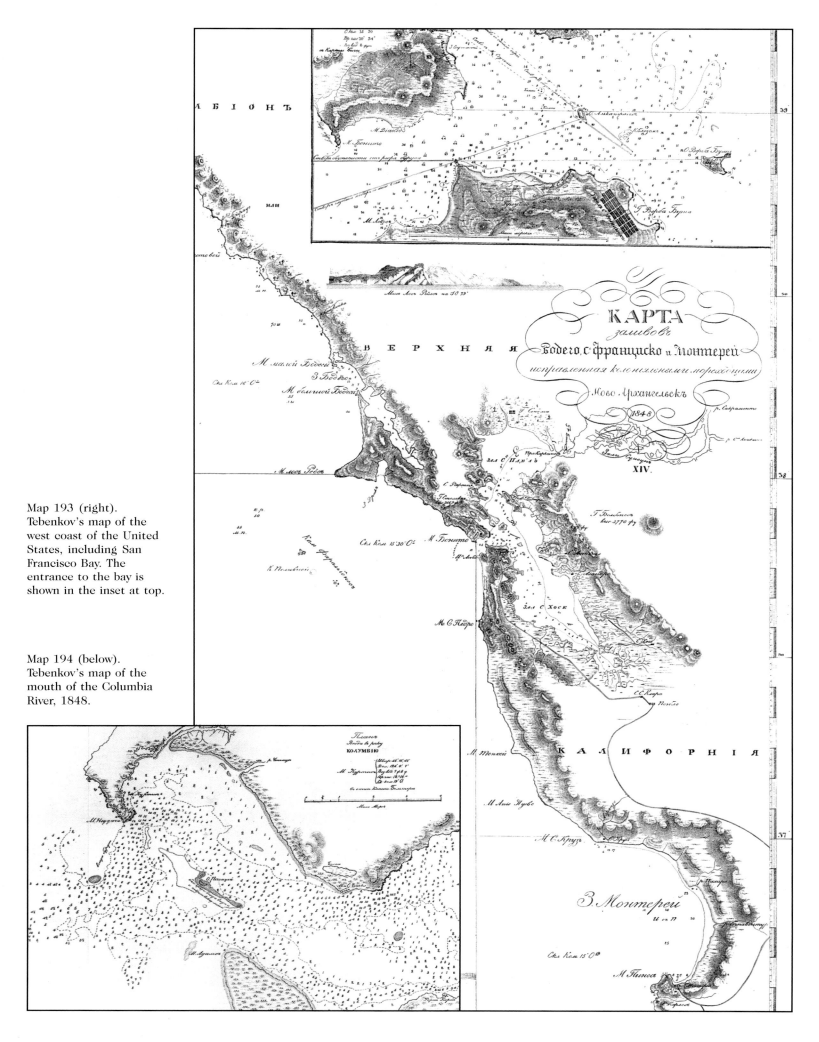

Map 193 (right). Tebenkov's map of the west coast of the United States, including San Francisco Bay. The entrance to the bay is shown in the inset at top.

Map 194 (below). Tebenkov's map of the mouth of the Columbia River, 1848.

Commodore Perry's Black Ships – The U.S. Japan Expedition

Map 195. Part of a mid-nineteenth-century Japanese world map showing the Pacific Ocean and Japan, with Perry's steamships – the "black ships."

The U.S. Japan Expedition under Commodore Matthew Calbraith Perry was an American effort to open Japan for trade. Japan was a closed society, where foreign ships that came within range had, by law, to be fired upon. The American government resolved to put an end to this situation, and Perry, with his squadron of what the Japanese called "black ships of the evil mien [main]," black smoke-belching ships, moving without the help of wind or the hand of man, arrived off the coast of Japan on 8 July 1853. The idea was to display a sufficient show of force that the Japanese would think it better to negotiate than fight.

The expedition was not intended to be a scientific one; Perry wrote that the expedition was

altogether of a naval and diplomatic character, and was never intended to embrace in its operations scientific researches.

But, he said,

Still I have determined that all shall be done under the circumstances to subserve the objects of science,

and so he issued orders that his officers collect hydrographical, meteorological, botanical, ichthylogical, zoological, ornithological, and other information. The result was that his expedition brought back many specimens and much information scientists could analyze.

There were few charts to guide the way; the American government purchased some inadequate ones from the Dutch for the astounding sum of $30,000.

The squadron steamed into Toyko Bay, repulsing all attempts to board them, until contact was made with a Japanese official who could speak Dutch. He had been brought from Nagasaki, the one place in Japan where Dutch merchants were allowed (see page 36). He was sent off with a copy of a letter from U.S. President Millard Fillmore to the Japanese emperor, but it seemed unlikely that it would actually be presented to the emperor.

While waiting for the Japanese to decide if the emperor would respond to their demands to negotiate, surveys and soundings were made in Tokyo Bay, protected by deployment of some of the squadron's ships.

At long length permission was given to meet a high official at Kurihama Bay, and Perry went ashore with as much pomp and circumstance as the Americans could muster, but at the same time defensively covered by his ship's guns. Here he met with Toda, the provincial governor, and officially delivered the letter to the emperor.

After more surveying, the squadron left, telling the Japanese that they would return the following spring for the emperor's reply.

Map 196 (right).
Perry's map of Tokyo wan (Tokyo Bay), which is here named "Jeddo Bay," from his first visit in 1853. The ships at anchor are named, and "Reception Bay" is shown. The land area on the map is today part of Yokohama.

Matthew Perry, commander of the U.S Japan Expedition.

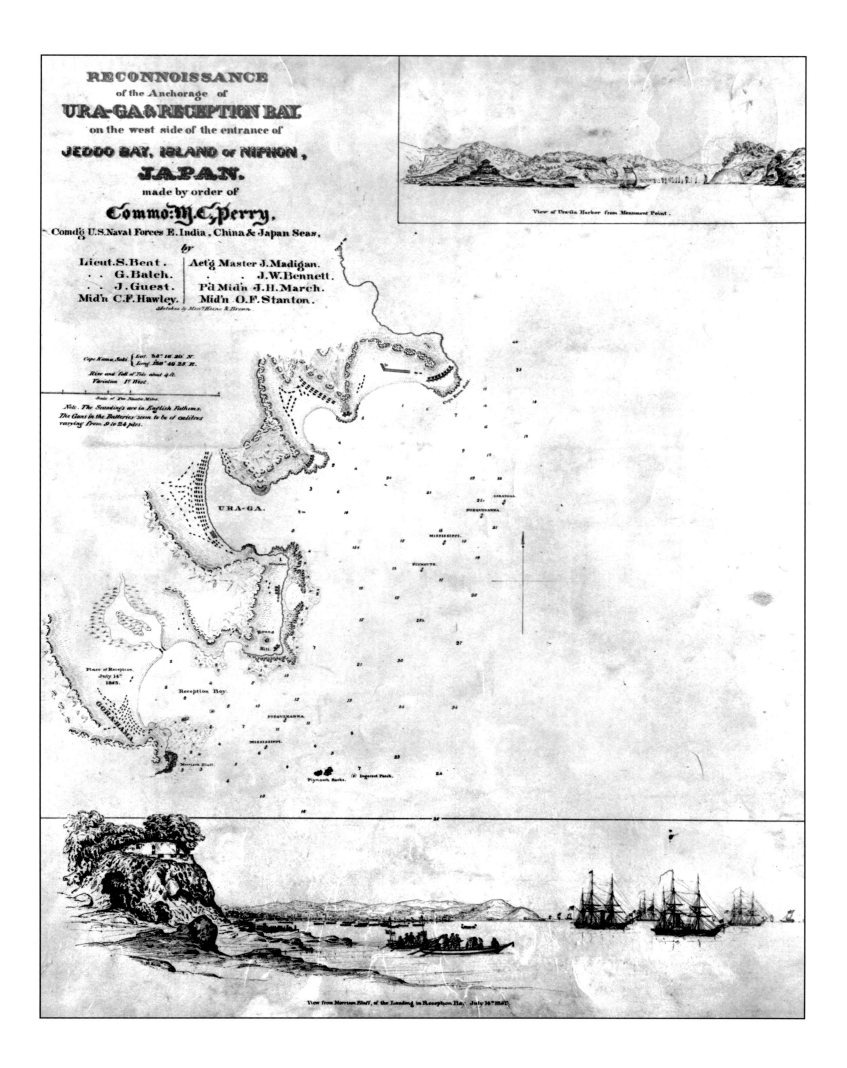

RECONNOISSANCE

of the Anchorage of

URA-GA & RECEPTION BAY

on the west side of the entrance of

JEDDO BAY, ISLAND of NIPHON,

JAPAN.

made by order of

Commo. M. C. Perry,

Comd'g U.S. Naval Forces E. India, China & Japan Seas,

by

Lieut. S. Bent .   Act'g Master J. Madigan.
. . G. Balch.   . . J. W. Bennett.
. . J. Guest.   Pd Mid'n J. H. March.
Mid'n C. F. Hawley.   Mid'n O. F. Stanton.

Sketches by Mess'r Heine & Brown.

Cape Kama Saki { Lat. 35° 16' 30" N.
                { Long. 136° 49' 35" E.

Rise and fall of Tide about 4 ft.
Variation 1° West.

Scale of Two Nautic Miles

Note. The Soundings are in English Fathoms.
The Guns in the Batteries seem to be of calibre
varying from 9 to 24 prs.

URA-GA.

Round
Hill.

Place of Reception
July 14th
1853.

Reception Bay.

SUSQUEHANNA

MISSISSIPPI.

Morrison Bluff.

Plymouth Rocks.   Ingersol Patch.

SARATOGA
SUSQUEHANNA

MISSISSIPPI.

PLYMOUTH.

View of Ura-Ga Harbor from Monument Point.

View from Morrison Bluff, of the Landing in Reception Bay. July 14th 1853.

In February the next year, 1854, they were back. This time they went ashore at Kanagawa, Yokohama. Accompanied by a well-armed retinue – even the band had pistols and swords – Perry went ashore, where he received the emperor's answer to President Fillmore's letter, in which he agreed to some of the American demands.

But Perry wanted more, and after weeks of further negotiations and military display, he got what he really wanted, a treaty.

The Treaty of Kanagawa between the United States and Japan was signed on 31 March 1854. It had twelve articles, including provisions that "there will be a perfect, permanent and universal peace, and a sincere cordial amnity, between the United States of America and Japan"; that the ports of Shimoda and Hakodate would be granted by the Japanese "as ports for the reception of American ships"; and that if U.S. ships were shipwrecked, Japan was to assist them, and shipwrecked sailors were not to be confined.

Although essentially forced upon the Japanese government, the treaty negotiated by Perry did in fact open up Japan to trade. For, once the Japanese started to trade with the outside world, there was no looking back.

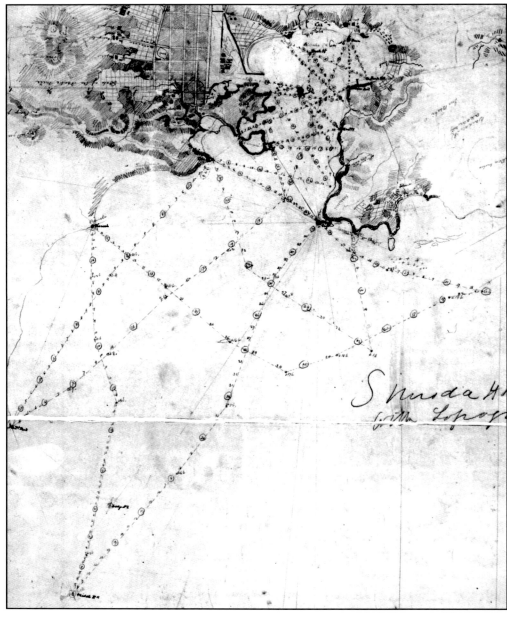

Map 197 (top).
"Simoda Lt. Bents Survey with Topography," a pencil copy of a survey of the small port of Shimoda, at the tip of the Izu Hanto (Izu Peninsula) on the east coast of Honshu, a little south of Tokyo. Silas Bent, one of Perry's officers, surveyed this new treaty port in April 1854.

Map 198 (right).
Harbor of Hakodadi Island of Yesso Surveyed by order of Commodore M. C. Perry By Lieut. W. L. Maury, Lieut. G.H. Preble, Lieut J. Nicholson, Lieut A. Barbot 1854. A rough plotting sheet showing lines of soundings, shoreline features, settlement, and topography of the harbor of Hakodate, the other harbor opened by treaty to American ships. It is at the south end of Hokkaido, on Tsugaru-kaikyo (Tsugaru Strait).

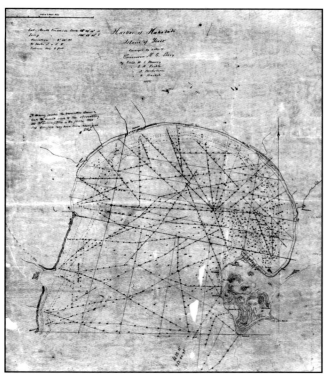

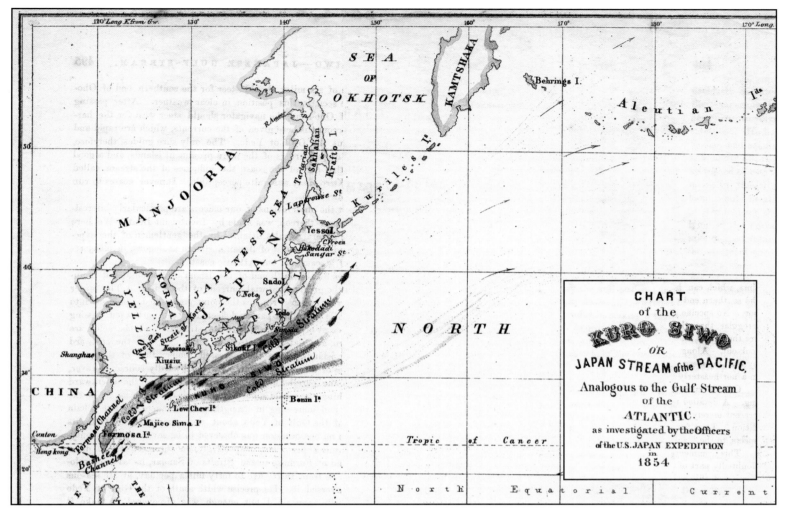

Map 199.
Chart of the Kuro Siwo or Japan Stream of the Pacific Analogous to the Gulf Stream of the Atlantic as investigated by the Officers of the U.S. Japan Expedition in 1854. From Perry's published reports, one of the first "scientific" mappings of the Kuroshio Current off the coast of Japan. An 1832 translation of a Japanese book Perry quoted in his journal noted the existence of a strong current between the islands of Mikura and Hachijojima "called Kouro se gawa (Kuroshio), or the black gulf current. It runs so rapidly that seamen regard it as the most difficult passage in these seas to get over."

Perry's book about the expedition was published in three large volumes in 1856–58. They contained a vast amount of information, sailing directions, illustrations of fish and other marine life, a whole volume of "observations of the zodiacal light," many maps and charts, reports on possible commercial features, such as coal deposits in Formosa, and even a copy of the treaty in Japanese.

Three fish caught and classified by the Perry expedition, beautifully illustrated and hand painted, from Perry's book. At left is (from Perry's descriptions) *Sebastes inermis,* 5¾ inches (142 mm) long, from Hakodadi (Hakodate). At right top is *Serranus tsirimenara* [*Epinephelus fasciatus,* blacktip grouper], 7¼ inches (181 mm) long, from Port Lloyd, Bonin Islands; and right bottom is *Serranus marginalis* [?], 8⅝ inches (216 mm) long, from Simoda (Shimoda).

The U.S. North Pacific Exploring Expedition

The U.S. North Pacific Exploring Expedition was authorized by Act of Congress in August 1852 for

the reconnaissance and survey for naval and commercial purposes of such parts of Behring's straits, of the North Pacific Ocean and of the China Sea as are frequented by American whaleships and by trading vessels in their routes between the United States and China.

The American government was trying to open the Orient, and especially Japan, to trade, and there was a need to test the treaty with Japan that Perry was expected to negotiate. In addition, the expedition was to chart the trans-Pacific routes to China. Whaling had become of considerable importance to the American economy at this time, and the uncharted islands of the Japan archipelago and farther north were a hazard to whaling ships.

Eager to acquire more information about the Pacific Ocean, Matthew Fontaine Maury, in charge of the Depot of Charts and Instruments (see page 152), undoubtedly had much to do with the decision to send out the expedition.

The expedition, the government explained to Cadwalader Ringgold, appointed to command it, was "not for conquest but discovery. Its objects are all peaceful, they are to extend the empire of commerce and of science; to diminish the hazards of the ocean."

Five ships formed the expedition, which left the United States in mid-1853. The flagship was *Vincennes,* the same as that of the Wilkes expedition fifteen years before (see page 136). Another was *Porpoise,* which had also been on the Wilkes expedition, under Ringgold. *Fenimore Cooper* was a smaller ship, intended as a tender. Only one of the ships, *John Hancock,* was a steamer.

Before the ships reached Hong Kong, Ringgold became ill and command devolved onto Lieutenant John Rodgers, who also took over command of *Vincennes.*

In September 1854 *Hancock* took American representatives to China to ask for revisions to treaties to open Chinese ports made in 1842–44. The

Map 200.
Straits of Tsugar Japan, 1855. This is the manuscript chart reduced for engraving. Tsugaru Strait is between Honshu and Hokkaido.

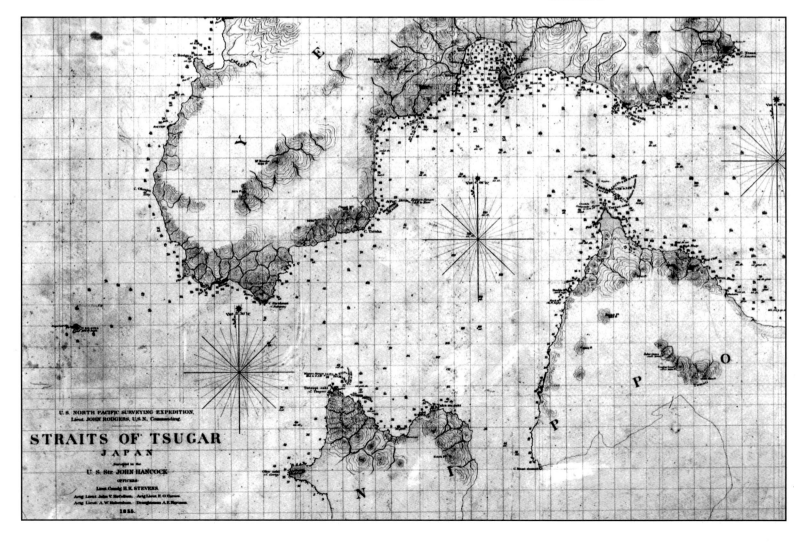

revisions were refused, but the opportunity was taken to sound around the mouths of several rivers, including the Yellow River and the Yangtze, and a survey was made in the Gulf of Chihli.

Meanwhile *Vincennes* and *Porpoise* had been surveying in the area south of Japan; *Porpoise* was lost, probably in a typhoon. Rodgers continued to chart islands between Okinawa (which they called Liu Ch'iu) and the Bay of Kagoshima, at the southern tip of the southernmost large Japanese island of Kyushu.

In 1855, the major surveying

Map 201 (top left).
Mouth of the Teen-Tsin-Ho (Yangtze-Kiang), surveyed by *John Hancock* and *Fenimore Cooper* in October 1854.

Map 202 (below).
Reconnoissance of the East Coast of Nippon, Empire of Japan, From Simoda to Hakodati By the launch of the United States Ship Vincennes, under the command of Lieutenant John M. Brooke, U.S.N., assisted by Edward M. Kern, Artist, and Richard Berry, Sailmaker. May 29th to June 17th 1855. Original Working Sheet. This is the map produced by Brooke from his epic voyage up the east coast of Japan in a small boat, *Vincennes Junior*.

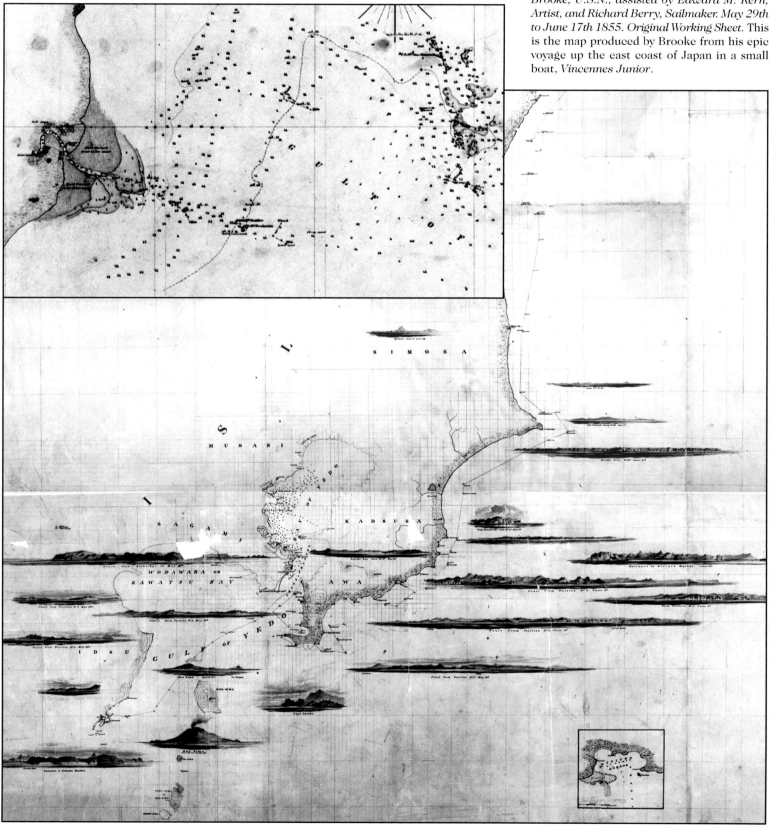

work began on the coasts of Japan. *Hancock* and *Vincennes* sailed north along the Ryukyu Islands and entered the new treaty port of Shimoda in May. Despite Japanese objections the two ships also visited the nearby port of Heda, charting into Suruga Bay.

At this time *Fenimore Cooper* surveyed parts of Kyushu and small islands, including the Goto Islands at the extreme western tip of Japan. Continuing northwards through the Korea Strait between Korea and Japan, *Cooper* surveyed the northwestern coast of Honshu and offshore islands such as the Oki Islands, meeting up with *Vincennes* and *Hancock* again at Hakodate, in Tsugaru Strait.

The southeastern coast of Honshu is often shrouded in fog, making it too hazardous to survey inshore with large ships, so men in one of *Vincennes'* boats, called *Vincennes Junior,* were ordered to survey the coast in detail from Shimoda to Hakodate. This somewhat epic voyage in an open boat, with fifteen men aboard, encountered some heavy weather in its 720-km or 450-mile survey. The boat was commanded by Lieutenant John M. Brooke, also the expedition's astronomer, who had two years before invented a new sounding apparatus that detached a weight used to sink a sounding line when it reached the seabed, allowing a relatively light line to be used to haul up the sampling tube. Now he put his sounding device to good work. This device would also be used to haul up seabed samples from 3,500 fathoms in the Japan Trench.

From Hakodate *Vincennes* surveyed north along the Kuril Islands to Petropavlovsk and the coast of Siberia to Bering Strait, and even farther, into the Arctic Ocean. Deep-sea

soundings were made off the Aleutian Islands before the ship returned to San Francisco, which it reached on 13 October 1855.

Fenimore Cooper had arrived two days before. They had surveyed in the Aleutians and searched for places where coal might be found. Coal had been found by the Russians at vari-

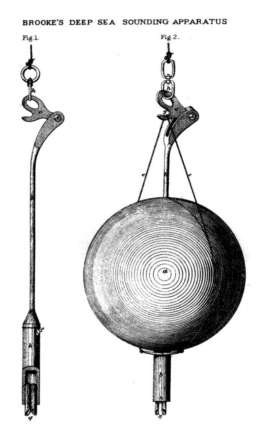

BROOKE'S DEEP SEA SOUNDING APPARATUS

Fig. 1. Fig. 2.

ous places on the Alaska coast, notably in Cook Inlet, information which was given to the ship's captain William Gibson by the Russian-American Company governor at New Archangel'sk (Sitka), which they had also visited.

John Hancock charted Tsugaru Strait, between Honshu and Hokkaido, surveyed the northern part of Honshu, and then proceeded up the

west coast of Hokkaido, charting La Pérouse Strait between Hokkaido and Sakhalin. Then the western coast of Sakhalin was surveyed, the approaches to the Amur River, the northern coast of the Sea of Okhotsk, and the western coast of Kamchatka. Here a search was made for coal to supply steamers, but only a small amount of inferior coal was found.

In September, surveying was finished and *Hancock* also made for San Francisco, arriving there on 19 October 1855.

Important information about the Great Circle route between the newly acquired west coast American ports (California was ceded to the United States in 1848) and Asia had been gained, at least, in addition to the surveys and the knowledge of the lack of coal sources.

In December 1855, Rodgers received orders to transfer the men and stores of *Fenimore Cooper* to *Vincennes* and return to the Atlantic coast. He was authorized to return by "any route as [he] may deem advisable," and in his letter of reply to the Secretary of the Navy is a very interesting observation.

An island has been reported to lie in Latitude 40° 40´ N, and in about Longitude 150° 50´ West. The report wears an appearance of authenticity. Should it accidentally contain a harbor, its examination before it has been landed upon or taken possession of may have political importance. In any case it is of consequence to know of its position. The probability is that the Island has no harbor; it is possible that it has a fine one. We shall look for it.

Look for it they may have; unfortunately for them not only did the island have no harbor, but the harbor had no island!

Although the work of the Perry expedition was published in three large volumes, that of the U.S. North Pacific Exploring Expedition was never published; it was in preparation when the American Civil War intervened. Disagreements between John Rodgers and Cadwalader Ringgold

We were rapidly clearing the land when a sea was observed to break about two points on our weather bow, a column of white foam high in the air. The helm put down, the sails lowered and the main quickly reefed to weather it, we were relieved in seeing the jet of a spouting whale in the hollow of the sea: it was upon his back that the sea had broken and not upon a rock.

– John Brooke, from his report to Commander John Rodgers on his small boat surveying between Shimoda and Hakodate, 22 June 1855

may have also contributed to delays; Rodgers thought Ringgold wanted to usurp his work.

John Brooke was involved in another foray into the North Pacific, however. The expedition had been intended to also survey proposed steamship routes from California to China, and this had not been done. Thus *Fenimore Cooper* was sent from San Francisco with Brooke in command in 1858 to chart this route. The purpose was to verify the existence or otherwise of reported reefs and shoals on the routes normally taken by steamers. Three months were spent surveying and correcting charts of islands and reefs northwest of Hawaii, and much deep-sea sounding was done using Brooke's invention. After surveying and sounding to Hawaii and to Hong Kong, a visit was made to Yokohama, Japan, in August 1859; ten days later *Fenimore Cooper* was destroyed in a typhoon. Her crew, instruments, and records were all saved, however. In February 1860 Brooke returned to the United States as a naval advisor on the *Kanrin Maru*, the first Japanese steamer to cross the Pacific Ocean.

The U.S. North Pacific Exploring Expedition was also active in collecting natural history specimens. A total of 5,211 species of vertebrates, insects, crustacea, annelids, molluscs, and radiates were collected, totalling over 12,000 specimens. When the botanical specimens were transferred to the Smithsonian Institution near the end of the nineteenth century, they took up more than 2.8 m³ or 100 cubic feet in their original packages.

Sir!

The Government of the United States sent five vessels, of which this is the chief, to examine the dangers of the Ocean. We have been round more than half the Globe. We have at last arrived at one of the Japanese ports. If the Islands of Japan with the rocks and shoals which surround them, were out of the paths which our vessels must follow across the Ocean, the world could say nothing, but as these dangers remain in the road of ships, we must examine them, and tell our countrymen where they lie. Otherwise our vessels would be wrecked, and many valuable lives might be lost.

– Letter addressed to "The Honourable Secretary of State for Foreign Affairs, Kingdom of Japan, by Commander John Rodgers, on board *Vincennes*, Kago Sima Bay, January 4th 1855," from a copy sent to the Secretary of the Navy. Rodgers said, in his covering letter, "It did not appear necessary that such an officer exist"; he was simply trying to persuade the Japanese government of his peaceful intentions.

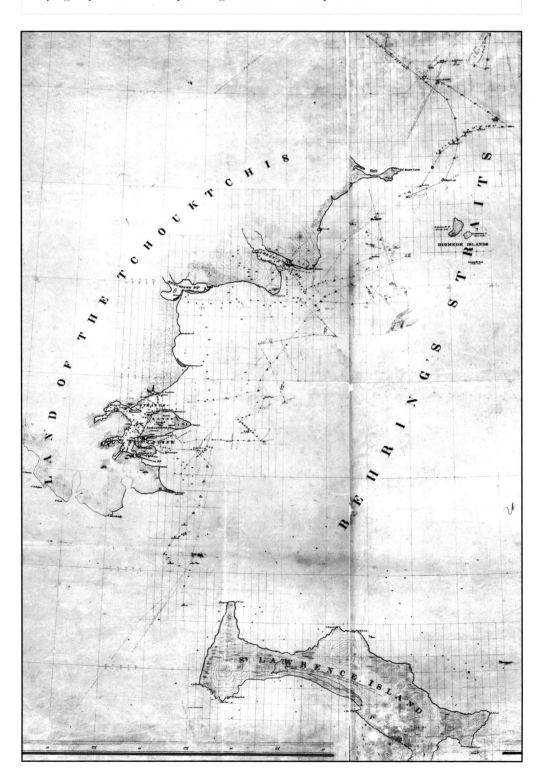

Map 203.
The Asiatic Coast of Behring's Straits. Surveyed in the U.S. Ship Vincennes July and August 1855. St. Lawrence Island is at the bottom.

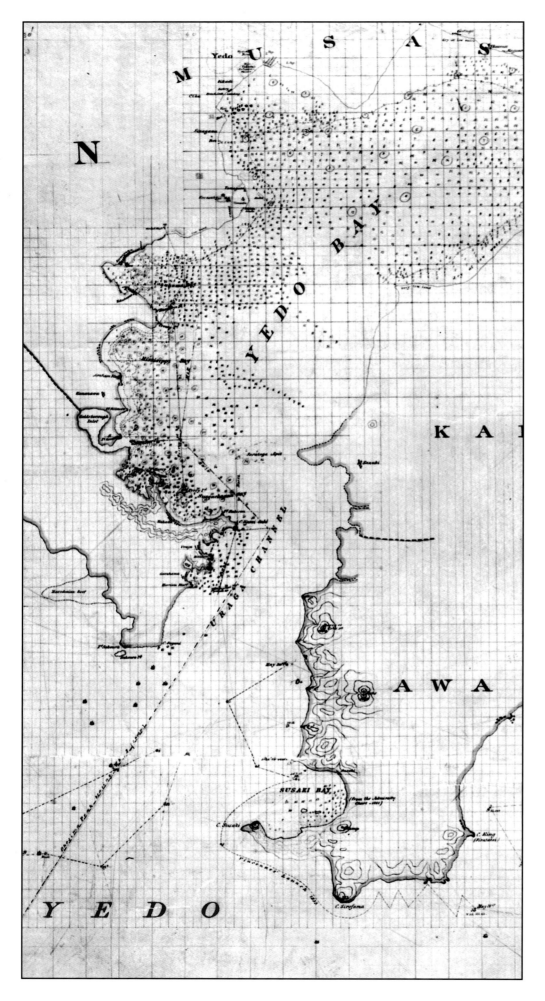

Map 204 (left).
Gulf of Yedo [Tokyo Bay] *and Approaches.*
A joint surveying effort by *Vincennes* and
John Hancock, May 1855, with additions by
John M. Brooke in *Fenimore Cooper,* 1859.

Map 205
S.W. Part of Japan from the Surveys of the Expedition in 1854–55 with additions by Lieut. Comdg. John M. Brooke, U.S. Schr. F. Cooper, 1859, and from Dutch, English and Russian Authorities.
A smaller-scale map of the whole of southern Japan, nevertheless with a lot of detail. It is made up of three large sheets.

Matthew Fontaine Maury's Wind and Current Charts

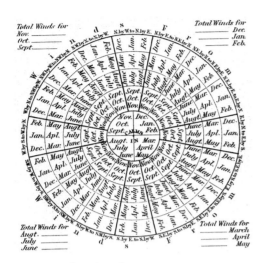

Maury's *Pilot Chart* key
(see Map 208, overleaf).

Matthew Fontaine Maury is widely regarded as being the father of modern ocean meteorology, if not oceanography as a whole.

After circumnavigating the globe between 1826 and 1830 as a midshipman in the U.S. Navy, Maury sailed around the Pacific Ocean extensively in the 1830s, and the information he gathered led to the publication in 1836 of a definitive book entitled *A New Theoretical and Practical Treatise on Navigation.*

In 1842 Maury was appointed Superintendent of the U.S. Navy Depot of Charts and Instruments (later the Hydrographic Office). Here he saw the potential in the mass of ships' logs and similar records gathered by ships crossing the world's oceans. The challenge was to gather the right information in a way it could be analyzed and used. He was responsible for a navy circular issued in late 1842 that invited ship owners and captains to send to the U.S. Bureau of Ordnance and Hydrography ten categories of hydrographical information that they might collect while at sea. Maury set copyists to work extracting the information these records contained. In the Pacific, information provided by whaling ships was valuable, because they tended to go where regular trading ships did not.

By 1847 Maury had enough information to begin to produce the *Wind and Current Charts* for which he is best known. They were an instant success; in a world of sailing vessels they were invaluable in reducing the time taken to sail from one point to another.

Simply knowing the locations of winds and currents enabled ships to sail an optimal route to take advantage of the winds or currents or both. This was particularly valuable for ships with time-sensitive cargoes, such as the clippers, which were built for speed. Even for the new-fangled steamships beginning to make their appearance on the world's oceans, the knowledge of currents made a big difference both in time saved and the amount of coal that had to be burned.

Maury's charts were soon in high demand. Five thousand were distributed, but they could not be bought except at the price of cooperation, which of course meant that more and more information flooded in to Maury. The U.S. Navy offered free charts to all who sent in data. A proud Maury was later to comment, "Never before was such a corps of observers known."

A pamphlet was prepared that told mariners not only how to use the charts but how to make observations at sea and how to record them. Maury knew that standardizing the format in which data was collected would increase the utility of the information.

The North Pacific Ocean chart was completed and issued in 1849.

In 1849 Maury began another method of plotting currents, one still in use by oceanographers today. He enlisted seamen on cooperating ships to mark their position and date on a piece of paper, and then seal it in a bottle and throw it overboard. Finders were asked to record the date and location the bottle was found, and send the information to Maury. Amazingly, the system worked, and

yet more information came to Maury. "In the absence of other information as to currents, that afforded by these mute little navigators is of great value," wrote Maury in 1855.

Maury then produced his so-called *Whale Charts,* which provided information on breeding habits, migrations, and the places where whales were most likely to be found from one season to the next. Naturally enough they proved a big success with the American whaling fleet, although Maury ran into some criticism from those who thought science should not assist commerce. But he was happy with his role as a practical scientist and laughed off the critics.

Also in 1849, Congress began to authorize the use of navy vessels for Maury's oceanographic investigations, a move prompted by the California gold rush, which meant that hordes of ships were in a big rush to get to California. The territorial designs of the American government on that region no doubt assisted Maury here. At the same time, Maury was advocating a railway across the

Map 206.
Maury's *Wind and Current Chart* for the middle of the North Pacific Ocean, 1849. The east coast of Japan's principal island, Honshu, is at top left, and the chart reaches eastwards to 170° E and south to the equator. The concentration of tracks in the trade winds is very apparent. Maury's charts were almost pictorial. In his words:

The winds are denoted by small brushes, the head of the brush pointing to the direction from whence the winds blow, the length of the brush showing the comparative force.
Currents are denoted by arrows, the length of the arrow being proportionate to the strength of the current: the figures beside the arrows show the number of knots.
The Roman numerals denote the degree of Magnetic Variation as recorded by the vessel near whose track they are placed.
The figures with a line drawn under them thus 80 show the temperature of the water.
The name of the ship which has supplied the route and the year of the voyage is recorded.

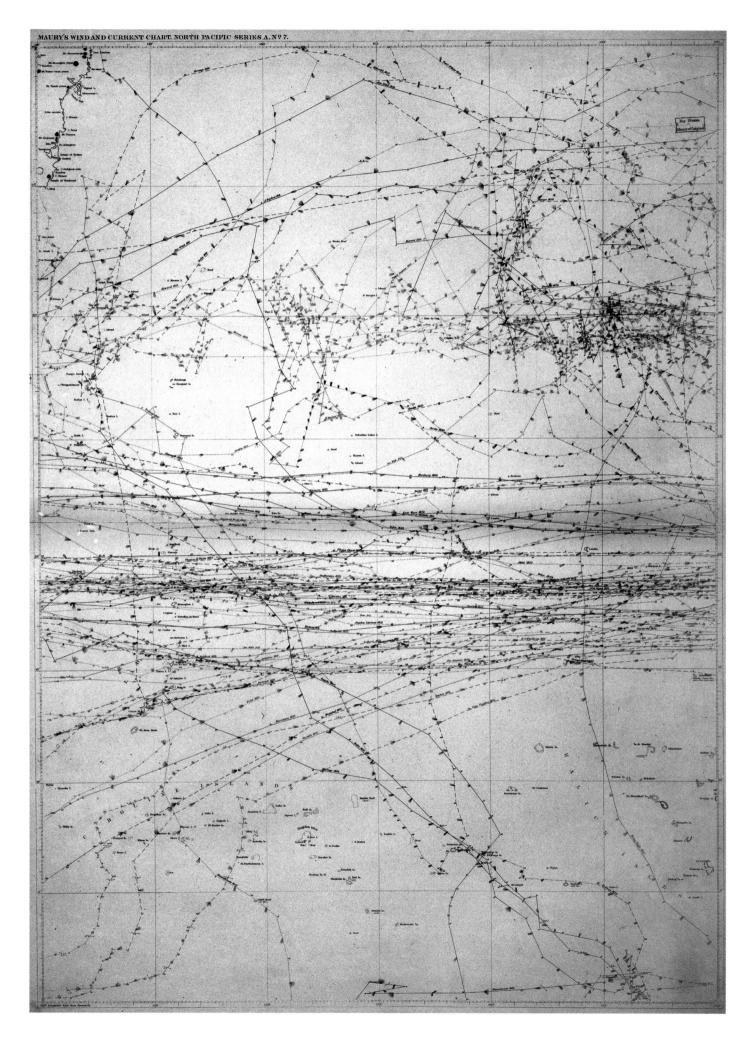

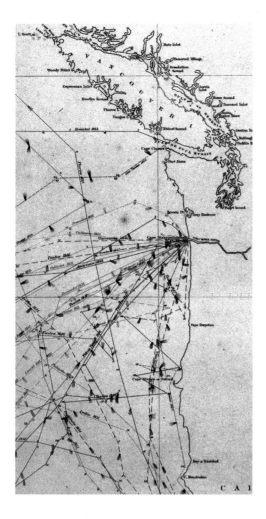

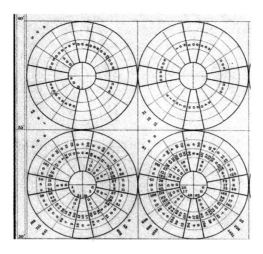

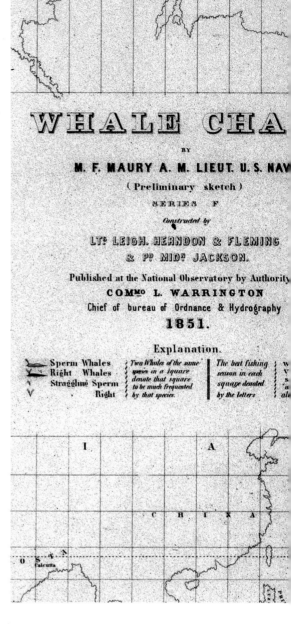

Map 207 (left).
Another of Maury's *Wind and Current Charts*, for the area off the Northwest Coast of North America. The concentration of tracks to and from the mouth of the Columbia River is distinct.

Map 208 (above).
Not looking like a map at all, Maury's 1851 *Pilot Chart* was a plotting of what were essentially glorified wind roses. A key is shown on page 152. This portion of the map of the North Pacific is for the area between 50° and 60° N and 155° and 165° W, for four 5° quadrants.

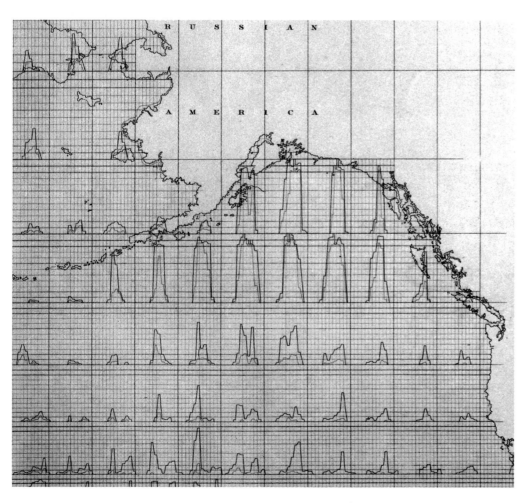

Map 209 (left).
Maury's *Whale Chart*, 1852. The data graphed refers to each square on the map. The top graph shows the number of days for which whales were searched, and the graphs below show the number of days when whales were sighted. A lot of information, all gathered from whaling ship logbooks, but a map that is not easy to interpret.

Map 210 (above).
A more pictorial version of Maury's *Whale Chart*, produced the year before, showing the distribution of sperm (red area) and right whales (green and blue), again by square. The map is printed but hand colored. Two whales per square indicates high frequency; a letter denotes season (see key).

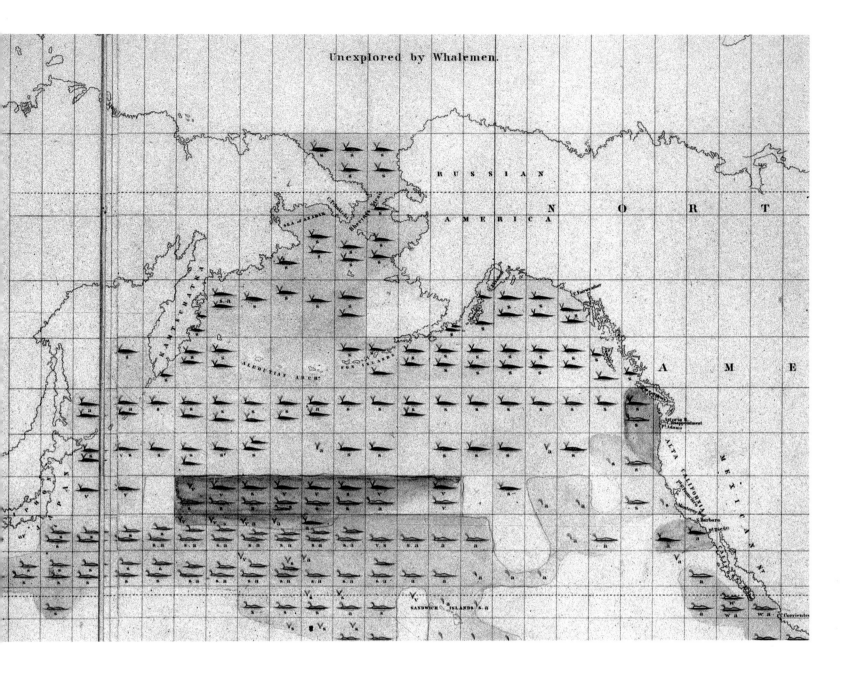

Isthmus of Panama and supported calls being made for the building of a canal.

By 1851, Maury's work had shortened the passage from New York to San Francisco by forty to forty-four days. The average time for ships *not* using the *Wind and Current Charts* was 187½ days, as compared to only 144½ days for those that did. In 1850 one ship sailed the 24 000 km or 15,000 miles in only ninety-seven days.

Also in 1851, Maury published the first edition – seven more would follow – of a voluminous work entitled *Explanations and Sailing Directions to Accompany the Wind and Current Charts,* which was distributed to the seamen who had helped compile his data.

In 1852 Maury played a major role in persuading the American government to send out the North Pacific Exploring Expedition (see page 146) and provided that expedition with charts and data to assist them.

In 1853 Maury's reputation was further enhanced by his correct prediction of the location to which a ship, disabled in a hurricane, would drift, enabling rescuers to find her.

The amount of money shipowners saved by following Maury's charts continued to mount; marine insurers also benefited, the latter presenting Maury with a handsome silver service and a check for $5,000 in 1853.

In 1854 Maury made another oceanographic "first"; he published a contour map of the North Atlantic

from Yucatan to the Cape Verde islands, using, as was his style, soundings from many ships. Though necessarily generalized, with data being available for only 200 points, and with contours only every 1,000 fathoms, it was the first contour bathymetric map to be drawn of an entire ocean basin. Not surprisingly, the map immediately attracted the attention of telegraph companies planning to lay cable across the Atlantic Ocean.

Utilizing the work on his *Wind and Current Charts,* in 1855 Maury published his *Physical Geography of the Sea,* a pioneering attempt to formulate a general theory of the circulation of the atmosphere. Although not accepted by many scientists, the book was immensely popular. It went

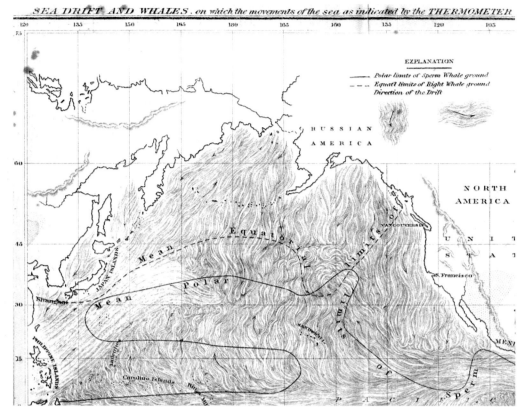

Map 211.
North Pacific Ocean part of Maury's map of *Sea Drift and Whales* from his *Physical Geography of the Sea*, published in 1855.

Map 212 (below).
North Pacific part of Maury's map of *Winds and Routes*, also from his 1855 book. As published, these maps were world maps, with much condensed information from his larger charts, which were issued in sections.

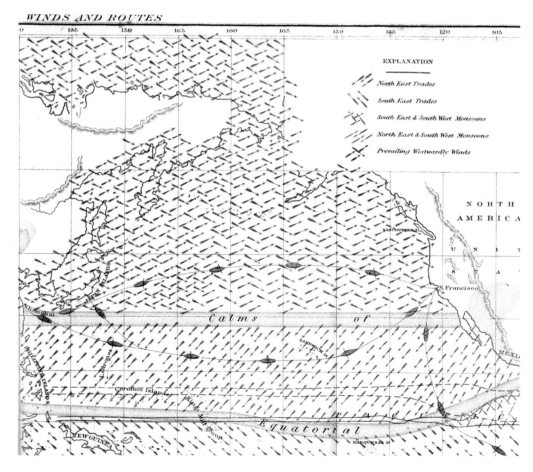

through eight editions at the time, and has been reprinted since.

Set out in the point-by-point deterministic format so common in the nineteenth century, Maury's text nevertheless provided an immense amount of information about the world's oceans for the first time. About the Pacific Maury wrote:

The currents of the Pacific are broad and sluggish, those of the Atlantic swift and contracted . . . [The Pacific] is a very much wider sea [than the Atlantic] and its Gulf Stream not so warm, nor so sharp, nor so rapid; therefore the broad Pacific does not, on the whole, present the elements of atmospherical disturbance in that compactness which is so striking in the narrow North Atlantic.

Under a heading "Average Depth of the North Pacific" he calculated, from tsunamis from an earthquake in Japan in 1854, the depth of the ocean over which the waves had traveled, concluding that

the average depth of the North Pacific between Japan and California, is, by the path of the San Francisco wave, 2149 fathoms, by the San Diego, 2034 (say 2½ miles).

Long after Maury's death in 1873, U. S. navigational charts bore the inscription

Founded upon the researches made in the early part of the nineteenth century by Matthew Fontaine Maury.

It was a fitting and long-lasting epitaph for a true oceanographic pioneer.

Becher's Navigation of the Pacific Ocean

Alexander Becher was a British Royal Navy captain working in the Admiralty Hydrographic Office. In 1860 he published a book entitled *Navigation of the Pacific Ocean with an Account of the Winds, Weather, and Currents Found Therein Throughout the Year.* Its purpose was stated in rhyme:

That seamen may with steam or sail
Know where to meet the favoring gale;
May take instruction from the skies,
And find the path where swiftness lies.

The book was clearly popular with Pacific navigators, going through several editions into the 1880s.

Essentially a generalized sailing directions manual, Becher's book compiled much of the known infor-mation into one easy-to-access source for practical use.

But there were still parts of the Pacific with insufficient information. "The Frigid Zone of the North Pacific Ocean has been little visited and the remarks consequently are few," wrote Becher. "Northward of 60° N the breadth of the ocean diminishes rapidly and it terminates in a basin of small extent. It is only during the fine season that these latitudes have been explored."

The striking thing about Becher's book to modern eyes is that although it is the essential authority of the late nineteenth century, much of the text is anecdotal, describing one captain or another's experiences in one place or another. It was not until Matthew Maury began the process of continuous surveying of the ocean (see page 152) that information began to be more comprehensive and based on much more available data.

Map 213.
The general map of winds and currents in the Pacific Ocean, from Becher's book. There are a number of fictitious islands shown on this map.

Becher's book included a table of the "comparative mean rates of the currents in twenty-four hours":

North Equatorial Current	*30 miles*
Counter Equatorial Current	*15 miles*
Monsoon Current of the Carolines	*3 miles*
Japan Current	*31 miles*
Cold Current of the American and Californian Coast	*16 miles*
Kamtschatka Current	*8 miles*
Behring Current	*14 miles*

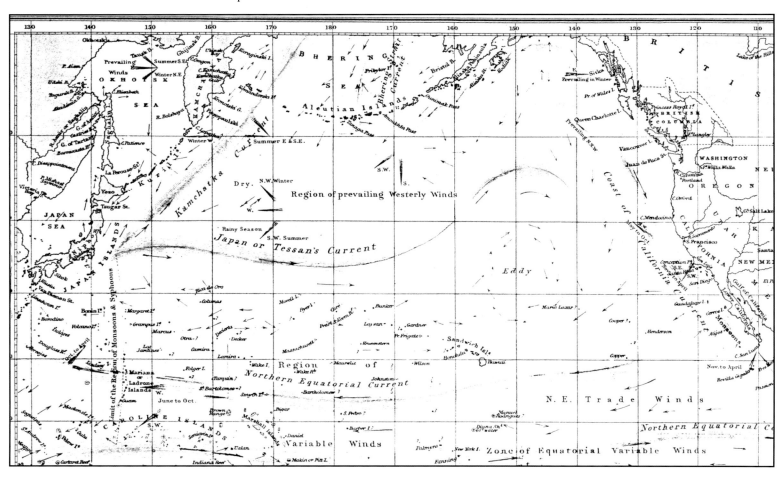

British Admiralty Hydrographic Surveying

British Admiralty charts have been used the world over for 175 years, and not just by British seamen; they have a deserved reputation for accuracy. These charts have been for sale to the merchant fleets of the world since 1823.

Some of the early charts were made by Frederick Beechey, who in his ship *Blossom* in 1825–28 completed a voyage of 117,000 km or 73,000 miles, principally in the Pacific Ocean, on his way to wait for the Franklin and Parry Arctic expeditions, which were expected to find their way to the coast north of Bering Strait. Beechey made surveys of most places he visited, including Avatcha Bay (Petropavlovsk Harbor) in Kamchatka, shown on the facing page.

In 1829, perhaps the most famous British hydrographer took over as Hydrographer of the Navy. He was Francis Beaufort, inventor of the Beaufort wind scale, and he oversaw the surveying efforts until 1855.

During his tenure, surveys were made all over the world, and there was a considerable increase in the number of charts available.

In the Pacific, Richard Collinson was surveying off the coast of China, and later, during a war with China that resulted in the British acquisition of Hong Kong, Collinson and fellow hydrographic surveyor Henry Kellett were able to pilot a British naval squadron 320 km or 200 miles up the uncharted Yangtze-Kiang River.

After this war, the ports of China, reluctantly opened to trade, were surveyed for the British Admiralty by William Bate.

Under Beaufort, there was increased precision in reproducing survey information. Every chart was scrutinized and checked by him before final printing and publication, improving the reliability of the charts.

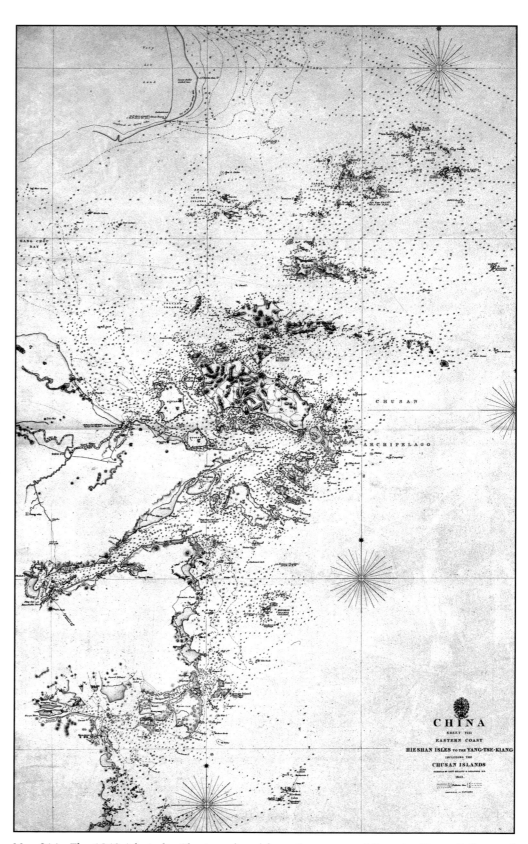

Map 214. The 1843 Admiralty Chart produced from the surveys of Captains Henry Kellett and Richard Collinson on the coast of China, including the mouth of the Yangtze-Kiang River (at top). The chart demonstrates with its incredible detail the amount of work that went into surveying an intricate coast such as this. The incongruity of names such as "Nimrod Sound" that the British bestowed on far-flung capes and bays did not seem to occur to them; they were British, and the British navy ruled the world!

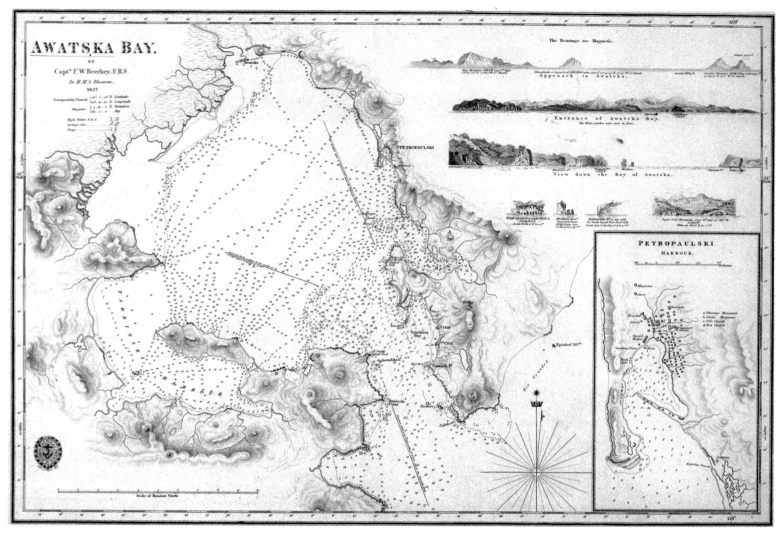

Map 215.
Early British Hydrographic Office chart, made by Frederick Beechey in 1827. This is Avatcha Bay ("Awatska Bay") or Avachinskaya Guba, the harbor of Petropavlovsk, in Kamchatka. Compare it with others made earlier by Vitus Bering (of the inner harbor only, page 69), Edward Riou in 1779 (page 99), and Vasillii Lovtsov in 1782 (page 101).

Map 216.
A map of the Point Roberts area of the Strait of Georgia, surveyed for a British Admiralty Chart in 1858 by Captain George Henry Richards. It is interesting to note that this British survey was being carried out at the same time as the American survey for the map on page 162 (Map 218), which is slightly east of the area surveyed here. This is perhaps not surprising, since both countries were surveying their new mutual boundary at this time.

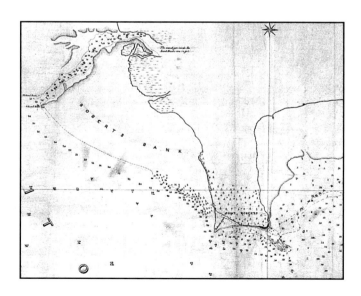

Coastal Surveys of the United States

The United States Coast Survey was created in 1807 primarily to assist in the navigation of the nation's merchant shipping.

In 1878 the organization's name was changed to the United States Coast and Geodetic Survey, responsible to this day for the production of navigational charts.

The United States just having acquired a west coast, Alexander Bache, the Coast Survey's first superintendent, initiated surveys of the Pacific coast in 1848 and 1849. William McArthur and George Davidson were responsible for beginning a proper triangulation of the coast. A chart of Point Pinos harbor was completed in 1851 and one of the rest of Monterey Bay in the following year. In 1851 the first map of the entire coast, at least from Monterey to the Columbia River, was produced. Part of this map is shown in Map 219, overleaf.

In 1853 accurate fixing of positions at close intervals along the coast was completed from San Diego to the Columbia, and surveys of all the main harbors were begun, this being of critical importance due to the relative dearth of proper harbors on the west coast. Lieutenants James Alden and George Davidson were responsible for much of this work.

In 1853 and 1854, enough surveying had been carried out to enable the production of a larger-scale reconnaissance map of the entire coast, issued in three sheets complete with coastal views. Half of one of the sheets is shown here (Map 217, above).

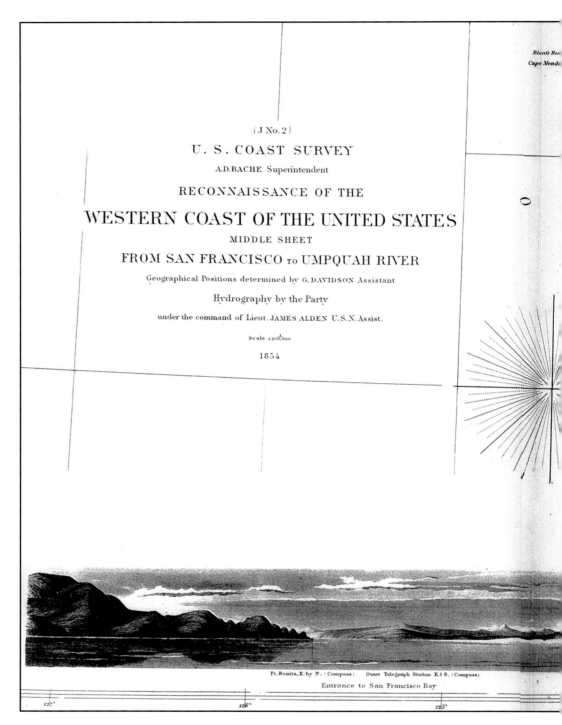

Permanent self-registering tide gauges were installed in 1854 at three places on the coast – Astoria, at the mouth of the Columbia; San Francisco; and San Diego. These revealed the large diurnal inequality in the tides characteristic of the west coast of North America.

Map 217.
A sheet of the *Reconnaissance of the Western Coast of the United States,* published in 1854, showing the coast from San Francisco to the Umquah River in southern Oregon. Complete with twelve engraved views, designed to aid mariners in recognizing where they were, the map was surveyed by James Alden. The bottom half only is shown here. Below, at right, is Cape Arago, from the same map.

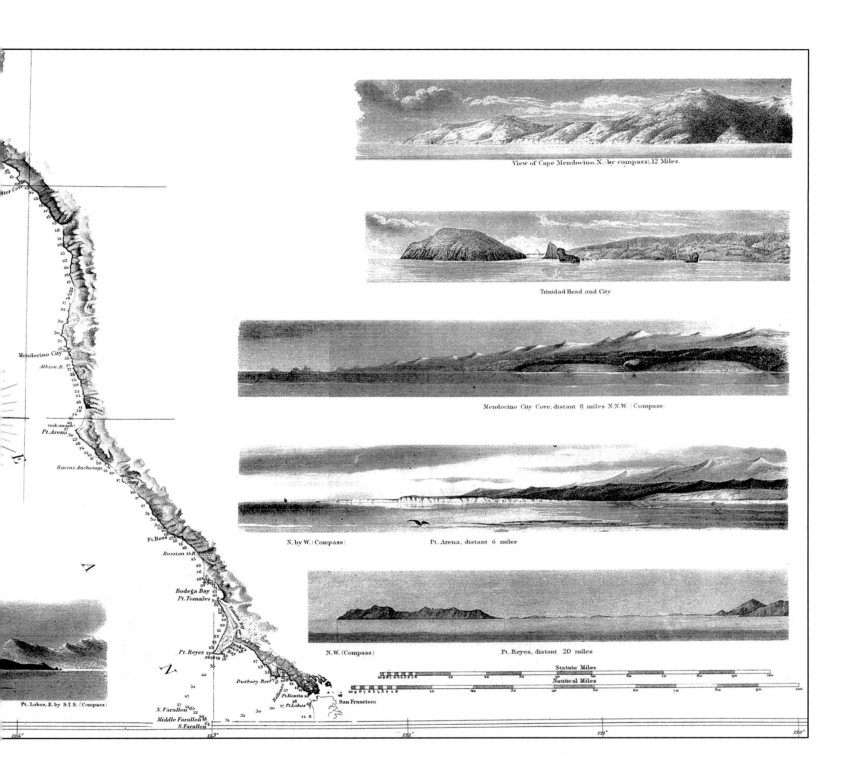

View of Cape Mendocino, N. (by compass), 12 Miles.

Trinidad Head and City

Mendocino City Cove, distant 8 miles N.N.W. (Compass)

N. by W. (Compass)   Pt. Arena, distant 6 miles

N.W. (Compass)   Pt. Reyes, distant 20 miles

Pt. Lobos, E. by S.? S. (Compass)

Statute Miles

Nautical Miles

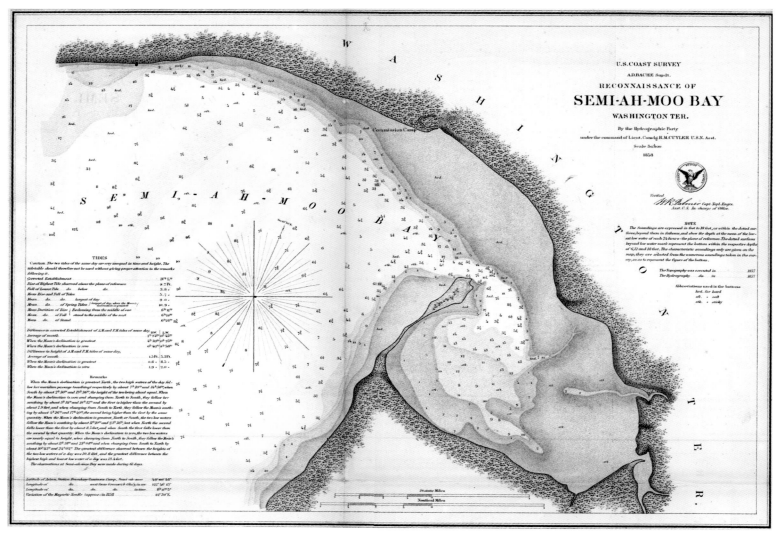

U.S. COAST SURVEY
A.D.BACHE Supdt.
RECONNAISSANCE OF
SEMI-AH-MOO BAY
WASHINGTON TER.
By the Hydrographic Party
under the command of Lieut. Comdg. R.M.CUYLER U.S.N. Asst.
Scale 3 inch to a
1858

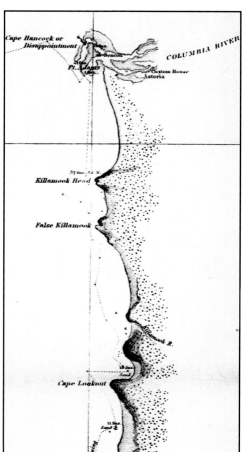

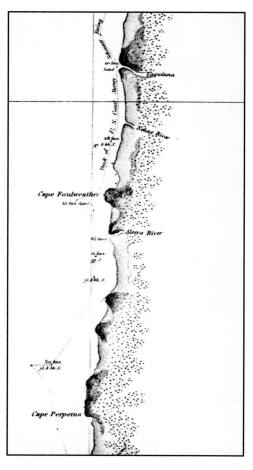

Map 218.
Surveying of harbors that could be used by shipping was a particular concern of the Coast Survey. This is a U.S. Coast Survey map of Semi-ah-moo Bay, Washington Territory, 1858, today's Drayton Harbor, Blaine, Washington State. The surveyed area actually crosses the 49th parallel, where the boundary between American and British territory had been drawn in 1846. You would never know it looking at this map, however. The "Commission Camp" is that of the Boundary Commission, which began surveying the boundary in 1858. Naturally, there is much more detail in the water area, with many detailed soundings.

Map 219.
These sections of an early U.S. Coast Survey map were produced by W. P. McArthur and W. A. Bartlett in 1851, as part of a three-sheet summary or reconnaissance map of the west coast of the United States from Monterey to the Columbia River. Shown here in two sections is the Columbia River to Cape Perpetua, on the Oregon coast.

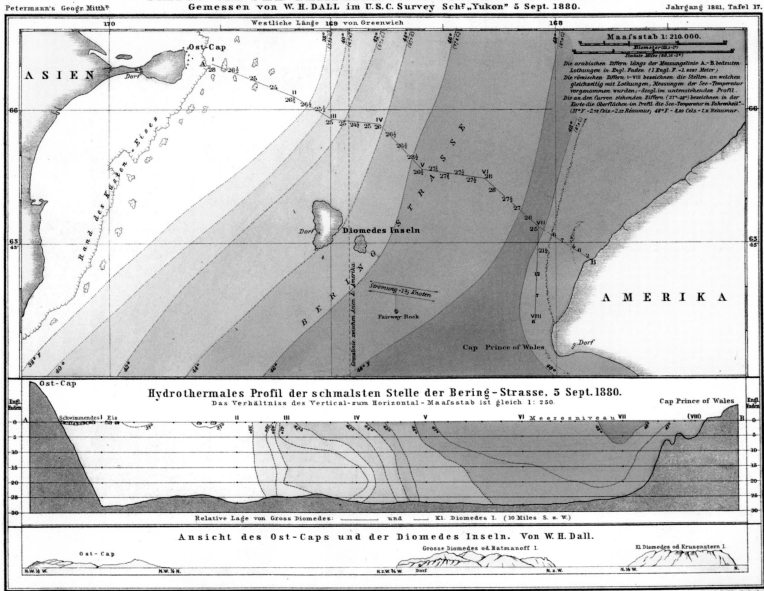

Map 220.

This map is a German edition of a hydrographic survey carried out by William Dall of the United States Coast Survey in the schooner *Yukon* in September 1880. It shows a depth profile across Bering Strait at its narrowest point, between East Cape and Cape Prince of Wales, and water temperatures with depth. The warmest and most ice-free channel is that nearest to the American shore. Lower water temperatures towards Siberia are manifested on the surface by pack ice.

Map 221.

Cortez Bank On the Western Coast of the United States By the Hydrographic Party under the command of Lieut. James Alden Assistant U.S.C.S. 1853. This is part of a U.S. Coast Survey map of 1853, showing the sounding and charting of Cortez Bank, about 200 km or 125 miles off the coast of southern California. This bank was in the path of steamers from Panama northwards. The shallowest water on the bank was 9 fathoms.

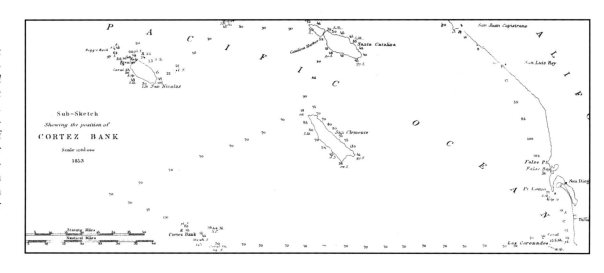

Tuscarora Discovers the Deeps

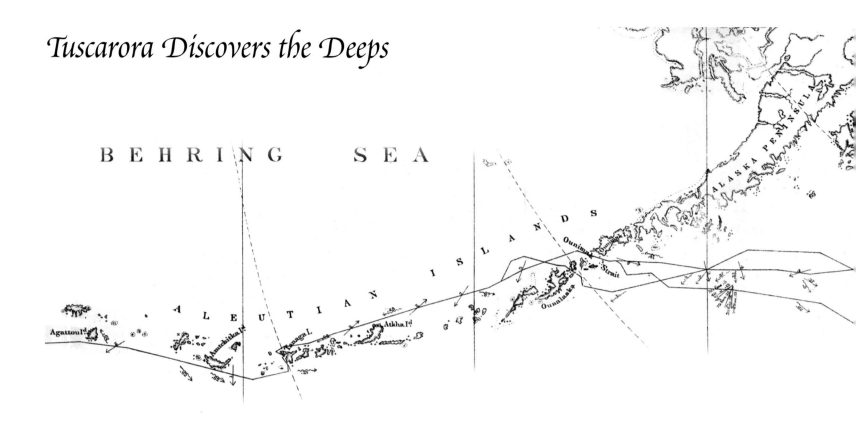

The success of a new submarine telegraph cable across the Atlantic in 1866 spurred the idea that a similar cable could be laid across the Pacific. The U.S. Congress passed a special resolution allowing the use of naval vessels for survey work.

In 1873 George Belknap was given command of the U.S. steamer *Tuscarora* with instructions to survey a route from America to the Far East.

New sounding equipment was installed, and in particular a sounding machine that used piano wire rather than much more springy and bulky hemp rope. The use of piano wire had been incorporated into a sounding machine the year before by a British scientist, William Thomson. After a series of shake-down trials in 1873, Belknap began the survey in January 1874, which was to cover a north and south Great Circle route to Japan, a plan later abandoned as impractical due to water depths.

One hundred and thirty-five soundings later, they arrived in Yokohama. On 8 June they began the return survey, but after eighteen soundings they found the water too deep, having determined that it was over 4,600 fathoms (8 400 km or 27,600 ft) deep. This was not going

THE BROOKE-SAND'S SOUNDING APPARATUS AS FIRST MODIFIED BY COMDR. BELKNAP.

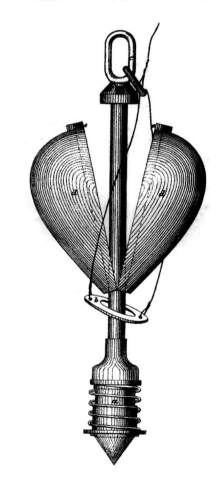

to be a possible route for any submarine cable. They had discovered the Japan Trench, one of the great ocean deeps.

In an attempt to avoid this trench, Belknap decided to try his luck on a more northerly route following islands, where he thought there was less likelihood of encountering such tremendous depths. Accordingly, a survey was begun from Hakodate on 30 June via the Kurils to the Aleutians, Tanaga Island in the Andreanof Group, then to Unalaska, and thence to Cape Flattery. But in the process Belknap, trying hard to avoid ocean deeps, discovered yet another, the Aleutian Trench.

Belknap recorded that they had to run a line of soundings to the northwards and to the southwards of the first line of soundings "to ascertain how a deep hole of 3,359 fathoms [6 150 m or 20,150 feet] might be avoided"; this was the Aleutian Trench.

(left and far right)
Sounding equipment used aboard *Tuscarora*.

(right)
Commander Belknap provided this rather daunting list of the equipment carried by *Tuscarora*.

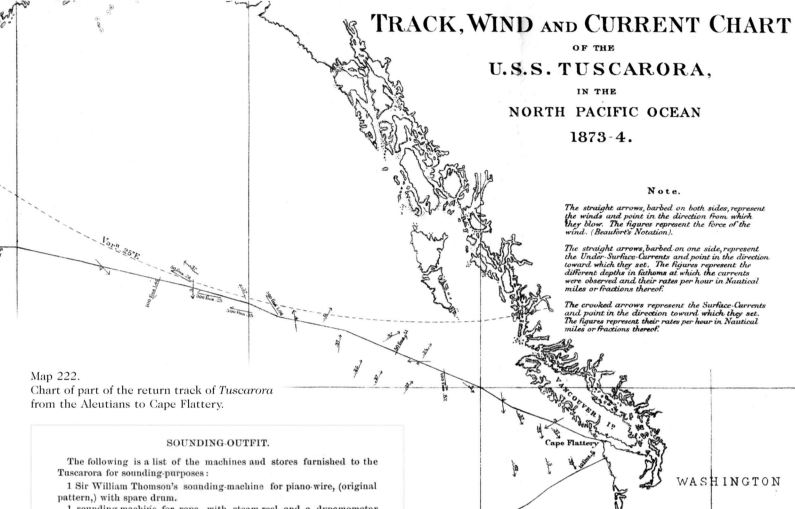

TRACK, WIND AND CURRENT CHART
OF THE
U.S.S. TUSCARORA,
IN THE
NORTH PACIFIC OCEAN
1873-4.

Note.

The straight arrows, barbed on both sides, represent the winds and point in the direction from which they blow. The figures represent the force of the wind. (Beaufort's Notation).

The straight arrows, barbed on one side, represent the Under-Surface-Currents and point in the direction toward which they set. The figures represent the different depths in fathoms at which the currents were observed and their rates per hour in Nautical miles or fractions thereof.

The crooked arrows represent the Surface-Currents and point in the direction toward which they set. The figures represent their rates per hour in Nautical miles or fractions thereof.

WASHINGTON

Map 222.
Chart of part of the return track of *Tuscarora* from the Aleutians to Cape Flattery.

SOUNDING-OUTFIT.

The following is a list of the machines and stores furnished to the Tuscarora for sounding-purposes:

1 Sir William Thomson's sounding-machine for piano-wire, (original pattern,) with spare drum.

1 sounding-machine for rope, with steam-reel, and a dynamometer designed by Passed Assistant Engineer T. W. Rae, (originally fitted for the Juniata.)

10 Brooke's sounding-rods.
6 Brooke's sounding-rods, (long.)
15 Brooke's modified attachment and sinkers.
210 slings for Brooke's sounding-apparatus.
11 Sands' cups for sounding-purposes.
1 spare spring for sounding-purposes.
6 Fitzgerald's sounding-apparatus.
8 sounding-cylinders.
100 copper sleeves for sounding-rods.
1 Massey's registering-apparatus.
1 Trowbridge's registering-apparatus.
600 bored shot, VIII-inch, for sinkers.
50 bored shot, 32-pounder, for sinkers.
25 bored shot, XV-inch, for sinkers.
Square sinkers, 18 to 30 pounds, for the Fitzgerald apparatus.
Split sinkers, from 20 to 300 pounds.
1 200-pound sounding-lead.
2 150-pound sounding-lead.
2 100-pound sounding-lead.
6 90-pound sounding-lead.
1 80-pound sounding-lead.
1 50-pound sounding-lead.
180 pounds piano-wire, Birmingham gauge No. 22.
950 pounds Albacore line, (¾-inch untarred hemp, 9 thread.)
2,270 pounds 1½-inch Manilla whale-line.
1,700 pounds 2⅛-inch Manilla carbolized line.
3,750 pounds 1⅛-inch carbolized line.
2,800 pounds 1½-inch carbolized line.
1,575 pounds 1¾-inch carbolized line.
665 pounds 1¼-inch lead-line.
590 pounds 1½-inch lead-line.
9 dozen cod-line.
1 Burt's buoy and nipper.
3 accumulators.
3 iron dredge-frames.
22 swivels.
1 galvanized-iron tub.
12 Miller-Cassella thermometers.

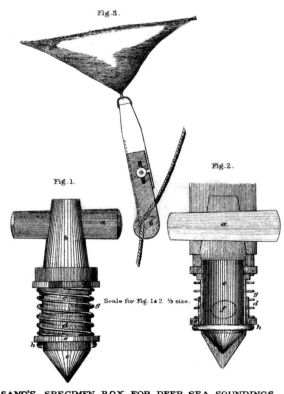

BURT'S SOUNDING NIPPER.

Fig.3.

Fig.1.

Fig.2.

Scale for Fig. 1 & 2 ⅓ size.

SAND'S SPECIMEN BOX FOR DEEP SEA SOUNDINGS.

SIDE ELEVATION
OF THE
FLYING BRIDGE OF THE U.S.S. TUSCARORA.
Showing its position and the arrangement for reeling in , using Sir Wᵐ Thomson's machine and piano wire
Note.:The reeling-in apparatus constructed on board the vessel.

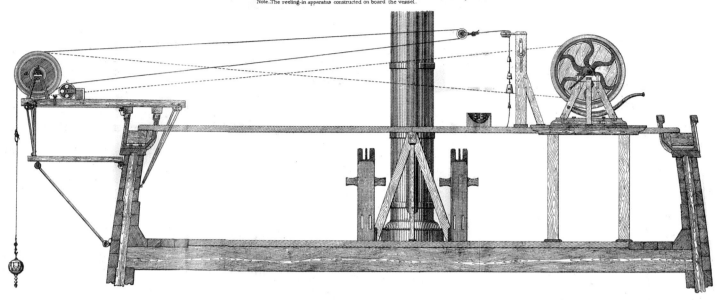

Tuscarora was the first ship to use piano wire for sounding. This is the machine invented in 1872 by William Thomson and installed aboard the ship.

The voyage of *Tuscarora* was immensely fruitful; surveyors carried out nearly 500 soundings, to depths not before possible, which they were able to do because of the Thomson piano wire machine. As the direct result of this application of new technology, not one but two major submarine features of the Pacific Ocean were discovered. Bottom specimens of considerable zoological interest were also collected, and records obtained of water temperatures both at the surface and at immense depth.

(right)
This straightforward though hardly simple table records the discovery of the Japan Trench. It shows data recorded aboard *Tuscarora* on 17 June 1874, off the east coast of Japan. A depth of 4,356 fathoms (7 940 m or 26,136 feet) is recorded, using the piano wire machine. It took an hour and a half to reel the wire back in. The real discovery of the trench took place a few days before, on 11 June, when a depth of 4,643 fathoms (8 500 m or 27,850 feet) was reached without hitting bottom. Belknap's journal recorded: "Wire broke. Bottom not reached."

Journal of deep-sea soundings, North Pacific Ocean, by United States steamship Tuscarora,
Commander George E. Belknap, commanding ;
Yokohama, Japan, to Cape Flattery,
via Aleutian Islands.

CAST NO. 28.—JUNE 17, 1874.

Number	28.	Latitude, 42° 57′ N., obs.	
Hour	9 h. 50 m. 54 s., a. m.	Longitude, 148° 23′ E., chro.	
Wind	Variable.	Barometer, 30.18 ; ther. att'd, 55°.8.	
Force	0.5 to 1.	Temperatures:	
Weather	b c f clouds, cirrus. Prop. clear, 8.	Air, 54°.6, D. B.; 55° W. B.	
Sea	Smooth.	Sea-surface, 49°.5.	
Line	Piano-wire, No. 22.	Under-surface 700 fms., 34°—0°.49=33°.51. (18143.)	
Sinker	8-inch shot and 19 lbs. lead weight on casting.	Depth, 4,356 fms.	
Weight	74 lbs.	Bottom, yellowish mud with sand and specks of lava.	
Machine	Sir William Thomson's.	Surface-current, 3 fms: N. E.	
App. for spec.	Belknap cylinder, No. 1.	Under-current:	

Value of sounding, undoubtedly good.

Under-current:
10 fms., 3 fms. NE. by N.
20 fms., ¾ fms. N. W.
30 fms., 1 fm. W.
50 fms., 1½ fms. W.
100 fms., 2 fms. W. by S.
200 fms., 6 fms. SW. by S.

Current shown by observation during past 24 hours, N. 45° E., 3 fms. per hour.

Fathoms or revolutions.	Time. Hour.	Time. Min.	Time. Sec.	A. m. or p. m.	Interval. Min.	Interval. Sec.	2d Diff. Min.	2d Diff. Sec.	Time hauling in. Hour.	Time hauling in. Min.	Time hauling in. Sec.	Remarks.
	9	50	54	a. m.	...	...	...	...	...	...	...	Fine calm weather ; engines moved occasionally ; Lieutenant F. M. Symonds went out in whale-boat to try under-surface currents.
100	9	52	02	a. m.	1	08	...	...	...	1	12	
200	9	52	53	a. m.	...	51	...	17	...	1	08	
300	9	53	43	a. m.	...	50	...	1	...	2	02	Before beginning this cast, wound 706 fathoms more of wire on the reel. Reel so much strained by these deep casts that the wire will have to be wound upon a new one.
400	9	54	33	a. m.	...	50	...	...	...	1	23	
500	9	55	25	a. m.	...	52	...	2	...	1	29	
600	9	56	19	a. m.	...	54	...	2	...	1	26	
700	9	57	14	a. m.	...	55	...	1	...	1	29	At end of cast kept on course under fore and aft sail, foresail, and steam ; wind very light.
800	9	58	10	a. m.	...	56	...	1	...	1	28	
900	9	59	07	a. m.	...	57	...	1	...	1	52	
1000	10	00	08	a. m.	1	01	...	4	...	1	59	SERIAL TEMPERATURES.
1100	10	1	11	a. m.	1	03	...	2	...	1	59	Surface, 49°.5.
1200	10	2	16	a. m.	1	05	...	2	...	1	48	10 fms., 42°.7—0°.00=42°.7. No. 18145.
1300	10	3	22	a. m.	1	06	...	1	...	1	54	15 fms., 36°.5—0°.01=36°.49. No. 18145.
1400	10	4	29	a. m.	1	07	...	1	...	2	02	25 fms., 33°.6—0°.02=33°.58. No. 18145.
1500	10	5	36	a. m.	1	07	...	...	...	2	07	50 fms., 32°.7—0°.03=32°.67. No. 18143.
1600	10	6	47	a. m.	1	11	...	4	...	2	19	100 fms., 33°.4—0°.07=33°.33. No. 18143.
1700	10	7	57	a. m.	1	10	...	1	...	2	20	300 fms., 33°.8—0°.21=33°.59. No. 18145.
1800	10	9	10	a. m.	1	13	...	3	...	2	00	500 fms 34°.5—0°.35=34°.15. No. 18145.
1900	10	10	23	a. m.	1	13	...	...	...	2	04	700 fms., 34°—0°.49=33°.51. No. 18143.
2000	10	11	37	a. m.	1	14	...	1	...	2	08	
2100	10	12	53	a. m.	1	16	...	2	...	2	10	Weights on pulley. Dyn. ind.
2200	10	14	10	a. m.	1	17	...	1	...	2	18	125 lbs 48 lbs.
2300	10	15	28	a. m.	1	18	...	1	...	2	19	90 lbs 44 lbs .... 50 fms.
2400	10	16	47	a. m.	1	19	...	1	...	2	11	65 lbs 36 lbs .... 70 fms.
2500	10	18	07	a. m.	1	20	...	1	...	2	37	50 lbs 30 lbs .... 90 fms.
2600	10	19	24	a. m.	1	17	...	3	...	2	43	25 lbs 18 lbs .. 170 fms.
2700	10	20	43	a. m.	1	19	...	2	...	2	27	40 lbs 18 lbs .. 970 fms.
2800	10	22	00	a. m.	1	17	...	2	...	2	15	90 lbs 35 lbs ..3,390 fms.
2900	10	23	23	a. m.	1	23	...	6	...	2	14	112 lbs 40 lbs ..3,600 fms.
3000	10	24	45	a. m.	1	22	...	1	...	2	51	150 lbs 47 lbs ..3,985 fms.
3100	10	26	09	a. m.	1	24	...	2	...	2	49	
3200	10	27	33	a. m.	1	24	...	...	...	2	47	Number of revolutions, 4,071.
3300	10	29	01	a. m.	1	28	...	4	...	2	41	
3400	10	30	43	a. m.	1	42	...	14	...	2	40	
3500	10	32	25	a. m.	1	42	...	...	...	2	56	
3600	10	34	05	a. m.	1	40	...	2	...	2	54	
3700	10	35	55	a. m.	1	50	...	10	...	2	31	
3800	10	37	48	a. m.	1	53	...	3	...	2	50	
3900	10	39	46	a. m.	1	58	...	5	...	2	59	
4000	10	41	51	a. m.	2	05	...	7	...	2	51	
4071	10	43	30	a. m.	1	39	...	...	...	2	02	

	Min.	Sec.		Hour.	Min.	Sec.
Time going out	52	36	Com'g in	1	30	10
Finished				12	17	51	p. m.
Total time of cast					2	26	57

Number of revolutions, 4,071.

Number of measured fathoms 4,331

Stray line 25

Depth 4,356

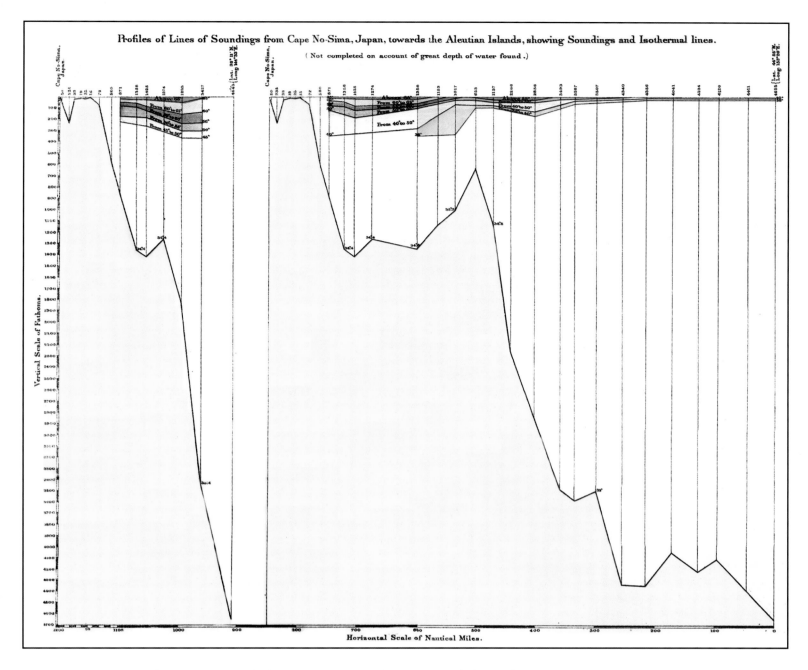

Profiles of Lines of Soundings from Cape No-Sima, Japan, towards the Aleutian Islands, showing Soundings and Isothermal lines.

(Not completed on account of great depth of water found .)

Tuscarora's survey lines from Japan towards the northeast had to be discontinued due to the inability to deal with the immense depths encountered. Above are two of the depth profiles, and at right (Map 223) is part of the track map with the tracks to which the profiles refer. Another part of this map is shown on the previous pages (164–65).

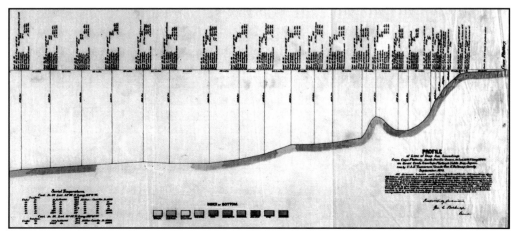

Part of the soundings profile approaching Cape Flattery.

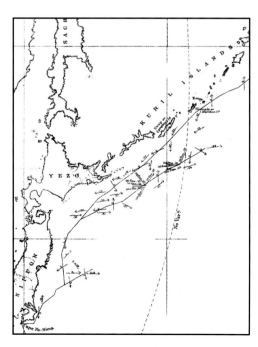

Exploring the Depths – The Challenger Expedition

On 23 March 1875 at 11° 24′ N, 143° 16′ E, *Challenger* sounded the greatest depth ever before reached. This was the Mariana Trench, and the sounding was of 4,475 fathoms (8 190 m or 26,850 feet). Joseph Matkin, a young ship's steward, recorded the event in his diary.

The 23d was a great day on board, at 6 am we sounded at the enormous depth of 4,600 fms, but as there was a doubt about it, the line was hauled up again. It was sent down again more heavily weighted, & 2 patent Thermometers were attached. The depth was decided to be 4,550 fms (5¹/₆ miles) – the greatest reliable depth ever obtained. One of the Therm'trs burst owing to the tremendous pressure on it.

Until the late 1850s, the common belief, which seemed eminently sensible, was that the "black abyss" of the deep sea below the reach of fishing nets could not possibly contain any life. What could be expected to live in such cold and completely dark conditions?

This concept changed dramatically in the 1860s, such that by the end of that decade the bottom of the ocean promised to become a cornucopia for the naturalist. An extensive sheet of living slime named *Bathybius* was thought to cover the seabed, forming the base of a food chain, a hypothesis that was to be disproved by *Challenger* while in the Pacific. It is therefore not surprising that in the 1860s oceanographic expeditions were proposed to explore these apparently newly alive deeps. By far the most famous and the most significant was that of *Challenger*.

The round-the-world voyage of the specially converted British ship HMS *Challenger* in 1873–76 is considered by many scientists to have inaugurated modern scientific research in the oceans. The Royal Society in Britain persuaded their government to outfit *Challenger* as a floating scientific laboratory.

After the voyage the scientific results were published in an enormous forty-volume report that was not completed until 1895.

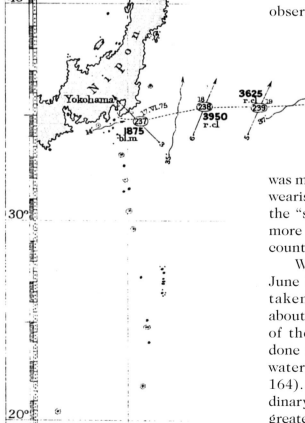

Challenger entered the North Pacific in April 1875, arriving in Japan and staying there some two months. William Spry wrote "even to ordinary observers of the picturesque there was much to compensate for the long wearisome voyage." Matkin thought the "shores of the Gulf of Yedo look more like England than those of any country we have visited."

When *Challenger* left Japan in June 1875, a course was deliberately taken approximately due east at about 35° N to not duplicate the track of the USS *Tuscarora*, which had done much surveying work in these waters the previous year (see page 164). *Tuscarora* had found extraordinary depths; *Challenger* found even greater depths in the Mariana Trench, and almost as great depths in the Japan Trench.

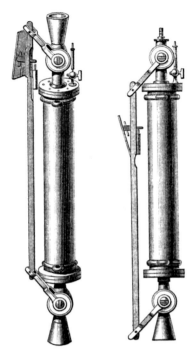

Water samplers used by *Challenger*. The top and bottom on the tube were open while being lowered (left), but as soon as the sampler was pulled up, both ends closed (right) and trapped a sample of water from that depth.

Map 224 (across page, below). Track of *Challenger* from Japan to Hawaii. Numbers in circles are sounding station numbers, bold number are depths in fathoms, and letters under the depth indicate bottom type (r. cl. is red clay; bl. m. is blue mud). Straight arrows are wind direction, with force according to the Beaufort scale; squiggly lines are surface current directions, with the number being rate in miles per 24 hours.

CHART

Showing the track of

H. M. S. CHALLENGER

in 1872-3-4-5 & 6.

Map 225 (above). The track of *Challenger* in the Pacific Ocean.

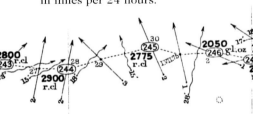

YOKOHAMA

to the

SANDWICH ISLANDS

June , July 1875.

For explanation of abbreviations &c. see Appendix 1.

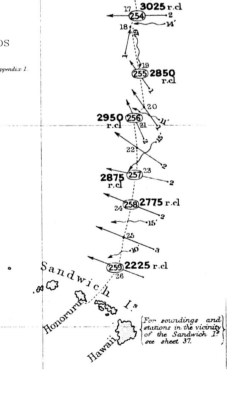

The day after leaving Japan, one of the sailors on board died, and on 18 July was buried at sea. Matkin noted that

directly after the funeral we took soundings at the enormous depth of 3,900 fathoms [7 140 m or 23,400 feet], 4½ miles, the second deepest sounding we have ever obtained.

The straight eastward track across the North Pacific after leaving the Japan Trench was relatively uneventful, even monotonous. Spry wrote that

very little of interest occurred from day to day, and the results of the trawling and additions to the natural history collection were very scanty.

They had crossed 180°; Matkin observed:

Last week with us contained 8 days, & we had two Sundays as the Admiralty allow us no pay for that day.

Generous lot, the British navy!

169

The observations and soundings made by *Challenger,* in conjunction with those made by *Tuscarora,* showed the Pacific to be different from other oceans. It was deeper, and much of the seabed was found to be covered with a characteristic deep-sea clay. Contained in this clay were larger mineral particles including quartz, mica, and pumice. This led John Murray to believe that its source was volcanic. Also present in large quantities were manganese nodules, precipitated around a nucleus of detritus.

By the time *Challenger* returned to Britain in May 1876, the ship had traveled 110 000 km or 69,000 miles, at an average speed, it has been pointed out, of little better than walking pace. She brought home an enormous scientific booty: 13,000 kinds of animals and plants, 1,441 water samples, and hundreds of sea bottom samples.

An animal called *Monocaulus imperator* retrieved from depth by *Challenger* in the North Pacific. In the report is the following:

Among the results of the Challenger dredgings must . . . be specifically recorded the discovery of a gigantic Tubularian, which was dredged in the North Pacific from depths of 1875 to 2900 fathoms. It is referable to the genus Monocaulus . . . One of the specimens whose dimensions were noted . . . was found to measure 9 inches from tip to tip of extended tentacles . . . while its stem rose from its point of attachment to a height of 7 feet 4 inches. This great Tubularian affords indeed an example of a Hydroid attaining dimensions far exceeding the maximum which would have been hitherto thought possible in Hydroid life – a character to which the vast depth whence it was obtained gives additional significance.

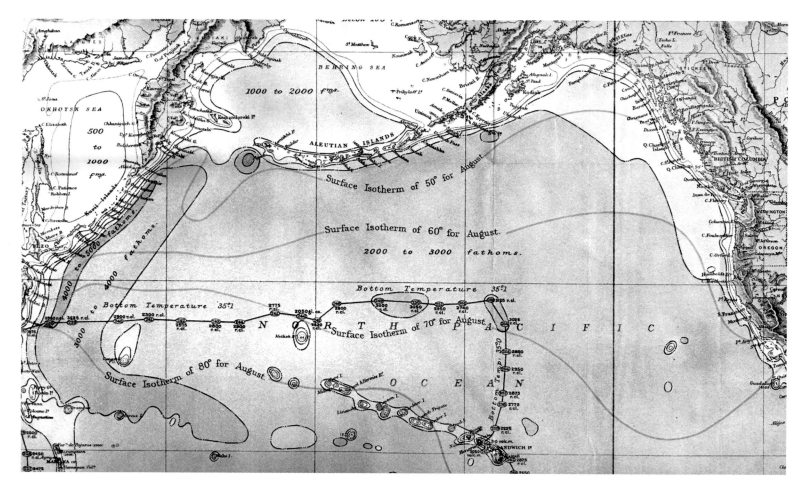

Map 226.
Map of the North Pacific Ocean showing information collected by *Challenger* augmented by that collected by others. It shows surface water temperatures (in °F) for August, bottom temperatures, and an elementary mapping of seabed depths, good enough to show the Japan Trench discovered by *Challenger*'s pioneering oceanographers.

William Spry wrote in his book about the expedition, published on its return in 1876:

When the deep sea dredge appears above the surface, there is usually great excitement amongst the "Philos", who are ever on the alert with forceps, bottles and jars, to secure the unwary creatures who may by chance have found their way into the net . . . We have no lack of wonderful things.

The method used for sounding is clear from the wonderful engraving of a deck scene on board *Challenger,* which was included in the expedition's report, and the diagram below.

Challenger's boat, complete with steam engine.

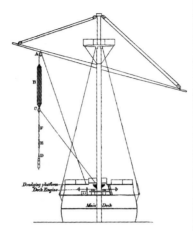

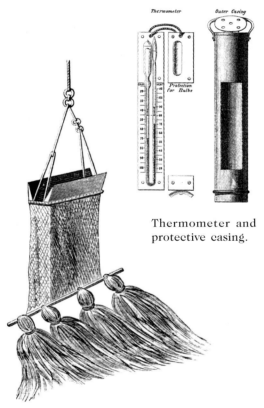

Thermometer and protective casing.

A deep-sea dredge. The brushes below the net were intended to sweep the seabed and bring up small animal life into the net.

East-west bottom profile obtained by *Challenger* from Japan, following the eastward track shown in Map 224 on pages 168–69. It shows the vast depth of the Japan Trench discovered by the expedition.

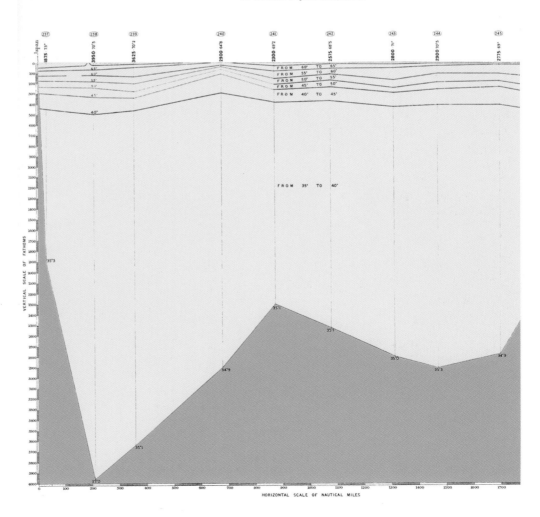

PACIFIC OCEAN

Longitudinal Temperature Section . Japan to a position in Lat. 35°49′N. Long. 180°

For explanation of Symbols see Appendix 1.

HORIZONTAL SCALE OF NAUTICAL MILES

The Maps of Sir John Murray

John Murray, a geologist, was one of the scientists on *Challenger*. He and Alphonse Renard wrote the volume of the *Challenger Report* on marine deposits. But, not satisfied with data from *Challenger* alone, Murray embarked on a long-term project to gather, in Maury-like style, all available data from any ship.

Both scientific and telegraph-company ships sent him their samples. With each was information as to the location and depth from which it came, and Murray used this data to construct topographical maps of the world's oceans.

Maps of the Pacific, Atlantic, and Indian Oceans were published in 1886, based on about 6,000 soundings. The map shown below is part of a world map, not much revised, published in 1899.

Maps 228 and 229 (facing page).
John Murray also produced other maps based on data from the *Challenger* expedition and other data he collected later. At right are shown two maps of the Pacific he published in 1899. The top one shows the distribution of minimum surface water temperatures and the bottom one shows maximum surface water temperatures.

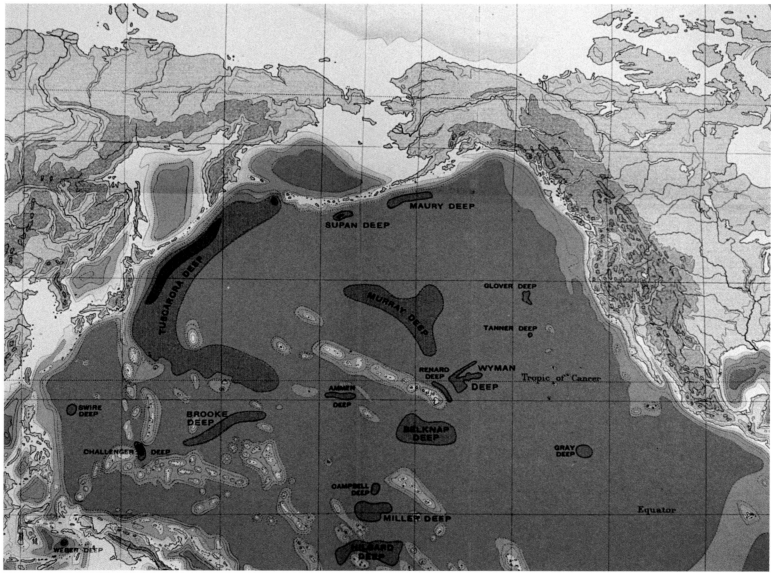

Map 227.
The 1899 edition of Murray's map, the first bathymetric map of the North Pacific that tried to be comprehensive in its scope. The recently discovered Aleutian and Japan Trenches are shown, but for all its apparent authority this map was very generalized, being based on remarkably few actual soundings considering the vast expanse of ocean covered.

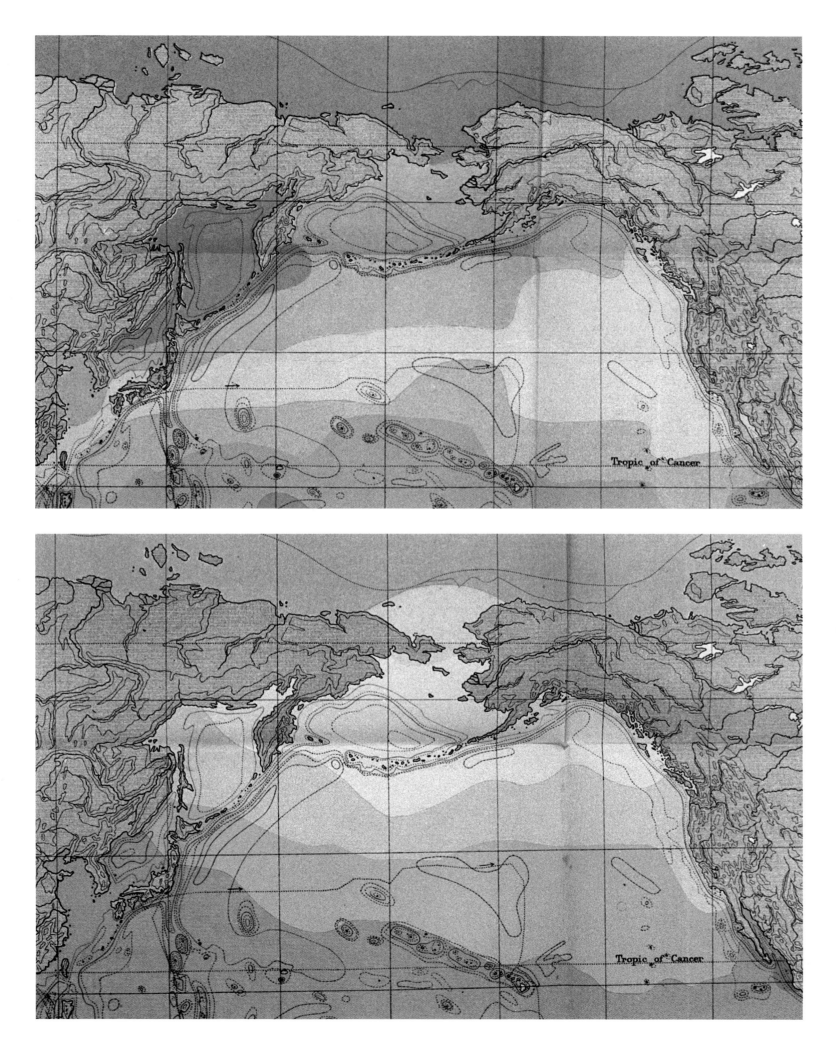

Tropic of Cancer

Tropic of Cancer

The Voyage of the Nero

Following the pioneering deep-sea surveying work of the *Tuscarora*, several other surveys were made to establish the best routes for trans-Pacific telegraph cables.

In 1899, the U.S. Navy fitted out a steam collier named *Nero* as a deep-sea surveying ship. The ship was to survey a route for a submarine telegraph cable between the United States, the Philippines, and Japan.

The route from the west coast of America to Hawaii was considered known by this time, so *Nero* began its survey from Honolulu.

The ship sailed to Midway, Guam, and the Philippines; back to Guam, then to Yokohama, Japan; back to Guam; then to Midway and back to Honolulu. Thus every part of the pos-sible route was surveyed twice. Over these routes, soundings were taken, on average, every ten miles.

The return route in each case was planned to cross the primary route zigzag at 45° angles with soundings taken at the change in direction; in this manner an examination was made of a belt of ocean about 22 km or 14 miles wide and over 9 650 km or 6,000 miles in length. This detailed a survey had never before been attempted on any ocean.

About 50 km or 30 miles to the west and south of Midway a "very bold peak" was discovered, rising abruptly from the sea floor at 2,000 fathoms (3 650 m or 12,000 feet) to only 82 fathoms (150 m or 500 feet).

Nearing Guam, four soundings below 5,000 fathoms were made, one at 5,269 fathoms (9 650 m or 31,600 feet), the deepest ocean discovered at that time. This was a trench now known as the "Nero Deep," and its discovery is what the voyage of the *Nero* is most remembered for. The report of the voyage noted that this depth was "only 66 feet less than 6 statute miles."

An extract from the sounding log for the *Nero* on 17 September 1899, shown below, gives some idea of the level of detail and the work involved in making deep-sea soundings. The crew of *Nero* made a total of 2,074 soundings across the Pacific. Equipment was often lost, and in particular, the notation "thermometer failed to work" appears frequently. Given the huge changing pressures to which these relatively sensitive intruments were subjected, this is hardly surprising.

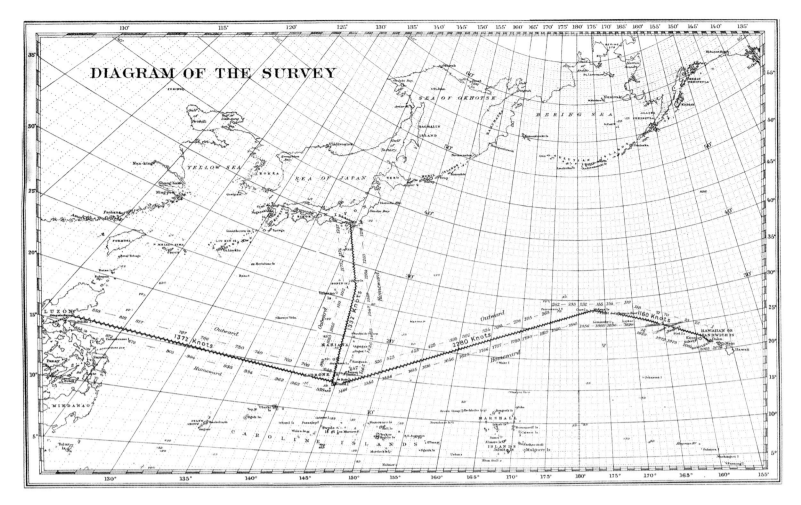

Map 230.
Map showing the track and the zigzag return track of the *Nero*.

RAPHIC OFFICE.

Pacific

RD.

30°-16'-30" Lat. Long. 141°-41'-15" E.

Lt. Bowdr. U.S.N. _____, commanding.

at *1* hours *0* minutes _____ Date, *Sept. 21" 1899*

Amount of Clouds, Scale 0-10.	State of the Sea by Symbols.	Time of stopping to Sound. H.	M.	Time of starting ahead after Sounding. H.	M.	Time occupied in making distance from last Sounding. H.	M.	Compass Course from last Sounding.	Correction.	True Course from last Sounding.	Reading of Patent Log.	Distance from last Record of P. L.	Corrected Interval.	Initials of Officer of the Deck.	REMARKS.
6	hv	1	06	2	04	1	12	N. 3. E.	1/4 W.	N. 7 E.	82.8	9.5	8.9	J.P.M.sy	last good, withstanding N.
4	hv	2	36	3	18	0	22	"	"	"	84.8	2.	2.	J.P.M.sy	" up & down.
5	hv	4	39	5	21	1	11	"	"	"	94.1	9.3	8.9	J.J.R.	"
5	hv	5	38	6	13	0	14	"	"	"	96	1.9	2.	J.J.R.	" " mainly
5	S.	7	20	7	53	1	07	"	"	"	2.1	6.1	8.9	J.H.R.	" Log fouled by piece of waste, destr... by turns 9.3 knots about.
4	S.	8	18	9	35	0	20	"	"	"	4	1.9	2.	J.H.R.	good withstanding slightly to E.
4	L.	10	03	10	35	1	08	"	"	"	13.6	9.6	8.9	J.H.R.	" up & down
4	L.	10	53	11	20	0	18	"	"	"	15.4	1.8	2.	J.H.R.	" " mainly
3	L.	0	28	1	59	1	08	"	"	"	24.9	9.5	9.25	M.J.	
4	L.	1	20	1	59	0	18	"	"	"	26.8	1.9	2.	M.J.	

Whaling and Sealing in the North Pacific

WHALE FISHING.

Although natives had hunted whales for centuries, whales were first commercially hunted in the North Pacific in 1835. It was the return to New England of Captain Barzillai Folger in his ship *Granges* loaded with whale oil and whalebone that first publicized the commerical possibilities of whale hunting in the region. After 1845, whaleships moved into the Bering Sea also, and soon up to 250 vessels each season were following the receding ice favored by the bowhead whale as a feeding ground. In 1848 the first whaler, now tracking rapidly diminishing whale stocks, entered the Arctic Ocean.

In the 1840s and 1850s, New England whale hunters killed bowhead whales by the thousands, outraging the Russians in the process. The hunt peaked in 1852, when 278 whaling ships were in the North Pacific, but by the 1860s the decline in whale numbers was such that fewer and fewer ships found it economic to make the long voyage to the whaling grounds. A further spur to the decline of the whale hunt came from the new petroleum industry in the 1880s.

When whales were hard to find, the whalers often turned to the walrus, hunted both for its oil and its tusks. It has been estimated that 200,000 walruses were killed in the twenty years between 1860 and 1880. Out of the water, in particular, the walrus was no match for a rifle-toting gunman.

Russians had hunted the sea cow to extinction, and there had been no outcry over the decimation of the whale and walrus stocks, but when the hunters turned to the fur seal, massive and complicated international controversies resulted. It is fair to say, however, that international difficulties developed as much for political and territorial reasons as for a concern for the seal herds, which were a convenient and nobler excuse for complaints.

Canadian intrusion into fur seal hunting led in short order to diplomatic incidents, as American naval vessels attempted to maintain their new sovereignty over Alaskan waters after the purchase of Alaska from the Russians in 1867.

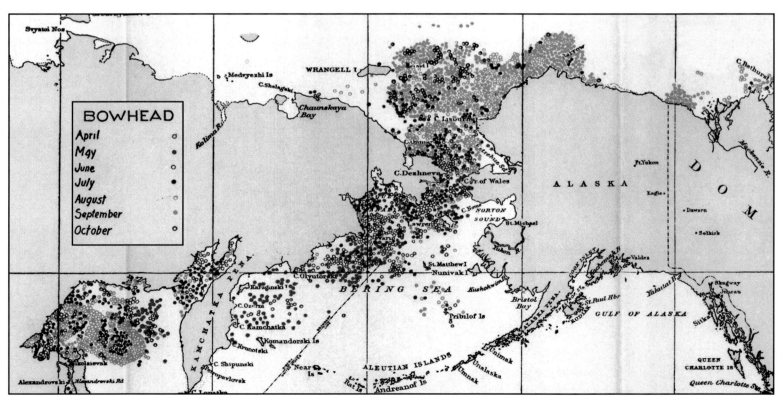

Map 231.
Distribution of bowhead whales by month of the year, as compiled from nineteenth-century whaleship logbooks by Charles Haskins, the director of the New York Aquarium, in 1935. The colored circles indicate the whale location and month.

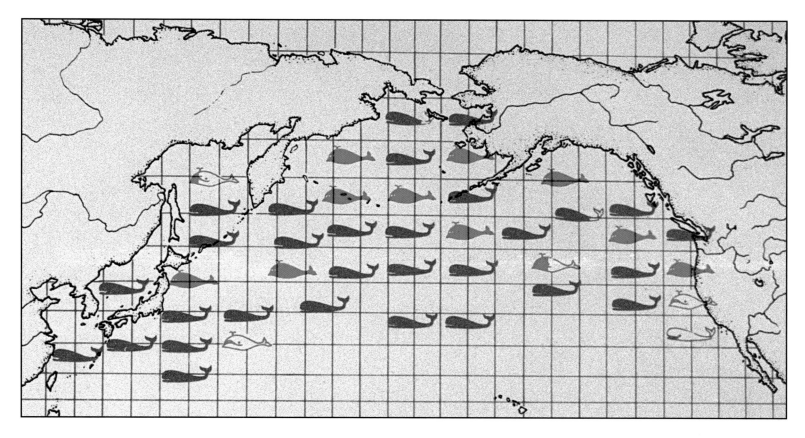

Map 232 (above).
Map of the whale catch in 1970, from the Food and Agriculture Organization of the United Nations, published in 1972. Blue whale symbols are sperm whales, red are baleen whales. Each completely colored symbol represents a catch of 500 whales. It may seem surprising to some today that the whale hunt was still going on as late as this.

(top left)
An engraving from the border decoration of a map entitled *British America*, drawn by John Tallis and published in 1851.

Map 233.
Map from the British counter case (see page 179) showing the places where seals were caught near the (Russian) Commander Islands in the Bering Sea in 1892.

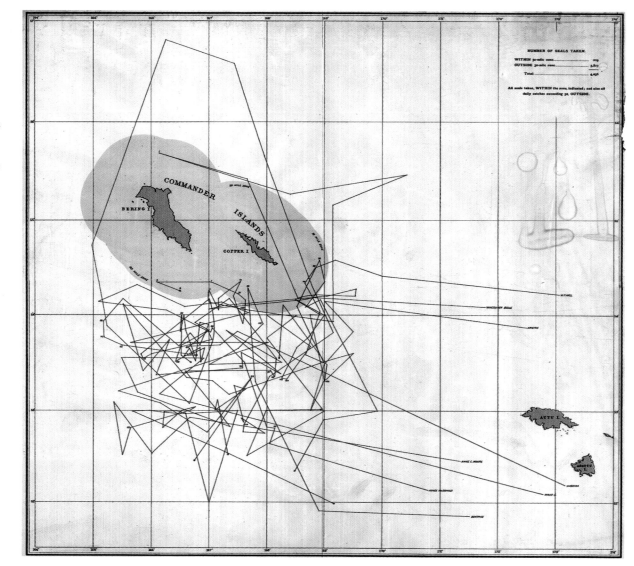

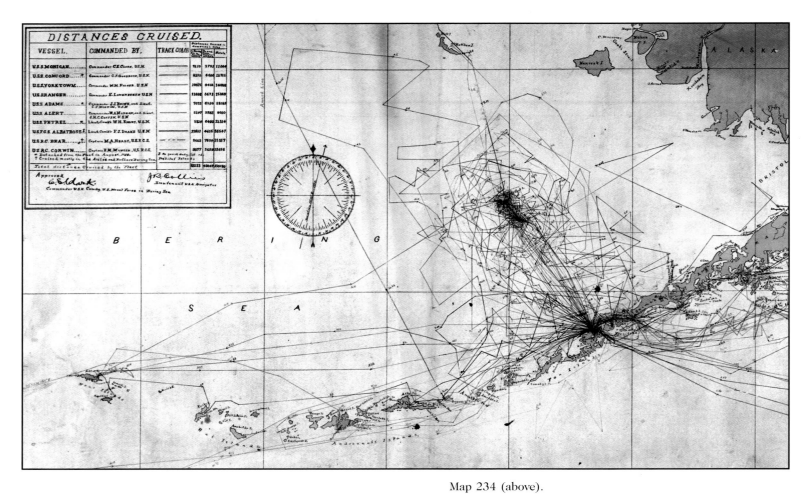

DISTANCES CRUISED.

VESSEL.	COMMANDED BY,	TRACK COLORS

Map 234 (above).
Tracks of American naval vessels in the Bering Sea in 1894. This shows the incredible amount of patrolling that occurred as the U.S. Navy tried to prevent poaching of seals.

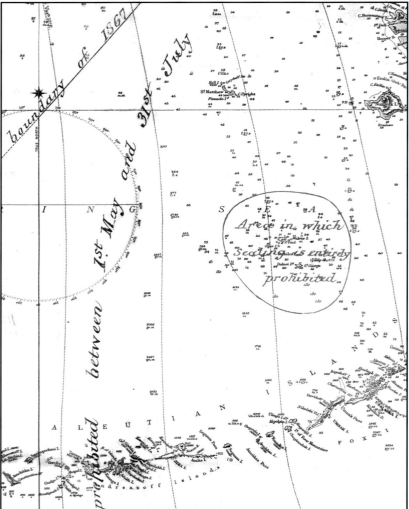

Map 235.
Map showing exclusion and restricted zones for sealing proposed in the 1892 arbitration.

In 1870, in order to protect an exclusive lease granted to the Alaska Commercial Company, the American government prohibited the killing of seals within its territory. The problem was in defining American territory. The 1867 treaty with Russia had appeared to give jurisdiction over much of the Bering Sea to the United States, but international law gave only a three-mile exclusion zone. American claims that the Bering Sea was a *mare clausum,* a closed sea surrounded by one country, did not carry much weight now that both Russian and American territory bordered that body of water. Nevertheless, there were significant economic reasons for arguing for total ownership. The British navy became involved, protecting Canadian and thus British interests, and the American navy sailed to protect its government's point of view.

Fur seals breed, now as then, in relatively few places in the Bering

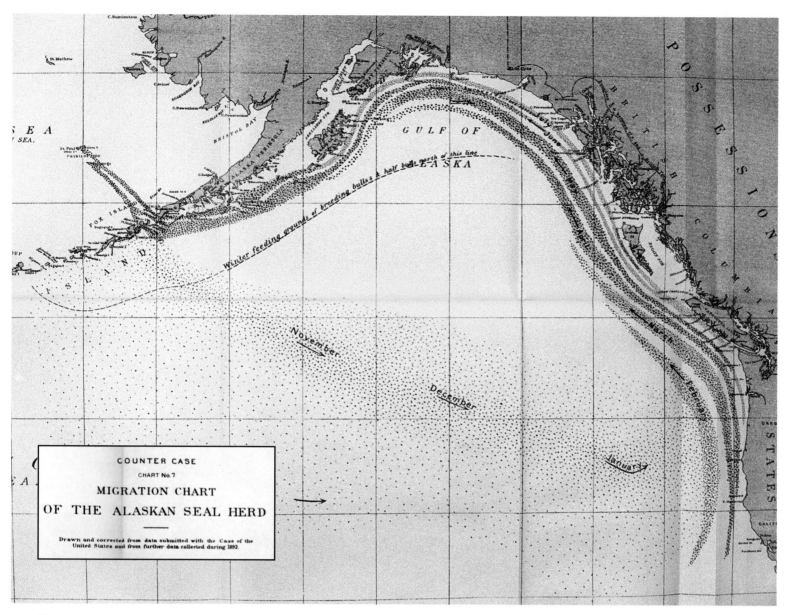

Map 236.
Map of seal migration for the 1893 arbitration, prepared in 1892.

Sea, most notably the Pribilof Islands and the Commander Islands. The Alaska Commercial Company had negotiated exclusive leases and rights to hunt seals on these islands first with the American government and then the Russian. The seals inhabit these islands during May, June, and July, but the rest of the year they migrate long distances southwards.

In 1874, Henry Elliott, who considered himself the premier scientist of the Bering Sea, even if others disagreed, had grossly overestimated the population of fur seals in the Pribilofs, and this was to lead to severe depletions of the rookeries in later years.

From 1879, ships began to engage in what was called pelagic seal-ing, the hunting of these migrating seals while they were at sea, an immensely wasteful hunt in which perhaps only 10 percent of the seals killed were actually recovered. So wasteful was this type of hunting that it rapidly threatened the survival of the Pribilof Islands herds.

In 1886, three Canadian ships were seized and taken to Sitka by a U.S. Revenue cutter, *Corwin*. Britain immediately protested this violation of the freedom of the seas, and the Bering Sea became for the next twenty years a focus of international attention.

The American government's claims of *mare clausum* were thrown out by an international arbitration tribunal in Paris in 1893. During the 1890s huge volumes of words and data were produced to buttress the claims of all sides. Heavy naval involvement, standoffs, and intimidation continued. The 1893 arbitration was ineffective, for by 1910 the Pribilof seal herd, which once numbered four million, was down to only one hundred thousand. Something had to be done, and fast. At the invitation of the United States, representatives of Britain, Russia and Japan met in Washington, D.C., to work out an agreement to save the herd from extinction. The result was the International Fur Seal Convention of 1911. Killing seals at sea was prohibited, and the Pribilof lessee, the Alaska Commercial Company, had to share furs with the Japanese, Canadians, and Russians.

The Prince Maps the Depths

John Murray compiled the first worldwide maps of the ocean floor in 1886 (page 172). In the ensuing years several others were produced, notably one in 1890 by James Dana, who had been Charles Wilkes' geologist, and another by Alexander Supan, in 1899. These were mainly based on the same sounding data.

In an attempt to coordinate bathymetric mapping, the International Geographical Congress in 1899 struck a commission to compile a general map of the world's oceans. Prince Albert of Monaco undertook this project and, perhaps as importantly, agreed also to bear the cost.

Prince Albert was one of the early benefactors of the science of oceanography, combining a personal interest with his own research, and funding all manner of others. He even had his own yacht fitted out for oceanographic work, and later he founded an oceanographic museum in Monaco.

Soundings from all over the world were again compiled, and by 1904 charts had been completed for all oceans, based now on some 18,400 locations. The result was the *Carte Generale Bathymetrique Des Oceans* (GEneral Bathymetric Chart of the Oceans, or GEBCO).

The task of keeping these maps up-to-date was later taken over by the International Hydrographic Bureau, with sixteen countries pooling data.

Four sheets of this map, shown here in part, form the North Pacific portion of the *Carte Generale*. The division of sheets is at 46° N and 180°.

The striking thing about the North Pacific sheets is how little actual information is recorded, as there are still relatively few sounding paths. Generalizations yet hide the unknown.

A new international effort was launched in the 1970s to bring the GEBCO up to modern standards, and

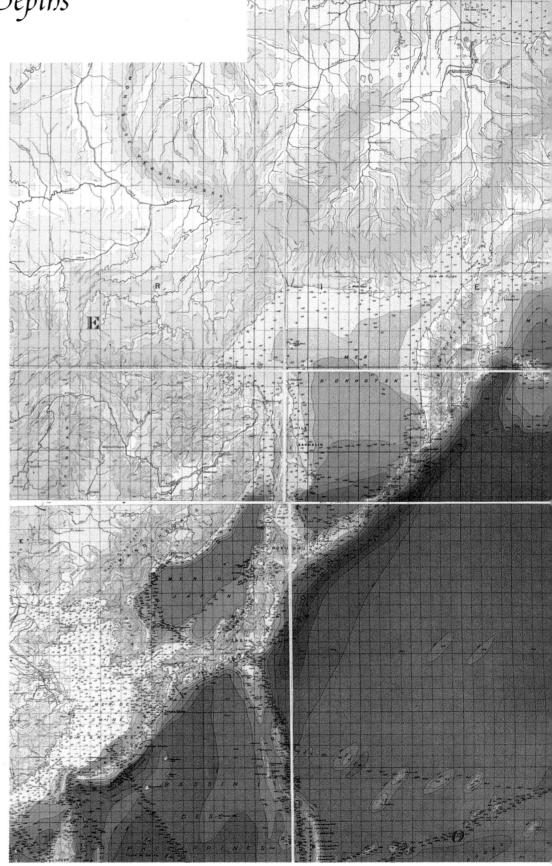

a new map appeared in 1982. Now the map has been digitized, following the release of a digital version of the map in 1994 on CD–ROM, and is much more regularly updated.

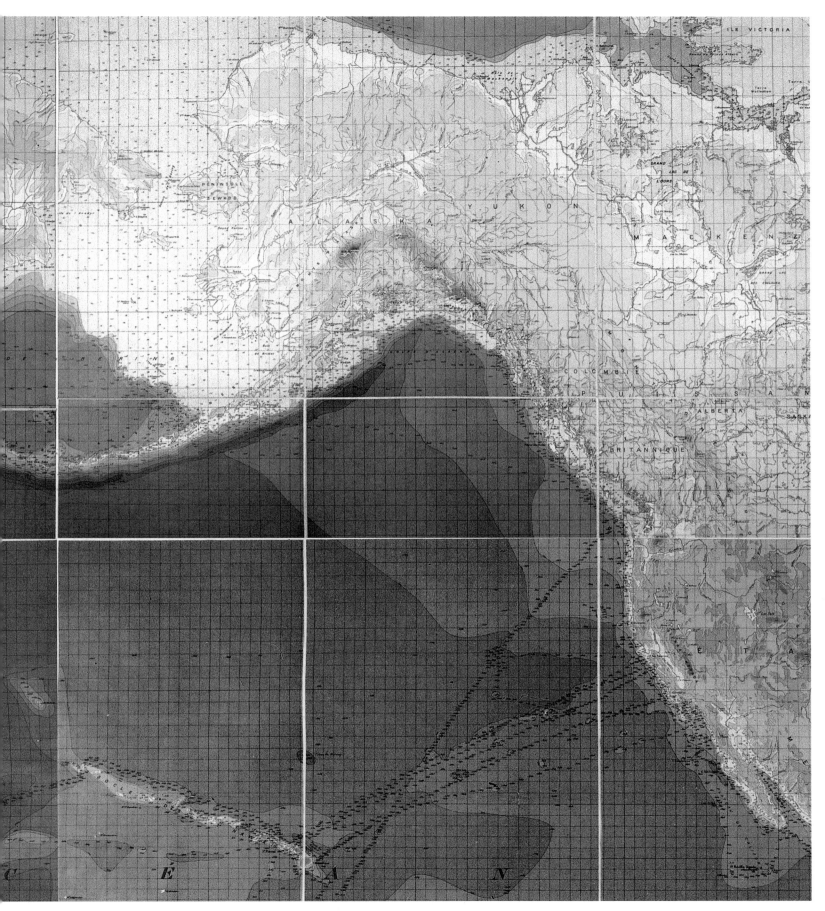

Map 237.
Part of four sheets of the *Carte Generale Bathymetrique Des Oceans,* the GEneral Bathymetric Chart of the Oceans, or GEBCO. The regime of constant updating meant that sheets were usually of different dates. Here the northeast (top right) sheet is dated 1 July 1927; the northwest (top left) sheet 1 July 1923; the southeast sheet (bottom right) 1 May 1912; and the southwest (bottom left) sheet 31 December 1912.

The Coming of Sonar

The electronic sound-generating and echo-recording apparatus today known as sonar (for "SOund Navigation And Ranging") was invented by Canadian-born American physicist and electrical engineer Reginald Fessenden. He is known for his early work in wireless communication. A prolific inventor, he gathered over 500 patents in his lifetime.

One of these patents was for the "fathometer," a device for measuring the depth of water under a ship. It had originally been developed to detect icebergs following the *Titanic* tragedy in 1912. By 1914 Fessenden was able to successfully test his "Iceberg Detector and Echo Depth Sounder," and by 1915 his device had been installed in British submarines and warships.

After the war, the application of Fessenden's invention to oceanography was recognized. A physicist, Harvey Hayes, developed an improved model called the "Hayes Sonic Depth Finder," which used Fessenden's sound-generating oscillator. In June 1922 this was used aboard the U.S. Navy vessel *Stewart* to make the first continuous depth profile across an ocean, the Atlantic, drawn from the 900 soundings made in *eight days* during the crossing. To put this in perspective, *Challenger* in 1873–76 had made a total of less than 300 soundings in *three years*.

Suddenly, the view that the sea floor was flat and featureless changed dramatically. Now any ship equipped with a depth finder could produce contour profiles of the seabed. The first bathymetric charts based on sonic soundings appeared in 1923, after which they were produced regularly as new information was collected and processed.

The first use of the new "Sonic Depth Finder" in the Pacific was made towards the end of 1922, when the naval vessels *Corry* and *Hull* made sonic soundings for a deep-sea contour map off the coast of California.

At the end of 1923, the U.S. Coast and Geodetic Survey ship *Guide* sailed from New England to San Diego, after testing the sonic depth finder in the Atlantic. The results were satisfactory except that some interference with radio broadcasts of the World Series had been reported!

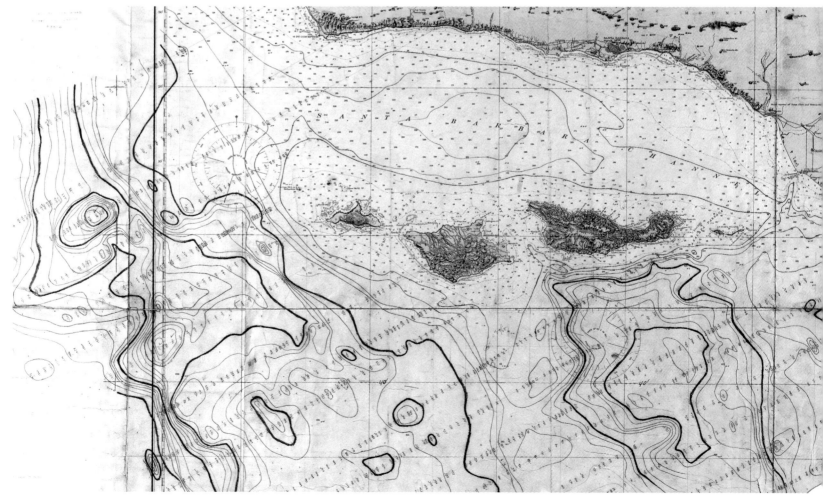

Map 238.
The first sonar map of any part of the Pacific Ocean.

On her voyage, via the Panama Canal, *Guide* compared sonic soundings with conventional wire soundings so that the accuracy of the new equipment could be assessed. It was found that the two types of soundings did not always agree, and it was recognized that variations in water temperature, salinity, and pressure could affect the speed at which sound traveled through water.

Off the Californian coast, further surveys were made while at the same time testing the water for temperature and salinity. Approximate corrections were made, and with further research into the way these factors affected sound transmission, the sonic method soon gained accuracy and, with it, acceptance.

In 1929 the U.S. Naval Hydrographic Office began regularly using this method to make bathymetric maps. Then, suddenly, map accuracy and detail improved dramatically.

This is part of a huge map, composed of seven irregular sheets made from cutting and pasting U.S. Coast and Geodetic Survey charts stretching from San Diego to San Francisco, and covering an offshore area to 2,000 fathoms (1 800 m or 6,000 feet). On these base maps, pencil annotations and seabed contours have been drawn, based on soundings made in 1922 by USS *Corry* with the Sonic Depth Finder, or Rangefinder, as they called it.

The Last Cruise of Carnegie

Variation of the compass, the difference between geographical north and magnetic north, is influenced by magnetic anomalies all over the Earth's surface. It had therefore long been considered useful to know how the Earth's magnetic field varied from place to place, in order to be able to compensate for compass errors. It was on the oceans that the data was most urgently needed, but there also that it was hardest to collect.

In 1904 the Carnegie Institution set up a Department of Terrestrial Magnetism to study this problem, and in 1909 built *Carnegie*, a specially constructed ship with a bronze engine, and wood and bronze nails. A ship without iron was required or else the very nails of its body could influence a compass and make observation of the magnetic field impossible. The crew even wore non-magnetic belt buckles and ate their meals with aluminum flatware.

Carnegie spent many years traversing the seas and in 1928 was also outfitted to carry out other oceanographic observations; in that year she sailed on a round-the-world cruise.

As part of that voyage she was in the North Pacific in 1929. In May of that year she discovered the Fleming Deep, 8 350 m (27,485 feet) deep, at 24° N, 144° E.

Carnegie – a seagoing non-magnetic observatory.

But the voyage was not to be completed. In November *Carnegie* was at Apia, Samoa, and a spark from an electrical switch thrown after refueling caused an explosion and a fire that killed the captain and destroyed the ship.

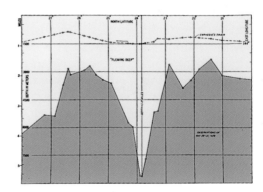

Chart showing the bottom profile and track of the *Carnegie* revealing the discovery of the Fleming Deep, the location of which is marked on the track chart below.

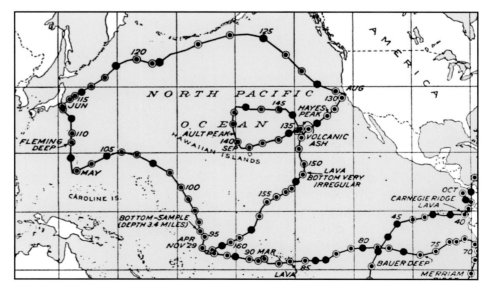

Map 239. Track of the *Carnegie* in the Pacific Ocean.

The Great Cooperative Effort – NORPAC

During the Second World War and in the period thereafter, the number of ships and scientists involved in oceanographic research increased dramatically, and in 1953 it was realized that if all the resources then available were combined at one time, better results might be achieved because a more complete and comprehensive "snapshot" of the state of the ocean might be obtained.

In 1953 Joseph Reid, an oceanographer at Scripps Institution of Oceanography, proposed a cooperative synoptic survey of the North Pacific Ocean be jointly undertaken in the summer of 1954 by ships from Canada and the United States. Although the project did not materialize in 1954, it did the following year, and with the additional resources of oceanographic institutions in Japan.

In total, some nineteen oceanographic research vessels took part. They did not stay in one location, for the belief was, partly correctly, that because of the greater amount of inertia inherent in ocean waters, simultaneity was less important than it would be in the atmosphere. Hence these nineteen ships covered some 1,002 hydrographic stations, or observation points, almost all during the course of three months, July, August, and September 1955. Fourteen oceanographic research institutions took part.

The venture became known as the NORPAC Expeditions. The area covered was the Pacific Ocean between 20° and 60° N.

For each oceanographic station, temperature, salinity, dissolved oxygen (a measure of productivity of the ocean), inorganic phosphate and phosphorus levels, and some other properties were all measured at standard depths, so that all the data would be comparable. In addition, biological data such as quantities and types of phytoplankton (microscopic plants that are the beginning of the food chain) and zooplankton (microscopic animals) were collected. Some geophysical data was also obtained.

Nearly half of the observations were made during the month of August 1955. The result was a far more comprehensive one-time look at the state of the North Pacific than had ever been achieved – or even attempted – before.

The data collected was published in two special tomes of a publication, published each year, known as *Oceanographic Observations of the Pacific*, which was the way information on oceanographic work was disseminated to other scientists in the days before the Internet. These were the *NORPAC Data* and the *NORPAC Atlas*. The maps shown here illustrate the vastness of the project's size and scope.

The information collected was used in applications ranging from fisheries to the understanding of ocean circulation and climate.

The project was considered so successful that a similar one, dubbed EQUAPAC, explored the equatorial region of the Pacific Ocean the next year.

Nowadays oceanographers can obtain a near-simultaneous comprehensive view of many of the parameters measured by NORPAC using satellites, but at the time the project was the most extensive ever attempted.

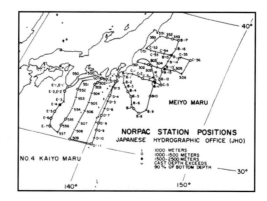

Map 240. Detail of the data collection points of one of the ships involved in NORPAC, *No. 4 Kaito Maru*, from the Japanese Hydrographic Office.

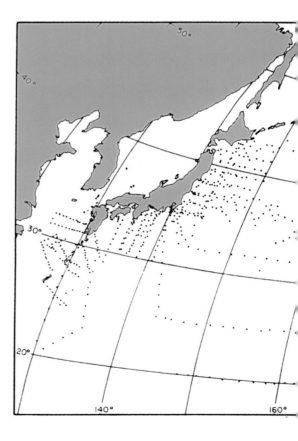

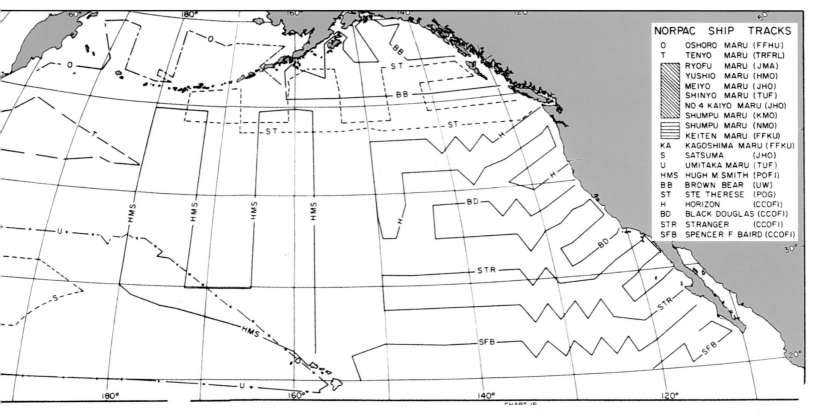

Nineteen ships from fourteen oceanographic institutions in three countries took part in NORPAC. It was the largest and most comprehensive attempt at near-simultaneous ocean data collection ever. The map above (Map 241) shows the actual tracks of the ships involved, and the one below (Map 242) shows the distribution of locations where data was gathered. The result of the rather haphazard-looking set of ship tracks above resulted, as planned, in the systematic distribution of data points below.

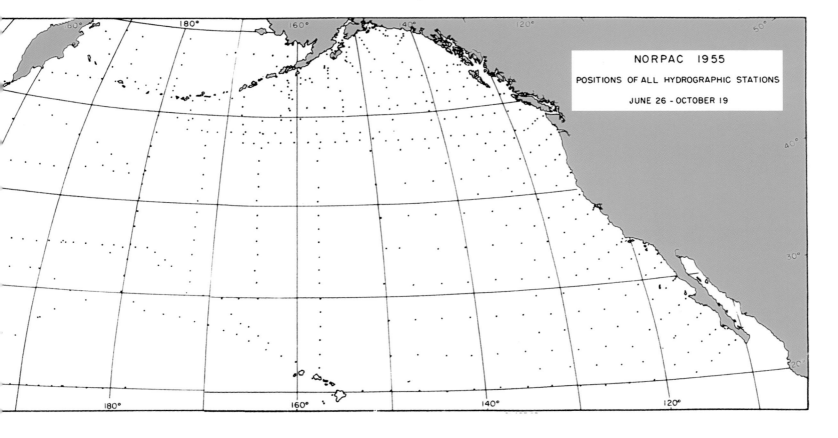

The Voyages of Vityaz

Vityaz has been a name for a succession of Russian oceanographic research vessels since the 1870s. The voyage of Stefan Makarov in the *Vityaz* of 1886–89 advanced knowledge of oceanography and the Pacific considerably.

In the period 1949 to 1955, a new *Vityaz* carried out more detailed surveys than had ever been done before in the northwestern part of the Pacific Ocean, as shown on Map 244 (right). The overwhelming coverage of the Russian ship is shown on the map that compares the tracks of that ship with those of other nations (Map 243, below).

A study of deep-sea fauna showed that life was possible at great depths despite their enormous pressures. A plot was made of the vertical distribution of animals in water 10 km (6 miles) deep.

After 1955 the *Vityaz* embarked on a survey of the whole North Pacific and was responsible for the discovery of a number of new trenches and seamounts. Map 245 (far right) shows some of the undersea features discovered by the ship.

In 1957 a new world record sounding of 10 990 m (36,056 feet) proved that the Mariana Trench was deeper than had previously been thought.

Bottom profile made by *Vityaz* from Tsugaru Strait, between Honshu and Hokkaido, and Adak Island, in the Aleutian chain. The two deeps are shown: the Japan Trench and the Aleutian Trench. Vertical exaggeration is 37x.

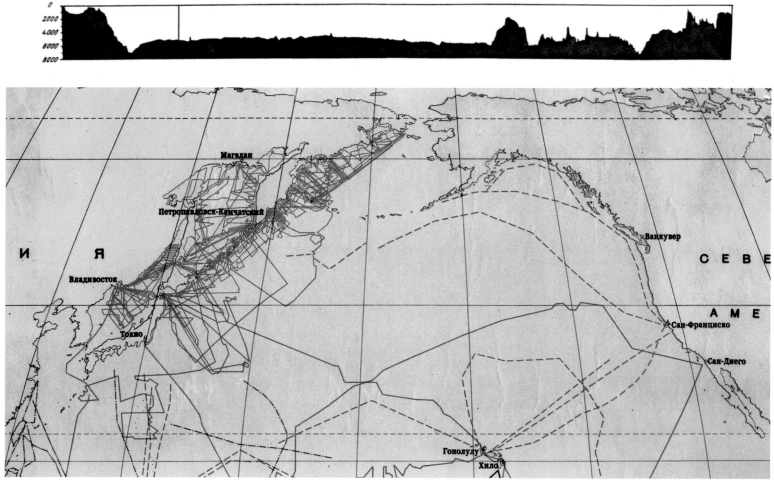

Map 243.
A Russian map dating from about 1960 showing the tracks of oceanographic vessels since *Nero* in 1899. The red lines are the tracks of *Vityaz*. The map shows dramatically, as it was no doubt supposed to, how much more comprehensive the Russian effort was to survey the oceans.

СХЕМА МАРШРУТОВ ЭКСПЕДИЦИЙ, ВЫПОЛНЯВШИХ ПОДРОБНЫЕ ТРОСОВЫЕ И ЭХОЛОТНЫЕ ИЗМЕРЕНИЯ ГЛУБИН, ИСПОЛЬЗОВАННЫХ ПРИ СОСТАВЛЕНИИ КАРТЫ

МАСШТАБ 1 : 40 000 000

400   0   400   800   1200   1600 км

СССР, „Витязь"

США „Хорайзн" (Horizon),„Атлантис" (Atlantis), „Арго"(Argo), „Альбатрос"(Albatross), „Карнеги"(Carnegie),„Неро"(Nero)

Швеция, „Альбатрос"(Albatross)

Дания,„Галатея" (Galathea),„Дана"(Dana)

Новая Зеландия, „Лахлан"(Lachlan)

Нидерланды, „Снеллиус"(Snellius),„Сибога"(Siboga)

Япония, „Синтоку-Мару" (Sintoku-Maru)

Германия, „Эди"(Edi), „Стефан"(Stephan), „Планет"(Planet), „Газелле"(Gaselle)

Map 244.
Map of the tracks of *Vityaz* in 1949–55.

Map 245 (right).
Summary map of Russian discoveries by *Vityaz* expeditions in the western Pacific.

Map 246 (below).
A simplified Russian bathymetric map produced as a result of the data collected from the intense activity of *Vityaz* in the northwest Pacific.

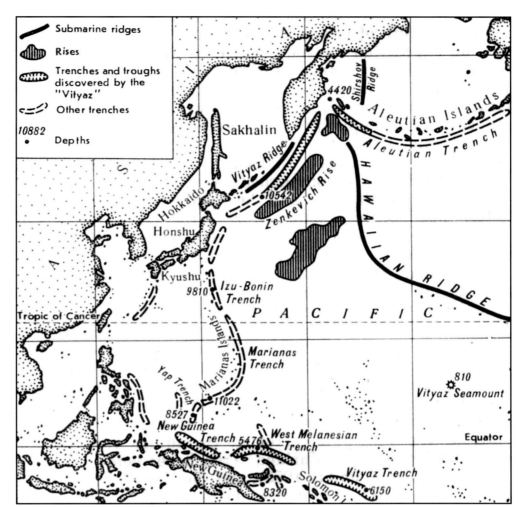

Envisioning the Sea Floor

This wonderfully artistic map is part of a map drawn by American marine geologist Bruce Heezen and his colleague Marie Tharp in 1971, as part of a continuing series of maps they drew of ocean floors.

Starting with the Atlantic Ocean in the early 1950s, Heezen and Tharp drew what they termed, with good reason, "physiographic diagrams" rather than maps, for the reality was that there was a good deal of imagination or at least informed guesswork that went into their construction, so limited was the data from which they were drawn relative to the detail that they show.

In 1953, Marie Tharp was working for Bruce Heezen. Tharp was laboriously plotting profile data from the Atlantic when she noticed a V-shaped notch in the crest of the Mid-Atlantic Ridge, a rift valley just like the one in East Africa. The theory of continental drift was not in vogue in those days, yet here was evidence for it. In addition, Heezen plotted records of earthquake epicenters, and most turned out to lie within Tharp's V-shaped notch.

As a result of this discovery, Heezen and another geologist, Maurice Ewing, made a logical leap. While they did not have detailed enough information as to the shape of the seabed for much of the world beyond the Atlantic, they did have earthquake records.

Thus they proposed that a continuous ridge, with a rift valley at its center, extended around the world, following the pattern of earthquake epicenters. It was the line from which the sea floor was wrenching apart, and generating earthquakes in the process.

In the Pacific it ran up the west coast of the Americas, in the north separating the North American Plate from the Pacific Plate, and across the Aleutians and south through the Kurils and Japan, separating the Pacific Plate from the Eurasian Plate.

Heezen and Tharp produced maps of the three major oceans of the world based on a painstaking plotting of any and all bathymetric data available at the time. But there were still huge holes in the vast expanses to be covered, and so Marie Tharp used her judgment to draw undersea mountains where she was sure they would be; she knew there was a range of mountains in a given location, but not the location of individual ones.

Thus the result they termed a "physiographic diagram" rather than a map, to admit the guesswork involved in some parts of the ocean.

The result was a series of artistically drawn maps that nevertheless gave an excellent impression of submarine topography. But the seabed was "envisioned," not mapped.

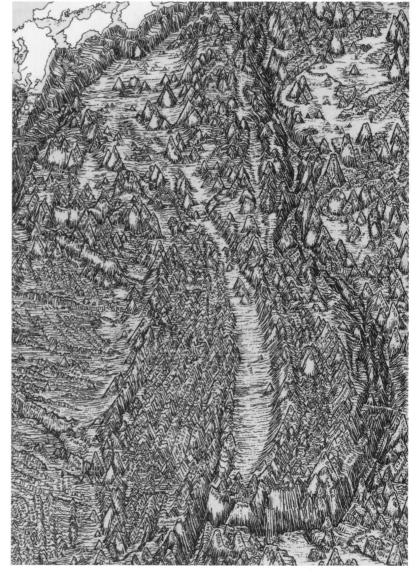

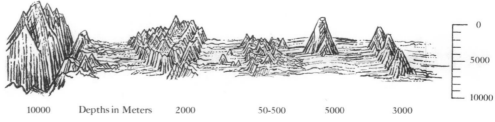

10000   Depths in Meters   2000   50-500   5000   3000

0
5000
10000

Map 248.
Part of a French world map of the oceans, drawn in 1979 based on the work of Bruce Heezen and Marie Tharp.

Map 247 (left).
Part of Bruce Heezen and Marie Tharp's "physiographic diagram" of the western Pacific Ocean, from a revised edition published in 1971. Shown is the area south of Japan (the land at the top of the map), including South Honshu Ridge (running down the middle); the Mariana Trench (bottom right); and the Bonin Trench (top right center, continuing northwards from the Mariana Trench). The ridge running down the left side of the map is the smaller Kyushu-Palau Ridge. Below is the map key.

The U.S. Navy's Climatic Atlas

During and after the Second World War, the use of the airplane revolutionized the collection of meteorological data in hitherto inaccessible places such as the North Pacific Ocean. Now information could be collected not only at sea level but at altitude.

Nevertheless, most data was still gathered at a finite number of "ocean station networks" established by the U.S. Navy, who had nine points only, and by other countries for the continuous observation of the weather. These locations were necessarily limited in number, but did allow collection of a time series of data from a single point, as on land. The rest of the information still came from transient shipping.

In the mid-1950s the U.S. Navy published a massive climatic atlas covering all the world's oceans; shown here are parts of just two of the many maps showing monthly conditions.

This situation was not to continue; the coming of satellites changed the observation of weather over the oceans forever. Now weather ships are gone, but the quality of information, now gathered remotely, has improved immensely.

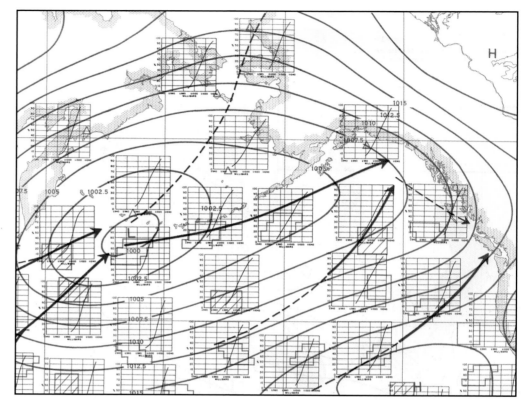

Two maps from the 1956 edition of the *U.S. Navy Marine Climatic Atlas of the World, Volume II, North Pacific Ocean*. Map 249, above, shows sea level pressure in January; storm tracks sweep towards the North American coast. Map 250, below, shows surface-level winds for April. The latter illustrates why it was difficult for Spanish and English voyages of exploration to sail close to the coast as they proceeded northwards in the springtime; the winds were contrary. The information shown on these maps is not as comprehensive as it looks, being based on a limited number of observation points. This was all about to change with the advent of satellites.

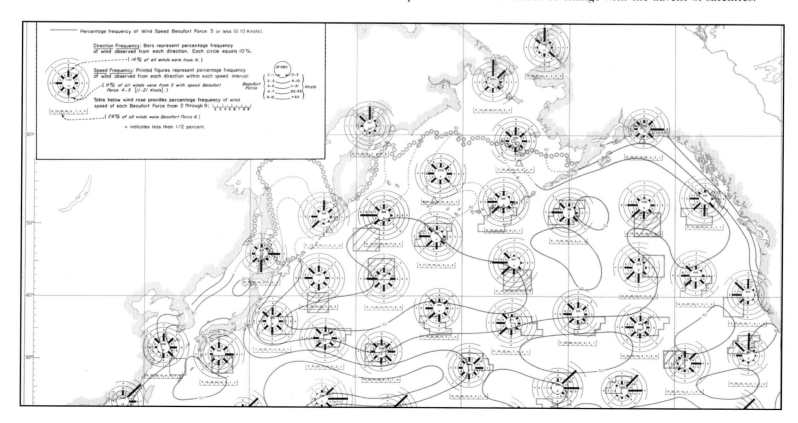

The Bathymetry of the North Pacific

In 1970, spurred by a considerably greater amount of information that had by then become available, scientists from Scripps Institute of Oceanography and Institute of Marine Resources compiled a large, multisection bathymetric map of the North Pacific Ocean.

The map was intended for use by scientists who were studying the emerging geological theories of sea floor spreading and plate tectonics and the various ocean sciences. Scientists on land had good geological maps, but those working on the ocean did not.

The maps were stated to be *an interpretation* of sea floor relief, and indeed they were, but nevertheless a much better interpretation than anything before. The map below shows the tracks of ships that contributed data to these maps; there are a huge number of tracks now. The basic contour interval was 200 fathoms (365 m or 1,200 feet), with contours at 100 fathoms where the quality of the data allowed.

These charts showed many previously uncharted submarine features such as seamounts and trenches. Aside from their obvious scientific value, these maps are works of art as well.

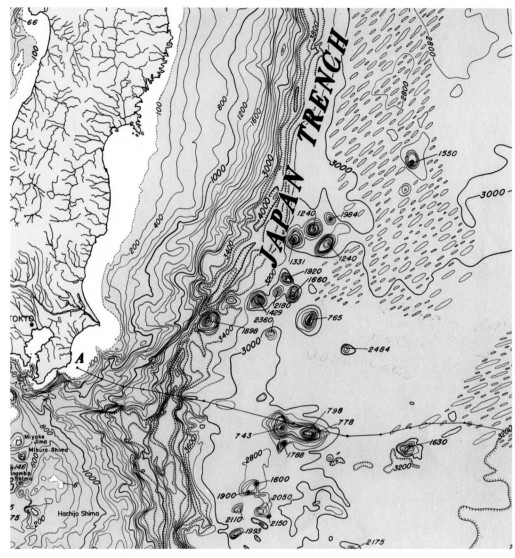

Map 251 (above).
A portrayal of part of the Japan Trench, off the southeast coast of Japan. The map key is shown overleaf.

Map 252 (below).
Key map showing the tracks of ships whose information was used to construct the Scripps bathymetric map.

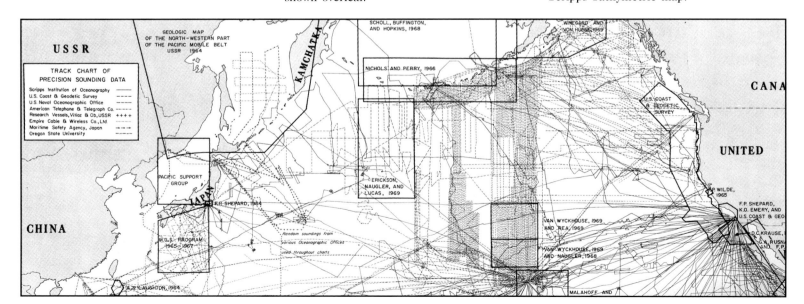

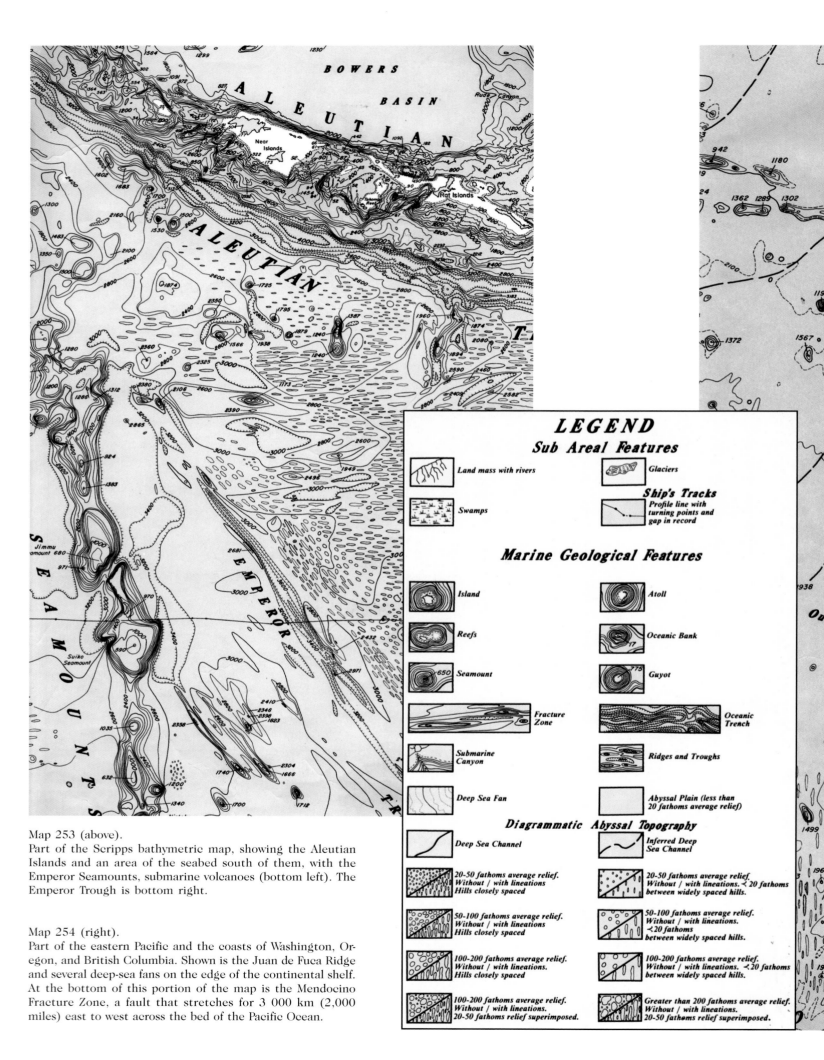

Map 253 (above).
Part of the Scripps bathymetric map, showing the Aleutian Islands and an area of the seabed south of them, with the Emperor Seamounts, submarine volcanoes (bottom left). The Emperor Trough is bottom right.

Map 254 (right).
Part of the eastern Pacific and the coasts of Washington, Oregon, and British Columbia. Shown is the Juan de Fuca Ridge and several deep-sea fans on the edge of the continental shelf. At the bottom of this portion of the map is the Mendocino Fracture Zone, a fault that stretches for 3 000 km (2,000 miles) east to west across the bed of the Pacific Ocean.

LEGEND
Sub Areal Features

Land mass with rivers   Glaciers

Swamps

Ship's Tracks
Profile line with turning points and gap in record

Marine Geological Features

Island   Atoll

Reefs   Oceanic Bank

Seamount   Guyot

Fracture Zone   Oceanic Trench

Submarine Canyon   Ridges and Troughs

Deep Sea Fan   Abyssal Plain (less than 20 fathoms average relief)

Diagrammatic Abyssal Topography

Deep Sea Channel   Inferred Deep Sea Channel

20-50 fathoms average relief. Without / with lineations Hills closely spaced   20-50 fathoms average relief. Without / with lineations. < 20 fathoms between widely spaced hills.

50-100 fathoms average relief. Without / with lineations Hills closely spaced   50-100 fathoms average relief. Without / with lineations. < 20 fathoms between widely spaced hills.

100-200 fathoms average relief. Without / with lineations. Hills closely spaced   100-200 fathoms average relief. Without / with lineations. < 20 fathoms between widely spaced hills.

100-200 fathoms average relief. Without / with lineations. 20-50 fathoms relief superimposed.   Greater than 200 fathoms average relief. Without / with lineations. 20-50 fathoms relief superimposed.

The Ocean Drilling Program

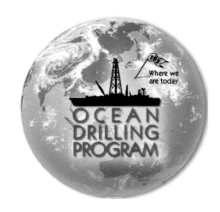

In 1957 the American Miscellaneous Society, a group of prominent ocean scientists, wanted to determine the physical properties of the discontinuity that exists between the Earth's crust and the underlying mantle, the Mohorovicic seismic discontinuity, as it is called. The scientists proposed to the U.S. National Science Foundation the aptly named Mohole Project, which was to drill a hole through the crust to the discontinuity and retrieve rock samples.

JOIDES Resolution, successor drilling ship to *Glomar Challenger*.

This project, though much promoted, never came to fruition, but it did generate interest in the idea of deep drilling, and in 1964 JOIDES (Joint Oceanographic Institutions for Deep Earth Sampling) was created to drill deep into the seabed, to help decipher the geologic history of the planet and look for evidence of ongoing processes such as sea floor spreading.

The thickness of the Earth's crust under the oceans is about 5 km or 3 miles, much less than it is under the continents, and so the record held in the crust could hopefully be accessed with considerably less drilling. However, the only way this could be done was from a ship, and the drill would first have to traverse the waters to the sea floor. A major challenge would be to keep the drilling platform in position.

In 1966, the U.S National Science Foundation, at the urging of JOIDES, approved construction of a specially designed ship. The Deep Sea Drilling Project, as the program was now called, contracted with Global Marine Inc., a commercial marine drilling company, to supply the ship, which was christened *Glomar Challenger*, in honor of the nineteenth-century pioneering oceanographic research vessel *Challenger* (see page 168).

Glomar Challenger went first to the Atlantic, where the cores drilled supported the new sea floor spreading hypothesis.

In the Pacific the crust far from centers of sea floor spreading was investigated, and from sediment-thickness data, epoch by epoch, a quantitative estimate of the rate of plate motion could be made.

Changes in the composition of sediments reflect changes in the productivity of the ocean above them, changes in the temperature of deep waters, and changes in large ocean-scale currents. Information from drill cores has been used to reconstruct the history of the Earth's climate. It has also provided records of cataclysmic events such as volcanic eruptions.

The Deep Sea Drilling Project was restructured in 1975 and with international participation became the International Ocean Drilling Program, with more than ten countries involved.

By the end of the program in 1983, *Global Challenger* had drilled a total of 325 km (200 miles) at 624 sites worldwide, and had penetrated as deep as 1 741 m (5,700 feet); the ship had traveled a total of nearly 700 000 km, or 435,000 miles.

But the drilling program was not finished; in 1985 a new ship was commissioned. This ship has been renamed *JOIDES Resolution*, this time named after James Cook's ship *Resolution*.

The deepest hole drilled by the new ship was one of 2 111 m (6,926 feet), in the eastern Pacific. The greatest water depth encountered at a drill site was 5 980 m (19,620 feet), in the western Pacific. Over 1,400 holes have been drilled.

Drilling in the modern era is made easier by the use of satellite technology to locate drill sites, and seabed sonar transmitters are used to maintain the ship in exactly the same position in all weathers.

Drilling today continues to explore the evolution and structure of the Earth below the world's oceans.

Map 255.
Drill sites of *Glomar Challenger* (blue) and *JOIDES Resolution* (red).

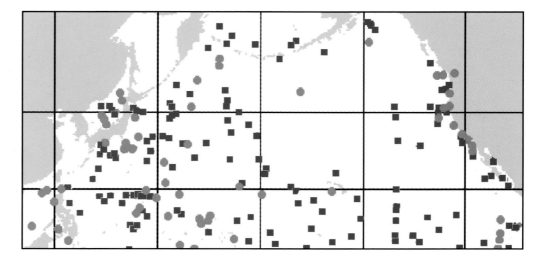

The International Decade of Ocean Exploration

The success of the International Geophysical Year in 1957–58 was the inspiration for a number of other scientific projects involving international cooperation. The International Decade of Ocean Exploration (IDOE) was sponsored by the Intergovernmental Oceanographic Commission and lasted from 1970 to 1980. It was an umbrella for an array of cooperative projects designed to further understanding of the processes that were taking place in the world's oceans and how these processes affected the environment.

Exploration of the sea was to be sustained rather than episodic and planned in a global context rather than as a collection of individual projects.

One project was termed the North Pacific Experiment, or NORPAX, and it was concerned with large-scale ocean-atmosphere interactions. Compared to the atmosphere, the ocean has an enormous capacity to store heat and energy, which can have a time-delayed effect on climate. NORPAX scientists discovered that they could predict El Niño (a warming of part of the ocean that materializes only once every four or five years) with tide-gauge measurements on certain islands near the equator. Just prior to an El Niño, mean sea level drops in

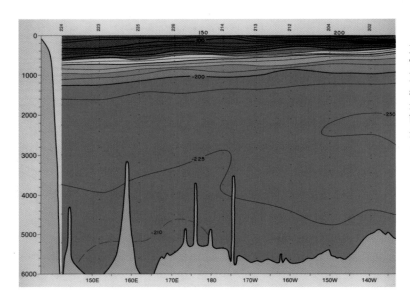

Map 256.
Track of Scripps' Research Vessel *Melville* in the Pacific Oceans during the GEOSECS project.

the eastern Pacific and rises in the western Pacific, a change associated with a failure of equatorial trade winds. The ability to predict El Niño assists in the forecasting of anomalous weather patterns that are typically associated with it.

Another IDOE project, partly in the North Pacific, was the Coastal Upwelling Ecosystems Analysis, or CUEA, whose observations included the waters off Oregon and Baja California as well as those in analogous areas off Peru and northwest Africa. These studies were directed towards predicting the biological productivity of upwelling ecosystems from observations of critical air-sea processes, mainly wind and currents.

Yet another program was the Geochemical Ocean Sections Study, or GEOSECS. This program was the idea of Henry Stommel, who thought that deep ocean currents and the whole thermohaline circulation of the oceans (large-scale water circulation driven by differences in temperature and salinity in three dimensions) could be tracked by the use of

trace chemicals, introduced into the ocean at one point, either naturally or artificially, and sampled at many other points. He realized that this would require a large-scale collaborative scientific effort.

Thus a global, three-dimensional survey of chemical, isotopic, and radiochemical tracers was initiated. Overall, the program lasted from 1972 to 1978, but in the Pacific the studies were carried out from August 1973 to June 1974. The Pacific survey was carried out by the research vessel *Melville*, from Scripps Institution of Oceanography.

GEOSECS was able to determine the rate and speed at which water sank, welled up, and moved laterally as currents in the deep ocean. In the process, it was found that in the northeast Pacific there was water at depth that had not been in contact with the atmosphere for a thousand years.

Map 257 (right, bottom).
The path of *Melville* while sampling water to compile the profile at left, which shows the vertical distribution of Carbon 14. The profile shows a very high surface maximum and a steep drop-off to a minimum in deep water. The high surface values are derived from nuclear bomb tests. The large area of minimum Carbon 14 represents water isolated from the surface for a long time.

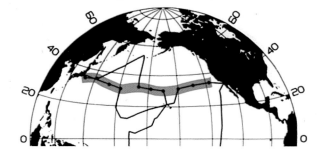

The Pacific Salmon

One of the great mysteries of evolution is how the salmon became anadromous, that is, living part of its life cycle in the salt of the sea and part, the beginning and end of its life, in the freshwater of the land.

Perhaps this was an adaptation to being driven from its streams by advancing ice during one of the ice ages. However it evolved, there is no doubt that the salmon has for millennia played a significant role in the diet and the culture of the peoples of the Pacific Rim.

In the nineteenth century, with the development of safe canning practices, the salmon spawned a major industry based on its capture and processing. More recently, there have been concerns about the maintenance of the resource for future generations.

As we have seen (page 70), it was Georg Steller who first described the life cycle of the Pacific salmon and identified the various species. But most of the major discoveries about salmon occurred two hundred years later as commercial salmon fisheries became an important economic force.

The first clear evidence that sockeye salmon returned to the stream where they hatched came at the beginning of the twentieth century. In 1903, an inquisitive technician at the Fortmann Hatchery on the Naha River, Alaska, removed some fins from 1,600 sockeye fry before they migrated seaward, and the fish reappeared as adult salmon in the same river in 1906 and 1907. But no one understood salmon behavior in the sea or the extent of their migrations until the middle of the century.

Following from a clause in the Peace Treaty of 1951 between the Allied Powers and Japan, the International Convention for the High Seas Fisheries of the North Pacific Ocean was signed in 1952 by Canada, Japan, and the United States. This led to the creation of the International North Pacific Fisheries Commission (INPFC) in 1953.

Between 1956 and 1958 scientists involved in INPFC began tagging salmon on the high seas to determine what line or lines at sea would best separate salmon originating in North America from those originating in Asia. This research led to the discovery that Pacific salmon and steelhead trout from Asia and North America migrate great distances and intermingle over broad areas of the North Pacific Ocean at certain times during their life. Tagging experiments now use more sophisticated tags that record depth, temperature, and even swimming speed.

During the twentieth century, humans have intervened increasingly in the natural life cycle of salmon. Eggs and milt are taken from returning spawning fish and incubated in hatcheries before being released to the ocean. Salmon production in Japan, largely chum salmon and pink salmon, relies almost entirely on hatcheries, while other nations have maintained both wild and hatchery production.

Map 258.
Distribution of recoveries of immature chum salmon, from a pioneer experiment carried out by American scientists in 1956–57. The salmon were tagged near Adak Island, in the Aleutians, in 1956, and caught at various locations in 1957, allowing plotting of the tracks they had taken.

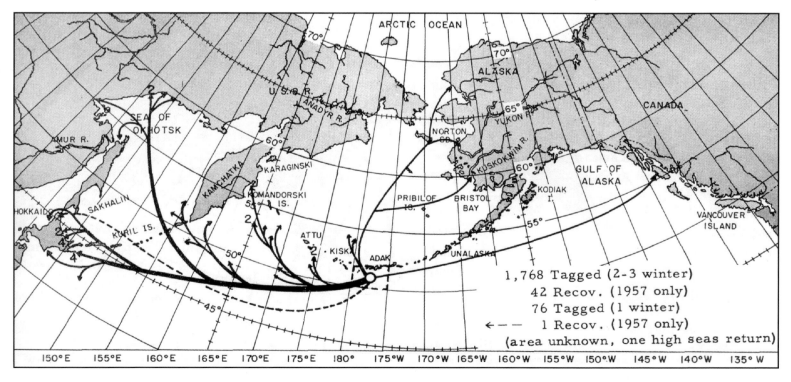

1,768 Tagged (2-3 winter)
42 Recov. (1957 only)
76 Tagged (1 winter)
← — 1 Recov. (1957 only)
(area unknown, one high seas return)

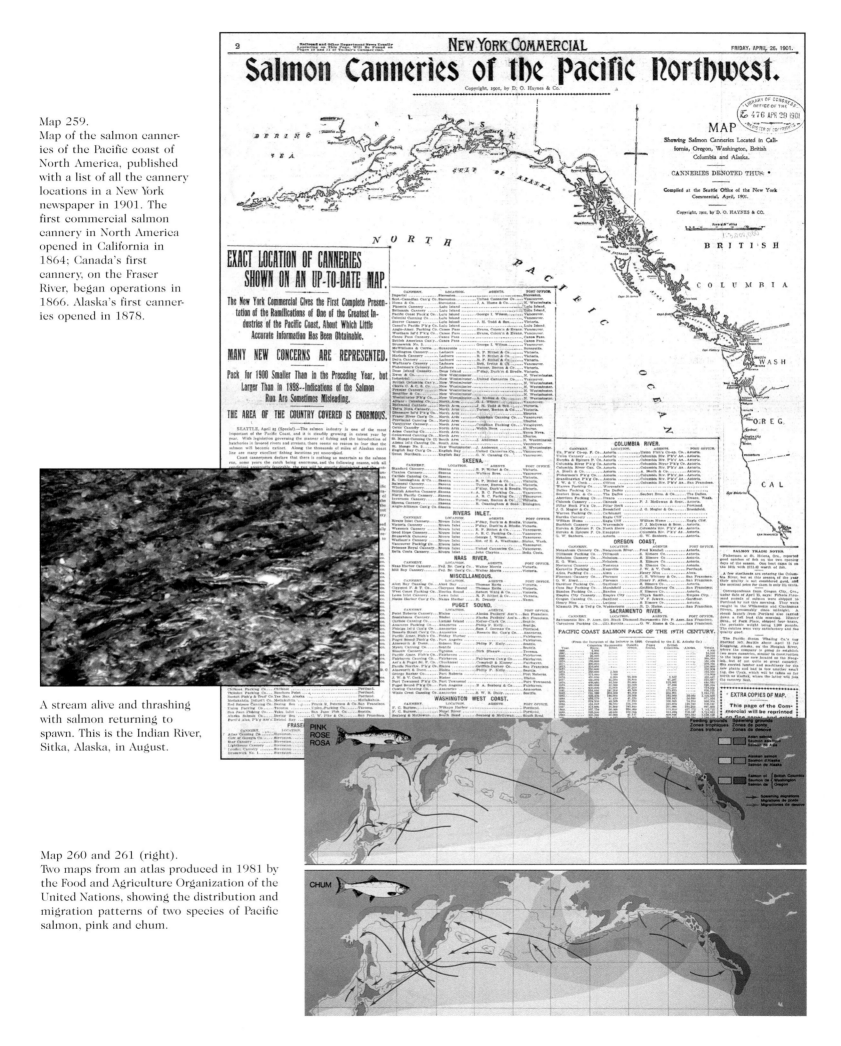

Map 259.
Map of the salmon canneries of the Pacific coast of North America, published with a list of all the cannery locations in a New York newspaper in 1901. The first commercial salmon cannery in North America opened in California in 1864; Canada's first cannery, on the Fraser River, began operations in 1866. Alaska's first canneries opened in 1878.

A stream alive and thrashing with salmon returning to spawn. This is the Indian River, Sitka, Alaska, in August.

Map 260 and 261 (right).
Two maps from an atlas produced in 1981 by the Food and Agriculture Organization of the United Nations, showing the distribution and migration patterns of two species of Pacific salmon, pink and chum.

The Origin of the Continents and Oceans

Two hundred million years ago there was only one continent, dubbed Pangaea, and one ocean surrounding it. The movement of the landmass and its breakup into separate continents formed the world's oceans, including the Pacific.

It was in 1915 that Alfred Wegener first proposed that the continents were originally one landmass, and that they are slowly drifting apart. In 1928 Arthur Holmes theorized that they moved because of convection currents in molten rock powered by radioactivity, thus laying the foundation from which modern ideas developed.

After more intensive surveying of the sea floor in the 1950s had revealed undersea topography to a previously unprecedented degree, a mechanism of sea floor spreading was proposed to explain the midocean ridges that had been identified in the world's oceans. In the process it explained continental drift,

continents moving away from each other because the ocean basins were expanding.

In the North Pacific, the midocean ridge comes inland at Baja California and is otherwise limited to a short stretch off the coast from Cape Mendocino to the northern tip of Vancouver Island. Here the Pacific Plate is expanding away from the Juan de Fuca Plate, which is in turn plunging under the North American Plate (see Map 264, pages 200–201).

Map 262 (right, top).
Earthquake probability clearly follows the Pacific Rim and the active zone of spreading or subduction.

Map 263 (right, bottom).
Part of a map showing the tectonic features of the Pacific Ocean, vividly demonstrating the Asian part of the "Rim of Fire." The key for this map and the eastern Pacific portion on the next page is shown below.

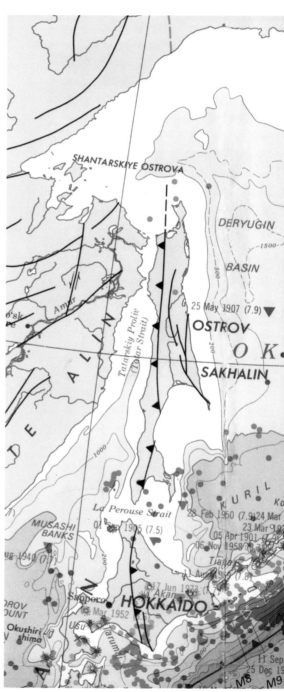

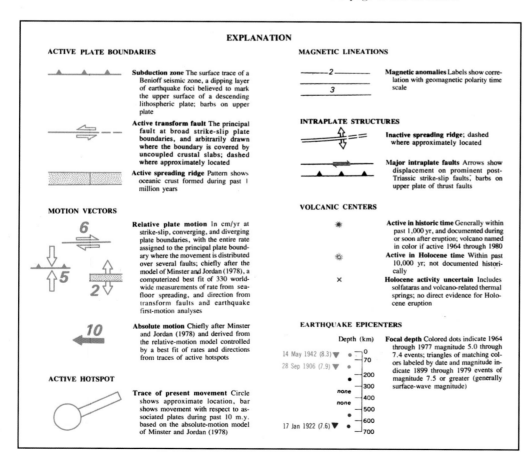

EXPLANATION

ACTIVE PLATE BOUNDARIES

Subduction zone The surface trace of a Benioff seismic zone, a dipping layer of earthquake foci believed to mark the upper surface of a descending lithospheric plate; barbs on upper plate

Active transform fault The principal fault at broad strike-slip plate boundaries, and arbitrarily drawn where the boundary is covered by uncoupled crustal slabs; dashed where approximately located

Active spreading ridge Pattern shows oceanic crust formed during past 1 million years

MOTION VECTORS

6
5
2

Relative plate motion In cm/yr at strike-slip, converging, and diverging plate boundaries, with the entire rate assigned to the principal plate boundary where the movement is distributed over several faults; chiefly after the model of Minster and Jordan (1978), a computerized best fit of 330 worldwide measurements of rate from sea-floor spreading, and direction from transform faults and earthquake first-motion analyses

10
Absolute motion Chiefly after Minster and Jordan (1978) and derived from the relative-motion model controlled by a best fit of rates and directions from traces of active hotspots

ACTIVE HOTSPOT

Trace of present movement Circle shows approximate location, bar shows movement with respect to associated plates during past 10 m.y. based on the absolute-motion model of Minster and Jordan (1978)

MAGNETIC LINEATIONS

—2—
3
Magnetic anomalies Labels show correlation with geomagnetic polarity time scale

INTRAPLATE STRUCTURES

Inactive spreading ridge; dashed where approximately located

Major intraplate faults Arrows show displacement on prominent post-Triassic strike-slip faults; barbs on upper plate of thrust faults

VOLCANIC CENTERS

✳ **Active in historic time** Generally within past 1,000 yr, and documented during or soon after eruption; volcano named in color if active 1964 through 1980

✴ **Active in Holocene time** Within past 10,000 yr; not documented historically

✕ **Holocene activity uncertain** Includes solfataras and volcano-related thermal springs; no direct evidence for Holocene eruption

EARTHQUAKE EPICENTERS

Depth (km)	
14 May 1942 (8.3) ▽ •	0 / 70
28 Sep 1906 (7.9) ▽ •	200
•	300
none	400
none	500
17 Jan 1922 (7.6) ▽ •	600 / 700

Focal depth Colored dots indicate 1964 through 1977 magnitude 5.0 through 7.4 events; triangles of matching colors labeled by date and magnitude indicate 1899 through 1979 events of magnitude 7.5 or greater (generally surface-wave magnitude)

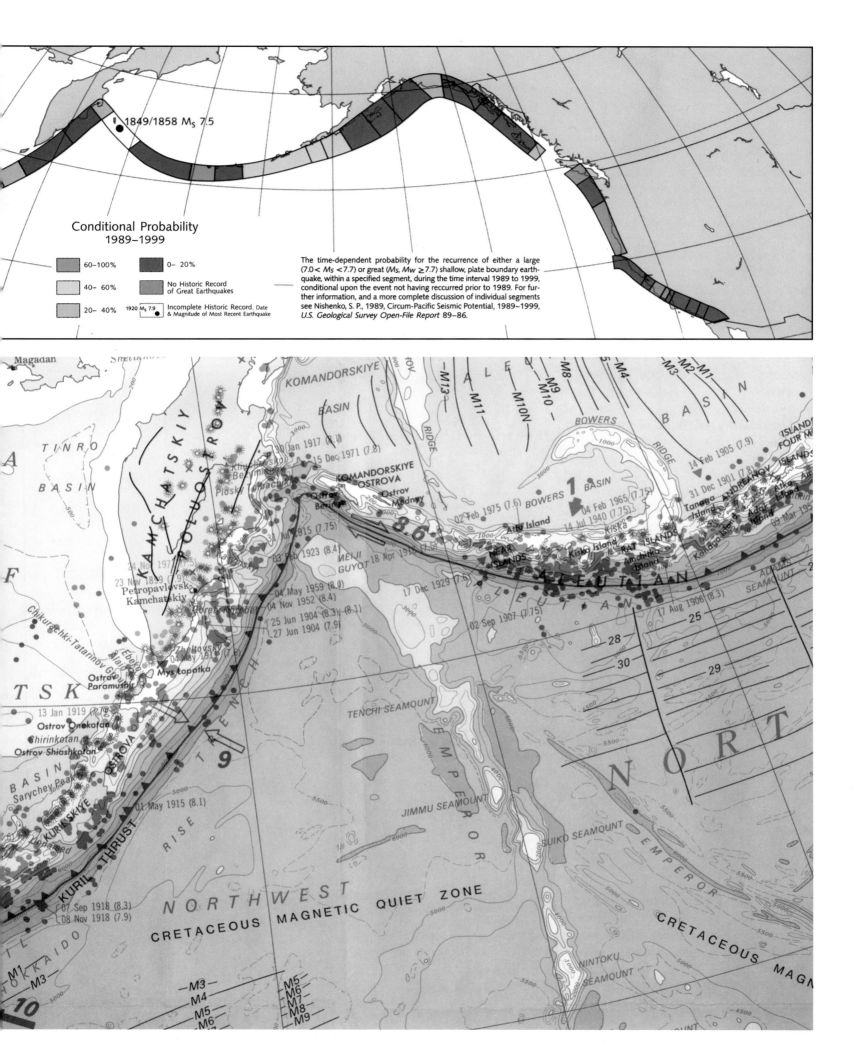

Conditional Probability
1989–1999

60–100%	0– 20%
40– 60%	No Historic Record of Great Earthquakes
20– 40%	Incomplete Historic Record. Date & Magnitude of Most Recent Earthquake

1920 M$_s$ 7.9 ● Incomplete Historic Record. Date & Magnitude of Most Recent Earthquake

1849/1858 M$_s$ 7.5

The time-dependent probability for the recurrence of either a large (7.0< M$_S$ <7.7) or great (M$_S$, M$_W$ ≥7.7) shallow, plate boundary earthquake, within a specified segment, during the time interval 1989 to 1999, conditional upon the event not having reccurred prior to 1989. For further information, and a more complete discussion of individual segments see Nishenko, S. P., 1989, Circum-Pacific Seismic Potential, 1989–1999, *U.S. Geological Survey Open-File Report* 89–86.

The theory of sea floor spreading was confirmed in 1963–66 by studies of the direction of ancient magnetism in rocks surrounding the ridges. This confirmation paved the way for modern theories of plate tectonics, which envision the Earth's crust as consisting of a series of plates that move relative to one another.

Around the Pacific Rim is the corollary of the expanding midocean ridge, the subduction zone, where plates grind together and one is dragged under the other. Under California and in a vast arc from the Alaska panhandle through the Aleutians and Kurils to Japan is a major subduction zone where ocean floor is being dragged under the North American and Eurasian Plates. In the process, ocean trenches such as the Aleutian Trench, the Japan Trench, and the Mariana Trench are formed.

The majority of volcanic activity occurs at these plate margins, as do earthquakes, hence the name "Pacific Rim of Fire."

However, some volcanic activity also occurs in the interiors of plates, over "hot spots," or weak points in the underlying crust. But the plate above the crust continues to move as a result of continuous sea floor spreading, and so volcanoes migrate away from the hot spots that gave rise to them, forming chains of seamounts such as the Emperor Seamounts and, eventually, islands such as the Hawaiian Islands.

Fracture zones of various magnitudes cover the sea floor of the northeast part of the Pacific Ocean (map at right). These are thought to be caused by slight changes in sea floor spreading direction, over a long period of time, which cause stresses between one part of a plate and another that eventually lead to cracking.

Along the line where the Pacific Plate and the Juan de Fuca Plate meet is a midocean ridge, at which upwelling is creating new sea floor and in the process pushing the two plates apart. Here geologists have found a number of hot vents, a form of volcanic activity. At what are essentially hot springs, superheated water is vented into the colder ocean water. The difference in temperatures causes an immediate precipitation of minerals, metal sulfides, held in solution, giving the appearance of dense black smoke. The rapid precipitation causes a solid chimney of rock to be built up from the seabed.

These "black smokers" have now been discovered all over the world, but one of the largest is on the Juan de Fuca Ridge; dubbed "Godzilla," it is sixteen storeys high.

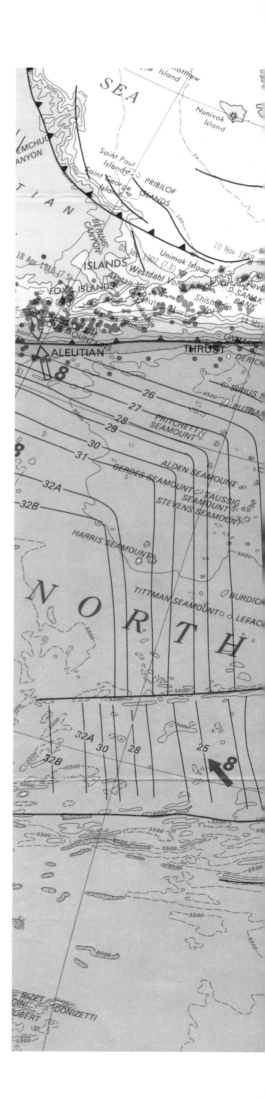

Map 264.
The eastern part of the tectonic map of the Pacific. The fracture zones are a nearly ubiquitous feature. The junction of the relatively small Juan de Fuca Plate with the much larger Pacific Plate to its west is the site of a midocean ridge, that is, a rift-type valley in the middle of a ridge, from which the plates are being propelled away from each other by the addition of new sea floor welling up from below. It is also the site of a line of volcanic activity, in this case hot vents. The red line with red triangles along the western coast of North America is a major subduction zone, where the Pacific and Juan de Fuca Plates are being dragged under the North American Plate.

Destructive Waves – Pacific Tsunamis

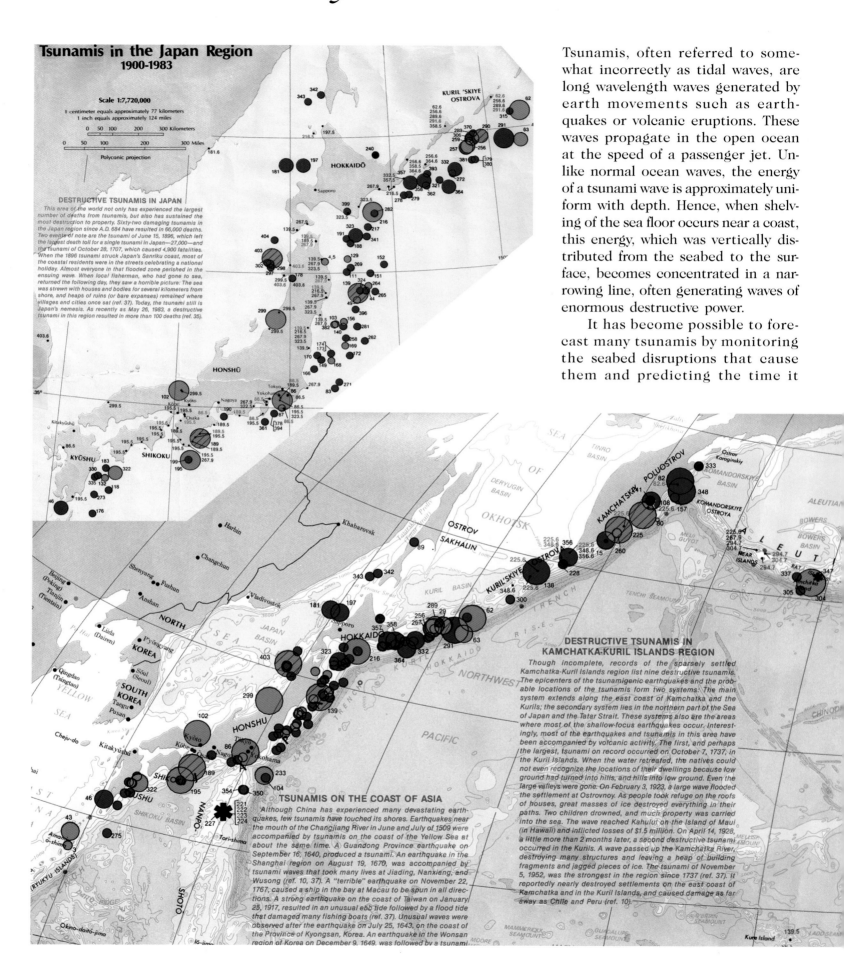

Tsunamis, often referred to somewhat incorrectly as tidal waves, are long wavelength waves generated by earth movements such as earthquakes or volcanic eruptions. These waves propagate in the open ocean at the speed of a passenger jet. Unlike normal ocean waves, the energy of a tsunami wave is approximately uniform with depth. Hence, when shelving of the sea floor occurs near a coast, this energy, which was vertically distributed from the seabed to the surface, becomes concentrated in a narrowing line, often generating waves of enormous destructive power.

It has become possible to forecast many tsunamis by monitoring the seabed disruptions that cause them and predicting the time it

Tsunamis in the Japan Region 1900-1983

Scale 1:7,720,000
1 centimeter equals approximately 77 kilometers
1 inch equals approximately 124 miles

0 50 100   200   300 Kilometers

0   50   100   200   300 Miles

Polyconic projection

DESTRUCTIVE TSUNAMIS IN JAPAN
This area of the world not only has experienced the largest number of deaths from tsunamis, but also has sustained the most destruction to property. Sixty-two damaging tsunamis in the Japan region since A.D. 684 have resulted in 66,000 deaths. Two events of note are the tsunami of June 15, 1896, which left the largest death toll for a single tsunami in Japan—27,000—and the tsunami of October 28, 1707, which caused 4,900 fatalities. When the 1896 tsunami struck Japan's Sanriku coast, most of the coastal residents were in the streets celebrating a national holiday. Almost everyone in that flooded zone perished in the ensuing wave. When local fisherman, who had gone to sea, returned the following day, they saw a horrible picture: The sea was strewn with houses and bodies for several kilometers from shore, and heaps of ruins (or bare expanses) remained where villages and cities once sat (ref. 37). Today, the tsunami still is Japan's nemesis. As recently as May 26, 1983, a destructive tsunami in this region resulted in more than 100 deaths (ref. 35).

DESTRUCTIVE TSUNAMIS IN KAMCHATKA-KURIL ISLANDS REGION
Though incomplete, records of the sparsely settled Kamchatka-Kuril Islands region list nine destructive tsunamis. The epicenters of the tsunamigenic earthquakes and the probable locations of the tsunamis form two systems: The main system extends along the east coast of Kamchatka and the Kurils; the secondary system lies in the northern part of the Sea of Japan and the Tatar Strait. These systems also are the areas where most of the shallow-focus earthquakes occur. Interestingly, most of the earthquakes and tsunamis in this area have been accompanied by volcanic activity. The first, and perhaps the largest, tsunami on record occurred on October 7, 1737, in the Kuril Islands. When the water retreated, the natives could not even recognize the locations of their dwellings because low ground had turned into hills, and hills into low ground. Even the large valleys were gone. On February 3, 1923, a large wave flooded the settlement at Ostrovnoy. As people took refuge on the roofs of houses, great masses of ice destroyed everything in their paths. Two children drowned, and much property was carried into the sea. The wave reached Kahului on the Island of Maui (in Hawaii) and inflicted losses of $1.5 million. On April 14, 1928, a little more than 2 months later, a second destructive tsunami occurred in the Kurils. A wave passed up the Kamchatka River, destroying many structures and leaving a heap of building fragments and jagged pieces of ice. The tsunami of November 5, 1952, was the strongest in the region since 1737 (ref. 37). It reportedly nearly destroyed settlements on the east coast of Kamchatka and in the Kuril Islands, and caused damage as far away as Chile and Peru (ref. 10).

TSUNAMIS ON THE COAST OF ASIA
Although China has experienced many devastating earthquakes, few tsunamis have touched its shores. Earthquakes near the mouth of the Changjiang River in June and July of 1509 were accompanied by tsunamis on the coast of the Yellow Sea at about the same time. A Guandong Province earthquake on September 16, 1640, produced a tsunami. An earthquake in the Shanghai region on August 19, 1670, was accompanied by tsunami waves that took many lives at Jiading, Nanxiang, and Wusong (ref. 10, 37). A "terrible" earthquake on November 22, 1767, caused a ship in the bay at Macau to be spun in all directions. A strong earthquake on the coast of Taiwan on January 25, 1917, resulted in an unusual ebb tide followed by a flood tide that damaged many fishing boats (ref. 37). Unusual waves were observed after the earthquake on July 25, 1643, on the coast of the Province of Kyongsan, Korea. An earthquake in the Wonsan region of Korea on December 9, 1649, was followed by a tsunami

will take for the tsunami to propagate from the source region to distant coastlines. This does not work, however, when the source is so near to a coastline that the tsunami arrives too quickly.

It is more difficult, however, to predict the height of tsunami waves, and sometimes alerts have been issued for massive evacuations of coastal areas only to find that the height of the arriving tsunami is inconsequential.

The solution to this problem lies in a network of moored ocean buoys supporting recording instruments on the seabed. Instruments are submerged, not on the buoy, because on the open ocean the unconcentrated tsunami wave can sometimes hardly be detected at the surface. The instruments detect the wave and send the information to the buoy, from where it is transmitted to a satellite.

Map 265.
The map on this page tells its own story. In several sections, the map shows the sources of tsunami-generating events around the Pacific Rim.

(inset)
A rare photograph of a tsunami coming ashore. This was the 1946 tsunami hitting Coconut Island, Hilo, Hawaii, an amazing image made by a no doubt fleeing photographer.

Pacific Tsunami Museum.

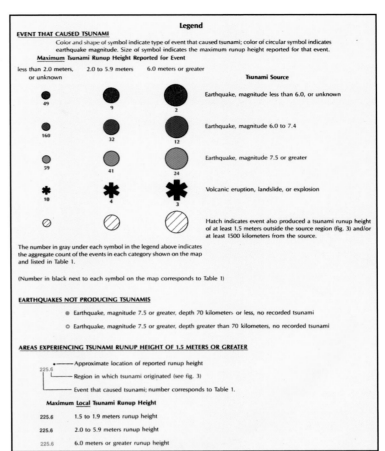

Legend

EVENT THAT CAUSED TSUNAMI
Color and shape of symbol indicate type of event that caused tsunami; color of circular symbol indicates earthquake magnitude. Size of symbol indicates the maximum runup height reported for that event.

Maximum Tsunami Runup Height Reported for Event

less than 2.0 meters, or unknown	2.0 to 5.9 meters	6.0 meters or greater	**Tsunami Source**
49	9	2	Earthquake, magnitude less than 6.0, or unknown
160	32	12	Earthquake, magnitude 6.0 to 7.4
59	41	24	Earthquake, magnitude 7.5 or greater
10	4	3	Volcanic eruption, landslide, or explosion
			Hatch indicates event also produced a tsunami runup height of at least 1.5 meters outside the source region (fig. 3) and/or at least 1500 kilometers from the source.

The number in gray under each symbol in the legend above indicates the aggregate count of the events in each category shown on the map and listed in Table 1.

(Number in black next to each symbol on the map corresponds to Table 1)

EARTHQUAKES NOT PRODUCING TSUNAMIS

- Earthquake, magnitude 7.5 or greater, depth 70 kilometers or less, no recorded tsunami
- Earthquake, magnitude 7.5 or greater, depth greater than 70 kilometers, no recorded tsunami

AREAS EXPERIENCING TSUNAMI RUNUP HEIGHT OF 1.5 METERS OR GREATER

- 225.6 ——— Approximate location of reported runup height
- ——— Region in which tsunami originated (see fig. 3)
- ——— Event that caused tsunami; number corresponds to Table 1.

Maximum Local Tsunami Runup Height

225.6	1.5 to 1.9 meters runup height
225.6	2.0 to 5.9 meters runup height
225.6	6.0 meters or greater runup height

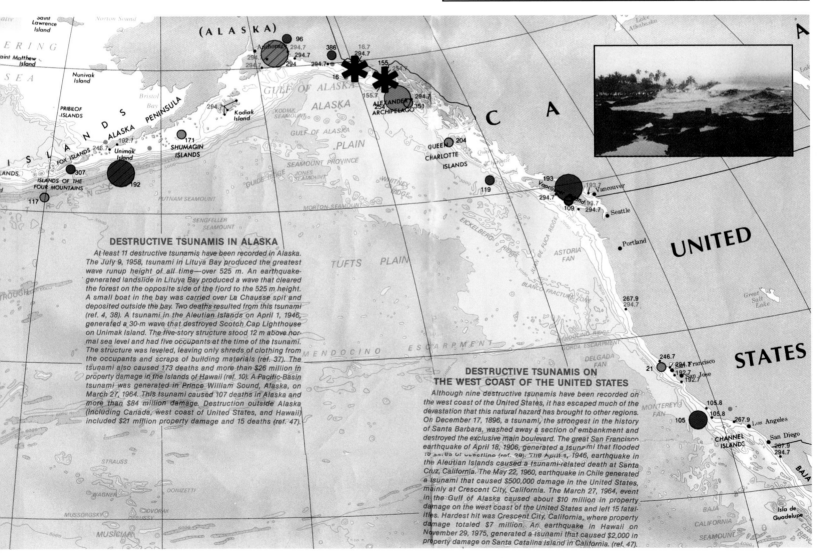

DESTRUCTIVE TSUNAMIS IN ALASKA

At least 11 destructive tsunamis have been recorded in Alaska. The July 9, 1958, tsunami in Lituya Bay produced the greatest wave runup height of all time—over 525 m. An earthquake-generated landslide in Lituya Bay produced a wave that cleared the forest on the opposite side of the fjord to the 525 m height. A small boat in the bay was carried over La Chausse spit and deposited outside the bay. Two deaths resulted from this tsunami (ref. 4, 38). A tsunami in the Aleutian Islands on April 1, 1946, generated a 30-m wave that destroyed Scotch Cap Lighthouse on Unimak Island. The five-story structure stood 12 m above normal sea level and had five occupants at the time of the tsunami. The structure was leveled, leaving only shreds of clothing from the occupants and scraps of building materials (ref. 37). The tsunami also caused 173 deaths and more than $26 million in property damage in the islands of Hawaii (ref. 10). A Pacific-Basin tsunami was generated in Prince William Sound, Alaska, on March 27, 1964. This tsunami caused 107 deaths in Alaska and more than $84 million damage. Destruction outside Alaska (including Canada, west coast of United States, and Hawaii) included $21 million property damage and 15 deaths (ref. 47).

DESTRUCTIVE TSUNAMIS ON THE WEST COAST OF THE UNITED STATES

Although nine destructive tsunamis have been recorded on the west coast of the United States, it has escaped much of the devastation that this natural hazard has brought to other regions. On December 17, 1896, a tsunami, the strongest in the history of Santa Barbara, washed away a section of embankment and destroyed the exclusive main boulevard. The great San Francisco earthquake of April 18, 1906, generated a tsunami that flooded 10 acres of coastline (ref. 29). The April 1, 1946, earthquake in the Aleutian Islands caused a tsunami-related death at Santa Cruz, California. The May 22, 1960, earthquake in Chile generated a tsunami that caused $500,000 damage in the United States, mainly at Crescent City, California. The March 27, 1964, event in the Gulf of Alaska caused about $10 million in property damage on the west coast of the United States and left 15 fatalities. Hardest hit was Crescent City, California, where property damage totaled $7 million. An earthquake in Hawaii on November 29, 1975, generated a tsunami that caused $2,000 in property damage on Santa Catalina Island in California. (ref. 47).

Multibeam Bathymetry Reveals the Details

The most detailed mapping possible is done with a camera. Over land, cameras can be mounted on planes, but in the ocean, lack of light means that cameras can only be used over extremely small areas that can be illuminated.

For larger areas, sonar mounted on a sled float at depth is towed behind a ship. The sonar scans the sea bed obliquely, producing a detailed topographical map. This is side-scan sonar.

A further method, utilized for larger areas, uses an array of sound sources and listening devices mounted on the hull of a ship. Every few seconds a strip of seabed perpendicular to the ship's direction is scanned. Because the ship is moving, a slightly different strip is scanned each time, building up a sort of stereoscopic picture of the sea floor. This is multibeam sonar, and it can produce remarkably detailed images of the seabed over a large area. It has been extensively used in the United States to map the undersea topography of the 200 mile (320 km) exclusive economic zone.

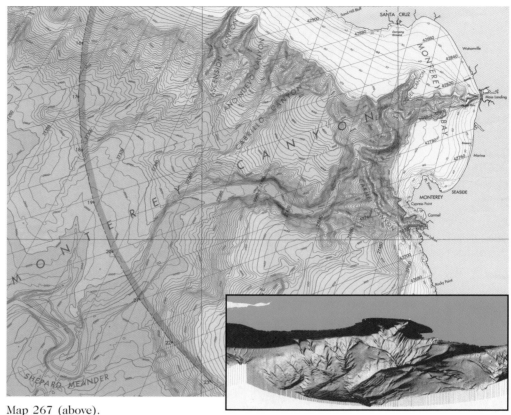

Map 267 (above).
Multibeam sonar allows the construction of very detailed maps of the sea floor, as this 1992 map of Monterey Canyon shows. The area is now the Monterey Bay National Marine Sanctuary. It covers an area the size of the state of Connecticut. Monterey Canyon cuts into the continental shelf on the scale of the Grand Canyon. Beginning just 100 m (300 feet) offshore, it extends westwards about 72 km (45 miles) and reaches depths of 3,000 m (10,000 feet). A three-dimensional view of the canyon is also shown above (Map 268).

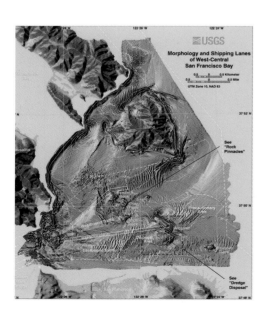

Map 266.
U.S. Geological Survey multibeam sonar image of part of San Francisco Bay.

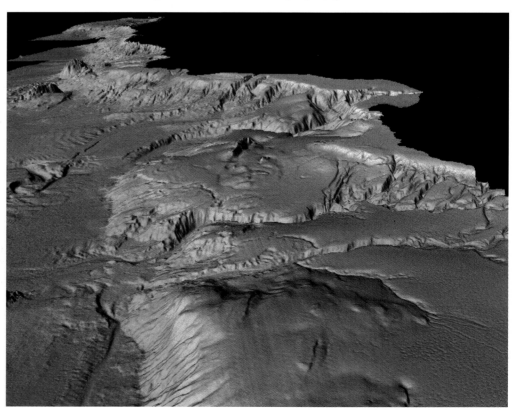

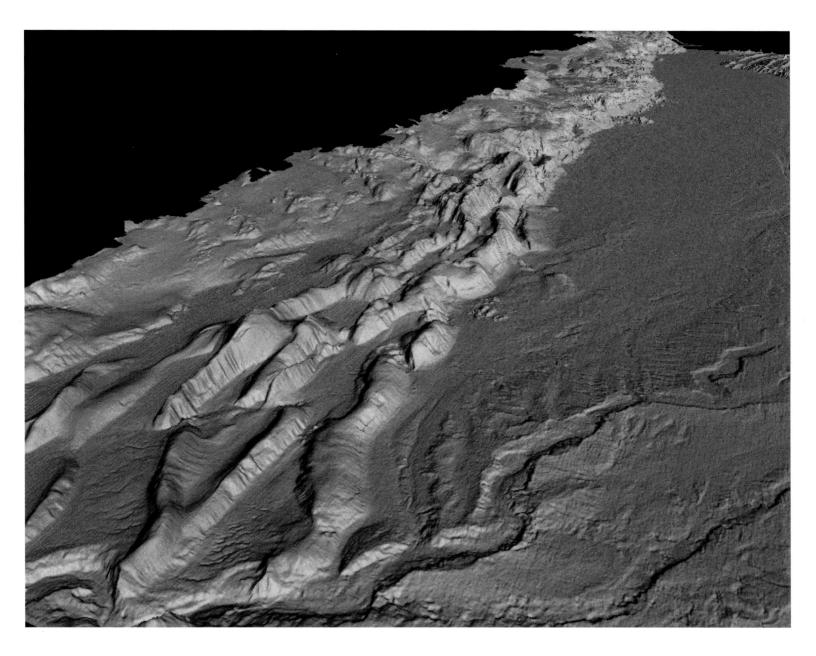

Map 269 (left, bottom) and Map 270 (above).
In 1981, the United States declared the waters and sea floor within 200 miles (320 km) of the shoreline to be an "exclusive economic zone." Between 1983 and 1993, NOAA, the National Oceanic and Atmospheric Administration, carried out detailed surveys of this zone using multibeam sonar. Computer-generated images like the two shown here allow the data to be interpreted as a three-dimensional "aerial view," producing revealing vistas of great beauty and detail. They were produced in 1996 by two geophysicists, Lincoln Pratson and William Haxby. Map 269, at left, is a view of the California coast, looking north from just south of Monterey. The Monterey Canyon shown in Map 267, above left, can also be seen in this view. Map 270, above, is a view of the Oregon coast, looking south, with the junction of the Juan de Fuca Plate, to the right, as it is dragged, or subducted, under the North American Plate, to the left. The ridges are the sediments that were on top of the Juan de Fuca Plate; they have been scraped off the sea floor by the North American Plate and accumulate as ridges. The vertical exaggeration in these images is 4x. A key for depths is given below.

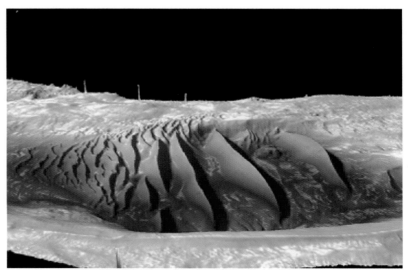

Map 271.
Multibeam imagery of a dune field off the coast of southern Vancouver Island, in the Strait of Juan de Fuca, off Victoria. The largest of these vertically exaggerated dunes is 8 m (25 feet) high.

3000   2000   1000   Depth (m)

The Satellite Sees All

The first Earth-observing satellites were launched in the 1960s and 70s. Since then, the capability of satellite sensors has increased dramatically, with a wide variety of instruments now covering almost all usable wavelengths of the spectrum, from ultraviolet light to microwaves. Nowadays, satellites play a key role in efforts directed at a better understanding of the ocean and climate.

Sea surface temperatures can be mapped to 1 000 m (3,300 feet) resolution by the thermal scanners carried by many weather satellites. Resolution of global composites is reduced to simplify processing and because features are in any case blurred from the month-long period typically chosen to allow all areas to be imaged be-

tween clouds (Maps 273 and 274). Periods of fine weather sometimes allows composite images to be made over a shorter time, in which smaller features are preserved (Map 272, below).

Sensitive optical instruments on the U.S. NASA *SeaWiFS* and Japanese NASDA *ADEOS* satellites have been designed to detect the colour change from clear blue to blue-green caused by chlorophyll in microscopic ocean plants – phytoplankton. Phytoplankton form the basis for the ocean food chain, and their distribution is an indicator of ocean productivity. Since life in the oceans affects many economic activities, such as fishing, being able to detect areas of increasing or decreasing productivity is very useful (Maps 275, 276, and 277).

Unlike visible imagers that are blocked by clouds and can operate only during the day, radar works day and night, and can "see" through cloud cover. High-resolution radar images of the ocean surface show roughness patterns due to winds, waves, oil slicks, current boundaries, and eddies, and are often used to track ships, especially those involved in commercial fishing. A more specialized radar scatterometer is now used to measure both wind speed and direction by looking at the sea surface from a variety of directions (Maps 278 and 279, page 208).

Most satellite data relate only to the ocean surface. Thermal measurements relate to less than the top millimeter of the sea; radar pen-

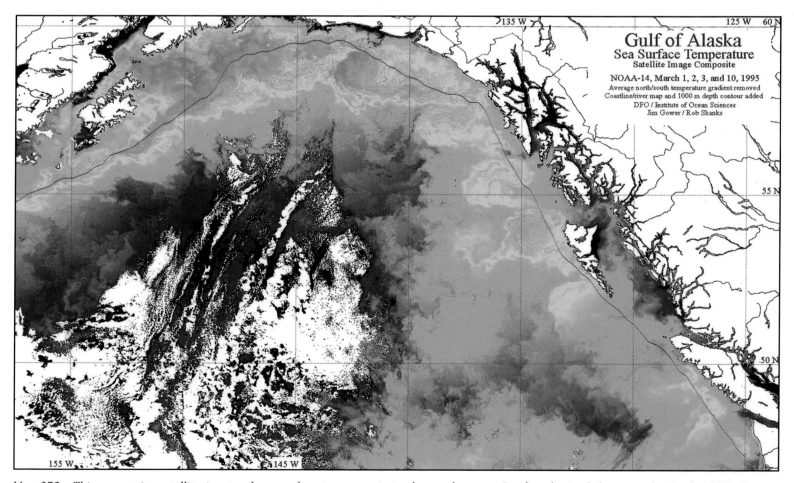

Map 272. This composite satellite image of sea surface temperature in the northeastern Pacific, obtained during early March 1995, shows a string of eddies along the B.C.–Alaska coast. At the top left of the image, the warmer water of the Alaska Stream can be seen moving westwards along the continental slope. The temperature differences in the image are about 4°C from the coolest (dark blue) to the warmest (red). An adjustment has been made to remove the effect of the normal north-to-south temperature gradient. The image was prepared by James Gower, Institute of Ocean Sciences, Fisheries and Oceans Canada.

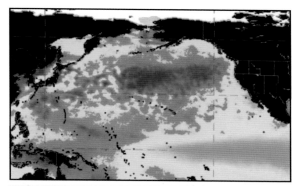

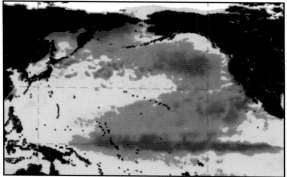

Map 273 (top) and Map 274. These images show the differences from the average sea surface temperature for the month, in the range ± 5°C. The top image is for November 1997, at the height of an El Niño, and the one below it is for November 1998, when warmer temperatures (red) along the equator have been replaced by colder (blue) La Niña conditions.

etrates a few centimeters. Visible radiation can "see" deeper, to a few meters, but this is still much less than the average 5-km (3 mile) depth of the ocean. Although unable to penetrate water to view the seabed directly, radar from, for example, the U.S. Navy's *Geosat* satellite can measure the distance to the sea surface to within 5 cm (2 inches). Sea surface height, which can vary as much as 200 m (650 feet), reflects small differences in the Earth's gravity caused by variations in undersea topography. For example, an underwater volcano 2 000 m (6,500 feet) high and 40 km (25 miles) wide will produce a bulge 2 m (6 feet) high in the seawater above it, due to its large mass and consequent increased gravitational attraction. But features less than 10 km (6 miles) across will not have sufficient mass to be detected. Sea surface elevation is measured over an area a few kilometers across, and this averages out the effects of waves.

Geosat satellite data was not declassified until 1995, but within two

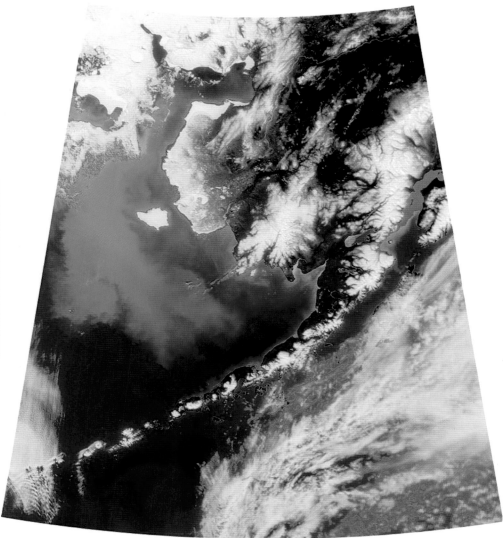

Map 275.
Coccolithophores, a type of phytoplankton, bloom in the Bering Sea in this NASA *SeaWiFS* satellite image. The sea has been turned whiter by the *coccolithophores* shedding their little chalk shields, the coccoliths.

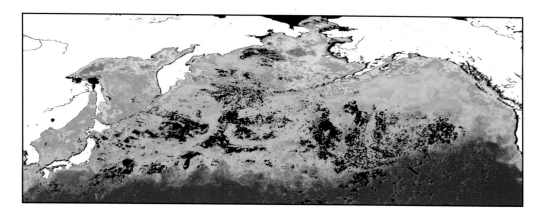

Map 276.
Monthly mean chlorophyll distribution in the North Pacific, May 1997. The *Advanced Earth Observing Satellite (ADEOS),* carrying the Ocean Color and Temperature Scanner (OCTS), which made this image, was launched by the National Space and Development Agency of Japan (NASDA) in 1996. Phytoplankton distribution is shown by the production of chlorophyll and is an indicator of ocean productivity. The image shows remarkable differences between the eastern and western subarctic circulation systems, or gyres. The map was prepared by Sei-ichi Saitoh and Kosei Sasaoka, Hokkaido University, Japan.

Map 277 (above). A composite image from the *SeaWiFS* satellite. The change in water color from clear blue to blue-green is caused by an increasing concentration of phytoplankton. A line of greener water can be seen along the equator, where a combination of wind and the Earth's rotation brings nutrients to the surface, and north of about 30 degrees latitude. The areas of highest productivity are the Sea of Okhotsk and the Bering Sea, where extraordinary "blooms" such as that shown on Map 275 sometimes occur.

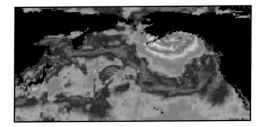

Map 280 (right).
This phenomenal view of the Earth was computer generated using several different sets of satellite data by Rudolf B. Husar, Washington University, St. Louis. Sea surface temperatures are shown particularly well here (yellow-orange-red being warmer water), with El Niño flaring eastwards across the Pacific to the South American coast. Data used were: a true-color image for the land from NASA-GSFC *SeaWiFS*; fire maps from the European Space Agency; aerosols from *NOAA-NESDIS* AVHRR data; plus clouds from four geostationary satellites, *GOES 8, GOES 9, METEOSAT,* and *GMS5,* from the University of Wisconsin SSEC KidSat Project.

Map 278 (center) and
Map 279 (right, bottom).
Images from a new NASA satellite called *QuickScat,* with a radar scatterometer which measures wind speed and direction twice a day. Map 278 shows wind speeds during a storm in the Gulf of Alaska on 8 October 2000. The red area is the storm. Map 279 was recorded at the same time and shows wind stream lines in the entire North Pacific, indicating direction as well as speed.

W. Timothy Liu and Wenquing Tang, NASA/NOAA-sponsored data system Seaflux at JPL, U.S.A.

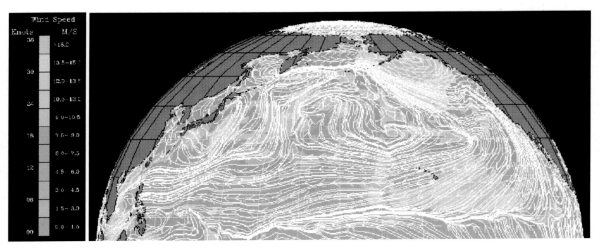

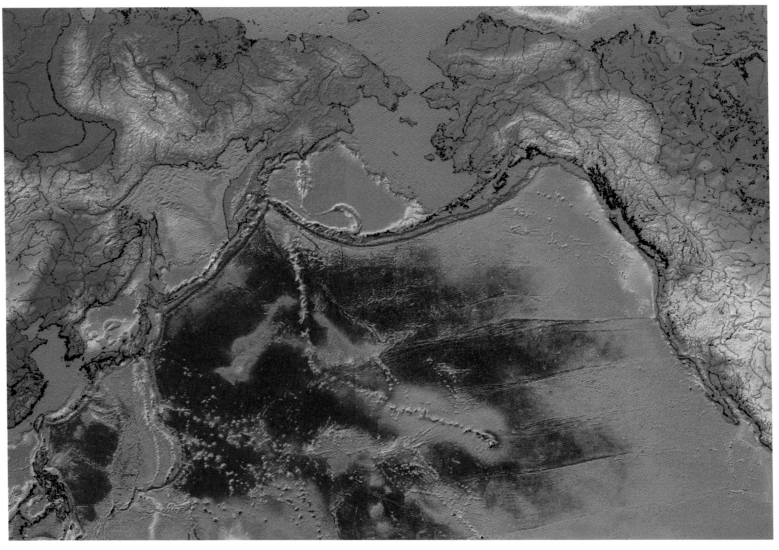

Map 281 (above).
A map of sea floor topography made from satellite gravity measurements supplemented with ship-based soundings, by Walter Smith of NOAA and David Sandwell of Scripps, published in 1997. The relatively shallow continental shelves are pink-orange; midocean ridges and seamounts are green and yellow; the abyssal plains, with fracture zones and deeper trenches, are blue and purple. This map showed thousands of seamounts worldwide that were not on the charts before.

months two geophysicists, David Sandwell of Scripps and Walter Smith of NOAA, had converted the data into a map. In order to improve its accuracy, they then correlated the data with known ship soundings. This eliminated errors due to, for example, increased gravitational pull that was due not to increased volume but to increased mass, that is, higher rock density. They also supplemented the map with data from a similar European satellite, *ERS-1*. The result is the rather beautiful map shown above (Map 281).

Radar altimeters have become an important source of data on water movement. Altimeters on U.S. *TOPEX/Poseidon* and European *ERS-2* satellites are more precise than *Geosat*, and are in orbits designed to detect changes in the height of the ocean surface to an accuracy that allows detection and tracking of eddies and other dynamic features.

Map 282. Radar altimeter map of the northeastern Pacific, from *TOPEX/ Poseidon* and *ERS-2* satellites. This map is an average for a 90-day period from November 1997 to February 1998, at the time of an El Niño. Sea level is 10 to 30 cm above normal

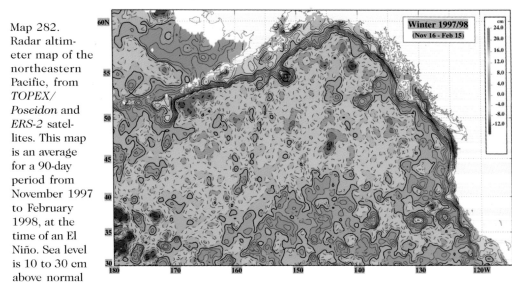

along the coast and in eddies, seen as areas 200 to 300 km wide. As this is the northern hemisphere, water in these eddies is slowly circulating in a clockwise direction. Images such as this are built up over a period of time as the satellite tracks overhead. Prepared by Josef Cherniawsky, Institute of Ocean Sciences, Fisheries and Oceans Canada.

The World Ocean Circulation Experiment

Concerns about the impact of increasing levels of carbon dioxide in the Earth's atmosphere, first documented in the 1960s, coupled with advances in weather prediction techniques, led in 1980 to the establishment of the World Climate Research Program (WCRP). The mission of the WCRP is to carry out the research needed to predict climate on time scales ranging from months to decades.

The oceans are an important part of the world's climate system, capable of storing and transporting large quantities of heat; they also contain 96 percent of the Earth's water. The lack of reliable models of ocean circulation was seen as a major obstacle to climate prediction.

In response, scientists from more than thirty countries planned, managed, and carried out the World Ocean Circulation Experiment (WOCE), with the goal of developing models useful for predicting climate change and to find methods for determining long-term changes in ocean circulation.

Observations for WOCE were carried out between 1990 and 1997, and these were followed by an interpretation, analysis, modelling, and synthesis phase, planned to end in 2002. However, the work of scientific interpretation of the data is expected to go on for many years.

One major component of the observing program was a global one-time ship-based survey of the distribution of ocean temperatures, salinity, and chemical tracers including nutrients, dissolved oxygen, chlorinated fluorocarbons, tritium, helium, and Carbon 14. The tracks of ships during this survey are shown criss-crossing the Pacific in the map below.

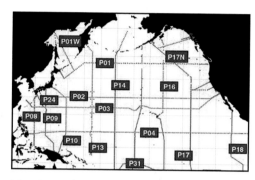

Map 283. The network of observational tracks made by research ships in the North Pacific during WOCE.

Specially launched satellites played an important part by making global observations of sea level, accurate to 5 cm, and the slope of sea level, which allowed changes in surface currents to be determined repeatedly over several years. Satellites also provided observations of sea surface temperature and winds and allowed precise navigation.

In addition, "repeat hydrography" was carried out; that is, multiple observations of temperature, salinity, and nutrients were made several times along the same ship track, in order to measure changes. Upper-ocean thermal structure was measured, in an interesting extension of work begun by Matthew Fontaine Maury in the mid-nineteenth century (see page 152), by merchant ships dropping expendable probes.

Satellite-tracked drifting buoys measured surface currents and temperature, acoustically tracked floats recorded conditions at various depths, anchored arrays of current meters measured ocean currents over time, and a network of tide gauges measured sea level.

With all this activity, naturally enough WOCE produced a massive amount of data that will be a scientific resource for many years to come.

One of its major achievements was developing a way of consolidating and storing this data, and distributing it over the Internet.

By the end of the observing phase, data from WOCE had already been used to improve estimates of the circulation of heat and water in the world's oceans. Another major result was a greatly improved understanding of the role of large eddies in the movement and mixing of heat (Map 272, page 206). A further important legacy of WOCE was the development of new techniques and equipment for ocean observation.

This WOCE profile is of water salinity in the North Pacific north-south along 179° E. It shows that nearer the surface, the northern part of the ocean is less salty than the rest.

Prepared by Alex Kozyr, CDIAC, University of Tennessee, using *Ocean Data View*, Version 5.1 - 2000, by Reiner Schlitzer, http://www.awi-bremerhaven.de/GEO/ODV.

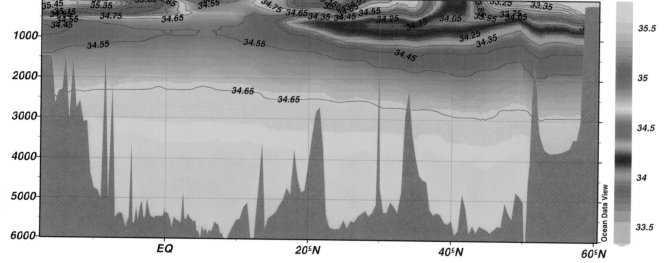

The Future – Project Argo

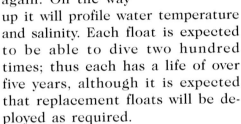

Project Argo, which is currently under way, aims to deploy floating observation robots at depth in the oceans around the world.

The idea of obtaining information on currents using floats was not new. The basic circulation, or gyre, of the Atlantic was determined in 1885–87 by Prince Albert of Monaco, who had released 1,675 bottles each with a polite message for the finder in ten languages, 227 of which were recovered.

Then in 1948 Henry Stommel, whom we have already met in our section on lost islands (page 59), produced a major theory explaining ocean circulation, which in the Atlantic predicted a southward counter-flow of cold water *under* the northward-flowing Gulf Stream. British oceanographer John Swallow had invented a device that would prove Stommel correct, a variation of one Stommel himself had suggested.

The device consisted of two aluminum scaffolding tubes, each 3 m (10 feet) long, bound together. One tube provided flotation and was designed to hold the other tube, which contained batteries and a transducer, at a specific depth. The transducer emitted a sound that could be picked up by a nearby ship and its position thus determined.

In this way, Stommel's revelatory abyssal circulation theory, the precursor of the modern theory of thermohaline circulation of the oceans (that ocean circulation is caused by differences in temperature and salinity, and requires deep counter currents as well as surface currents) was proven.

The floating devices being deployed as part of Project Argo are the modern high-tech descendants of Stommel and Swallow's tubes. They are called PALACE floats, an acronym for Profiling Autonomous LAgrangian Current Explorer.

The Pacific Ocean has a profound effect on the climate of many areas of the Earth, and changes in currents and water temperatures at depth as well as at the surface often are behind changes in climate on land. The Argo floats will provide, it is hoped, vital information in a much more comprehensive fashion than was possible before.

When a PALACE float is deployed, mainly from the air, it will sink to 2 000 m (6,500 feet) and drift at that depth for ten days. It will then rise to the surface, transmit its data to a satellite, and then dive again. On the way up it will profile water temperature and salinity. Each float is expected to be able to dive two hundred times; thus each has a life of over five years, although it is expected that replacement floats will be deployed as required.

The difference in the position of the float from one dive to the next shows the ten-day drift at depth, and thus the average deep current speed. Going up and diving, the float will give information on the complete internal dynamics of the top 2 000 m of the ocean, every ten days on a continuing basis. Such data will be used to initialize climate forecast models and, it is hoped, thus provide much-improved seasonal weather forecasts. All this data is to be made available on the Internet within twenty-four hours.

By the end of 2003 it is expected that 3,000 PALACE floats will have been deployed worldwide, 850 of which will be in the North Pacific. This will create an internationally-sponsored global ocean climate observatory of unprecedented proportions.

Map 284.
Map showing the proposed deployment of PALACE floats.

(above, right)
Cross-section of a PALACE float.

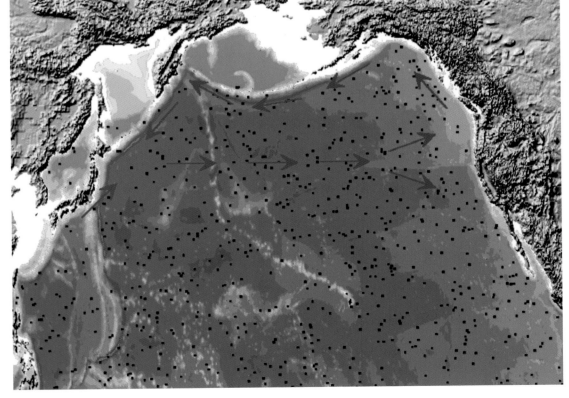

Map Sources

Sources for maps are stated in the individual listings in the map catalog. Where none is given, the map is from the author's or another private collection, or an original source is untraceable. All efforts were made to ensure proper credit for sources, and I apologize if any have been missed.

Abbreviations used in the map catalog:

AN — Archives nationales, Paris
ARA — Algemein Rijksarchief, Hague
ARSI — Archivum Romanum Societatis Iesu (Jesuit Archives), Rome
Bancroft — Bancroft Library, University of California
BCA — British Columbia Archives
Beinecke — Beinecke Rare Book Library, Yale University
BL — British Library
BNF — Bibliothèque nationale, Paris
Cabinet Library — Cabinet Library, Tokyo, Japan
Huntington — Huntington Library, San Marino, CA
JCBL — John Carter Brown Library, Brown University, Providence, RI
JFBL — James Ford Bell Library, University of Minnesota
KB — Kungl. Biblioteket (Royal Library), National Library of Sweden, Stockholm
Kobe Public Library — Kobe Public Library, Kobe, Japan
LC — Library of Congress
MMPH — Maritiem Museum Prins Hendrick, Rotterdam
NAC — National Archives of Canada
NARA — National Archives and Records Administration (U.S. National Archives)
NLC — National Library of Canada
NMM — National Maritime Museum, Greenwich
NYPL — New York Public Library
OHS — Oregon Historical Society, Portland
Princeton — Princeton University Library
PRO — Public Record Office, Kew, U.K.
UBC — Special Collections, University of British Columbia, Vancouver
UKHO — United Kingdom Hydrographic Office, Taunton, U.K.
VPL — Special Collections, Vancouver Public Library
Yale — Yale University Library

Map Catalog

Maps are listed by map number.

1 (Frontispiece)
[Map of the North Pacific Ocean]
Girolamo de Angelis, 1621
ARSI

2 Asia Novissima Tabula
Gerard de Jode, 1578. From: Speculum Orbia Terrarum, Plate #4.
LC G1015.J6 1578 vault

3 Carte Universelle du Monde
Pierre Du Val, 1684
LC GM Neg. 259

4 Carte de la partie Septentrionale et Orientale de l'Asie
Samuel Engel, 1764. From: Extraits Raissonnés Des Voyages, 1779.
NLC G606 E53 1779 Fol. Res.

5 Geographische Vorstelling eines Globi, welchen Anno 1492. Herr Martin Behaim
Johan Doppelmayer copy of Behaim globe, 1730
Nordenskiöld, 1889

6 [World map]
Giovanni Contarini and Francesco Rosselli, 1506
BL Maps.C.2.cc.4

7 [Gores for a world globe]
Martin Waldseemüller
JFBL

8 [World map, west sheet]
Diogo Ribiero, 1529. Copy made in 1886 or 1887.
LC G3200 1529.R5 1887 MLC

9 [World map]
Sebastian Münster, 1546
JFBL

10 [1520 Schöner Globe redrawn by Kohl]
LC Kohl Collection

11 [Map of East China Sea]
Cheng Ho, no date. From: Ying Yai Sheng Lan.
LC

12 [World map]
Battista Agnese, 1542

13 [Chart of the Patagonian Region]
Antonio Pigafetta, from his manuscript account of Magellan's voyage, c1525.
Beinecke Folio 21, recto

14 [World map]
Sebastian Cabot, 1544
BNF RES Ge AA 582 Rc C 2486

15 Descripcion de las Indias Ocidentalis
After Juan López de Velasco, 1601.
From: Antonio Herrera, 1622 edition.
LC G1100.H42 1622 vault

16 Descripcion de las Indias Del Poiniente
After Juan López de Velasco, 1601.
From: Antonio Herrera, 1622 edition, between folio 78 and folio 79.
LC G1100.H42 1622 vault

17 [Map of the Pacific Ocean showing galleon routes]
Juan López de Velasco, c1575
JCBL

18 Part of the Pacific Ocean between California and the Philippine Islands
La Pérouse, 1798, atlas, English edition.

19 Nova Totius Terrarum Orbis Ixxta Neotericorum Traditiones Descriptio
Abraham Ortelius, 1564
BL Maps.C.2.a.6

20 [Southeast Asia, part of world map]
Emery Molyneux, 1599. From: Principall Navigations, Richard Hakluyt, 1599 edition.

21 [Map of Southeast Asia]
Fernão Vaz Dourado, 1570
Huntington Library

22 Asiae Novo Descriptio
Abraham Ortelius, 1570
From: Theatrum Orbis Terrarum.
LC G1006.T5 1570b vault

23 Universale Descrittione di tutta la terra conosciuta fin qui
Paolo Forlani, c1562
LC G3200 1565 .F6 vault

24 [World map]
Giovanni Gastaldi, 1562

25 [World map]
Bolognini Zalterii or Paolo Forlani, 1566

26 [Map of California, Japan, and the Pacific]
Joan Martines, 1578
BL Harley MS 3450, Map 10 in atlas

27 Tartariae Sive Magni Chami Regni
Abraham Ortelius, 1570
From: Theatrum Orbis Terrarum.
LC G7270 1570.O7 vault

28 [Map of the world in two hemispheres]
Title page to Purchas His Pilgrimes, Samuel Purchas, 1625.

29 La Herdike [sic, Heroike] Enterprinse Faict par de Signeur Draeck d'avoir Cirquit Toute la Terre ("The French Drake Map")
Nicola van Sype, c1583
BL Maps Cs.a7(1)

30 Carta particolare della stretto di Iezo Pra l'America e l'Isola Iezo D'America Carta XXXIII
Robert Dudley, 1647. From: Dell' Arcano del Mare, Florence, 1647.
Engraved by Antonio Francesco Lucini.

31 Vera Totius Expeditionis Nauticae descriptio D. Franc. Draci . . . Addita est etiam viva delineatio navigationes Thomea Caundish . . . Iudocus Hondius
Joducus Hondius, Amsterdam, 1589
MMPH

32 Portius Nova Albionis
Inset on Hondius, Map 31.
MMPH

85 [Donna Maria Laxara Island]
John Green, 1776
From: *Chart containing part of the Icy Sea with the adjacent coasts of Asia and America.* Published by Thomas Jefferys, London, 1776.

86 *Nova et Accuratissima Totius Terrarum Orbis Tabula*
Reinier and Joshua Ottens, 1745
From: *Atlas van Zeevaert en Koophandel door de Geheele Weereldt,* 1745.

87 *Mar Del Zur Hispanis Mare Pacificum*
Joannes Jansson, 1650

88 *Mappe Monde ou Globe Terrestre en deux Plans Hemispheres. Dressee sur les observations de Mrss de L'Academie Royal Des Sciences*
Jean Covens and Corneille Mortier, c1780

89 *Carte Generale Des Découvertes de l'Amiral de Fonte et autres navigateurs Espagnols Anglois et Russes pour la recherche du passage a la Mer du Sud par M. De L'Isle del'Academie des Sciences etc.*
Robert de Vaugondy, 1755
Thought to be from Diderot's *Encyclopedié.*

90 *A Chart Containing the Coasts of California, New Albion, and Russian Discoveries to the North with the Peninsula of Kamschatka, Asia, opposite thereto And Islands dispersed over the Pacific Ocean to the North of the line*
Thomas Jefferys, 1775
From: *An American Atlas Engraved on 48 copper plates by the late Thomas Jefferys Geographer to the King, and others.*
BCA NW912.7 J45am

91 *La America Septentrional desde su extremo Norte hasta 10° de Latitud.*
Isidoro de Antillon, 1802

92 *Carte des Terres Aux Environs du Japon . . .*
Philippe Buache, 1752
From: *Considerations Geographiques et Physiques,* 1755.
LC G2860.B9 1755 copy 2 vault

93 *Carte du Geometrique . . .*
Philippe Buache, 1752
From: *Considerations Geographiques et Physiques,* 1755.
LC G2860.B9 1755 copy 2 vault

94 *Atlas Général a L'Usage Des Colleges et Museums D'Éducation . . . de J. B. Nolin*
Jean B. Nolin, 1783
From: *Amerique Septentrionale,* Plate 33.
LC G1015 .N68 1783

95 *A Map of the Country which Capt.n Beerings past through in his Journey from Tobolsk to Kamtschatka*
Joseph-Nicolas de L'Isle, based on a map by Jean-Baptiste Bourguignon d'Anville
From: *The General History of China,* Jean Baptiste du Halde, 1736.

96 [Map of Bering's 1728 voyage]
Anonymous, c1728
KB

97 [Sketch illustrating Bering's first voyage, in 1728]
Joseph-Nicolas de L'Isle, based on his conversation with Bering, c1732

98 [Map of Mikhail Gvozdev's voyage]
Martin Spanberg, c1734
From: A. V. Efimov, 1964, Map 69.

99 [Kamchatka and the Kuril Islands]
Martin Spanberg, 1739
From: A. V. Efimov, 1964, Map 105.

100 *Carte Dressee en 1731 Pour Servir a la recherche des Terres et des Mers Situees Au Nord de la Mer du Sud*
Joseph-Nicolas de L'Isle, 1731
From: A. V. Efimov, 1964, Map 78.

101 [St. Elias (Kayak) Island]
Sofron Khitrov, 1741
From: F. A. Golder, 1922/25.

102 [Shumagin Islands]
Sofron Khitrov, 1741
From: F. A. Golder, 1922/25.

103 [Map of Bering's 1741 voyage]
Probably by Sven Waxell, 1742
From: A. V. Efimov, 1964, Map 101.

104 [Petropavlovsk Harbor, Kamchatka]
Vitus Bering, 1741
From: F. A. Golder, 1922/25.

105 [East coast of Kamchatka and Bering Island]
Sven Waxell, c1742
From: F. A. Golder 1722/25

106 [Map of Alexei Chirikov's voyage]
Ivan Elagin, c1742
From: A. V. Efimov, 1964, Map 98.

107 [Map of Second Kamchatka Expedition (1)]
Anonymous, c1742
From: A. V. Efimov, 1964, Map 93.

108 [Map of Second Kamchatka Expedition (2)]
Anonymous, c1742
From: A. V. Efimov, 1964, Map 117.

109 *Carte de Nouvelles Decouvertes*
Joseph-Nicolas de L'Isle, 1752
NAC NMC 210056

110 *Carte des Nouvelles Decouvertes entre la partie Orient.le de Asie et Occid.le de L'Amerique*
Philippe Buache, 1755
From: *Considerations Geographiques et Physiques,* 1755.
LC G2860.B9 1755 copy 2 vault

111 *Chart containing part of the Icy Sea with the adjacent coasts of Asia and America*
John Green, 1753. Published by Thomas Jefferys, London, 1753.

112 *Chart containing the Coasts of California, New Albion, and Russian Discoveries to the North with the Peninsula of Kamchatka, Asia, opposite thereto; And Islands, dispersed over the Pacific Ocean, to the North of the Line*
John Green, 1753
Published by Thomas Jefferys, London, 1753.

113 *L'hydrographie françois: recueil des cartes générales et particulières qui ont éte faites pour le servire des vaisseaux du roy, par ordre des Ministres de la marine, depuis 1737, jusqu'en 1765*
Jacques Nicolas Bellin, c1766
LC G1059.B43 1772

114 *Nouvelle Carte de decouvertes faites par de vaisseaux Russiens aux côtes inconnues de l'Amerique Septentrionale avec les pais adjacents*
Gerhard Müller, 1754
JCBL

115 [Map of Ivan Synd's voyage]
Ivan Synd, 1768

116 [Geographical map showing discoveries of Russian seagoing vessels on the northern part of America]
Gerhard Müller, Imperial Academy of Learning, St. Petersburg
Russian edition, c1773.

117 *A Map of the New Northern Archipelago discover'd by the Russians in the Seas of Kamtschatka & Anadir*
Jacob von Stählin, 1774
From: *Account of a New Northern Archipelago Lately Discovered by the Russians,* 1774.

118 *Chart of Synd's Voyage towards Tchukotskoi Nos*
From: William Coxe, *An Account of the Russian Discoveries between Asia and America,* London, 1780.
VPL

119 *Map of Krenitsin and Levashev's Voyage to the Fox Islands in 1768 and 1769. Published April 13th 1780 . . . by T. Cadell. Engr by T. Kitchin.*
From: William Coxe, *An Account of the Russian Discoveries between Asia and America,* London, 1780.
VPL

120 [Potap Zaikov's map of the Aleutians]
1779
From: A. V. Efimov, 1964, Map 161.

121 [Map of the North Pacific Ocean]
Grigorii Shelikov, 1787
Yale *23 1787

122 *Magnum Mare del Zur cum Insula California*
Reinier and Joshua Ottens, 1750
LC G9230 1750 .R2 vault

123 *Plano del Puerto de S Diego . . .*
Anonymous, Spanish, no date
LC G3351.P5 1799.C vault

124 *Carta Reducida del Oceano Asiatico ō Mar del Sur que contiene la Costa de la California comprehendida desde el Puerto de Monterrey. hta la Punta de S.ta Maria Magdelena hecha según las observaciones y Demarcasiones del Aljerez de Fragata de la R.l Armada y Primer Piloto de este Departamento D.n Juan Perez por D.n Josef de Cañizarez.*
Josef de Cañizarez, 1774
NARA

125 *Plano del Puerto de Sn Francisco*
Josef Camacho, Spanish, c1779 or later copy
LC G3351.P5 1799.C vault

126 *Plano del Puerto de Sn Francisco*
Josef de Cañizarez, 1774
Bancroft

127 *Plano del Puerto de los Dolores*
Jacinto Caamaño, 1792, or anonymous later copy
LC G3351.P5 1799.C vault

128 *Plano de la Rada de Bucareli situado . . .*
Bruno de Hezeta y Dudagoitia, July 1775.
Archivo General de Indias, Seville

129 *Plano de la Bahia de la Asunciōn . . .*
Bruno de Hezeta y Dudagoitia, August 1775
Archivo General de Indias, Seville

130 *Carta que contiene parte de la costa de la California*
Bernabe Muñoz, 1787
LC G4362.C6 1787.M8 TIL vault

131 *Plano de la Entrada de Ezeta*
Esteban José Martínez, Spanish, 1793
LC G3351.P5 1799.C vault

132 *Carta reducida de las costas, y mares
septentrionales de California construida
bajo las observaciones, y demarcaciones
hechas por de Fragata Don Juan Francisco
de la Vodega y Quadra commandante de la
goleta Sonora y por el piloto Don Francisco
Antonio Maurelle . . . , 1775*
Archivo General de Indias, Sevilla
MP, Mexico 581

133 *Carte de L'Ocean Pacifique au Nord de
l'Equateur, et des Cotes qui . . . Espagnols,
les Russes, et les Anglois, jusqu'en 1780*
Tobie Conrad Lotter, 1781
NAC NMC 8607 H2 1-4000 [1781?]

134 *Esquisse d'une Carte* and *Extrait de la Carte*
Samuel Engel, 1781
Beinecke Zc86 781en

135 *Track from first making the Continent,
March 7th, to Anchoring in King George's
Sound*
From: Journal of James Burney, 1778.
PRO ADM 51/4528

136 *Chart of part of the N W Coast of America
Explored by Capt. J. Cook in 1778*
James Cook, 1778
PRO MPI 83 (removed from ADM 1/1621)

137 *Chart of the NW Coast of America and the
NE Coast of Asia explored in the years 1778
and 1779. The unshaded parts of the coast
of Asia are taken from a MS chart received
from the Russians.*
From: James Cook, *Voyage to the Pacific Ocean*,
1784.

138 *Chart of Norton Sound and of Bherings
Strait made by the East Cape of Asia and
the West Point of America, 1778/1779*
From: James Cook, *Voyage to the Pacific
Ocean*, 1784.

139 *General Chart exhibiting the discoveries
made by Capt. James Cook in this and his
preceding two voyages, with the tracks of
the ships under his command.*
Henry Roberts. Wm. Faden, 1784
BCA CM B1189

140 *A Plan of the Bay of A'vatch'ka by
Edward Riou*
Edward Riou, 1779
UKHO 524/1 on Rd
© Crown Copyright 2000. Published by
permission of the Controller of Her
Majesty's Stationery Office and the U.K.
Hydrographic Office.

141–147 (seven maps)
From: *Atlas, by Navigator Lovtsov
composed by him while wintering at the
Bol'sheretsk ostrog in the year 1782*
Seven watercolor plates from MS atlas.
Vasilii Fedorovich Lovtsov, 1782
BCA NW 912.722 L922

148 *Chart of the Coasts of America & Asia
from California to Macao according to the
Discoveries made in 1786 & 1787 by the
Boussole & Astrolabe*
G. G. and J. Robinson, November 1797

149 [Carte de la Côte Ouest de l'Amérique du
Nord, de Mt. St. Elias à Monterey, avec la
trajectoire l'expédition de La Pérouse et la
table des données de longitude compilées
par Bernizet and Dagelet]
Joseph Dagelet and Gérault-Sébastien
Bernizet, 1786
AN 6 JJ1: 34B

150 *Plan du Port des Français Située sur la
Côte du N.O. de l'Amerique Septentrionale*
Gérault-Sébastien Bernizet and Paul
Mérault de Monneron, July 1786
AN 6 JJ1: 30

151 *Plan de Baye de Castries Située sur la Côte
Orientale de Tartarie*
Gérault-Sébastien Bernizet, July 1787
AN 6 JJ1: 41B

152 [Northeast Portion of Siberia, the Arctic
Ocean, Eastern Ocean, and Northwest
Coasts of North America]
Gavriil A. Sarychev, 1802
From: *Puteshesvie flota kapitana Sarycheva
po severovostochnoi chasti Sibiri. . . flota
kapitana Billingsa s 1785 po 1793 god*,
2 volumes, St. Petersburg, 1802.
UBC Special Collections G9285 S2 1954 loc4

153 *Sketch of the Entrance of the Strait of Juan
de Fuca by Charles Duncan Master in the
Royal Navy 15th August 1788 Alexander
Dalrymple, publ.*
LC

154 *N. W. America Drawn by J.C. from his own
Information & what could be collected from
the Sloop Pr Royal & Boats in the Years
1787 1788*
James Colnett, 1788
UKHO p24 on 87
© Crown Copyright 2000. Published by
permission of the Controller of Her
Majesty's Stationery Office and the U.K.
Hydrographic Office.

155 *Chart of the N.W. Coast of America and the
N.E. Coast of Asia, explored in the Years
1778 and 1779 by Capt Cook and further
explored, in 1788, and 1789.*
From: John Meares, *Voyages made in the
years 1788 and 1789 from China to the
North West Coast of America*, 1790.

156 *A Chart of the Interior Part of North
America Demonstrating the very great
probability of an Inland Navigation from
Hudson's Bay to the West Coast*
From: John Meares, *Voyages made in the
years 1788 and 1789 from China to the
North West Coast of America*, 1790.

157 *Chart of the World on Mercator's
Projection Exhibiting all the New
Discoveries to the Present Time*
Aaron Arrowsmith, 1794 (dated 1790)

158 *Chart of the Pacific Ocean drawn from a
great number of printed and ms journals*
A. Arrowsmith, 1798, Sheet 11/9 [sic, 1/9]
LC G9230 1798.A72 vault

159 *Carta que comprehende los interiers y veril
de la costa desde los 48° de Latitud N hasta
los 50°. 1791*
José María Nárvaez, 1791
LC G3351.P5 1799.C vault, Map 12

160 *Num 9 Plano del Puerto del Desengaño
Trabasado de Orden del Rey*
From: *Relación*, atlas, 1802.
VPL SPA 970P E77r2

161 *Chart of the West Coast of North America,
with the Isles adjacent from the Latde 50
45'N & Longde. 30 [sic] copied from one
constructed . . . by Dn. Caamano . . . in . . .
1792*
Traced by an English draughtsman.
UKHO 355/3 on Ac 1

162 *Num. 2 Carta Esférica de los Recono-
cimientos hechos en la Costa N.O.
De América en 1791 y 92 por las Goletas
Sutil y Mexicana y otres Bruques de S.M.*
Dionisio Galiano, 1792
From: *Relación*, atlas, 1802.

163 *Carta general de quanto asta hoy se ha
descubierto y examinado por los Espanoles
en la Costa Septentrional de California,
formada . . . por D. Juan Francisco de la
Bodega y Quadra Ano de 1791*
Museo Naval, Madrid

164 *Carta que contiene parte de la costa de la
California. . .*
Bernabe Muñoz, 1787
LC G4362.C6 1787.M8 TIL vault

165 *Carta Reducida de la Costa Septentrional
de California . . .*
Juan Francisco de la Bodega y Quadra, 1791
or 1792
LC G3351.P5 1799.C vault, Map 1

166 *Carta de los Descubrimientos hechos en la
Costa N.O. America Septentrional*
Juan Francisco de la Bodega y Quadra, 1792
LC G3350 1792.B6 TIL vault

167 [Preliminary chart of N.W. Coast of
America from George Vancouver's landfall
to Cape Mudge, including the first mapping
of Puget Sound]
PRO MPG 557 (4), removed from CO 5/187

168 *A Chart Showing part of the Western Coast
of North America . . . George Vancouver in
the Summer of 1792. Prepared by Lieut
Josh Baker under the immediate inspection
of Capt Vancouver.*
UKHO 226 on Ac1
© Crown Copyright 2000. Published by
permission of the Controller of Her
Majesty's Stationery Office and the U.K.
Hydrographic Office.

169 [James Johnstone's first survey of
Johnstone Strait and Loughborough Inlet,
1792]
UKHO 231/4 Ac 1

170 *A Chart shewing part of the Coast of N.W.
America with the tracks of His Majesty's
Sloop Discovery and Armed Tender
Chatham Commanded by George
Vancouver Esq. . . . The parts not shaded
are taken from Russian Authority. [Cook Inlet]*
From: George Vancouver, *A Voyage of
Discovery to the North Pacific Ocean and
Around the World*, Plate 12 of atlas, 1798.

171 *A Chart shewing part of the N.W. Coast of
North America with the Tracks of His
Majesty's Sloop Discovery and Armed
Tender Chatham . . .*
[Summary map of west coast]
From: George Vancouver, *A Voyage of
Discovery . . .*, Plate 14 of atlas, 1798.

172 *A Chart shewing part of the N.W. Coast of
North America with the Tracks of His
Majesty's Sloop Discovery and Armed
Tender Chatham . . .*
From: George Vancouver, *A Voyage of
Discovery . . .*, Plate 7 of atlas, 1798.

173 *A Chart shewing part of the Coast of N.W. America with the tracks of His Majesty's Sloop Discovery and Armed Tender Chatham Commanded by George Vancouver Esq. and prepared under his immediate inspection by Lieut. Joseph Baker . . . The parts not shaded are taken from Spanish Authorities.*
Compilation chart for Plate 5 of the atlas for *A Voyage of Discovery* . . .
George Vancouver, 1798
PRO CO 700 British Columbia 1

174 *A Chart of the N.E. Coast of Asia, and Japanese Isles . . .*
William Broughton, 1797
From: William Broughton, *A Voyage of Discovery to the North Pacific Ocean*, 1804.

175 *A Chart of the East Coast of Japan with the Kurile and Liquieux Is. explored by Captn Broughton in His Majesty's Sloop Providence 1796* [Volcano Bay portion, 1796]
William Broughton, 1796–97
UKHO 514/2 on Se
© Crown Copyright 2000. Published by permission of the Controller of Her Majesty's Stationery Office and the U.K. Hydrographic Office.

176 *A Chart of the East Coast of Japan with the Kurile and Liquieux Is. explored by Captn Broughton in His Majesty's Sloop Providence 1796* [with 1797 additions]
William Broughton, 1797
UKHO 514/2 on Se
© Crown Copyright 2000. Published by permission of the Controller of Her Majesty's Stationery Office and the U.K. Hydrographic Office.

177 *Map of the Globe, incorporating the latest descriptions from the Lisianskii fleet, with a display of the route of the Neva from 1803–1806*
From: *Collection of Maps and Drawings Relating to the Voyage of the Fleet of Captain (1st Order) and Gentleman Urei Lisianskii of the ship Neva*, St. Petersburg, 1812.

178 *Chart of the Northwest Part of the Great Ocean. Drawn by D.F. Sotzmann 1811. Reduced from Capt'n Krusenstern's Original Chart*
VPL 910.4R K94, Vol. 1

179 [Map of Russian possessions in North America]
From: Vasili Nikolayevich Berkh, *Atlas geograficheskikh otkrytii v Sibiri i v Severo Zapadnoi Ameriki*, 1821.

180 *Die Insel Krafto (Seghalien) und die Mundung Des Manko (Amur) Nach Original Karten von Mogami Tokunai und Mamia Rinzo* [Tokunai map]
Philipp Franz von Siebold, 1852
BL 14001.i.44, Vol. 7, Plate XXV

181 [Map of strait between Sakhalin and the mainland, with the Amur River]
Mamiya Rinzo, 1809
Cabinet Library, Tokyo

182 *Die Insel Krafto (Seghalien) und die Mundung Des Manko (Amur) Nach Original Karten von Mogami Tokunai und Mamia Rinzo* [Mamiya map]
Philipp Franz von Siebold, 1852
BL 14001.i.44, Vol. 7, Plate XXV

183 *Xᵉ feuille de la Tartarie Chinoise contenent le Païs de Ke-Tching l'embouchure du Saghalien-Oula dans al Mer Orientale et la grande Isle qui est au dedans*
Jean Baptiste d'Anville, 1737
From: *Nouvelle Atlas.*

184 *Chart of the Pacific Ocean drawn from a great number of printed and ms journals*
Aaron Arrowsmith, 1818

185 *Chart of Behring's Strait.*
Otto Kotzebue, August 1816

186 *Carte Générale de la Mer de Behring 1828*
Fedor Lütke, 1828

187 *Map Exhibiting Areas of Temperature of the Ocean and the Isothermal and Isocheimal Curves of the Continents by the U.S. Ex. Ex. 1850*
From: Charles Wilkes, *Meteorology*, 1850.
LC Q115.W6 folio

188 *Mouth of the Columbia River Oregon Territory Surveyed by the U.S. Ex. Ex. Charles Wilkes Commander. 1841*
Sheet #1
LC G2860.W52 1850 copy 2 fol., Vol. 2, Map #68

189 *Region of Fog North Pacific Ocean by the U.S. Ex.Ex., 1842*
From: Charles Wilkes, *Theory of the Winds*, 1856.
LC Toner QC931 W68 Copy 3 1856, between pages 102 and 103

190 *Chart of the World Shewing the Tracks of the United States Exploring Expedition*
Charles Wilkes, 1845
From: Charles Wilkes, *Narrative of the United States Exploring Expedition during the years 1838, 1839, 1840, 1841, 1842, 1845.*
VPL

191 *Map of the World Shewing the Extent and Direction of the Wind . . . 1856*
From: Charles Wilkes, *Hydrography*, 1856.
LC Q115.W6 vol 23, foldout map between pages 364 and 365

192 [Map of St. Lawrence Island, Bering Sea] 1849
From: Mikhail D. Tebenkov, *Atlas Severozapadnikh beregov Ameriki ot Beringova proliva do mysa i ostrov Aleutskikh*, 1852.

193 [Map of the coast of California, with inset of Golden Gate, San Francisco] 1848
From: Mikhail D. Tebenkov, atlas, 1852.

194 [Map of the mouth of the Columbia River] 1848
From: Mikhail D. Tebenkov, atlas, 1852.

195 *Sekai Bankoku Yori Kaijō Risu Kokuin Ōjō Jimbutsuzu* [Map of the world showing the distances of the various countries from Japan, their names, and inhabitants of their capitals; undated]
Kobe Public Library

196 *Reconnoissiance of the Anchorage of Ura-Ga & Reception Bay, on the west side of the entrance of Jeddo Bay, Island of Niphon, Japan, made by order of Commo. M.C. Perry, Comd'g U.S. Naval Forces E. India, China & Japan Seas*
1853
NARA Record Group 37, 451.36 #40

197 "Simoda Lt. Bents Survey with Topography"
NARA Record Group 37, 451.36 #34b

198 *Harbor of Hakodadi Island of Yesso Surveyed by order of Commodore M.C. Perry By Lieut. W.L. Maury, Lieut. G.H. Preble, Lieut J. Nicholson, Lieut A. Barbot 1854*
NARA Record Group 37, 451.36 #31

199 *Chart of the Kuro Siwa or Japan Stream of the Pacific . . .*
Matthew Perry, 1854

200 *Straits of Tsugar*
MS chart reduced for engraving.
NARA Record Group 37, 451.36 #36

201 *Mouth of the Teen-Tsin-Ho And Approach to the Sha-lui-tien Banks By the U.S. Str. John Hancock & U.S. Schr. Fenimore Cooper October 1854*
NARA Record Group 37, 451.36 #28

202 *Reconnoissance of the East Coast of Nippon, Empire of Japan, From Simoda to Hakodati By the launch of the United States Ship Vincennes, under the command of Lieutenant John M. Brooke, U.S.N., assisted by Edward M. Kern, Artist, and Richard Berry, Sailmaker. May 29th to June 17th 1855. Original Working Sheet.*
NARA Record Group 37, 451.36 #13; Yedo (Tokyo) Bay and coast north and south: #1/5 and #2/5

203 *The Asiatic Coast of Behring's Straits. Surveyed in the U.S. Ship Vincennes July and August 1855*
NARA Record Group 37, 181.36 #67

204 *Gulf of Yedo and Approaches By the U.S. Ship Vincennes, Lieut. John Rodgers Commanding U.S. Str. John Hancock, Lieut. Commanding H. K. Stevens May 1855. Additions by Lieut. Commdg. John M. Brooke, U.S. Schr. Fenimore Cooper, 1859.*
NARA Record Group 37, 451.36 #19, Sheet 2 of 4

205 *S.W. Part of Japan From the Surveys of the Expedition in 1854–55 with additions by Lieut. Comdg. John M. Brooke, U.S. Schr. F. Cooper, 1859, and from Dutch, English and Russian Authorities*
NARA Record Group 37, 451.36 #20, 3 sheets

206 *Wind and Current Chart*
North Pacific No. 7 Series A
Matthew Fontaine Maury, 1849
LC G9096.C7 svar.M3 vault

207 *Wind and Current Chart*
North Pacific No. 5 Series A
Matthew Fontaine Maury, 1849
LC G9096.C7 svar.M3 vault

208 *Pilot Chart of the North Pacific Sheet No. 5, Series C*
Matthew Fontaine Maury, 1851
LC G9096.C7 svar.M3 vault

209 *Whale Chart of the World*
Matthew Fontaine Maury, 1852
LC G9096.C7 svar.M3 vault

210 *Whale Chart by M. F. Maury A. M. Lieut. U.S.Navy* (Series F)
Matthew Fontaine Maury, 1851
LC G9096.C7 svar.M3 vault

211 *Sea Drift and Whales*
Matthew Fontaine Maury
From: *The Physical Geography of the Sea and Its Meteorology*, 1855.

Map 285.
During my searches for maps for this book I came across this intriguing manuscript on vellum map in the Library of Congress, where it is attributed to c1300. A palimpsest, the faintly visible and very hard to reproduce map is called "Map with Ship," from the ship on the left. It has been attributed in the past to some derivation of Marco Polo. Immediately suspicious because of the considerable geographical knowledge of the Pacific it shows (though it may have been added to later), it has been presumed by some to be a fake, though has not actually proven to be so. Not only does the map show China and Japan, but also what must be Kamchatka and eastern Siberia, the Kuril and Aleutian Islands, and Alaska. The map has a history all of its own; included in its file is a letter from J. Edgar Hoover of the FBI, to whom the map was at one time entrusted in order to have the inks tested. Unfortunately this analysis yielded little definite information, and the map, at least for now, remains an enigma.

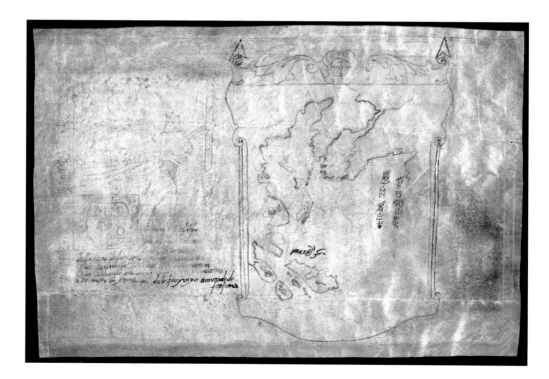

Bibliography

Bancroft, Hubert Howe
History of Alaska, 1730–1885
Bancroft & Co., San Francisco, 1886

Barkan, Frances B. (ed.)
The Wilkes Expedition:
Puget Sound and the Oregon Country
Washington State Capital Museum, Olympia, WA, 1987

Barratt, Glynn
Russia in Pacific Waters, 1715–1825
UBC Press, Vancouver, 1981

Beaglehole, John C.
The Exploration of the Pacific
Stanford University, Stanford, CA, 1966, third edition

Beaglehole, John C.
The Life of Captain James Cook
Hakluyt Society, London, 1974

Beaglehole, John C. (ed.)
The Journals of Captain James Cook on His Voyages of
Discovery: The Voyage of the Resolution *and the* Discovery,
1776–1780, Vol. 3
Hakluyt Society, Cambridge, 1967

Beals, Herbert K. (trans. and notes)
For Honor and Country: The Diary of Bruno De Heseta
Oregon Historical Society Press, Portland, 1985

Beals, Herbert K. (trans.)
Juan Pérez on the Northwest Coast.
Six Documents of His Expedition in 1774
Oregon Historical Society Press, Portland, 1989

Belknap, George E.
Deep-Sea Soundings in the North Pacific Ocean Obtained
in the United States Steamer Tuscarora
U.S. Hydrographic Office No. 54. Government Printing
Office, Washington, DC, 1874

Bishop, R. P.
"Drake's Course in the North Pacific"
British Columbia Historical Quarterly, 3, 1939

Black, Lydia (trans. and intro.)
The Lovtsov Atlas of the North Pacific Ocean
by Vasilii Fedorovich Lovtsov
Limestone Press, Kingston, ON, 1991

Breitfuss, L.
"Early Maps of North-Eastern Asia and of the Lands
around the North Pacific: Controversy between G. F.
Müller and N. Delisle"
Imago Mundi, 3, pp. 87–101, 1939

British Library
Sir Francis Drake: An Exhibition to Commemorate
Francis Drake's Voyage around the World, 1577–1580
Exhibition catalog.
British Museum Publications, London, 1977

Broughton, William Robert
A Voyage of Discovery to the North Pacific Ocean
Cadell and Davies, London, 1804

Challenger Office
Report on the Scientific Results of the Voyage of H.M.S.
Challenger *during the Years 1873–1876*
40 volumes in 44, London, 1880–95

Cortazzi, Hugh
Isles of Gold: Antique Maps of Japan
Weatherhill, New York, 1983

Cutter, Donald C.
Malaspina and Galiano: Spanish Voyages
to the Northwest Coast, 1791 and 1792
Douglas & McIntyre, Vancouver, 1991

Deacon, Margaret
Scientists and the Sea, 1650–1900:
A Study of Marine Science
Academic Press, London, 1971

Dickson, H. N.
"Prof. Pettersson on Methods of Oceanographic Research"
Geographical Journal, 14, No.2, pp. 185–90, August 1899

Divin, Vasilii A.
The Great Russian Navigator, A. I. Chirikov
Translated and annotated by Raymond H. Fisher.
University of Alaska Press, Fairbanks, 1993

Dmytryshyn, Basil, and E. A. P. Crownhart-Vaughan
(trans. and notes)
Colonial Russian America:
Kyrill T. Khlebnikov's Reports, 1817–1832
Oregon Historical Society Press, Portland, 1976

Efimov, A. V. (ed.)
Atlas geograficheskikh v Sibiri i severo-zapadnoy Amerike
XVII–XVIII vv. [Atlas of geographical discoveries in Siberia
and northwestern America in the 17th–18th centuries]
Nauka, Moscow, 1964

Erickson, Jon
Plate Tectonics: Unraveling the Mysteries of the Earth
Facts on File, New York, 1992

Falk, Marvin W.
"Mapping Russian America"
In *Russia in North America*. Proceedings of 2nd
International Conference on Russian America, Sitka,
Alaska, 19–22 August 1987

Fisher, Raymond H.
Bering's Voyages: Whither and Why
University of Washington Press, Seattle, 1977

Fisher, Raymond H.
The Voyage of Semen Dezhnev in 1648:
Bering's Precursor; With Selected Documents
Hakluyt Society, London, 1981

Fisher, Robin
Vancouver's Voyage:
Charting the Northwest Coast, 1791–1795
Douglas & McIntyre, Vancouver; University of Washington
Press, Seattle, 1992

Fisher, Robin, and Hugh Johnston (eds.)
From Maps to Metaphors:
The Pacific World of George Vancouver
UBC Press, Vancouver, 1993

Flint, James M.
A Contribution to the Oceanography of the Pacific
[The voyage of the *Nero*]
United States National Museum Bulletin, 55, 1902

Ford, Corey
Where the Sea Breaks Its Back: The Epic Story of a Pioneer
Naturalist and the Discovery of Alaska
Little, Brown, Boston, 1966

Friis, Herman R. (ed.)
The Pacific Basin:
A History of Its Geographical Exploration
American Geographical Society, New York, 1967

Frost, Alan, and Jane Samson (eds.)
Pacific Empires: Essays in Honour of Glyndwr Williams
UBC Press, Vancouver, 1999

GEOSECS Executive Committee
GEOSECS Atlantic, Pacific, and Indian Ocean Expeditions
Vol. 7, Shorebased Data and Graphics
National Science Foundation, Washington, DC, 1987

Goetzmann, William H., and Glyndwr Williams
The Atlas of North American Exploration:
From the Norse Voyages to the Race to the Pole
Prentice Hall, New York, 1992

Golder, Frank A.
Russian Expansion in the Pacific, 1641–1850
Arthur H. Clark, Cleveland, 1914

Golder, Frank A.
Bering's Voyages: An Account of the Efforts of the Russians
to Determine the Relation of Asia and America, 2 vols.
American Geographical Society, New York, 1922 and 1925

Gough, Barry M.
The Northwest Coast:
British Navigation, Trade and Discoveries to 1812
UBC Press, Vancouver, 1992

Gvozdetsky, N. A.
Soviet Geographical Explorations and Discoveries
Progress Publishers, Moscow, 1978

Hayes, Derek
Historical Atlas of the Pacific Northwest
Sasquatch Books, Seattle, 1999
Also published as *Historical Atlas of British Columbia*
and the Pacific Northwest
Cavendish Books, Vancouver, 1999

Hayes, Derek
"Hydrographic Surveying in British Columbia
from 1774 to 1870"
Resolution: The Journal of the Maritime Museum of British
Columbia, No. 48, pp. 3–6, Spring 2000

Hough, Richard
Captain James Cook: A Biography
Hodder and Stoughton, London, 1994

Hunt, William R.
Arctic Passage: The Turbulent History of the Land
and People of the Bering Sea, 1697–1975
Charles Scribner's Sons, New York, 1975

Kearey, Philip, and Frederick J. Vine
Global Tectonics
Blackwell Science, Oxford, 1996

Kendrick, John
The Men with Wooden Feet:
The Spanish Exploration of the Pacific Northwest
NC Press, Toronto, 1986

Kendrick, John
Alejandro Malaspina: Portrait of a Visionary
McGill-Queen's University Press, Montreal, 1999

Kendrick, John (trans. and intro.)
The Voyage of Sutil *and* Mexicana *1792: The Last Spanish*
Exploration of the Northwest Coast of America
Arthur H. Clark, Spokane, WA, 1991

Kerr, Adam J. (ed.)
"The Dynamics of Oceanic Cartography"
Cartographica, Vol. 17, No. 2, Summer 1980
Monograph 25.

Kohl, J. G.
History of Discovery and Exploration on the Coasts
of the United States
U.S. Coast and Geodetic Survey, Washington, DC, 1885

Kunzig, Robert
Mapping the Deep: The Extraordinary Story
of Ocean Science
Sort of Books, London, 2000

Kushnarev, Evenii G., and E.A.P. Crownhart-Vaughan
(ed. and trans.)
Bering's Search for the Strait:
The First Kamchatka Expedition, 1725–1730
Oregon Historical Society Press, Portland, 1990

La Pérouse, Jean-François de Galaup de
The Journal of Jean-François de Galaup de la Pérouse,
1785–1788, 2 vols.
Translated and edited by John Dunmore.
Hakluyt Society, London, 1984

Litke, Frederic [Lütke, Fedor]
A Voyage Around the World, 1826–1829
English translation of French edition,
Voyage Autour de Monde, Paris, 1835
Limestone Press, Kingston, ON, 1987

Longenbaugh, Dee
"From Anian to Alaschka:
The Mapping of Alaska to 1778"
Map Collector, No. 29, p. 28, December 1984

McConnell, Anita
Historical Instruments in Oceanography:
Background to the Oceanography Collection
at the Science Museum (London)
Her Majesty's Stationery Office, London, 1981

McDougall, Walter A.
Let the Sea Make a Noise: A History of the North Pacific
from Magellan to MacArthur
Harper Collins, Basic Books, New York, 1993

McEvedy, Colin
The Penguin Historical Atlas of the Pacific
Penguin Putnam, New York, 1998

Mathes, W. Michael
Vizcaíno and Spanish Exploration
in the Pacific Ocean, 1580–1630
California Historical Society, San Francisco, 1968

Matkin, Joseph
At Sea with the Scientifics:
The Challenger *Letters of Joseph Matkin*
Edited by Philip F. Rehbock.
University of Hawaii Press, Honolulu, 1992

Maury, Matthew Fontaine
The Physical Geography of the Sea and Its Meteorology
Harvard University Press, Belknap Press, Cambridge, MA,
1963. First edition 1855.

Meares, John
Voyages Made in the Years 1788 and 1789
from China to the North West Coast of America
Logographic Press, London, 1790

Menard, H. W.
Marine Geology of the Pacific
McGraw-Hill, New York, 1964

Ministerio de Defensa, Museo Naval
La Expedición Malaspina 1789–1794, 2 vols.
Barcelona, 1987/1993

Mourelle, Francisco Antonio
Voyage of the Sonora from the 1775 Journal
Translated by the Hon. Daines Barrington.
From Daines Barrington, *Miscellanies,* 1781, reprinted by
Thomas C. Russell, San Francisco 1920; also reprint of
this edition by Ye Galleon Press, Fairfield, WA, no date.

Müller, Gerhard Friedrich
Bering's Voyages: The Reports from Russia
Trans. of *Nachricten von Seareisen*, St. Petersburg, 1758.
Commentary by Carol Urness.
University of Alaska Press, Fairbanks, 1986

Müller, Gerhard Friedrich
Voyages from Asia to America, for Completing the
Discoveries of the North West Coast of America
Trans. by Thomas Jefferys, London, 1764.

Murray, Sir John
"On the Temperature of the Floor of the Ocean,
and of the Surface Waters of the Ocean"
Geographical Journal, 14, No. 1, p. 34–51, July 1899

Murray, Sir John
"Oceanography"
Geographical Journal, 14, No. 4, pp. 426–39, Oct. 1899

Needham, Joseph "Geography and Cartography"
In *Science and Civilization in China*, Cambridge
University Press, Vol. 3, pp. 497–590, 1959

Pallas, Peter Simon
Neue nordische Beyträge 1781-3
Trans. by James R. Masterson and Helen Brower.
In *Bering's Successors, 1745–1780: Contributions of Peter*
Simon Pallas to the History of Russian Exploration toward
Alaska
University of Washington Press, Seattle, 1948

Parry, J. H.
The Discovery of the Sea: An Illustrated History of Men,
Ships and the Sea in the Fifteenth and Sixteenth Centuries
Dial Press, New York, 1974

Paul, J. Harland
The Last Cruise of the Carnegie
Williams and Wilkins, Baltimore, 1932

Pethick, Derek
First Approaches to the Northwest Coast
J. J. Douglas, Vancouver, 1976

Pethick, Derek
The Nootka Connection:
Europe and the Northwest Coast, 1790–1795
Douglas & McIntyre, Vancouver, 1980

Pigafetta, Antonio
The First Voyage around the World:
An Account of Magellan's Expedition
Edited by Theodore Cachey. Originally published as
Viaggio intorno al mondo in 1522.
Marsilio Publishers, New York, 1995

Pineau, Roger (ed.)
The Japan Expedition, 1852–1854:
The Personal Journal of Commodore Matthew C. Perry
Smithsonian Institution Press, Washington, DC, 1968

Riesenberg, Felix
The Pacific Ocean
McGraw-Hill, New York, 1940

Ritchie, G. S.
The Admiralty Chart: British Naval Hydrography
in the Nineteenth Century
Hollis and Carter, London, 1967

Sarychev, Gavriil
Account of a Voyage of Discovery to the North-East of
Siberia, the Frozen Ocean, and the North-East Sea
Richard Phillips, London, 1806

Schlee, Susan
The Edge of an Unfamiliar World:
A History of Oceanography
E. P. Dutton, New York, 1973

Sherry, Frank
Pacific Passions: The European Struggle for Power
in the Great Ocean in the Age of Exploration
William Morrow, New York, 1994

Smith, Richard J.
Chinese Maps
Images of Asia series
Oxford University Press, Oxford, 1996

Spry, William J. J.
The Cruise of Her Majesty's Ship Challenger:
Voyages over Many Seas, Scenes in Many Lands
Marston Searle and Rivington, London, 1876

Stanton, William
The Great United States Exploring Expedition
University of California Press, Berkeley, 1975

Stejneger, L. H.
Georg Wilhelm Steller: The Pioneer
of Alaskan Natural History
Cambridge, MA, 1936

Stommel, Henry
Lost Islands: The Story of Islands
That Have Vanished from Nautical Charts
UBC Press, Vancouver, 1984

Svet, Yakov M., and Svetlana G. Fedorova
"Captain Cook and the Russians"
Pacific Studies, Vol. 2, No. 1, pp. 1–19, Fall 1978

Sysoev, N. N. (ed.)
"Oceanographic Research by the 'Vityaz' in the North
Pacific under the I. G. Y. Program"
Transactions of the Institute of Oceanology, Vol. 45,
Academy of Sciences of the U.S.S.R.
Israel Program for Scientific Translations, Jerusalem, 1969

Thrower, Norman J. W. (ed.)
Sir Francis Drake and the Famous Voyage
1577–1580
University of California Press, Berkeley, 1984

Tompkins, S. R., and M. L. Moorhead
"Russia's Approach to America"
B.C. Historical Quarterly, 13,
April, July, and October 1949

Tooley, R. V.
Maps and Map-Makers
Dorset Press, 1987, seventh edition

United Nations Food and Agriculture Organization
Atlas of the Living Resources of the Sea
UNFAO, first edition 1971; second edition 1981

U.S. Navy. Chief of Naval Operations
U.S. Navy Marine Climatic Atlas of the World,
Vol. 2, *North Pacific Ocean*
U.S. Government Printing Office, Washington, DC, 1956

Vancouver, George
A Voyage of Discovery to the North Pacific Ocean
and Round the World, 1791–1795, 4 vols.
Edited by W. Kaye Lamb.
Hakluyt Society, London, 1984
Also original edition, London, 1798

Vaughan, Thomas, E. A. P. Crownhart-Vaughan,
and Mercedes Palau de Iglesias
Voyages of Enlightenment:
Malaspina on the Northwest Coast 1791/1792
Oregon Historical Society Press, Portland, 1977

Wagner, Henry R.
Spanish Voyages to the Northwest Coast
in the Sixteenth Century
California Historical Society, San Francisco, 1929

Wagner, Henry R.
Spanish Explorations in the Strait of Juan de Fuca
Santa Ana, 1933. Reprint AMS Press, New York, 1971

Wagner, Henry R.
Cartography of the Northwest Coast to the Year 1800
University of California Press, 1937. Reprint 2000

Walworth, Arthur
Black Ships Off Japan:
The Story of Commodore Perry's Expedition
Archon Books, Hamden, CT, 1966

Whitfield, Peter
The Image of the World: 20 Centuries of World Maps
Pomegranate Artbooks, San Francisco;
British Library, 1994

Wilkes, Charles
Narrative of the United States Exploring Expedition
during the Years 1838, 1839, 1840, 1841, 1842
Lea and Blanchard, Philadelphia, 1845

Williams, Frances Leigh
Matthew Fontaine Maury, Scientist of the Sea
Rutgers, State University, 1963

Williams, Glyndwr
The British Search for the North West Passage
in the Eighteenth Century
Longmans, Green, London, 1962

Wroth, Lawrence C.
"The Early Cartography of the Pacific"
Bibliographical Society of America Papers, Vol. 38,
No. 2, pp. 87–268, June 1944

Index

MONGOL
CIRCVLVS

ANIAN AR

A

AJO

A

Rabana

Quanzu

Hic

Quinzai

40

Iapan

Cozones

TALIS

Liampo

Aua

Zaiton

30

Lichi

achuchina

Aynam

TRO

PICV

J.Aynam

20

L goma

Costa de Lacoes L

Gaspari

Pulosursir

Capan

S Bye

Quitas

Mindanao